SEAL OF THE PROPHETS

By Rev. J. T. Towers

When we walk the good red road, we walk with
the earth and not on it, with respect for
everything, from the stones to the stars.

June 2019

Seal of the Prophets

Cover Design by **Stands With Wings Graphics**

Art by Tony Black and Jose Rubio

Editing by Shanara Asherah Schmidt

ISBN : 978-1-7923-0936-6
© Rev. J. T. Towers
All rights reserved Good Red Road Publishing LLC
GoodRedRoadPublishing.com

In the name of God, The Beneficent, The Merciful.

JAMES A. MICHENER: "Muhammad, the inspired man who founded Islam, was born orphaned at birth; he was always particularly solicitous of the poor and needy, the widow and the orphan, the slave and the down-trodden. At twenty he was already a successful businessman, and soon became director of camel caravans for a wealthy widow. When he reached twenty-five, his employer recognizing his merit, proposed marriage; even though she was fifteen years older, he married her. As long as she lived he remained a devoted husband.

"Like almost every major prophet before him, Muhammad fought shy of serving as the transmitter of God's word, sensing his own inadequacy. But the angel commanded 'READ'. So far as we know, Muhammad was unable to read or write, but he began to dictate those inspired words which would soon revolutionize a large segment of the earth: "THERE IS ONE GOD."

"In all things Muhammad was profoundly practical. When his beloved son Ibrahim died, an eclipse occurred, and rumors of God's personal condolence quickly arose. Whereupon Muhammad is said to have announced, 'An eclipse is a phenomenon of nature. It is foolish to attribute such things to the death or birth of a human being'.

"At Muhammad's own death an attempt was made to deify him, but the man who was to become his administrative successor killed the hysteria with one of the noblest speeches in religious history: 'If there are any among you who worshipped Muhammad, he is dead. But if it is God you worshipped, He lives for ever.'" (Islam: The Misunderstood Religion, American Edition of Reader's Digest, 1955, pp.68-70)

MICHAEL H. HART: "My choice of Muhammad to lead the list of the world's most influential persons may surprise some readers and may be questioned by others, but he was the only man in history who was supremely successful on both the religious and secular levels." (The 100: A Ranking of the Most Influential Persons in History. New York, 1978, p.33)

DE LACY O'LEARY: "History makes it clear however, that the legend of fanatical Muslims sweeping through the world and forcing Islam at the point of the sword upon conquered races is one of the most fantastically absurd myths that historians have ever repeated." ('Islam at the Crossroads', p.8)

THOMAS CALYLE: "How one man single-handedly, could weld warring tribes and wandering Bedouins into a most powerful and civilized nation in less than two decades." (Hero's and Hero-worship')

GEORGE BERNARD SHAW: "He must be called the Savior of Humanity. I believe that if a man like him were to assume the dictatorship of the modern world, he would succeed in solving its problems in a way that would bring it much needed peace and happiness." ('The Genuine Islam', Singapore, Vol.1, no., 8, 1936)

LAMARTINE: Renowned Historian; If greatness of purpose, smallness of means and astounding results are the three criteria of human genius, who could dare to compare any great man in modern history with Muhammad? The most famous men created arms, laws and empires only. They founded, if anything at all, no more than material powers which often crumbled away before their eyes. This man moved not only armies, legislation, empires, peoples and dynasties, but millions of men in one-third of the then inhabited world; and more than that, he moved the alters, the gods, the religions, the ideas, the beliefs and souls. His forbearance in victory, his ambition, which was entirely devoted to one idea and in no manner striving for an empire; his endless prayers, his mystic conversations with God, his death and triumph after death; all these attest not to an imposture but to a firm conviction which gave him the power to restore dogma. This dogma was two-fold, the unity of God and the immateriality of God; the former telling what God is, the latter telling what God is not; the one overthrowing false gods with the sword, the other starting an idea with words."

"Philosopher, orator, apostle, legislator, warrior, conqueror of ideas, restorer of rational dogmas, of a cult without images, the founder of twenty terrestrial empires - of one spiritual empire that is MUHAMMAD.

"As regards all the standards by which Human Greatness may be measured, we may well ask, IS THERE ANY MAN GREATER THAN HE?" (Historire de la Turquie, Vol.2, pp.276-277)

SAROJINI NAIDU: famous poetess; speaking on the equality of women before God in Islam. "It was the first religion that preached and practiced democracy; for in the mosque, when the Call to Prayer is sounded and worshippers are gathered together, the democracy of Islam is embodied five times a day when the peasant and the king kneel side by side and proclaim: 'GOD ALONE IS GREAT'... I have been struck over and over again by this indivisible unity of Islam that makes man instinctively a brother." (Ideals of Islam, vide Speeches & Writings, p.169)

PROFESSOR HURGRONJE: "...the league of nations founded by the Prophet of Islam put the principle of international unity and human brotherhood on such universal foundations as to show candle to other nations... The fact is that no nation of the world can show a parallel to what Islam has done towards the realization of the idea of the League of Nations."

MAHATMA GANDHI: "I wanted to know the best of one who holds today undisputed sway over the hearts of millions of mankind... I became more than convinced that it was not the sword that won a place for Islam in those days in the scheme of life. It was the rigid simplicity, the utter self-effacement of the Prophet, the scrupulous regard for his pledges, his fearlessness, and his absolute trust in God and in his own mission. These and not the sword carried everything before them and surmounted every obstacle. When I closed the 2nd volume (of the Prophet's biography), I was sorry there was not more for me to read of the great life." ('Young India')

EDWARD GIBBON and SIMON OCKLEY: write; "I BELIEVE IN ONE GOD, AND MAHOMET, AN APOSTLE OF GOD, is the simple and invariable profession of Islam. The intellectual image of the Deity has never been degraded by any visible idol; the honor of the Prophet have never transgressed the measures of human virtues; and his living precepts have restrained the gratitude of his disciples within the bounds of reason and Religion (History of the Saracen Empires, p.54)

W. MONTGOMERY WATT: "I am not a Muslim in the usual sense, though I hope I am a 'Muslim' as 'one surrendered to God', but I believe that embedded in the Qur'an and other expressions of the Islamic visions are one vast store of Divine Truth from which I and other occidentals have still much to learn, and 'Islam is certainly a strong contender for the supplying of the basic framework of the religion of the future.'" (Islam and Christianity Today, 1983, p.ix)

A.J. TOYNBEE: "The extinction of race consciousness as between Muslims is one of the outstanding achievements of Islam and in the contemporary world there is, as it happens, a crying need for the propagation of this Islamic virtue." (Civilization on Trial, p.205)

ACKNOWLEDGEMENTS

All Praise and Gratitude is due only unto Allah, The Cherisher and Sustainer of the Worlds, without Whose Grace the writing of this work would have proven a task well beyond my abilities. I thank the esteemed Dr. A.S.Hashim of the Qur'an Account, Inc., Rockville, Maryland, U.S.N.A., for permitting the use of his material: A series of Islamic books for beginners, "The Life of Prophet Muhammad", Vols., 1&2, 1st and 3rd Editions, and "Ahlul Bayt", Vols., 1&2, 1st and 3rd Editions, upon which this work is based and whose direction provided invaluable assistance. I thank Muslim scholars, past and present, for points of references. I thank the renowned late great Scholar sage, Hujjatul-Islam Ayatullah Haji Mirza Mahdi Pooya Yazdi and S.V.Mir Ahmed Ali, (may Allah be pleased with them), for providing the MOST comprehensive Holy Qur'an with English Translation of the Arabic Text and Commentary According to the Interpretation of those Whom Allah Himself Specifically Purified, the Holy Ahlul Bayt, from which I quoted Qur'anic Verses and footnotes. I thank the Amana Corporation of North America for their edition of Holy Qur'an from which I also used the footnotes, appendices and commentaries. I thank Muhammad al-Tijani al-Samawi of Gafsa, Tunisia, North Africa, for information which otherwise may not have come to light. I thank Nazir Ahmed of Pakistan, for his constant support and encouragement, and Ali A. Agah of Manassas, Virginia, U.S.N.A., for his optimism, help and belief. Special thanks go to my dear friends and 'brothers', the Vallejo Brothers: Arturo 'Art', Efrain and Tony, of Sacramento, California, U.S.N.A., for their kindness, belief, suggestions, support, understanding, unending patience, and for being there whenever I needed them. I would also like to thank Marjorie Morakkabi of Millersville, Maryland, U.S.N.A., for her time in helping me prepare this work. And a very special heartfelt thank you to S. A. Schmidt, Washington State, USA., for her knowledge, determination, expertise, energy and graciousness in finalizing my work.

DEDICATED TO THOSE SEEKING TRUTH

INTRODUCTION

Following the creation of the worlds, God filled the earth with all manner of living things. He, next, took of the earth and formed man, fashioning him in ways representative of His own essence. Placing Adam in the Garden, the Lord then caused a deep sleep to fall upon Adam and took from his body and created him a mate. The Lord said: "Of every tree thou can eat freely of, but eat not from the tree of knowledge."

In the process of time, Satan, subtler than any other creature had been in communication with Adam and Eve, enticed them to eat of the tree which the Lord didst forbid. And it came to pass that they succumbed to Satan's temptation. When they ate the fruit of the tree their eyes were opened to knowing good and evil. Repentant, they fell to their knees and prostrated in submission to God. Thus, a Way of life began: submitting your will to God's Will.

Obedience to God's will has been promulgated all through the ages by His prophets in various ways for different times. But, as man populated the earth he grew hypocritical, overbearing, skeptical of the wonders structuring his world, and the true Way of life passed into superstitious amelioration. Before long, religious observance exploded in the forms of elemental and celestial worship; human sacrifices, apotheosis, zealotry, and cross worship, even going as far as naming the way after men. Blinded by ignorance and self-importance, man's corruption spread and he began asserting superiority over others. Then he started contending exclusive descendancy from Adam and set out to extinguish man's inherent affinity for one another. Thus, to set matters aright, God sent His Angel Gabriel with Divine Disclosure to a man born in history's coming of age. Muhammad ibn Abdullah, an unlettered man of the Arabian Desert, prepared by its no frills living, was that man chosen to proclaim the Final Message that would change the course of human history.

Hence, there is no question now of race or nation, of a "Chosen People" or the "Seed of Abraham", or the "Seed of David", or of Hindu ARYA-VARTA, of Jew or Gentile, Arab or Ajam (Persian), Turk or Tajik, European or Asiatic, White or Colored, Aryan, Semetic, Mongolian, or African, Australian, or Polynesian.(1)

With the end of Sacred Scripture, God not only perfected the Way to live, but named it Islam. So, as His Final Testament circulates throughout the world beware of those who teach "HIS-LAM" and not Islam. For Islam is the universal enlightenment for ALL humanity.

AUTHOR'S NOTE

This story has been based upon facts and recorded personages. Also, where history does not mention, I have for the purposes of dramatization introduced phenomena. And it must be noted that the Revelations written within this book were revealed PIECEMEAL over a twenty-three year period. Rarely was a complete Surah of Revelation revealed in its entirety, (except for the short ones.) For simplicity some of the longer Surahs were transcribed as whole. (*Surah is the term for Chapter in the Quran*)

"The lies which well-meaning zeal has heaped round this man (Muhammad) are disgraceful to ourselves only."
Thomas Carlyle

PROLOGUE

ABOUT GOD'S ONENESS:

"And Jesus answered and said unto him, Get thee behind me, Satan: for it is written, Thou shalt worship the Lord thy God, and Him only shalt thou serve." LUKE 4:8

"Thou shalt not bow down thyself to them nor serve them for I the Lord thy God AM a jealous God." EXODUS 20:5

"I am the Lord: that is My name: and My glory will I not give to another, neither My praise to graven images." ISAIAH 42:8

PROPHET JESUS ABOUT ISRAEL:

"But he answered and said, I am not sent but unto the lost sheep of the house of Israel." MATTHEW 15:24

"Therefore say I unto you, the Kingdom of God shall be taken from you, and given to a nation bringing forth the fruits thereof." MATTHEW 21:43

AND THE LORD SAID UNTO ABRAHAM:

"And I will establish My covenant between Me and thee and thy seed after thee in their generations for an everlasting covenant, to be a God unto thee, and to thy seed after thee. And as for Isma'il, I have heard thee: Behold, I have blessed him, and will make him fruitful, and will multiply him exceedingly; twelve princes* shall he beget, and I will make him a great nation." GENESIS 17:7, 20

AND THE LORD SAID UNTO MOSES:

"I will raise them up a Prophet from their brethren**, LIKE UNTO THEE and I will put My words in his mouth; and he shall speak unto them all that I command him. And it shall come to pass, THAT whosoever will not hearken unto My words which he shall speak in My name, I will require IT of him." DEUTERONOMY 18:18-19

FROM GOD'S FINAL TESTAMENT, THE HOLY QUR'AN:

And nor he (Muhammad) speakest of (his own) inclination; it (the wording) is naught but a revelation revealed (unto him)." CHAPTER 53:3-4

JESUS ABOUT MUHAMMAD:

"And I will pray the Father, and He shall give you another Comforter" JOHN 14:16

"...for the prince of this world cometh" JOHN 14:30

"Nevertheless I tell you the truth; it is expedient for you that I go away: for if I go not away, the Comforter will not come unto you... And when he is come, he will reprove the world of sin, and of righteousness, and of judgment... Howbeit when he, the Spirit of truth, is come, he will guide you into all truth: for he shall not speak of himself; but whatsoever he shall hear, THAT SHALL he speak: and he will show you things to come." JOHN: 16:7, 8, 13

* Guides, Holy Imams ** i.e. Isma'ilites

PART ONE:
MEKKAH (approx., 570 C.E.)

CHAPTER ONE

The ancient city of Mekkah, shielded from the scorching Arabian sun by a bulbous bank of cumulus clouds, bestirred itself as the aromatic scent wafted in from the flowering countryside. The unusual mild mid-afternoon filled the valley with an air of undefined exuberance. A deeply felt and tender comfort filled Abdul Mut'talib as he led his companion through the area. Waraqah ibn Naufal, sightless since childhood, was versed in Holy Scripture and frequently spent his time with Abdul discussing the various aspects of the known history of God and religion.

Now returning from the wilderness, the two walked arm in arm through the city's streets. Abdul slowed their pace to an amble, steering his friend through the maze of playing children. Waraqah, unhindered by the distractions, continued to speak. Immersed in thought, Abdul nodded absent mindedly and responded with grunts of acknowledgement. Ending his comments, Waraqah was saying, "...way for the city to become which cost Ashram dearly."

All the while, Abdul had been thinking of his daughter-in-law, Aminah bint Wahab. Then, suddenly and without thought to his friend, he spoke aloud in a voice full of pleading: "Oh, Allah! I beseech Thee to shower Thy mercy and blessings upon my daughter Aminah whom Thou knowest to be enduring a laborious pregnancy."

At the moment of Mut'talib's petition to the Almighty his daughter-in-law's water broke and she went into labor. Aminah never recalled traversing from the main room of the house to her bedroom where she collapsed in throbbing pain. She next remembered hearing the frantic whisperings of those around her. Drifting in and out of consciousness for the rest of the day and most of the evening, she abruptly became cognizant of a rasping, uneven sound roaring in her ears. For several seconds she lay prone trying to decipher the unfamiliar noise. To her relief she recognized the sound as her own labored breathing.

Aminah hadn't known how long she'd been abed, but by the room's darkened window she realized the lateness of hour. Turning toward the wavering candle light, she found herself amid pillows and covered with a thick woolen blanket. In spite of the pain she raised herself slowly, gasping at the effort, and propped her elbows to bear the brunt of her weight. She started to investigate the flickering taper shining in her face as if she'd never before seen fire light. It was quite obvious that Aminah's movements took all her strength and concentration. The midwives in attendance, alarmed at her unexpected motion, jumped from their seats and gently forced her to lie back down while appealing for her to remain calm.

Outside her room, in the main part of the house, family members, friends and their wives gathered to await the birth. Abdul, Lady Jahsh, Abu Lahab, and several others talked in hushed tones as they sat around worriedly, wishing a safe delivery. Then, without the usual onset of outcries accompanying delivery, Aminah started screaming at the top of her lungs as her womb dilated and the sharp pains of birth befell her. Instantly the household froze as the chilling screams of excruciating pain emitted from the next room. As quickly as it began the blood curdling shrieks stopped, replaced by a newborn's vigorous wailing, shattering the tensions of the birthing process.

Inside Aminah's room the midwives were chattering excitedly, relieved the ordeal was over with no complications. They cleansed and swaddled the baby, a healthy beautiful boy.

Wrapping him in soft lamb's wool, the infant was handed over to his mother. Aminah cradled her son next to her breast for nursing but the infant recognized the familiar heartbeat, yawned and fell asleep.

One of the midwives moved aside the curtain draped over the doorway and announced the news that the family's inquiring looks demanded. After a round of congratulations, she told Abdul that Aminah wished to speak with him. The remaining family members and friends erupted with lively conversation. The servants cheerfully resumed their duties before the strains of childbearing began.

"Father, wilt thou sit besides me?," Aminah asked her father-in-law with a voice weakened from exertion. Abdul quickly crossed the room and looking upon Aminah's face became overwhelmed with feelings of love and compassion as he took her dry, parched hands, in his. She focused her sight on his features, seeing the inner strength, maturity and peace earned across the years of pain and suffering. Wonder filled her thoughts, the wonder of life. Something benevolent emanated from him, something steady and full of understanding.

From eyes deep in their sockets, Abdul regarded her tenderly then shifted his vision to the sleeping baby. He gazed wistfully at the newborn thinking how perfect and handsome the boy was. Suddenly, as he beheld the child a fleeting shadow flashed across his face. Thoughts of Abdullah, the baby's father, untimely death raced through his mind. He walked over to the window, melancholy mushrooming over his face with each step, and peered out into the night. Able to glimpse the somber cast of her father-in-law's features before he completed his turn to step away, Aminah watched apprehensively while he stood next to the window staring off into the moonlit night. She wondered what was troubling him. "What troubleth thee, father?," Aminah inquired timidly.

Not wanting to taint the joyous event of birth with talk of the departed, Abdul inhaled a deep breath, sighed, and turned to face his daughter-in-law. "Daughter, wouldst thou name the child Muhammad?" Then he added to ease her concerns, "It is thy wretched custom of subjecting infants to outside influences which bringeth sadness upon me."

For longer than he knew, babies born into important families were taken out of the city to be raised in the desert area. Perceiving no better time he informed Aminah that Halimah al-Sa'diyyah, the nursemaid engaged for the child nurturing would be arriving within two months time to collect Muhammad. Meanwhile, baby Muhammad's first breath had coincided with a spectacular eruption of meteors streaking across the heavens; the magnitude of which had never been witnessed. The grand palace of Kisra shook violently, cracking from its foundation to its roof and toppling fourteen of its massive battlements. The thousand year old continuous burning flame of Persia's Fire worshiping Temple was extinguished.

An elderly Rabbi, awestruck by the sudden phenomena, reflected but a moment before becoming visibly excited. "Al-Hamdu lillah," he abruptly exclaimed. "Oh, ye men" the flushed Rabbi pronounced in a voice demanding attention.

Startled by the unexpected intrusion into their midst, the assembly of chieftains ceased all discussion and faced glaringly at the stranger. "What cause hast thou to overstep thy bounds!" said the eldest indignantly.

"Begging thy pardon, my lord," returned the Rabbi. "If thou wilt permit me to speak, I" – he was cut off.

"Saith what thou camest to say," voiced the eldest sheik irritably.

"Has there been a male child born unto thy tribe this day?"

"What affair is it of thine?" retorted the eldest.

The Rabbi observed many of the clan chiefs respond negatively. Then without acknowledging the elder's brusqueness, he addressed the group. "Thou must be mistaken, for it is written in the Torah, the Book of Moses, that when the Last Prophet Of God is born, the devilish forces will be repulsed with shooting stars from heaven and the entry of the devils into the higher regions will be closed for ever."[1]

Halimah arrived six and a half weeks later to take the baby into the hills where the desert air was pure and full of sunshine. It was considered among the influential that open air living gave the infant a healthy beginning and increased the child's chances to endure the rigors of life's hardships.

Upon entering Mekkah, Halimah began to feel uneasy as she traveled the narrow confines of the streets. It brought to mind the congestion, disease, and the fact of Abdullah's death. And now as she neared her destination she feverishly thought of the best way to back out of the prearranged agreement between their families about the child's fostering. Mercilessly, the thought of not being paid for her services edged all other thoughts out. Before realizing, she had dismounted and found herself knocking on the door to Abdul's house. Abdul opened the door and immediately saw Halimah's look of anxiety. He could almost hear the thoughts running through her mind; such was his uncanny ability to interpret the apprehensive looks of others around him. There was but a few seconds of uncomfortable silence before he graciously welcomed her in.

As the nursemaid stepped over the threshold, she began to speak. "Oh Abdul, I —"

Abdul raised his hand, cutting her off before she could complete her sentence. Correctly surmising the reason for Halimah's anxiety, he started to assure her before the subject could be raised. He said, "Concern thyself not, thy services wilt be paid for most generously."

Pleased with his sense of perception and not having to raise the delicate matter of money, she breathed a sigh of relief. Nervously, she followed him through the house to meet her charge. Halimah entered the room and saw Aminah rocking the child's cradle. She heard the soft cooing sounds only a baby could make and went to the cradle. Hearing a strange voice, baby Muhammad gurgled and smiled, which made him all the more lovable. She peered over the cradle's side. "Aah, the child is a pleasing sight to one's eyes," said Halimah. All at once she was delighted she had made the journey. Silently, she vowed to herself that she would lavish the child with love and care. Smitten with the smiling Muhammad, Halimah spent the better part of the day acquainting herself with him, and before she said good-by, she promised to return at dawn the following day.

Aminah and her father-in-law had watched the nursemaid closely and were satisfied that Muhammad would be well cared for. That evening, the entire household was in a state of repressed emotions. Abdul quietly directed the servants in packing supplies needed for the trip into the hills where Banu Sa'd, Halimah's tribe, was located. Aminah, forsaking her dinner, passed the time with Muhammad. She never once put him down until hours later when her arms began to cramp.

Halimah used the time to shop in the square, purchasing things for the members of her clan. The following day Aminah and Abdul were up before the crack of dawn. They waited in a small alcove off the main room, drinking hot tea to ward off the early morning chill. Halimah arrived just as the cover of darkness was giving way to the new day. Softly, as if afraid to wake the already awakened neighbors, she knocked on the door.

Abdul welcomed her in and invited her to sit and share tea while the servants loaded the packs of supplies. Then, both grandfather and Aminah began giving last minute instructions. What seemed a short time later to Aminah, one of the servants crossed the room and informed her provisions were stowed and that everything was in readiness for departure. Aminah sadly rose to her feet, her emotions in turmoil. She looked from her father-in-law's face to the nursemaid's then without saying a word, left the alcove.

Minutes later a rooster crowed piercingly at the sun's rising. Aminah returned carrying the bundled up Muhammad. Lost in thought, she started outside towards the waiting animals.

Abdul looked to Halimah and said, "Thou must be anxious to begin thy journey home." "Yeah, for it is a long ride," returned Halimah

With the small talk ended, Abdul escorted her to the waiting mount. Heavy-hearted with thoughts of separation, Aminah started to silently weep as she handed her son up to Halimah's outstretched arms.

Abdul, fearing the display of an emotional outburst in front of the women, hastily retreated back to the pack animals and busily engaged himself inspecting the bonds holding the supplies in place. Tearfully Aminah bid farewell and broke into sobs as she watched her son and Halimah ride off. Meanwhile, Abdul, unable to control the feelings washing over him let the tears fall. He gathered his daughter-in-law in his arms, and together they stared after Muhammad until he was lost in the rising sun.

Riding off, Halimah and her charge joined up with other travelers leaving the city. Together they formed a small caravan, more out of necessity than of convenience, for there were always the nomadic Bedouins of the desert seeking the unwary. As the wayfarers pressed forward across the dry, sandy plains of the desert, a hot, heavy wind started to blow, flinging bits of sand and dust particles. There was no escaping the elements as the earth found its way into every crack and crevice, stinging the exposed areas of skin and just falling short of blinding them and their beasts.

The caravan's leader, a veteran of desert travel and its storms, thought it best to halt the train's progress and let the onslaught of sand filled winds pass them over. He led them to a small hollow between the dunes where the half-gale winds were less violent. Halimah, clinging the baby to her breast with one arm, trying to protect her vision with the other, while sitting side-saddle on a skittish horse, was more than she could handle. On the verge of tears, she looked around helplessly. She opened her mouth to call for help, only to have it filled with grit. The train's leader, seeing her difficulties, rushed over to aid her dismount. He then forced her animal to the ground so she could use the mass of horseflesh as a windbreak against the flurry.

Some hours later, the blustering storm blew itself out. Injuries were minor; the men receiving some sand-papering for their efforts in helping the women. Within the hour the travelers reformed their train to continue the journey. With the sandy tracts of desert stretching on and on, several women in the caravan began to while away the time gossiping. The mindless prattle soon shifted to Halimah. They conversed in low tones behind her back. Shamelessly they ridiculed her, thinking her foolish to have provided services to a household with no father to pay for her troubles.

Before reaching their destination, the desert heat, hot dry winds and tediousness of travel, gave rise to the worst in the loquacious women. Abandoning all regard for Halimah's feelings, the women began to openly mock her with scorn in their voices. Their notion of sensitivity and love precluded them from understanding why anyone would undertake the responsibility of rearing a fatherless child.

Eventually, after crossing through the arid land, the caravan reached the withered hills and valleys belonging to Banu Sa'd. Going through the highlands, it was apparent the area had not seen rain for a long time. Everything was dead or dying. Subsoil showed in large patches and dust blew with sirocco-like winds. Nonetheless, the scenery raised smiles on everyone's faces.

As the vestige of dust trailed behind the caravan, it attracted the settlement's attention and many of its inhabitants turned out to greet the riders. Excited by the end of the long arduous journey, Halimah prompted her mount to go a little faster. As she drew closer to the crowd of people that gathered to welcome the caravan, she recognized several faces and impulsively began to wave. The gathering, drawn by the motion of Halimah's waving, directed their vision toward her and the small bundle in her arm. The closer they got the more of baby Muhammad's smiling face came into focus. It was at that very moment the heavens reverberated across the valley with thunder and started dropping the much-needed rain. Throughout the settlement cries were heard thanking the gods for the sudden shower. Old and young alike danced in circles, laughing as the rain soaked them to the bone. In their exhilaration, most forgot the caravan's arrival except for several elders; they declared the smiling child in Halimah's arm an omen of good fortune.

During the following years, Muhammad's presence among Banu Sa'd generated a lively and carefree existence. The skies rained more than usual, ripening the hills and valleys with sumptuous, verdant pasturage. Livestock fattened, date palms produced an abundance of dates each year. All in all, the general welfare of the tribe was one of happiness and prosperity.

In Muhammad's third and fourth years, his command of the language became most impressive. He was able to understand the nuances of speech much better than older children, and in some cases, surpassed the adults in comprehension. His powers of retention became the talk of the colony and his extremely gentle nature endeared him to all. At about that time Halimah started to instruct Muhammad according to Aminah and Abdul's wishes.

Through her guidance, he began to mold into an exceptional child. His developing disposition was evolving into one of friendliness and diplomacy, so much so that at the beginning of each day, children rushed to his tent first asking him to play. He never wanted to see anyone hurt and more often than not, often took pains to arbitrate the petty squabbles between the other children. Never known for subtracting or embellishing the facts of any given situation, the adults first turned to him whenever there were accidents or the rivalry of children got out of hand, for he continually told the truth, even when involved.

Nearing the end of his stay, so accurate was his memory that the tribe's elders looked to Muhammad to recall events of certain days when disputes arose. His honesty and straightforwardness earned him the love and admiration of the community. In him they detected something special yet to emerge; even the children sensed a distinctiveness about him.

After five years of open air living, Muhammad was strong, healthy and vibrant. Many of Banu Sa'd had come to regard young Muhammad a true blessing, for they had never before known such fullness of life until his arrival. And when Halimah announced their departure with the traders leaving for Mekkah, they showered him with gifts and tokens of remembrances.

Traveling along the long snaking road out of the hills and valleys, the procession finally emerged on the last slope; descending toward the wide expanse of desert by late afternoon of their first day out. The immensity of sand filled land and dunes stretching to the horizon filled Muhammad with wonder and a sense of adventure. His imaginative questions and antics kept Halimah and the accompanying travelers occupied from the monotony of travel. However, the novelty of the journey soon faded and the repetitiousness of their animal's hooves and pads rhythmically plopping on the sand induced one to reflection as a means to escape the weariness.

Halimah reminisced of the memories with Muhammad, while every now and then asking him to recite one of the many narratives she taught him just to hear the sound of his voice. It always amazed her that he could repeat anything word for word after hearing it once.

Muhammad thought of the children he played with, the friendships he made, how Halimah cared for him and about the stories she had him learn.

He distinctly remembered one in particular, because Halimah emphasized its importance: "Never be afraid nor show the slightest fear, for a scared man is mean,and cruel, and will never have peace in his home."

A few days later, while Muhammad watched the caravan's captain rise and fall with each of his mount's gait, he noticed far off in the distance a break in the horizon's continuity. Abruptly he called out excitedly, pointing in the direction he wanted his nursemaid to look. Then exclaimed: "Halimah! Halimah! What lieth over there?" Startled by the sudden sound of his voice, Halimah's musings vanished and comprehension of their whereabouts set in. Knowing the answer to his query, even before shifting her vision to where he indicated, she responded sadly, a lump in her throat, "It is the Holy City of Mekkah. In ancient times the ancestors of our people restored the foundation of Allah's House. There wilt we find thy mother and grandfather."

Realizing his kin were less than a day's travel away, he worked himself up into a fluster and started asking nonstop questions. The steady flow enabled Halimah enough time to think that her life with Muhammad was coming to an end; the tears began to spill down her cheeks.

Anxious for answers, Muhammad ripped his attention away from the sight and looked up at his nursemaid expectantly. He was surprised to see her weeping. He didn't understand, but sensitive to the needs of another's pain, he restrained his excitement and quietly waited for her to regain her composure. Mindful of his behavior, Halimah summoned her reserve and answered his many questions until he could no longer think of new ones. Hours later, the caravan arrived at the city's outskirts. The spectacle of stone buildings looming toward the heavens overwhelmed Muhammad with fascination. To him, the sight of two and three story structures was absolutely amazing.

Plodding on, they soon found their way into the heart of the city. Muhammad had never seen such a densely populated area with an environment completely devoid of grass, shrubs and trees, or angular streets with thread-like alleys haphazardly going in every direction, or houses built side by side, back to back, intermingled with niches occupied with merchants and tradesmen of every description noisily hawking spirits, foodstuffs, and an array of life's necessities.

In the midst of all the distractions were screaming children, running and playing unchecked by supervision. Trying to look everywhere at once, Muhammad noticed the caravan's captain standing with a small group of people who kept staring his way, looking tense, on edge. Suddenly, a middle-aged lady and an old man separated themselves from the group and started toward him and Halimah. The nursemaid squeezed her charge's hand gently. Muhammad's inner core began to beat, his heart pounding with excitement.

"Halimah, is that my mother and grandfather who come this way," asked the young boy to confirm his feelings. But before she had the opportunity to respond, Abdul was there lifting him from the animal's back and helping her dismount.

Bursting in tears of happiness and cries of joy, Aminah embraced both her father-in-law and Muhammad. She showered them with hugs and kisses. Abdul, embarrassed by the display of affection, relinquished his hold on the boy and turned him over to his mother. Aminah continued to lavish him with love. Finally, after several minutes time, the reunited family and Halimah entered the house.

Muhammad's homecoming was a joyous occasion, filling the household with an air of festivity. Even the normally sedate servants were affected by the boy's arrival, and upon word immediately began preparations to celebrate his return. Hoping to add gaiety, Aminah asked one of the servants to spread the news among their clan and friends, inviting them to share in the evening meal.

Late that evening the household was still filled with company. People passing by, who heard the hubbub of activity, thought some momentous event was taking place, such was the laughter and talking going on. It wasn't long before Halimah began to unwind and reveal her precious memories of Muhammad. Every once in a while the assembled guests would erupt with questions, laughing after Halimah related the details of his amusing escapades. Everyone sat and listened, absorbing the details. Then on a more serious level she began to tell them of the characteristics he demonstrated and his remarkable ability to retain information. Had it not been for her honesty and integrity, they would have attributed her accounts to mere exaggeration.

Later, after the servants had cleared away the table, Aminah turned to Muhammad and said: "My son, the hour is late and thou dost need thy sleep." Grudgingly Muhammad rose from the table and bid everyone a good night. Next, he looked toward Halimah who watched him with a curious expression, her eyes shone with unshed tears.

Sensing he might not see Halimah again, he rushed over and hugged her with all his strength. His embrace and show of affection spoke more eloquently than words. Turning, he saw his mother's outstretched arms and moved toward her shyly.

Aminah clutched Muhammad at the shoulders, holding him at arms length, caressing his small frame. Timidly, he leaned into her, reciprocating her motions. Sitting as she was, her eyes were nearly level with his. She thought the look in them was one of gentleness, understanding, and of wisdom beyond his years. "Good night my love," said Aminah softly. She kissed him on the forehead and pivoted him toward his grandfather.

Late into the night the household was still, the night silent, Muhammad could not fall asleep. The heart stirring day, new surroundings, all worked to magnify his restlessness. He rose from bed and quietly went to his room's window where he gazed out at the flickering stars. Involuntarily his sight shifted from the heavens to take in the scene at window level. He saw a shadowy world dimly illuminated under a crescent shaped moon. He thought the crescent and stars symmetry punctuated the earth's beauty. Even the blacks and grays of night were amazing. Feeling joyful and somewhat self-conscious for staring out the window in the middle of the night, he giggled, spun around and scampered back to bed.

Just before dawn, Aminah silently stole her way into Muhammad's room. She stood near the head of his bed for several long minutes watching him sleep. The blankets were entwined about his small arms and legs. She thought that he slept with complete abandon and then bent over and tenderly moved aside the thick mass of curls from his forehead to kiss him on the cheek. She could not help but feel the fleshiness of babyhood which caused her to experience a feeling of the deepest satisfaction. Smiling, she turned and crept out of the room.

Muhammad awoke to the sound of chattering sparrows, barking dogs, crowing roosters and the bawling of herd animals being led out to the countryside. Lying inertly, he waited for the cloudiness of sleep to clear away when he saw the nut-like face of his grandfather appearing from around the door's framework. "Ah ha! So thou hast awakened at last," said the rusty voice of Abdul. Smiling affectionately, Abdul crossed over to the boy's bed and stood looking down at him balled up beneath the blankets. Reaching down he tousled the mass of hair, splaying it over Muhammad's forehead. The youngster grinned up at his grandfather, cast aside the bed covers and jumped spryly to his feet. It seemed that before his feet contacted the floor he had asked several questions. In the excited jabber, Abdul only heard something about the big city of Mekkah. Laughing, he said: "Come on, thy mother awaits us with the morning meal."

CHAPTER TWO

In the course of time, Muhammad discovered his grandfather to be a font of knowledge. When other children were out playing, young Muhammad would often be found in the company of Abdul under the eaves of their house, deep in conversation. He learned many things but was particularly distressed over the custom of burying female infants alive and the superstition of abandoning the blind or those afflicted with serious diseases. For the life of him, he could not understand why people were so cruel to those less fortunate. However, he did take pride in his clan: the Hashim; part of Quraysh, the largest and noblest tribe in Arabia.

Frequently their evenings together were interrupted by people stopping to pay their respects and chat a few moments with Abdul. It was during one of these visits that Muhammad learned his grandfather was chief of Quraysh, with the responsibility as keeper of the Ka'bah, the First House of God. Fascinated over discussion about the Ka'bah, Muhammad would listen intently whenever one of the well-wishers raised the subject. One evening soon afterwards, after learning all he could, he began to question his grandfather in depth with an intensity uncommon in children. He left no stone unturned in his pursuit of answers. Taken aback with the shrewdness of questions posed, Abdul smiled inwardly with pride at his grandson's intelligence. He said simply, "On the morrow wilt I show thee so thou mayest understand better."

Early next day, the riotous noise of wildly chirping birds squabbling over the grain which Muhammad had placed on the window's sill woke him. Jumping out of bed, he crept toward the window with and peeked from behind its curtain. He smiled in satisfaction; the birds had finally discovered the crumbs of food he continually left there. For a few moments he watched the covey of birds swarming down, in and out as they pecked at the food in a blur of feathers. Sighing happily, he turned and bolted from the room.

Eagerly he had anticipated his first visit to the city's square. The suspense worked his stomach nervously, affecting him like the fluttering birds of moments ago. He could not eat any of his breakfast. "Should I ask thy mother to serve thee another portion, my boy," Abdul asked teasingly. Without missing a beat, Muhammad slid his bowl of uneaten food toward his grandfather, saying: "Nay grandfather! Take ye my bowl of food. I cannot eat for the excitement of learning new things has hindered my hunger."

Aminah smiled and Abdul chuckled in mirth at the seriousness of the expression he used. "Very well, thou must eat all thy noon meal, Muhammad," said his mother.

"Aminah, dost thou need anything from the marketplace," Abdul questioned.

Nay father, but keep thine eye on Muhammad," she returned, concern emanating from her expression.

"Art thou ready boy?" Abdul said to Muhammad's back as he raced for the door. Shaking his head in amusement, he rose from the table as the youngster impatiently called for him to hurry.

As the two started out for the square where the Ka'bah was located, Abdul began to study his grandson. Until falling asleep the night before, he had thought the boy still too young to grasp the significance of the Ka'bah's history or the principle of One God. But while he walked, he started contemplating the boy's talent to retain information. He decided what Muhammad didn't understand now he'd understand later.

"Muhammad," began Abdul tentatively, "there is nothing closer to one's heart or self than Allah and his own heart. It is the center of man's being and governs ones actions. As ye grow, thou wilt undergo many passions. A good man will control these passions and be at peace with himself. He will be calm, caring, truthful, and free of the lusts which drive the ones who have lost control. Always follow thy impulses of reason and they will guide thee to understanding, forbearance, generosity and security. Thou must bear this simple truth in mind and look further afield to prepare thyself against the passions of those who have given into their desires."

"Just as surely as men strive for sons and riches there are others who seek the truth and reality of existence. Thus, every day is another day to begin searching for truth. Seen from thy point of view no doubt it appears a difficult journey to seek for that which is unseen. But if ye wish truth and peace it is a journey worth traveling. For the man not true unto himself provides many reasons for delay and hesitation, and frequently becomes absorbed in his thoughts for selfish gain. He eventually becomes a treacherous, shameless, deceitful, greedy and vengeful man, despised by those whom he considers friends and loved ones. On the history of this city which dates back to ancient times, I only know what has been handed down to me from my father. There are others who are more knowledgeable in its lore and thou wilt meet them. But for now my meager store of knowledge will have to suffice thee.

"Abraham and his son, peace and blessings be upon them, came to this city and repaired Allah's House. But with time men started falsifying the belief in One God and tolerated its change which killed the spirit. Alas, my boy, regrettably this most holiest of cities has fallen

14

under the influence of merchants who seek only worldly gain. Daily, men squander their lives pursuing pleasures of the flesh and needless luxuries, or contrive mischief. It is an outrage against man's dignity and spirit!"

Nearing the square, Abdul ended his discourse, much to Muhammad's displeasure. Directly ahead, just visible over the rooftops, Abdul pointed out the huge imposing structure of the Ka'bah in the skyline.

Tearing his attention away from his grandfather, Muhammad looked to where Abdul pointed. In silence he stared, flashing on all Abdul had told him. He was awed by its history. Upon entering the square, Muhammad's senses were assaulted by the pungent odors of excrement exuding from wooden enclosures holding a variety of animals, of rotting vegetables, of meats made rancid by the burning sun. He then noticed a profusion of people dressed in tattered rags lining the inner walls of the square begging for Dirhams, shrieking infants clutched by their mothers, children of all ages scrambling about wildly competing with yelping dogs for scraps of food, others eating out of piles of refuse, and drunken men acting lewdly with the women as they stumbled about.

"Muhammad...Muhammad!" Abdul called solicitously as he watched the various expressions come and go on the boy's face. "Seest thou the young boy with the mark of the pox, the one beating upon the younger child? Stay ye clear of him for evil minded he is. So much so, his own kin and clan hath forsaken him. He is named Russal and he is known as the one who transgresses all bounds."

At first Muhammad hadn't heard his grandfather calling him: for the malodorous smells; the poor; the hungry, the immorality, had totally bewildered and left him feeling nauseous. Before he realized it, he and Abdul had arrived at the steps leading up into the Ka'bah, a massive stone edifice, cubical in shape and draped with black cloth. Once inside, Muhammad paused to allow his vision time to adjust to the darkened interior. He then began surveying the spacious chamber, scrutinizing the multi-formed images of stone along the walls. For a few moments he struggled to keep control of himself. He shivered involuntarily, repugnance striking his mind like a cudgel against the fragile barrier of his rationality. His emotions convulsed, churning into the caustic taste of shame and loathing. For the first time in his young life he felt an urge to destroy. So compelling was the impulse that he unknowingly clenched his fists and felt like screaming out against those responsible for erecting the hideous images. He thought to himself: how couldst they put such wickedness in the One God's House?

It took all his power of concentration to regain control of his thoughts. Then, with a detachment rare in adults let alone children, he began to see the idol worshippers' actions for what they really were. Thinking it utter nonsense, a hint of a smile started to crease the corners of his mouth as he observed people offering sacrifices. Others were earnestly conversing with the ugly shapes of human-like forms and weird caricatures of animals, pleading for wealth, health and happiness. Overwhelmed by the sheer silliness of it, he lost control and exploded into spasms of giggles.

A sudden silence fell, impregnating the Ka'bah with indignation. Men and women, young and old alike, turned toward the source of laughter with venomous looks filling their faces and Abdul, hoping to avoid an incident, hastily departed the Ka'bah with Muhammad in tow. He descended the few steps thinking it prudent to leave the area and return home. Stepping quickly, he held onto Muhammad's small hand firmly. He steered their flight through the square's center where Muhammad witnessed a scene that would ever come to mind when he saw a person with the mark of pox. Russal had knocked an old woman to the ground and ripped away the food she had for her family from her arms. But what really made the act all the more despicable was him kicking her about the face to silence her cries.

Exiting the square, Abdul looked over his shoulder searching for anyone from the Ka'bah. Satisfied they were out of harm's way, he slowed the pace.

"Wouldst thou like to visit Waraqah," asked Abdul, hoping to remove the disappointment of having cut short his first visit to the bazaar.

Muhammad welcomed the opportunity, for he particularly enjoyed the blind man's wit and knowledge of times past. He started to ask his grandfather a question but before he could mouth the words, Abdul asked: "What didst thou think of Allah's House?"

Giving the question deep thought, Muhammad's young face assumed the appearance of sagaciousness for several seconds before answering. He replied to his grandfather's question with one of his own. "There is only One Allah, so why are people worshipping false gods?"

Pleased with the boy's acuity, Abdul smiled warmly. He said, "Thou dost know which question to ask. I know but little of this matter, but of what I do wilt I tell thee and Waraqah can tell thee the rest."

A few minutes later, Abdul was knocking on Waraqah's door. At first Waraqah was unsure of who was rapping at his door, but when he heard the small knuckles accentuating the harder knock, he smiled in pleasure. "Abdul, Muhammad! Enter my friends," said the blind man from inside the house.

Taken aback by the blind man's ability to correctly name his guests without the benefit of sight, Muhammad cautiously opened the door as if expecting someone behind it. He peeked around the door and scanned the interior. Seeing no one, he inquired: "Waraqah, how didst thou know it was me and my grandfather?"

"Ah, man doth not see only with the eyes, for a man without sight learns to see with his ears," answered Waraqah.

Abdul burst into laughter at the confusing look on Muhammad's face. Waraqah, suspecting the reason for Abdul's peal of laughter, also began laughing. Muhammad didn't understand the cause for such risibility, but being the child he was, he too started giggling. Finally, when the moment of mirth passed, Abdul 'a-hemmed' a couple of times to clear his throat.

"Waraqah my friend, Muhammad would like to ask thee some questions," voiced Abdul. "Speak up Muhammad," said Waraqah seriously toward the sound Muhammad last made and added, "knowledge will open many a door."

"Saith grandfather there is only One God. Yet, people worship all manner of things in the Ka'bah. Why?"

"My boy," began Waraqah, "it is a question which hath its answer dating back thousands of years. When Allah, the One God, commanded the Prophet Abraham, peace and blessing be upon him, to come and purify the Mother of cities, he and his first born Isma'il, peace and blessings be upon him, restored the Ka'bah for the exclusive worship of Allah. But, with the passage of time and influences from other cultures, man became corrupted and superstitious in belief. Men began adorning themselves with baubles which are for women. They grew obstinate, giving themselves to arrogance, surrounding themselves with people who wouldest flatter their vanities. Then, as a means to reach the One God, man fashioned idols, images, crucifixes and numerous representations, in spite of Allah's Curse upon the practitioners of idolatry.

"And yet the Disbelievers say Allah came in the form of a man! Allah is not a man, nor is He many in one."

With every day living, Muhammad soon grew accustomed to his new surroundings and ways of life. His qualities which brought him a certain distinction among the Banu Sa'd began to manifest itself in the new community. His friendly disposition and truthfulness won him many new friends, young and old alike.

One evening a friend of Abdul's arrived as the family ended their meal. He was full of excitement as he revealed the fair's upcoming date. Together, he, Abdul and Aminah, excitedly discussed the many events the fair would bring. Muhammad, unfamiliar with the concept of a fair, paid close attention while the grownups talked. Anxiously, he waited for a break in dialogue to start asking questions.

Recognizing Muhammad's nervous fidgeting while he tried to contain his mounting excitement, Abdul grinned and asked: "Hast thou something on thy mind, Muhammad?" "What is a fair, what is a fair?" Muhammad returned in a flow of nonstop words.

Simultaneously the elders convulsed into laughter at the tumble of Muhammad's words. His mother then explained that the fair was really called the Ukadh which was only held during the four holy months of each year, and turned to continue her conversation with their guest.

Unsatisfied with his mother's meager explanation, Muhammad's face filled with an inquisitive look. He started squirming, his brow creasing in discontent. Abdul noticed the look and picked up where Aminah left off. "People from all Arabia and surrounding countries sojourn in Mekkah. This territory, especially during these special months well known is free from fear, danger, and the ravages of war or private feuds. It is the place where everyone feels safe to gather at one time. They bring goods, wares and livestock, to sell, trade or purchase."

Muhammad mentally restrained his natural curiosity from asking any more questions. Instead, he began to consider his grandfather's explanation and its implications. And during the coming days, before the Ukadh officially got underway, Muhammad frequently went with Abdul to the square. Usually left to his own devises, he wandered about the marketplace marveling over the different preparations for the fair while his grandfather went from stall to stall searching for the best bargains.

On one occasion, with a Dirham in his pocket, Muhammad sought out his favorite confectioner. While he walked to the square's far side, he observed a woman of advanced years, dressed in soiled rags. The old woman was quietly weeping for no apparent reason he could discern. It was a pitiful sight and he felt an overpowering sense of compassion. He approached the woman intending to offer comfort and give her his Dirham. When out of nowhere a drunken man started to curse and abuse the old lady with the foulest language he'd ever heard. Shocked at the treatment the poor lady was receiving, he left the area seeking the safety of his grandfather. Flushed and disturbed, he stepped in behind Abdul and silently followed him from each of the booths.

Aware that Muhammad was trailing close behind, Abdul pretended not to notice the boy. He waited, knowing the boy's inquisitorial nature would soon surface. After a time, the silence between them in the noisy square seemed to have become extraordinary profound. Growing curious as to the boy's reticence, he turned around to face him. It was immediately clear that Muhammad was troubled by something. He stopped and crouched down to his level. "What aileth thee, Muhammad," asked Abdul.

Muhammad recounted the incident involving the old woman, and then asked: "Why?" Not knowing how to explain a society where there are so many injustices, Abdul just answered: "The man was in a state of inebriation and knewest not his actions."

Muhammad weighed his grandfather's explanation and found it wanting. Try as he might, he could not understand. Finally unable to comprehend the reasons why the man would act as he did, he questioned Abdul again, probing for more information. What he didn't realize was that his young mind could not grasp the abstract meaning of hate, yet.

Eventually, opening day of the Ukadh arrived and households all throughout the city were alive with excitement. In anticipation of the fair's commencement and attractions, Aminah rose before dawn and prepared a huge, nourishing meal to see her father-in-law and son through to the end of the evening. But discussion at the table about the fair's events curbed Muhammad's appetite and served as fuel to fire his imagination.

Aminah flung her arms in the air, feigning exasperation, and dispensed with the effort to feed Muhammad. She and Abdul could only smile at the boy's enthusiasm as he kept running from the window and table to see if they had finished their breakfast. At the last, Abdul rose, indicating departure. Muhammad squeaked in delight. Aminah smiled and the trio left for the fair.

Almost immediately they found themselves swallowed up by hordes of people, camels, goats, sheep and barking dogs, sweeping them towards the square. Muhammad, spellbound by the pulsating life around him, flowed absently along with the mass of humanity and animals. A succession of ideas came and went as he threaded his way through the menagerie of life until he entered the square.

It was a scene straight out of the times of antiquity. Men and women were attired in colors of scarlet and purples, decorated with finger rings, toe rings, nose rings and bracelets of hammered gold. Many of the women dressed unchastely, baring their legs and shoulders, provoking the men into making obscene gestures and causing numerous altercations.

Animals were being butchered and roasted over open pits, and adding to the disorder, groups of men roamed the bazaar in a drunken stupor.

Seeing another group of people standing in front of a man "oohing" and "aahing", Muhammad's intellect burned with curiosity. He moved in closer, wiggling his way through the crowd to investigate. The man was speaking in rhyme: relating stories of war; valor; kings; and, carnality. He learned later that such men were called poets and their tales, poems. He wasn't much interested in the poems but was captivated by the poet's ability to keep peoples attention. He watched the bard's performance, studying and committing to memory the man's demeanor.

Moving on, he came across several men deep in their cups, effusively using foul language and boasting about the wealth of their tribes. People around them were becoming angry, resentful, and feeling the air thicken with malice he quit the area. Finding himself near the Ka'bah, memories of the silly idol worshippers came flooding back, making him smile. He decided to enter. Again, he found people exhorting the carved images of stone and wood. He thought the offerings were a waste, especially when the poor and hungry could have used them so much better. Withdrawing as quietly as he entered, he felt disturbed by the wretched things taking place.

By late afternoon, Muhammad returned home to find his mother and grandfather in conversation, expressing their delight over the new items the fair had to offer and new friends each had made. He couldn't understand why they didn't suffer the same ill-effects and it confused him. He knew they were kind and loving people, yet they acted as if nothing untoward was taking place. How couldst that be, he thought.

Aminah saw the perplexed cast to Muhammad's face and mistakenly thought him ill. She stopped in mid-sentence and gathered Muhammad in her arms, questioning him about what he'd eaten. Soothed by his mother's affections, his thoughts diverted from confusion to contentment.

Mollified by his features expanding into a bright smile, Aminah asked him: "Wouldst thou go to the well for water and aid thy grandfather in building the fire for dinner?" Muhammad was only too happy to comply with his mother's wishes and skipped off to do her bidding.

With the servants having the day off, dinner was later than usual. All through the meal Muhammad's eyes drooped, and he nearly toppled off his seat in exhaustion from his day in the square. His mother then picked him up and carried him off to bed.

Lying in bed, Muhammad sleepily asked his mother for a story as she drew up the blanket and tucked it in around him. Sitting next to him, she began telling him about his father. In a matter of minutes he was lulled to sleep by his mother's voice. Aminah extinguished the candle, kissed him softly, and as an afterthought voiced, "Soon my son wilt we visit thy father's grave and thy relatives in Yathrib."

In the morning, Muhammad woke to an unusually silent house. Gone were the familiar voices of the servants, his mother and grandfather. Imagining the extreme, he perked up his ears, tuning in on any sound, but there was only the faint rattling of utensils to be heard. Silently he got out of bed, crept to the doorway like a leopard stalking its prey. Peeping around the casement, he saw his grandfather in the small alcove eating breakfast. With an audible sigh of relief, he skipped toward Abdul and joined him at the table.

Aminah, before leaving for the marketplace with the servants, left Abdul in charge of making sure Muhammad ate his breakfast. So when the boy sat down he served up the hot pottage. But still troubled from his visit to the fair, Muhammad picked at his food soundlessly. Abdul had to admonish him to eat several times before his meal grew cold.

Subtly Abdul watched him, thinking the boy too sensitive for his years, virtuous with characteristics that indicated forbearance and patience, yet embodied with an uncommon inner strength. Puzzled by the absence of his grandson's customary early morning chatter, he probed for an answer.

"Why art thou so quiet, Muhammad," he asked.

For the lapse of many seconds Muhammad just stared into his grandfather's judicious old eyes, gathering his thoughts. Then, in a release of pent-up emotions, he confided in Abdul, telling him his trouble understanding why people treated the poor with so much cruelty and abuse. Intuitively Abdul knew the boy would not be appeased with another simple explanation. He sat back against the wall of the alcove and regarded his grandson in mute contemplation, considering his response. Finally, he said: "Oh, Muhammad, these are people who behold themselves better than others observe them.

They live their lives without concern for the plight of others less fortunate than themselves. And when they behold someone not conforming to their desires, evil minded and abusive they become. Man by himself..."

After the sobering conversation, Muhammad had gained a little more insight into man's behavior and soon became his usual cheery self again. Abdul pleased at the boy's response, spent the day with Muhammad, telling him what he knew of the story of the Prophet Abraham and his progeny.

Days later, while Aminah aided the servants in preparing the morning meal, she told the sleepy headed Muhammad of her friend's arrival to help them pack and travel to Yathrib. Quick as lightening the youngster's sleepiness evaporated. He ran to the room's window and pushed aside the curtains, expecting to see his mother's friend, Umm Ayman, to magically appear. The servants grinned, Abdul chuckled outright, and Aminah smiled at her son's antics. Muhammad's zest for life was like a force unto itself. "Wilt she be here soon enough, my son. But now it is time for thee to eat," said Aminah.

Muhammad reluctantly turned away from the window and returned to the table. Upon hearing approaching footfalls, he jumped from his seat and nearly knocked his chair to the floor. He ran to open the door and before his mother or grandfather could reach the door, Muhammad had already welcomed Umm Ayman into the house. Aminah and Abdul nevertheless welcomed her again. Then they retreated to the alcove for tea and to renew their friendship before beginning their preparations for the trip.

As the packing got underway, Muhammad's animation charmed Umm Ayman. Busily he ran back and forth between her and his mother, asking what he could do to help. Umm Ayman watched the excited boy with admiration, thinking: never before hadst I known a six year old child to be so considerate and helpful. About an hour before noon they were ready to depart. Relaxing, they joined Abdul and chatted until the scheduled hour for their departure arrived which came all too fast for Abdul.

At the appointed hour, Abdul fervently embraced his daughter-in-law and grandson. For him, the moment was too reminiscent of an earlier time. Somberly he helped the three of them mount their animals. He asked again if they needed a guide but the women assured him they'd all be safe. Thus, bidding farewell, he wished them a safe journey and watched them ride off.

The road to Yathrib, well traveled by caravans, was relatively free of highwaymen. Nonetheless the journey in and of itself was treacherous and dangerous as it snaked its way up and along the high rugged mountains. At sunset of their first day out they were still scaling the heights when Umm Ayman deemed it too risky to continue. Finding an area level enough to sleep the night, they dismounted. The women made ready their evening meal, Muhammad tended the animals.

The setting sun filled the sky with beautiful hues of red and gold, clouds reflecting the colors added to the majesty. Muhammad stood lost in amazement as he took in the unsurpassed beauty of the heavens. It was his first time viewing the sunset from so high up, and in years to come he would equate the mountains with tranquility, a place of sanctuary. That night the air was cool as he slept peacefully under the crystal clear skies.

In the days following, the going was slow and tedious. Blowing winds brought desert sand up into the mountains, making everyone uncomfortable. One could only endure the abrasive sand pricking the exposed skin with annoyance. Conversation was nearly impossible without the grit filling one's mouth. The camels, half blinded, snorted in displeasure at the elements as the granulated winds howled through the craggy ridges, forcing them to seek protection along the sharp outcroppings of rock. Two weeks later, they arrived in Yathrib.

CHAPTER THREE

Aminah's youngest sister, drawing water from the city's well, saw the small caravan. She raised her hand to block out the early morning glare and screamed with delight, surprised by Aminah's unexpected arrival in Yathrib. She ran back to her home, shouting all the way: "Aminah is here! Aminah is here!"

Family members emerged from different parts of the house and joined up in the courtyard. Happily they welcomed Aminah, the matronly lady and small boy. Amid the hugs and kisses, Aminah presented her son and friend. After the introductions, the family took her rare visit as an occasion to celebrate.

Abu Ayyub, one of Muhammad's uncles, asked him if he would like to accompany him and his friends, Itban and Kharijah, to select a young ewe for the evening meal. Without a moments hesitation Muhammad agreed then sheepishly looked toward his mother for permission. She acquiesced genially and the four went off to butcher their meal. Aminah, her sisters and Umm Ayman, left for the family's orchard to gather fruits while her parents returned into the house to make ready for the night's festivities.

Aminah, during dinner and for much of her stay, spent the time recounting the years since her last visit. Umm Ayman rendered her time informing the household of past and current events in Mekkah. Muhammad played, explored the city and made new friends.

Three weeks later, Aminah sadly told her family time had come for them to return home. The family appealed for her to extend their visit, for they had grown to love and admire Muhammad, lauding his honesty and unselfishness. Almost swayed by their request and affection for her son, she nevertheless remained steadfast in her decision.

Aminah and Umm Ayman resolutely began assembling their provisions for the journey back to Mekkah. The womenfolk joined in and the evening passed at a leisurely pace until Aminah shrieked with pain. She sank to her knees clutching her abdomen and crumbled to the floor. She was so frightened, she didn't hear the cries of alarm and pounding footsteps running toward her or feel herself being raised and moved.

All through the night Aminah tossed, turned, and groaned in sufferance. Her family, doing all they could, grew increasingly alarmed by the pallor of her skin. Periodically regaining her sensory faculties, she felt cool poultices pressed across her head. She was not sure exactly when she first realized the light of dawn spilling into the room or why it suddenly mattered. By sunrise her color partially returned and she awoke feeling a bit better. She found herself surrounded by family members trying to persuade her to delay her departure a few days in order to recover her strength. But not realizing the seriousness of her condition, she declined, explaining her malady away as a minor upset stomach.

After a hot breakfast, Aminah, Umm Ayman and Muhammad, departed for Mekkah. Upon clearing the city, Aminah turned their small train toward the grave site of Muhammad's father. It was during their stop at Abdullah's resting place that Aminah again started to feel in a bad way. But unwilling to alarm anyone, she remained silent about her suffering and continued on.

Within a week's travel time from Yathrib, she could no longer endure the rigors of traveling. Umm Ayman, against Aminah's bidding, halted their journey, hoping the stop would give her friend the opportunity to recover. Umm Ayman considered how far they had traversed, their remoteness, and then forsook her notion of returning to Yathrib for help. For, in all Arabia there were few if any that understood the loss of health and she could not leave a child to care for his ailing mother. She and the boy's only option was to make Aminah as comfortable as possible and hope for the best.

For two days Aminah struggled against her illness before surrendering her life. Muhammad wept with grief. His mother's death and having just visited his father's grave shattered his senses. With Muhammad sobbing and Umm Ayman weeping, they both began to dig up the rock imbedded ground for Aminah's burial. The task was all the more difficult because they were lacking proper implements to use. With bleeding hands and shredded fingers, they lay to rest Aminah's body and continued on to Mekkah.

In the stillness of the mountains, the full impact of his mother and father's death struck Muhammad heavily. Inundated with thoughts of death, his head sagged ponderously, and ever so gradually he began to withdraw into himself.

Umm Ayman helplessly watched in growing alarm as the young boy regressed further and further into himself. Redoubling her efforts to console him, she tried drawing him into conversation about anything that came to mind, but nothing worked. His refusal to engage in discourse, his loss of appetite, made her uneasy and she began fearing for his health.

Fortunately, Muhammad and Umm Ayman arrived in Mekkah before his deterioration reached the point of no return. Thin and worn down from the ravages of grief, Muhammad felt no joy in the familiar sight of his home. If anything he felt a wave of retrospection wash over him, for he burst into tears. Umm Ayman, at her wits end, heard the pitiful sobs and she too began to weep. Thus with heavy hearts they dismounted and entered the house.

As the door opened the servants turned to face them. Every one of them broke into smiles and started to happily greet Muhammad and Umm Ayman until they noticed his tear stained face and somber appearance. One by one they smothered their spirited welcoming and looked at each other with curiosity, wondering what had befallen them.

Abdul, elsewhere in the house, dropped what he was doing when he heard the servants hailing his grandson. He rushed as fast as his old legs would allow to welcome his daughter-in-law's homecoming. Upon entering the main room, he stopped dead in his tracks, fear clutching at his heart. He saw Muhammad and Umm Ayman's faces utterly distressed. With a pervading sense of dread he asked the suspected whereabouts of Aminah. At the mention of his mother's name, Muhammad whimpered and fled the room, leaving the distraught Umm Ayman to answer his grandfather's questions.

With the passage of time, Muhammad soon overcame the vacuum left by his mother's death. He, more often than not, spent his days outside his house watching the activities of people around his neighborhood, studying and analyzing their actions.

Abu Talib, Muhammad's favorite uncle, had of late heard through family members of the boy's inactivity. Concerned over Muhammad's welfare, he decided to make some time for his nephew. Misunderstanding the boy's indolence, he arrived on Muhammad's seventh birthday intending to spend the entire day with him at the bazaar, hoping to foster a livelier disposition.

Seldom did Muhammad's uncle Talib ever take time off from his duties. To Muhammad, the visit was indeed special. Even though he was unable to fully appreciate the significance of his uncle's consideration, he nevertheless wanted nothing to mar the occasion. Imposing his will, he refrained from thinking of the city's malignity as they headed toward the square. But it was not meant to be. The first thing he saw upon entering the marketplace were men fighting, heatedly cursing one another with every pummel of their fists. He turned his head in disgust only to see a wealthy man in a litter lashing his bearers. Seeing the violence, Abu Talib twinged involuntarily and steered Muhammad in the opposite direction.

Muhammad attempted to dismiss the brawl from his mind as his uncle's hand guided him over to a confectionery stand. But while waiting in the small queue he heard a group of men boasting of their exploits in the desert. In and of itself, the self praise was trivial but they were crowing over the pillaging, debauchery, and killing of innocent people. Disgusted with the offensive braggarts, he was only too happy to move on.

Abu Talib stopped at a booth in the shade of food stalls where games of chance were being played. Visibly growing excited, he soon forgot about Muhammad at his side and elbowed his way through the men surrounding the gaming table.

Muhammad watched a few minutes, running his eyes over the men who were all whooping and yelling. Losing interest, he ambled away. Wending his way through the crowd, he came across a startling scene of brutality. Two men were stomping an old crippled beggar. Incapable of halting the savagery, he lost command of his emotions and soundlessly started to cry. Deploring man's maliciousness toward his brother, the incident amplified itself to the point of torturing his young soul. Not knowing how to deal with it he snuffled, wiped away the tears and continued on. After a few steps he walked into Russal, the evil one. Russal looked into his red rimmed eyes and started jeering, calling him effeminate names. Muhammad stood his ground, staring him back coldly in the eye. Seconds passed, tensions mounted, the evil one blinked, turned and tread a hasty path feeling intimidated and belittled by Muhammad's unrelenting stare.

An hour or two later, Abu Talib came upon Muhammad sitting on the Ka'bah's steps. He stopped to watch and as before, wondered over the boy's seriousness.

"Muhammad, why art thou so unhappy?" Talib called out in a voice trying to conceal his concern.

"It is a strange world we live in," returned Muhammad. Double taking his nephew, Talib arched his brow and suddenly thought the stories of his perceptivity held true. "In time thou wilt come to understand the strangeness. But for now, enough is it to say men know not Allah."

As the two returned to their home, they encountered several members of their clan along the way; hurrying toward the house. Abu Talib instantly sensed trouble from the looks on their faces. Muhammad, no stranger to death's rattle, instinctively tensed, his flesh beginning to crawl. Picking up the pace, Talib called out worriedly to his kinsman: "Abu Lahab, what saith thou for thy haste?" Well-to-do, influential, Abu Lahab spun around haughtily and answered back contemptuously, "By the gods, how shouldst I know? I was summoned but a moment ago, by one of Abbas' brood to make haste for father's house."

Stung by the sharp retort, Talib nevertheless continued on, stepping up his pace until reaching his father's home. There, he met numerous members of the family speaking in hushed tones, anxiety filled their faces. Dreading what he suspected, he entered Abdul's room. He found the patriarch of the family bed stricken, weak with fever and coughing feebly, each spasm racking his body.

Nearly eighty years old, Abdul had fallen ill in the span of a short time, seized with an unknown ailment. His children who were all grown had come to be by his side. Feeling helpless, they surrounded his bed, worried and upset over his rapid discoloration and waning breath. With no medical practitioners skilled in the art of medicine, they did their best to care for him.

Abdul listlessly moved his head around, scanning the room until his weak sight rested on Muhammad. Smiling a special smile reserved for the boy, the corners of his eyes crinkled, making his eyes shine with love. Struggling against the weight of the woolen blanket, he raised himself onto his elbows. He extended his frail arms, his hands looking like gnarled claws, and gestured Muhammad to step forward.

Muhammad stepped toward his grandfather falteringly, tears spilling down his cheeks. Then, all at once, he rushed into the outstretched arms, sobbing and fearing the unseen King of Terror.

Abdul's shock of white hair flounced with each of Muhammad's convulsive inhalations. Patting his small back, he temporarily soothed the raging emotions playing havoc within his grandson.

"There, there, weep not my son," cooed Abdul.

"B-but gr-grandfather," began Muhammad before he was cut off.

"Shh, little one," returned the hoary voice of his grandfather as he maneuvered Muhammad to sit besides him on the bed. With a strength belying his infirmity, Abdul clutched the boy's hands in his knotted, palsied-like fingers. "Talib?" He called out with tears in his eyes, while staring into Muhammad's frightened face.

"I am here, father," answered Talib.

"Take thou charge of Muhammad's rearing," expelled Abdul with his last breath.

Feeling greatly honored by his father's vote of confidence, Abu Talib readily consented. Then before adding anything further, he realized his father, Abdul Mut'talib, Chief of Banu Quraysh, had breathed his last breath.

The women wailed in anguish. Abbas and several others cleared the room, and started preparations for burial. Muhammad was especially hard hit, having lost the two people he loved most in the world. The city as well, in days to come, would feel the repercussions of Abdul's death.

The city's fathers, merchants and tradesmen, fearing an end to their many years of prosperity as Abdul's death created an air of general insecurity. Mekkah, centrally located on the Peninsula of Arabia and near the Red Sea, facilitated trade which gave the city honor and profit. (1) Trade caravans enriched the city, bringing much knowledge of the world and it's many arts, and perfected their language as a polished medium of literary expression(2) which drew people from distant parts to Mekkah.(3) Thus, the transition of chieftain-ship, like anywhere else, left many wondering if any could match Abdul's skill and diplomacy. For through his prestige and integrity had he maintained the covenants of security and safe passage from the Rulers of neighboring countries which protected their trade routes in all seasons. (4)

CHAPTER FOUR

Muhammad's life soon returned to normal after moving in with his uncle Talib and the many children. The new found freedom to move about without supervision increased his time in examining people's ways, and added to his knowledge dramatically. The experiences he gained, however, deeply affected his views on life. He had come to dread the yearly Ukadh gatherings simply because he loathed what he saw and heard.

And after two years, the smiling child began to develop into a contemplative young man, mature beyond his years. He started disassociating himself from most of the people around him, preferring to keep to himself. Daily, he mentally recorded the immorality and tyranny of the oppressed. His only happiness coming from helping his uncle and family.

Abu Talib, busily engaged pursuing a living and raising his children, noticed the emergence of Muhammad's serious nature and outlook on life. Stumped as what to do about the boy's solemn comportment, he asked him if he would like to care for the family's herd of sheep, hoping the change of scenery would enliven the boy's spirits. In fact, the change was exactly opposite of what he wanted. For it would give the young Muhammad time to refine his thoughts in the solitude of Najd's pastures.

Muhammad happily accepted the offer, pleased that he was trusted with the family's livelihood. He knew from previous occasions helping his cousins the responsibilities of shepherding were not difficult and would afford him more than enough time to ponder the complexities of life without distractions.

Within days of his appointment he began taking advantage of his spare time while the sheep grazed for hours on end. He'd sit on an elevation staring off into the horizon; deep in thought as the warm breezes flowing across the meadows refreshed his spirits.

After a time he noticed people looking at him in a different way every time he ventured into the city's square. They no longer treated him as a meddlesome adolescent. He wasn't sure but it seemed to him people respected and listened to him. Always they greeted him and tried to act civilly around him. Eventually he reasoned the cause for the difference being that he invariably fulfilled his obligations and never caused harm to anyone.

Shortly following his twelfth birthday, he was in the square when he overheard a group of men discussing a trade caravan leaving for Syria in a week's time. Roused by their stories of far away places, he stepped in among the men and listened.

Unexpectedly one of the men addressed him. "Art thou Muhammad?"

"Yea," Muhammad replied.

"Is thy uncle in readiness for the expedition," questioned the stranger.

"I know not, sir."

A moment later Muhammad spun around, creating a small whirlwind of dust in his haste to get home. Bubbling over with excitement, he found his uncle going over the accounts. Breathlessly he asked if he could accompany him to Syria.

Abu Talib fondly looked at his nephew in silence, thinking the boy had indeed grown up in the past years and would someday be a man to contend with. Then as Muhammad began to shuffle his feet back and forth, he grinned at his excitability and granted permission.

Delighted by his uncle's indulgence, Muhammad thanked him and energetically bounded off to prepare for the journey. Less than a minute later, embarrassed and red faced, he sheepishly returned to ask his uncle what to pack.

Talib could not help himself from convulsing in laughter over his nephew's blushing face. Holding his sides, he explained what would be needed for the trip.

At week's end all was in readiness, and on the day of departure, following the day's first light, men, beasts of burden and livestock commenced the trek to Syria. Before long, Muhammad started to comprehend the desert's vastness, the heaven's immensity. The miraculous sunrises and sunsets filled him with wonder as he thought how beautiful the One God's world was. He inwardly marked the proficiency with which all creatures sought the bounty of Allah.

As the caravan languidly traversed its route under the blazing sun, the heavily laden camels had to be rested frequently. During these stops the men erected tarps to veil themselves from the sun's heat and launched into conversations about every thing under the sun while they waited for people of nearby settlements to come and trade.

Muhammad was always interested in learning something new and wandered in and out of the various shelters, stopping only when the topic of discussion was serious and new to him.

After several weeks travel the collection of men comprising the caravan came to rest on the outskirts of Busra, a small town in the Mountain Druze district of Syria, some seventy miles south of Damascus.(1) The lush vibrancy of hills, valleys and trees, and flowing streams were markedly different from the Arabian expanse of arid desert. And to Muhammad it brought to mind his life with Halimah and her tribe.

Buhaira, a Christian monk, and his coenobitical order learned of a caravan setting up camp in the vicinity and set off to invite the travelers to share dinner with them back at the monastery. Grateful for the opportunity to partake in a decent cooked meal, the men expressed their appreciation and thanked Buhaira, promising to join them once their camp was in order. After taking a head count, he sent his brothers back to the monastery with the numbers, then pitched in to help the Bedouins make their camp. Following an hour of strenuous work, the men washed themselves and set out for the basilica, leaving the young boys behind to tend the animals.

"Captain! Captain!" Buhaira called out as he ran after the caravan's leader.

"Buhaira, how can I help thee," asked the Captain."

"The young men are also invited to break bread, Captain."

"Then, see the curly headed boy spreading feed for the livestock?"

"Yea!"

"Tell him to care for the animals and to tell the others to join us."

"Begging thy pardon Captain, he is yet but a mere boy," Buhaira commented with raised brows.

"It is the truth thou saith. However, he is the most responsible."

Surprised by the Captain's choice, Buhaira walked back towards the young boy and relayed his instructions, then waited for him to return.

"What is thy name son," Buhaira questioned curiously.

"Muhammad."

Buhaira, known and respected for his deep knowledge of the Christian faith, gulped air as his heart accelerated to twice its normal beat. He knew the Books given to Moses told of a Prophet's advent from the Isma'ilites and prophet Jesus himself in his original teachings named the Prophet to come "Ahmad".

Excitedly he began asking many questions, probing for answers that would conclusively fulfill the Prophecies. Exultant, he swiftly beat a path back to the priory and commenced to ask the caravan's elders, "Unto who is the boy, Muhammad, related to?" All eyes turned to Abu Talib.

"He is my nephew."

The monk impassionedly began to impart information from his readings: "He is the promised Prophet whose universal Prophethood, conquests, and rule have been foretold in the heavenly Books and the signs which I have read in the Books apply to him. He is the same Prophet, about whose name and about the name of whose father and regarding whose family, I have read in the religious books, and I know from whence he is to rise and in what manner his religion will spread in the world. However, you must keep him hidden from the eyes of the Jews; for, if they learn about him, they will kill him."(2)

Abu Talib was astonished at what he heard and numbly responded with Muhammad's acts of good deeds, fairness, and honesty, which confirmed the monk's beliefs all the more. Talib knew well the probity of Muhammad's mind and soul, and assured Buhaira he would use his utmost power and skill protecting the boy. That night he was unable to sleep and spent the time meditating under the stars. He kept remembering Buhaira's words and realized Muhammad was steadfastly growing in virtues. He thought: with no instruction Muhammad put to shame the knowledge of learned men; he was able to learn from men and teach them in turn; always, he won the love of people he worked and lived with. Ever loyal to the core, he never lost his way to truth and righteousness(3) amid the equivocating society of Mekkah. Turning to face the sleeping boy, his heart filled with compassion and his eyes looked in admiration. Shortly thereafter he drifted off in slumber.

Skirting the plains of Al Laja, the caravan arrived in Muhajjah, their last business stop before returning to Mekkah. The few days they were there, Muhammad noticed the variations in customs and ways of living between his countrymen and the people of Syria. Yet, what stayed uppermost in his mind was even though the two peoples were different, corruption remained the same.

CHAPTER FIVE

Back in Mekkah, Muhammad resumed his shepherding duties. The ensuing years spent out in the grasslands were years of spiritual awakening and insight into man's ingratitude when he rebelled and held as naught the Signs of God, turning his gift to baser uses. Ofttimes, driving rarer souls to hermit life, clouding the heavenly mirror of pure affections with selfish passion, mad unseemly wrangles, and hard unhallowed loathsome tortures of themselves.(1)

He worked with joy in honest labor, traded with integrity to himself and to others. He joined the throngs of cities and their busy lives, seeing theirv good and evil as an aspect of an inner and more lasting life hereafter. He despised not wealth but used it for others. He was happy in poverty and used it as his badge as a man among men. (2)

One day near Muhammad's fifteenth birthday, while the sheep grazed, he
stooped over the water hole to wash the dust from his face. Midway down, he suddenly stopped and stared at his image reflected by the water. Mesmerized, he thought of how others saw him. He was the picture of health with a muscular frame. A velvety soft thatch of hair lightly shadowed his cheeks, creating a look of dignity. Next, he noticed his pain filled eyes staring back at him. The minutes slipped away as he glimpsed the inner reaches of his soul. Finally, to break the grasp of heavy feelings clutching his mind's eye, he rubbed his eyes rigorously like he was trying to erase what he envisioned. Disturbed, he got up and walked to a nearby boulder and perched himself atop. Looking out over the gently swaying grasses and sheep filled landscape, his mind refused to release the depiction of depravity, ignorance, and selfishness of others.

Thinking he must do something, he picked unmindfully at a loose thread on his tunic with one hand while resting his chin on the other. It wasn't fulfilling to offer a kind word or provide an occasional meal to those stricken with poverty. Powerless, he felt webbed in inexperience to solve or at least help remedy man's plight. Forlornly he shook his head, causing him to return to the here and now. He was surprised, for more than an hour had elapsed unnoticed, the sheep had returned from their foraging and were at the water hole.

In the past four years, his many trips to the marketplace kept him abreast of the current hostilities raging on and off between his tribe and the Hawazin. To him, the reasons for fighting were foolish and resulted in meaningless deaths. Realizing its absurdity, he declared his position and spoke to those who'd listen about the arrogance and corruption of both tribes, which kept the feuding alive. One day, his uncle Talib informed him that when the fighting resumed he would have to join in now that he was fifteen years of age. He agreed but insisted he would not take up arms and only do what he could in clear conscious.

When the call to arms went out, Muhammad, true to his word joined the throng of men heading out of Mekkah. Mostly, he stood at his uncle's side, probing the reasons for placing men in certain areas of the battlefield. From the information he received and through his observations, he collected a great deal about the tactics of war which in years to come would be called to mind.

After three days of savage fighting, the battling stopped. Relieved, he welcomed the break wholeheartedly, yet the cessation filled him with bitterness. Women screamed and cried as they grieved over the deaths of their sons, brothers and husbands. The wailing women so depressed his spirits he left the city, seeking the remembered solace in the adjacent mountains.

Meanwhile, the city's square was alive with discussion of ways to end once and for all, the senseless war of which the contending tribes had long forgotten the reasons. During the latest round of battle twice as many men were either killed or maimed than in all previous skirmishes added together. The knowledge terrorized the tribes' leaders and in an effort to reconcile their differences, they met on the Ka'bah's steps.

Throughout the afternoon they heatedly argued with each other concerning the causes for hostilities, and after nearly coming to blows, an agreement was reached. In one week's time, Ga'dan, a respected elder of a nonpartisan tribe, would host a special council where he would arbitrate the differences.

Muhammad reappeared late that afternoon to find an unaccustomed calm permeating the city; even the women were restraining their lamentations. Suspecting a turn for the worse, he rushed home, the anxieties of earlier taking its first steps in constraining his peace. The moment he walked through the door, Abu Talib excitedly began recounting the day's events, describing every detail. Relief flooded Muhammad's face, the worst of his fears had been allayed and for the remainder of the evening the two talked over the ramifications of peace.

On the scheduled day of the meeting, Muhammad awoke to the sound of squalling sparrows, disturbed by the influx of men coming into Mekkah. Realizing the day for the unique meeting had arrived, he scrambled out of bed, stepped to the window and listened to the numerous voices passing by. Determining the tone the council would take, he was pleased. Smiling, he hastily dressed, losing no time in his hurry to catch the groups of men headed for Ga'dan's house.

Upon entering their host's huge house in the hilly, well-to-do section of Mekkah, Muhammad seated himself amid the crowd of men. As he listened to different bits of conversations, he gradually became aware of his surroundings. The interior was truly a work of craftsmanship: walls were draped with exquisite tapestries of Persian and Asian origin; small potted palms and flora endemic to the area were everywhere, filling the house with a fragrance of lush gardens; chairs made from rare exotic woods were lined to face an impressively carved table where Ga'dan himself sat.

All in all, Muhammad thought the beautiful surroundings would serve as a reminder of what could be lost if the warfare didn't stop. Being fifteen years of age and the youngest present, it wasn't long before Muhammad began to notice some of the elders eyeing him with raised brows. Only his excellent reputation arrested any comment.

As the meeting progressed, it severed into several small groups. Ga'dan, sensing the council was making no headway toward its goals, stood and clamored for order. The assemblage, surprised by the authoritative voice, settled down and gave their attention as he put forth ideas.

In the interim, they started gaining ground, and following hours of suggestions and opinions, several resolutions were passed: 1.) to help the poor and needy; 2.) to defend the weak; 3.) to establish peace and promote harmony; and, 4.) to end oppression.

After the last resolution had been voted in, the small convention of one time enemies embraced as a seal to the agreements. To Muhammad, it was more than expected to see the men's camaraderie especially when just a week ago these same men were trying to kill each other. Satisfied at the outcome, he departed for home in high spirits thinking that now the city would become a better place to live.

The next few years brought meager changes if any to Mekkah. Muhammad, recalling that memorable meeting at Ga'dan's thought with no hope the city's present conditions would not change in the years to come. He had really believed things were going to improve but corruption still ran rampant and the hapless seemingly suffered greater indignities. It was then he decided to take in tow the poor, sick and disadvantaged.

CHAPTER SIX

Upon attaining the considered age of maturity, Muhammad had grown into a well proportioned young man of medium height. Tanned, broad shouldered and powerfully built, he refused to don the clothes characteristic of up and coming men. He preferred to dress simply in garb purchased from the poor.

Known for his disarming personality, Muhammad was well loved, respected, trusted and very highly appreciated. His reputation for impartially, candor and reliability preceded him wherever he went, be it to Mekkah's far side or to neighboring settlements and towns. And as his popularity grew, his honesty and exemplary life put him beyond suspicion to such an extent that people sought his counsel and began to call him "Al-Amin". This title of honor had never before been bestowed on anyone and indicated his status among his peers.

A few years later while in the city's marketplace purchasing goods for his family, Abu Talib learned from his sister Jahsh that the widowed lady Khadijah needed an agent of the highest integrity to transport her caravan of merchandise to Syria. Jahsh had smiled impishly, a secretive gleam in her eyes making him think along the same lines: it was time for their nephew to have a wife. Knowing Khadijah to be highly respected, affluent and just in her business affairs, he thanked Jahsh for the information and left her to her leather work.

That evening after the day's heat started to dissipate, Abu Talib departed for Khadijah's residence intending to offer Muhammad's services as Captain of her caravan.

Maysara, the lady's manservant, went to answer Talib's knock. Khadijah intervened, asking him to prepare refreshments for the company. Unassumingly she answered the door herself despite a household full of servants.

"Abu Talib! Good gracious, it has been many a day since thou hast darkened my doorway," said Khadijah.

"Yea, my lady, and I do apologize," he returned. "Nay, my old friend, Thou hast no need for amends. Gracious me! It is I whom asketh forgiveness. Enter, enter," she intoned embarrassingly.

Put at ease, Abu Talib followed Khadijah to the sitting room where they small talked until Maysara returned with refreshments. With the amenities completed, Talib tactfully broached the subject of her need to employ someone as representative for her caravan. Confirming her need, he began to acquaint her with Muhammad's qualities. His integrity had reached her ears many, many times before, nevertheless she allowed him to continue uninterrupted. Ending his account of Muhammad's attributes, he waited with bated breath for her response.

"Wouldst I be delighted to employ al-Amin, and furthermore, wouldst I give him double of what I would give another man," (1) replied Khadijah.

Pleased with the results of his efforts, Talib apologized for the lateness of hour and took his leave. Excited by the possibilities Muhammad would be afforded, he rushed home to inform his nephew of his appointment as Captain to Khadijah's caravan. "Nephew," enunciated Abu Talib tentatively upon seeing Muhammad. "Doth thou knowest Khadijah bint Whuwaylid?"

"Aye, she is a woman of fine standing, and strong of character," Muhammad answered.

"Good, good. Hath she a caravan ready for Syria and is in need of someone trustworthy to captain it. If thou were to offer thy services, she wouldst readily accept thee."(2) Muhammad nodded his head, implying that he would do just that.

"Then, thou wilt be pleased to know she hath chosen thee to represent the caravan as her Captain."

Elated with the prospect of travel and its opportunities to meet new people, Muhammad thanked his uncle for speaking in his behalf and promised to visit and personally thank Khadijah on the morrow.

Talib tried to keep his delight from showing itself but his eyes crinkled in secret amusement, betraying the mystery of his thoughts.

Muhammad saw the smug look his uncle tried so hard to conceal, and knowing him the way he did he knew there would be no chance of getting him to reveal whatever he was keeping to himself. So he bid a good night and retired to his room. He wondered what his uncle schemed for the next hour until sleep overtook him.

The next morning Muhammad meticulously groomed and dressed, then set out for Khadijah's home. On the way he brought to mind all the things he knew or heard of her. But as he walked through the city, his thoughts were constantly interrupted by the many people calling to him in greeting or stopping to ask his advice on some matter. And before he could collate his study any further, his self-communing had gotten as far as thinking about her being twice widowed, around forty years of age, quick-witted, made prosperous through astute business ventures and pleasing to the eye, when he arrived. For some reason he couldn't fathom, he looked around feeling embarrassed then knocked on the courtyard gate.

Within seconds the bondsman was there to answer. Muhammad explained his business and Maysara permitted him to pass on into the courtyard. As he walked the length of the enclosure, he glimpsed Khadijah standing on the second floor balcony before going under the eaves of the house. He thought: her posture was straight and held in such a way as to suggest a magnanimous temperament; her hair, thick, black and wavy, shone like light reflecting off a smooth pond's surface as it fell in long waves down her back.

Once in the house, Maysara seated Muhammad, informed him that Khadijah would be down shortly and left the room to bring refreshments. While Muhammad waited for Khadijah's appearance, his fascination with her large house occupied his thoughts. Impregnably built of stone, her house was located in the hilly section of Mekkah, and so situated, it overlooked the city below. Rising, he walked over to the oblong window which afforded a panoramic view.

Admiring the picturesque scene, he could distinctly see in all its detail the city below with its snaking, black streets and alleys, threading their way between the buildings. Returning to his seat, he began to examine the interior. He should have known but he was nonetheless surprised by its warmth and elegance. Then, as he turned his attention to the statuary, Khadijah swept into the room. Muhammad stood and introduced himself formally. Blushing at her stir of feelings, Khadijah quickly mastered control of her thinking and business-like began to relate the duties expected of him.

Muhammad listened attentively, bearing in mind the details and interrupting only to clarify certain points.

Ending her list of duties, she and Muhammad awkwardly attempted to small talk for a while but both being inhibited by their feelings for one another made excuses to end the conversation. She summoned Maysara and informed him he was to accompany Muhammad to Syria.

Early next morning Maysara joined Muhammad, and for the next few days spent their time at the caravansary outside the city, overseeing the packing of merchandise and supplies. Being a bondsman, Maysara had become accustomed to abusive behavior by those in authority, but when the unexpectedness of Muhammad's courtesy and treatment as an equal befell him he was astounded to no end and was only too happy to carry out his orders.

Finally all was in readiness. At dawn on the day of departure, the caravan's workmen were alert and prepared for the drudgery of the long journey across the desert. Khadijah, Abu Talib, Jahsh, and their families, and a multitude of Mekkanese turned out to wish friends or loved ones farewell. But it was two hours later when the genuine goodbyes were said.

Muhammad, who was positioned at the point, looked back along the train of dromedaries, livestock and men, and issued the command to launch the caravan forward.

All through the following week the crossing was hard and tedious. The pace, steady but slow as the animals floundered through the shifting sands. Throughout the trip the caravan had to stop for rest and nourishment which allowed for Muhammad and Maysara to develop a warm friendship.

After weeks of hot, dusty traveling, the large caravan reached the small town of Busra where long ago Muhammad had enjoyed the kindly old monk's conversation. Recalling the intensity of their discussion, Muhammad decided to invite Buhaira and the monks to share in their evening meal, hoping for the same type of lively dialogue between himself and Buhaira. Muhammad scanned the terrain, selected the location to encamp, and relinquished the reins of power to Maysara, instructing him to establish camp. Cleansing the grime of travel off, Muhammad dressed in clean garments and departed for the monastery to call upon Buhaira. To his sorrow, he learned that the gentle old monk had recently passed away. Disconcerted, he forgot to invite the monks to dinner.

Muhammad returned to find Maysara directing the men in setting up camp. Wanting to rid himself of the sadness he felt over Buhaira's death, he elected to join in and assist the workmen while Maysara continued the direction.

The men admired Muhammad for his hard work and permitting a bondsman to supervise the task while he labored as hard as the rest of them. To them it only proved his worthiness as Captain. Several hours later, the strenuous exertion of raising tents so exhausted Muhammad, he retired earlier than usual and overlooked his customary check on the men's welfare.

Maysara, quick to notice Muhammad's preoccupation, excused himself from his friends and followed al-Amin to his tent. "Muhammad is something troubling thee," he asked.

"An old friend..."

After nearly a month of days filled with oppressive heat and shivering nights, they entered the lush green lands of Syria. Its luxuriousness induced Muhammad's mind to flood with pleasant memories of his first trip thirteen years earlier. Absorbed in thought, he nigh missed the familiar landmarks indicating the first leg of their journey was close at hand. Muhajjah, their final destination lied northeast, within a half day's travel. Thinking it better to reach the city's outskirts during the daylight hours he ordered the caravan's halt. That evening the men were in high spirits. With no serious mishaps to speak of, the men began to celebrate their arrival. Muhammad allowed the merry-making and unwinding to continue for more than an hour before stepping in and ordering the camp to turn in, thinking it prudent for the men to be well rested for the day ahead. He explained the morrow held promise of a hard day.

Decamping with the crack of dawn, the caravan arrived at the city's environs in early afternoon. Leaving Maysara in charge, Muhammad entered Muhajjah to investigate his competition. First he circled the marketplace searching for the best possible location in which to set up his stalls. Next, he mingled in among the crowd, examining the quality of goods and wares. To his shock he discovered that most merchants employed dishonesty to sell their wares. Back in camp, Muhammad issued orders for the merchandise to be loaded onto carts for easy transport. Then spent the remainder of the day instructing the men he'd use in selling Khadijah's cargo.

The next day, Muhammad, Maysara and several others moved out before dawn with carts in tow. Bearing in mind his earlier visit, Muhammad chose his site for his business where people were most apt to pass. Muhammad's honesty in relating good and bad points of the commodities people wanted and is fair prices soon had the crowd flocking to his stalls. His tactics yielded brisk sales and the rising ire of other merchants.

Never had they seen or heard of anyone dealing goods in such a straightforward manner. Grumbling and complaining, they feared him setting a standard for business which would cut into their profits. Fortunately for them he soon sold out his stores, and at a respectable gain. He paid the members of his caravan and allowed a day's leisure before returning to Mekkah. Using the rest of the day, he searched out the items Khadijah had requested and bought gifts for his family.

In the meantime, Khadijah had been quite busy back in Mekkah. Almost every day since the caravan struck their tents she had gone into the square to speak with storekeepers and the more reputable elders, thoroughly investigating Muhammad, not because she suspected his honesty but subliminally she hoped for a future with him.

Through her inquiries she uncovered first hand accounts of his integrity, stories of his grace and wisdom, his being held in the highest esteem, his generosity to those in need, his stand on humanity. It came as no surprise why he had been honored with the title of "Al-Amin".

Curious, she began to wonder about the reasons why he had remained unmarried for so long when thoughts of his handsomeness invaded her mind. Embarrassed by the ardent theme crossing her mind, she flushed with color and looked around coquettishly, wanting to avoid any conversation while attempting to deny the reality of her ardor. As she entered the courtyard, she voiced aloud her concern:

"Wouldst it appear unbecoming to wed a man fifteen years younger than myself!" She then smiled secretly.

The animals, no longer burdened with heavily laden packs traveled sure footed and Muhammad's caravan reached Mekkah within a few weeks time. Muhammad and Maysara, the only two heading into the hilly section, laughed and recounted the particulars of their journey as they rode towards Khadijah's home. Al-Amin was the first to see Khadijah as they came up the small knoll leading to the forepart of her residence.

Khadijah, after calculating the approximate date of Muhammad's return, had begun to wait out on the balcony of her home which overlooked the roadway leading to her house. Daydreaming, she suddenly heard some animals snort and spit in displeasure at the short climb. She turned and gasped in surprise, then rushed down to welcome Muhammad. Succumbing to his good looks and rugged masculinity, her breath started to come faster as she watched him dismount. She wished now that she had shown a little restraint in her eagerness to receive him.

The two just looked at one another, warm in their thoughts, until she spoke, her voice catching as if her control had slipped: "Muhammad, come into the house and refresh thyself before telling me of thy journey." While she waited for him, she had the servants bring a small ewer of cold water and several platters of cheeses, dates and meats.

Having washed the grittiness of travel from his face, Muhammad briskly brushed the dust from his clothes. Feeling invigorated, he returned to the room where Khadijah awaited him. Sitting in the proffered seat, he sighed audibly as he relaxed upon the cushioned chair.

"Muhammad, wouldst thou like cold water with thy food," Khadijah ceremoniously asked. "Lady Khadijah, water would be most welcome for the dust of travel still layers my throat," Muhammad returned.

Inwardly pleased, she promptly summoned one of the servants and requested another carafe of water. And while Muhammad ate, in between bites, he articulated the details of his trip to Syria. At the last, happy and pleased with the outcome of his travels and their business venture, Khadijah graciously thanked him and completed their deal.

Rising to take his leave, he suddenly stood rooted in silence. He forced himself to meet the sparkle of her eyes with some semblance of composure. He drew a deep breath hoping the intake of cool air would dampen the suffusion of color tingling his cheeks. Khadijah heard the sharp intake of breath and regarded him a moment longer before smiling and snapping the tension.

Muhammad bid goodbye and took his leave. Mixed with various feelings, he laid awake long into the night thinking of Khadijah. He kept envisioning her. He was sure beyond a shadow of a doubt that she was strong and principled. A woman filled with the knowledge of life who expressed herself through imagination, gentleness and compassion.

Feverish with activity, Maysara gradually worked his way into Khadijah's current of thought as he cleaned the house. Observing this incredible manifestation of energy on the part of her servant, she asked him the cause for his buoyancy. Grinning like he'd been waiting for her to ask, he began to tell her how wonderfully Muhammad had treated him during their trip to Syria. Once he started expounding on Muhammad's qualities he wouldn't stop until she reminded him of an errand he needed to take care of.

That night her mind was alive with speculation. Thoughts of marriage twittered in and out of her head causing her to flush hotly. She was almost prepared to admit their difference in age would be a hindrance to them becoming betrothed, but that inconsistent admission melted away by thinking sensible people didn't allow the opinions of others to guide their lives. Finally she conceded to herself the affection she felt for Muhammad, and before drifting off in slumber she was in the belief that the thoughts she entertained were radical to the point of being revolutionary. Nevertheless, they gave birth to an exhilaration and wild unrestrained happiness.

The following morning Khadijah awoke slowly. Desperately, she tried to clear away the sluggishness of sleep as the memories of her dreams fluttered on the edges of her consciousness. It was at that instant she realized her affections for Muhammad had grown by leaps and bounds during the night. All at once, she was wide awake with excitement. In a hurry, she completed her morning rituals, dressed and departed for her best friend's house to reveal her secret love.

After Khadijah greeted Nafisah with a warm embrace, she took hold of her hands, leading her into a small recess in the room where they could speak out of hearing range from any passing servants. Nafisah was surprised over the air of mystery and repressed the urge to start in with questions of her own. Instead, she took a seat and waited for Khadijah to begin the conversation. Khadijah glanced around, her hands linked as the excitement of revealing her feelings overwhelmed her. Satisfied no one lurked about within earshot, she drew the alcove's only other chair close to her friend and sat down, immediately forgetting the possibility of someone entering the room.

Nafisah studied her friend's face and sighed happily at its glow. Being a woman, she recognized the signs, surmising Khadijah was in love. Unable to hold her tongue any longer, she said cheerfully, "Do I know the lucky man?"

"B-but how didst thou know," Khadijah asked in astonishment.

Nafisah looked down at Khadijah's hands twisting in her lap, glanced back up to her face, taking in the rosy sheen of her cheeks and smiled knowingly. "Dost thou not remember that I too have been in love," she replied.

Khadijah inhaled a deep breath, drawing heavily on reserves of courage and began to put into words her admiration and affections for Muhammad.

Realizing her friend loved Muhammad, Nafisah proposed herself to act as intermediary between her and Muhammad. Relieved like a weight lifted from her shoulders, Khadijah gladly accepted her offer. And within days of their conversation, Nafisah paid a visit to Abu Talib's home to speak with Muhammad.

Welcoming Nafisah into his home, Talib directed her to the sitting room where one of his daughters served them up a pot of fresh tea. For the next fifteen minutes she talked nonstop about the heat and Muhammad's trip to Syria while glancing around every so often hoping to see Muhammad. Curious as to why she wanted his nephew, he inquired about her reasons before telling her his whereabouts.

"Doth thou wish to know in concern or curiosity," Nafisah asked in mock seriousness. She herself aware of Muhammad's frequent visits to the poorer section of Mekkah, now smiled and added, "Wilt thou tell me his whereabouts so that I can tell the lady Khadijah?"

Talib burst into laughter and said, "Is it concern or curiosity that prompts thy question?"

"Oh Abu Talib, wilt Khadijah want to know," she replied jovially.

"Tell thy lady Muhammad consoles the less fortunate of the city."

Promising to return the next day, Nafisah bid good day and took her leave.

When Muhammad came back from Mekkah's poor section darkness had already fallen. He found it was the only time he could walk through the city without hearing the anguished cries of the children which affected him so badly. Upon reaching his home he entered quietly, not wanting to disturb anyone. As he passed into the main room, he stopped in mid-stride wondering why Talib sat there with his youngest son sound asleep in his arms. He noticed then, his uncle eyeing him with a peculiar look on his face.

"Uncle, why art thou not abed," asked Muhammad, puzzlement inflecting his voice. Abu Talib smiled mysteriously, and not wanting to spoil his surprise, simply answered: "My baby is restless."

Since the child was sound asleep with his head lulling to its side, Muhammad looked at his uncle speculatively, doubting the veracity of his answer. And seeing that familiar gleam in Abu Talib's eyes, he forewent the questions burning in his mind and retired, wondering at his uncle's cryptic looks.

Nafisah returned as promised and encountered Muhammad walking out the door. Determined not to keep Khadijah waiting any longer than necessary, she asked him outright if she could speak with him in private.

Intrigued by the force of her statement, he agreed amiably and turned to reenter the house with her following. After the observance of amenities she initiated the conversation, coming straight to the point.

"Why hast thou never married?"

Taken by surprise, Muhammad smiled and replied, "What have I to offer a body?" Smiling back in return, she responded with another question. "If wealth concerned thee not, what wouldest thou say?"

Misunderstanding her direction, a look of disbelief filled Muhammad's face as he thought: scarcely do I know thee! Nafisah, noticing his look, tittered softly. She said: "I inquire on the behalf of lady Khadijah."

Muhammad bolted upright in his seat, his nerve endings alive. He never suspected that Khadijah might feel so strongly about him. He just sat there mutely relishing the sensations of happiness coursing through his mind.

His silence and bedazzled look distressed Nafisah as she waited for some kind of response. Unsure of the significance his reticence indicated, she quickly began a short chronicle of Khadijah's qualities, amplifying the areas of her integrity, wisdom, strength and courage.

Interrupting her flow of words, Muhammad simply said,"I accept."

Nafisah breathed a sigh of relief and said her goodbye, then hurried to tell Khadijah the good news.

The while, Khadijah had been anxiously awaiting in anticipation. Finally, at what seemed hours, she saw her friend treading up the small knoll leading to the courtyard. She ran down the stairs and out of the house to meet Nafisah.

"Thou art betrothed!" Nafisah exclaimed. As the two linked arms, she began to recount the morning's events while they strolled back into the house.

Muhammad continued with his plans before Nafisah's arrival. He made his way toward the impoverished section of Mekkah thinking it was a trial unto itself to pass the invisible line separating those who have and those who have not. And now as before he unconsciously clenched his fists, pressing them to his sides to keep from screaming out against man's injustices toward his brother. He loathed the miserable conditions and malodorous smells of open sewers they were forced to live by. Silently he vowed again to do all that was humanly possible to comfort and ease the suffering of those who have not.

First in Muhammad's long number of stops was the adobe brick structure where Abu Rayyah shared his one room hovel with another family, more out of loneliness than convenience. Though Abu Rayyah was an emaciated, frail and forever exhausted old man, he invariably rose from his pallet at the sound of Muhammad's voice. Welcoming him in with a toothless smile, Muhammad had to help him back to the pallet where they would sit and converse. Whenever Muhammad could speak to Abu Rayyah without the family's children interrupting, he would impart some bit of news which made the old man beam with gratification and satisfaction. His wrinkled old face would glow as if some heaviness or affliction had been displaced. To Muhammad, that alone was ample reward.

The stops seemed endless as he consoled the sick, gave sympathy, friendship and encouragement to the hapless. And not wanting to quit the area during the light of day, he continued his rounds until the cover of darkness made smooth the lines of faces contorted by hunger. It was their despair, suffering and pain, in trying to survive the harshness of life that drove Muhammad to turn away from Mekkah's aristocracy.

Abu Talib the night before sat in his favorite chair waiting for al-Amin's return from the poor section. But as the hours passed he fell into a light sleep. Awaking when Muhammad opened the front door, he yawned and smiled as he watched his nephew come through the door.

"Muhammad, had I hoped to speak with thee last night's eve, but now is just as well," said Talib groggily.

"Hadst I known thine wishes wouldst I have returned earlier," answered Muhammad conscientiously.

"Concern thyself not, here," Talib said, indicating the chair next to him. "Sit besides me," he ended in a calm and affectionate voice. As Muhammad came toward him, his brows were nearly united in scrutiny. Silently he studied the young man, his life under his guardianship flashing by.

"Nephew, art thou going to wed the lady Khadijah," he asked after a moment.

"Yea, but thou already knewest it," answered Muhammad.

"I confess that I had some inclination," replied Talib. Shifting in his chair seeking a comfortable position, he asked, "Wilt thou get me something to drink?"

Muhammad rose to do his uncle's bidding and returned with a tumbler of cold water.

"Many thanks," rendered Talib. After he took a small sip, Muhammad distinctly felt a subtle change in the air. Looking straight into his nephew's eyes, he started the conversation.

"Over the years hadst I watched thee and now thou art unto me as my own son. Proud of thee am I, for thou hath grown into a virtuous and kindly man. Here and abroad thy benevolence is known. It is a goodly thing but men wilt hate thee for it. So be not afraid in times to come of those who wilt oppose and try to frighten thee."

"Now, in regards to Khadijah, have I known her for a number of years. She is an honest and enterprising woman without pretense. There is an openness and straightforwardness about her which leaves no room for hypocrisy. Never hadst I heard her utter a single word of maliciousness toward anyone even in times of anger."

Stopping to indulge in another sip, Talib conveyed the rest of his feelings about the matter through his eyes as he affectionately regarded his nephew. Customarily a reserved man, Talib surprised Muhammad with the delivery of his long winded comments. Muhammad held his tongue thinking how pleased he felt that Khadijah met his uncle's approval.

As the unseen essence of sentience dispelled itself, Muhammad said: "All that remains now is setting the date."

"Were I a young man wouldst I not be able to withstand her wishes," Talib returned pleasantly.

CHAPTER SEVEN

In the succeeding months winter arrived with a vengeance that kept all but the most hearty Mekkans indoors. Muhammad, when the weather allowed spent the cold dreary days between his intended, the destitute, and his place of sanctuary.

One evening the chilled air caused Muhammad to leave the wilderness' solace earlier than he liked. On the way back home he watched in fascination the formation of dark, ugly, gray clouds in the distance. Boiling and twisting in monsoon-like appearance, they came rumbling over the mountains. Resounding with deafening claps of thunder, the heavens convulsed and began dropping enormous amounts of rain, soaking him to the bone.

The ensuing storm raged for several days and nights without pause, deluging the city with water. The downpour fell in sheets of glistening beads, obscuring the sight of water rushing down from Mekkah's hilly parts which streamed towards the Ka'bah, eating at its foundation. Had the Mekkans known of the Ka'bah's eroding base, they would have braved the inclement weather by the hundreds to protect their place of worship with countermeasures to stem the torrent of water. The Ka'bah, a far more ancient place of worship than any existing holy place had survived through thousands of years of meteorological changes. And already being in need of repairs, the heavy rains latest effects made the need all the more urgent.

Shortly after noon of the fifth consecutive day, the rain showed its first signs of abating when the clouds thunderously reverberated off the mountains in a final blast of fury. Several more days passed before people began stirring from their homes as they waited for the ground to dry. Then, in convivial-like atmosphere, nearly all the Mekkans first order of business was to visit the Ka'bah to pay homage to their idols for escaping the storm's violence. It was then that the Ka'bah's damage was discovered and the cries of alarm sounded.

Banu Quraysh, having the sole responsibility for maintaining the Ka'bah, dispatched messengers to its various leaders, summoning them to council. Following a short recitation of their obligations as keepers, an agreement was reached: each clan would send ten men to restore the structure's foundation.

The reconstruction progressed rapidly and well enough until arguments heatedly erupted about which clan would enjoy the distinction of returning Prophet Abraham's Black Stone of Remembrance to its proper place. Several hours passed in a discursive war of words. The mood turned ugly and emotions were raging near the flashing point. Clan members started to group up thinking weapons would be drawn at any moment, such was the tension. None of the clan representatives were willing to change their position. They regarded the matter as a grave insult if they didn't have the honor of placing the Stone on its resting place. Finally Abu Umayyah ibn Mughirah, hoping to avoid the call to arms and blood shed, suggested that the first man to enter the Ka'bah would judge and decide who returned the Stone of Remembrance.

Seeing the logic of impartiality behind his proposal, every one unanimously agreed and squatted down on the floor to wait. At first there were muted whisperings but as the minutes dragged by the Ka'bah fell tomb-like in silence while they anxiously listened for approaching footsteps. Shortly thereafter they heard the sound of steady footfalls coming toward them. As one they turned to face the Ka'bah's entrance. Full of expectation, their hearts started to pound in anticipation of being selected for the honor. Abruptly, outcries of "Al-Amin" echoed throughout the chamber and shattered the silence.

Upon Muhammad's crossing the Ka'bah's threshold, his title of respect boomed out, startling him with its suddenness. Before his surprised senses could recover, everyone at once started clamoring for his attention. Chaotically they yelled out their reasons why their particular clan should be designated above the others. Muhammad raised his arms over his head for order and when the pandemonium subsided, he asked: "What hath befallen ye for thy deafening cries?"

Again the assemblage exploded into a riot of noise. Muhammad, with exaggeration flung his arms into the air once more and implored for discipline. Ibn Mughirah, who worked more in a supervisory capacity than laborer, stood and explained: "Oh, al-Amin, to preserve the tribe's harmony, each clan hath consented to allow the first man entering the Ka'bah to act as judge and render a decision appointing which clan would return the Stone of Abraham to its place."

Thinking for all concerned, Muhammad thought something had to be done right away to cleave the underlying animosity which had developed. Prudently he considered the consequences of choosing one clan over the other. During the minute he self consulted, the men grew inpatient and started voicing the dilemma he was in when unexpectedly he asked for a robe.

The crowd for a span of several heartbeats' length didn't react. Lost in their own thoughts they started looking at one another in disbelief. Whispers of "How strange his request," "Why doth he call for a robe," and "Didst I not tell thee the problem could not be solved," were some of the sentiments rippling through the throng.

"Oh, people, are ye going to yield over a robe or not," Muhammad ventilated. Given a robe more to humor him than in seriousness, someone snidely called out: "Art thou cold Muhammad, or perhaps thou needest another robe."

The remark generated but few snickers. For the most part they watched in quiet wonder as Muhammad, unruffled, proceeded to the chamber's center and splayed the robe on the floor. He, then, retrieved the Stone, gently laying it in the robe's center, and saying: "Oh, ye of Quraysh! Leaders of thine clan, take ye a portion of the robe and together lift it." Once the Stone's elevation equaled its pedestal, Muhammad removed it and set it in its proper place.

In all its intents and purposes, Muhammad's splendid maturity of mind displayed his capacity and propensity to quickly resolve the hardest of problems. His method of dispensing such even handedness extremely impressed all who witnessed the event. For it not only permitted equal representation, a share of honor, but it checked the likelihood of spilling blood. And when all was said and done, each member of the different clans personally acknowledged his achievement and thanked him.

With the rainy season coming to an end, news of Muhammad and Khadijah's forthcoming nuptial spread like wild fire through the city.

Abu Jahl, a tall wiry individual with a satanic looking face, whom the populace regarded as a sadistic tyrant, had for the past two years been instituting a course of action to produce the right conditions that would make his character look favorable in Khadijah's eyes. But news of her wedding plans upset his designs and infuriated him to the point where he stormed over to her house in anger. His manner was ominous as he came straight to the point, forgetting his customary habits with her. "Khadijah, for thy own good wed not this upstart Muhammad."

Khadijah listened politely, but at his last words she colored violently, her face turning crimson in suppressed acerbity and tightened in repugnance. She automatically started to retort in angry reproof but closed her mouth before her rage became unwomanly. She thought: he surely would have been ostracized from the city had his wealth not purchased the strength needed to remain a part of the community. She, then, coolly replied in a voice exuding strength, "What kind of creature art thou, without propriety and behavior becoming a man in thy position. Even the humblest at least pretends to some semblance of respect."

Jahl stared back haughtily and feigning like he hadn't heard a word, interjected, "He plans to take thy wealth and squander it amongst his wretched friends of the city's sewers."

Khadijah's breath accelerated. She answered his look with contemptuous scrutiny and moved toward the door leading out of the house. "Abu Jahl! How obdurate art thou," Khadijah asked rhetorically.

"What indeed hath Muhammad done unto thee to merit such aspersions upon his character?"

Jahl remained nastily silent and returned the question with a look of derision. Discerning his look, Khadijah scathingly spoke. "Wilt I not waste any more time discussing my affairs or quarrel with thee. Thou deserveth not the effort. Thus, take ye thy leave and henceforth address me not except in the company of others."

Jahl realized the error he'd made and not wanting to compound his mistake any further, lamely said: "Was I only concerned for thy welfare Khadijah." Embarrassed over his failure to change her mind about Muhammad, he bowed insolently and took his leave.

The day of Muhammad and Khadijah's espousal arrived a few months after his twenty-fifth birthday. It was an auspicious beginning as pale gray skies surrendered to brilliant sunshine. The servants were bustling with activity in a flurry of preparations which promised a day of festivities.

Around mid-afternoon, Muhammad and Khadujah began receiving guests. Abu Talib was visibly excited and vibrated with energy as he thumped Muhammad's back in fatherly affection. Then, turning to the bride, he welcomed her to the Hashim clan.

Nafisah followed Talib's arrival. She was bursting with good cheer and crowded in around the well-wishers who were presenting gifts.

Hamzah, noted for his hunting prowess, made his entrance with a load of luxurious pelts on one arm while the other led Waraqah. Following them, more friends with their families started arriving, all bearing gifts.

All through the afternoon, Khadijah was in constant smiles when of a sudden the flashing smile altered ever so slightly. It became frozen in place as she stood fixedly, quietly watching Abu Jahl and his cronies arrive. His entrance along with the others introduced a noticeable chilliness into the air as their very presence reminded not only her but others as well of unpleasant experiences.

Abu Lahab, Abu Sufyan, Russal, and especially Abu Jahl, were dreaded, avoided, or feared by many Mekkanese attending. Known for their ruthlessness and oppressive ways, the guests could only gape as the four men made their way toward the hosts.

"I presume this is the young man ye intend to wed," Abu Jahl churlishly asked Khadijah with emphasis on Muhammad's youth.

Muhammad's hair on the nape of his neck bristled in resentment at the slight. Khadijah and several others within earshot stiffened. But before anyone could react, Abu Lahab laughed and sarcastically interjected: "It is a good thing to entertain us so lavishly."

The moment passed and tensions ebbed with each step the four men took away. Muhammad resumed his conversation. Khadijah, recalling her encounter with Abu Jahl, looked away with a curious expression.

From across the courtyard, Talib witnessed the incident and saw Khadijah's look as she turned away. Surmising the situation, he excused himself from a small group of Mekkan traders who had the men enthralled with news of the merchandise that would be arriving soon from Damascus. Approaching Khadijah, he asked: "My dear, is there some one troubling thee?"

"It is nothing," she replied hollowly. Then turned and disappeared into the house.

Soon thereafter Khadijah reappeared and took her place next to Muhammad. The guests began quieting down. Abu Talib stepped to the front and delivered a short speech.

At the last, the marriage officiator cleared his throat importantly as he marched to the forepart of the gathering. Khadijah's entire countenance softened, becoming youthful. Muhammad was dressed simply and looked dignified with an aura of unshakable strength surrounding him. The officiator regarded the couple to be but a moment then articulated the marriage contract that would seal their lives in wedlock. And as the solemnity of the occasion ended, tears of joy trickled down lady Khadijah's cheeks and the two were joined in matrimony.

CHAPTER EIGHT

In the ensuing five years, Muhammad's life with Khadijah was exceptionally gratifying as each year blessed them with children. Three boys: Qasim, Tahir and Tayyib, who resembled their father; and, two girls; Zaynab and Ruqayyah, who took after their mother. It was a time of great happiness for the proud parents until shortly after Ruqayyah's birth when tragedy struck. The boys, within a span of two months died one after the other from some unknown sickness. Khadijah spent hours on end sitting idly near the second floor window fondling the boys clothing. She existed in a capsule of silence. Eating her meals alone, she isolated herself from the rest of the household fearing the Hand of Death's return.

Muhammad, his own spirit heavily weighted and nearly broken by the deaths, did all in his power attempting to restore the family's established routine. Day in, day out, he suffused normality into his voice whenever he spoke with household members. But nothing he said or did seemed to break the awful silence. In his grief he spent a considerable amount of time at Abu Talib's house where his many children, along with Zaynab and Ruqayyah, soothed away the pain.

Talib thought Muhammad's real reason for his frequent visits was to be near his youngest son Ali. An active and handsome boy of two years, Ali was full of charm and vitality. And every time al-Amin came to call the toddler would shriek in delight and run into his arms. Thus, in time the boys death lessened in its intensity and life returned somewhat back to normal. Khadijah conceived and gave birth to another daughter: Umm Kulthum.

Muhammad, with his girls in tow, increased his time at his uncle's house. Before long he realized his uncle was having financial difficulties in supporting his family and never forgetting the many years he himself spent in Talib's house, he wanted to help. So one day while his uncle labored over the cost of living, he said: "Uncle, thy hardships are mine and if thou wouldest allow Ali to live in my household, perchance thy burdens would be eased."

After a few seconds thought, Talib agreed to the suggestion gratefully. He knew Muhammad loved Ali deeply and that he would be well cared for, protected and in the best of hands.

Ali was close to three years of age when he joined Muhammad's family. Soon afterwards his buoyancy and amusing escapades had the household back in high spirits. And following his first year with the family, Khadijah gave birth to another child. She was named Fa'timah.

Muhammad, meantime, was undergoing changes both mentally and spiritually. He sought out with zeal the mysteries of human understanding through God's bounty. He continued calling on the poor and unfortunate of Mekkah, and more often than not, took the young Ali along to show him man's injustice against those who have not. Abu Rayyah had passed on but he habitually stopped at his shack first to comfort the family that had remained. Throughout his visits, it dawned on him that the oppressive conditions invariably remained the same. It was then, through growing enlightenment, his huge house with all its splendors started troubling his conscious. He didn't like envisioning himself living in such grand surroundings while the greater number of his brethren lived in squalor. Living as he did, in the affluent part of the city, he observed the avariciousness of his neighbors. A number of them started to stand out above the rest and in his mind he regarded them as the city's chief source of corruption and its ills.

Abu Jahl, arrogant beyond reason, was the kind of man who never pardoned nor forgot. His beliefs, once made were impossible to change even when faced with the truth. When evidence was presented showing the inaccuracy of his opinions, he felt personally set upon and adhered to his preceding assessment, doubly sure he was being intentionally duped.

Abu Sufyan, a distant relative from Yathrib, was short, spindly, and all sharp points with cadaverously thin features. He, having an exaggerated opinion of his importance, believed his way best and relentlessly imposed his way upon others.

And Russal, the evil one, was an undersized brutal man with a gaunt and ruddy complexion. The pox craters filling his face made him look all the more sinister. He was as vicious and unscrupulous as a fiend in human form. Always thirsting for power, he patronized those wielding authority, nurturing their approbation for self aggrandizement. Muhammad could never think of him without the memory of his attack upon the old helpless woman coming to mind.

The three older men with Russal functioning in an underling capacity, operated in junta-like fashion, enforcing their wills upon the populace by any means necessary. And whenever interfering in the affairs of the community, Russal frequently hired on Umar ibn al-Khattab, in case of violence, to do their bidding. Umar, a particularly rough and cruel individual often made the difference in swaying opinions toward the self styled oligarchy's views.

Muhammad had now amassed a tremendous amount of experiences in dealing with man's injustices. It pained him deeply to watch man in discord with nature, following the distorted path of contention. Nor did he grieve less for the weak's oppression.

Often speaking with Khadijah, he revealed his innermost thoughts. In her presence he felt at ease, knowing that she understood the ache troubling his soul. But the comfort received was short lived and offered no solutions to the problems. Many times she had awakened in the dead of night to find him missing from bed. Aware of his night time habits, she'd rise from bed to step outside on the balcony overlooking the courtyard where she'd silently watch him walk the grounds submerged in thought.

One particular night while Muhammad paced along the courtyard's walls it dawned on him suddenly that the injustices kept repeating themselves in one form or another. Thus, with the new found comprehension he delved into himself searching for the elusive key that would unlock the door to man's suffering and set his spirit free to see his true nature within. However, the proximity of his family and the city's distractions impeded his mind's freedom to explore the realm of possibilities. Left so, he sought out the comforting solitude of the mountains where he could think without swerving from the direction his mind wanted to take.

Quietly opening the gate, he slipped into the darkness toward the mountains. As he walked along the alleys, he invariably gazed at the stars, recalling the discovery of the small cave with its long torturous climb up the mount's rugged sides and the beautiful hues of sunset filling the sky when he reached the crest. Then, he'd think of the tranquilizing effect he found from simply being there enjoying the wilderness and cool breezes from the desert.

Disgusted with the iniquitous city, he increasingly found himself spending more time in the mountain's solitude. Its tranquility had soothing qualities his old soul desperately needed, and with each succeeding trip he acquired more insight into man's struggles, seeing patterns of evil in everyday living shape and mold man's character. He identified skepticism, suspicion, lust and despair, as the poisons perverting life. Yet, he was not deluded into believing things could not be rectified.

Some three miles north of Mekkah, in a valley which turns left from the road to Arafat,(1) Muhammad found a small unused cave in the side of Mount Hira.(2) Near its top, the cavern provided an imposing view of Mekkah and the Ka'bah, and he made it his place of sanctuary.

Upon attaining the cave's entrance, dawn was filling the horizon. Sighing contentedly, he sat down exhausted, his back against the cave's wall. There alone, hard were the problems he resolved in his mind, harder and more cross-grained than the red granite around him.(3) He recognized the unending struggle of good rage against evil. Man in his lust for power and influence against man trying to survive. He conceded there was a need for men with power to regulate society, but they were not the ones who counted. It was evident that the weak despaired of equity in law to redress the injustices inflicted but what could he do to ease their pain and fear?

He knew all too well that people in their climb for prestige, demoralized others, frequently infusing them with avarice. He had seen ordinary people once affected, dress their small children in rags and turn them out to the streets to beg in their passion for substance. And the poor suffered immediately at the hands of merchants who raised the cost of their goods and wares beyond reason. No wonder, he thought sadly, the impoverished in their strife to endure life had no time to ponder the higher things and turned to idolatry, hoping to be favored.

One underlying problem stood out which affected him the greatest: the ceaseless desecration of the Ka'bah's sacredness. It seemed to him the most crucial point which caused the deterioration of moral rectitude among the Mekkans. Their ways of worshipping were alien to him and didn't make any sense. He felt the oblation of idols a waste of time and energy. The feeling caused him to wonder aloud: "How could anyone pay homage to graven images, crosses, or likenesses of men that they themselves made? Worshipping aught but the Creator seemed the more sensible. How can I find the Creator?..."

One evening Abu Talib after having many times in recent years watched Muhammad return from the mountains direction, always in a state of peacefulness, at the last became curious. Knowing nothing but sand and mountains existed in the line of march his nephew returned from asked of his activity in the wilderness.

"Uncle, it is the Mount Hira whence I goest," Muhammad answered. "There I while away the time in an undersized cavern seeking in contemplation the truth of man's existence through nature's law."

Muhammad's solemn response triggered a chain of memories to flood Talib's mind. He looked at his nephew and saw Buhaira's countenance who so long ago told him of the signs the coming Prophet would exhibit. He stared at Muhammad and seriously began considering if indeed his nephew was the Prophet foretold in Holy Scripture.

During the years, world conditions were creating the stage for God's Final Testament. The Roman Emperor Maurice had his army revolt against him, placing in his stead a centurion named Phocas who introduced a reign of oppression. In India, Harsha Vardhana's influences fountain-headed the furthering of sciences, literature, art, political power, which brought China into a closer relationship through religious inquiry. Yet, for all this gloriousness and glitter, the seeds of destruction had started to germinate. The Persian Empire was embroiled in war with Abyssinia in Yemen.(4) In Egypt, a new and different kind of Christianity evolved from the simple teachings of the holy prophet Jesus. The native Egyptian Church turned contemplative, ascetic and mystical in nature. Monasticism became so rampant it affected the population's growth and down graded the position of women. The Roman Catholic church, having rejected the doctrine of Unity espoused irrational distinctions of the One Eternal God and invented the Trinity.(5)

PART TWO
PROPHETHOOD

CHAPTER NINE

A few years before Muhammad's fortieth year, he was recognized as a man whose integrity could not be compromised. Yet, he was unfulfilled. He started feeling a compulsion to do something. It was no longer enough to merely help his fellow man with food and shelter. He felt helpless against man's obstinate desire to pile up fortunes which he had to leave behind. Has man's soul transcended beyond redemption, he frequently asked himself. Surely I think not these thoughts alone, for there must be others who believe as I! Thus accustomed to the land's hardships and resistance to man, Muhammad gradually increased his visits to Cave Hira, sometimes for days on end.

Alone in his cave of solace overlooking the city below, he'd fast and through contemplation, probe the Creation, the Divinity, the moral, physical and spiritual worlds, for that elusive key to man's existence. He sat pondering the great world around him. As he thought of mankind in general, he gave credit to the young for instinctiveness who fathomed the mystic forces in the world. But those in the decline of life, he realized, suspected reason and nature's law and preferred to escape the fight for life. It was sad they only recognized the beauty, greatness and value of existence when they were close to departing from it. Only then, he thought, when the spirit of life ebbed from its body did they suddenly visualize everything in its clarity. He glanced heavenward, taking in the grandeur and instantly felt at peace. Unfolding his legs, he massaged the pinched muscles, then made his way home.

Ali, all the while, spent his days and evenings playing and listening to Muhammad and Khadijah's stories. He found the tales fascinating, garnering many lessons on life. But above all, they furnished him with a unique sense of regard toward the sanctity of life.

Having grown up in his cousin's household, he'd come to think of Muhammad and Khadijah as his surrogate parents. Muhammad, however, to insure a healthy relationship between Ali and his womb relatives, repeatedly took him to visit his father, mother, brothers and sisters, thereby fostering their kinship as Ali grew with the years.

Between his father's home and play time, Ali would accompany Muhammad to the marketplace and visits to the impoverished section of the city. Each time they called upon the dilapidated homes, he'd watch Muhammad with growing respect, giving solace, comfort and any help he could. Strongly affected by Muhammad's actions, he unconsciously started to pattern himself after his cousin and develop a meaningful perception of justice.

One evening after returning from their excursion into the poor section, Ali wondered why they never called upon the huge houses around their neighborhood. He asked, "Muhammad, why do we not ever visit those around us?"

"Ali," said Muhammad, "I like not to speak ill of anyone, but thou needest to know the truth. Thou hath no doubt assumed that we live in the well-to-do section of Mekkah. This in itself is of no concern. However, many of our neighbors art overbearing, puffed up with self-importance and repulsive in their behavior toward the needy. It is through their greediness that they keep the people on the verge of starvation, in low spirits, and more than not drive them into the streets where they beg to survive. It is they who prevent the city from reaching true prosperity in their desire for servility. Doth thou understand?"

Ali nodded in reply and remained silent for several moments. He took to heart Muhammad's response and started thinking of the deplorable conditions the poor lived in. He asked more questions, thus opening the door for Muhammad to indoctrinate him in the moral decay consuming society. And in the numerous conversations that followed, Muhammad detected no hypocrisy in his personality and was developing analytical powers that could solve problems quickly.

A time later, Ali and Muhammad were in the marketplace to purchase some items Khadijah requested. As they wandered around, going from stall to stall, Muhammad came upon a frightening scene. His friend, Zayd ibn Harith was being viciously beaten and kicked by his master. Without thinking Muhammad shoved Ali back out of harm's way and stepped in between to stop the man from further assaulting his friend.

Outraged by Muhammad's intervention, the man shrilly screamed out his indignation: "B-by what right dost thou dare interfere with a man reproving his bondsman?"

Muhammad looked at the man incredulously and calmly answered, "I heard no words of reprimand, and thus thy actions affected me as if thou wert a robber out to steal my friend's purse." His rejoinder seemed to increase the man's anger for he stammering articulated, raising his voice several octaves higher: "If t-thou hath so much concern, ye can ob-obtain his freedom for a price!"

"What is thy price," Muhammad asked without hesitation, knowing Khadijah would understand the expense.

"F-five gold dinars!"

"Fine," said Muhammad. He then bent down to whisper in Ali's ear, telling him to run home and tell Khadijah he urgently needed three more gold dinars. While he waited for Ali he began negotiating, and by the time Ali returned with the coins he'd persuaded the man to lower his price to three gold dinars. Upon completion of their transaction

Muhammad loudly declared to those that had gathered around, "Oh, ye people! Hearken unto my words. The bondsman Zayd ibn Harith is from this day on, a freed man!"

The crowd of onlookers, surprised, started chattering in their astonishment. They had never seen anyone pay gold coin for a slave just to set him free. Ali, during the time, had been tending Zayd and now assisted him to stand. Bruised and battered, he hobbled over to Muhammad where he fell to his knees in thankfulness.

Embarrassed by Zayd's display of gratitude, Muhammad carefully slid his hands under his friend's arms and raised him to his feet. He said: "Zayd, thou hath no cause to bow down before me. I am but a man as thyself." Then led him away toward his home. Before stepping twenty paces Zayd faltered and stumbled against a nearby stall. Paying no mind to Zayd's claims that he could walk unassisted, Muhammad and Ali put their arms around him in support. As they started on Ali fell into deep thought. He considered Muhammad the kindest man ever alive and felt himself very lucky to have him teaching him the ways of the world. The experience, unlike Muhammad's other acts of charity, embedded a conscientious regard for all life in his young mind.

Khadijah, meanwhile, had become immensely curious as to why Muhammad needed the extra coins. It is not like him to be frivolous in matters of money, she thought abstractedly. She paced up and down anxiously awaiting his return. On hearing the courtyard gate creak open, she looked out the window and gasped in alarm. At first sight she saw the battered features of the man between Muhammad and Ali. "Maysara!" Khadijah called out, "Put water to boil." Then swiftly covered the ground to meet them. Muhammad caught sight of Khadijah's frightened looks as she ran toward them. Quickly explaining what happened, he managed to soothe her fears before she became frantic.

Following a week's recuperation time, Zayd fully recovered from his injuries. His rapport with the girls, Ali and servants, so impressed Muhammad and Khadijah that they asked him if he would consider staying on with the household.

Now at the mature age of forty, Muhammad's wisdom, depth of character, and view points, were well known. And try as he might, he could not stop the problems or even dent the malefic forces overrunning the city. Without warning his visits to the poverty stricken area started sinking his spirit lower and lower as the oppressive conditions took its toll. He felt uneasy about what he was going through and discussed his concerns with Khadijah. Mostly, she let him talk as she gazed at him with compassion. She saw in him gentleness and intelligence so profound, she realized he'd rather understand than blame or criticize. She always listened to him, assuring and supporting him. And following their conversation she invariably knew he'd soon be leaving for the mountains.

One afternoon in Cave Hira Muhammad had been for hours contemplating divine Justice and Mekkah's wretched conditions. After repeatedly beseeching the Creator for guidance, he fell asleep exhausted. At night fall he awoke rubbing his throbbing temples, feeling that every thing around him was strange, out of harmony. The wind seemingly whispered as it danced, swirled small eddies of dust all around him. Then, all at once, he was wide awake tingling with apprehension. His head began to pound. He sat up rigidly, looked around bewildered, felt brushed by phantoms of unknown origin. Abruptly, there was a deviation in density of atmosphere. The earth lost its scent, the moon cast an ethereal aurora of light, everything about him took on a look of insubstantiality. The ground suddenly started to vibrate underneath him. Startled, he scrambled to his feet thinking the earth was quaking. But just as quick as it began the tremors subsided and he sank to the ground in relief, wondering if the shaking was just a figment of his imagination for everything looked as it should have.

As the furor slowed its beat in his veins, he again thought of the Creation, the Divine, the city's ignorance, immorality, disorder, corruption and idolatry. He felt strongly the need to bring about the down fall of the evil forces directing man's destiny. Then without warning, something unseen closed around his breast, squeezing, strangulating, like tightening bands of steel.

"Iqraa!" Resounded throughout the small cave from a deep, powerful and electrifying voice.

Instinctively alert, Muhammad began to rise, his heart pounding violently. The winds suddenly came alive, screaming through the mountain's crags in their intensity. Shaking all over, he sat but saw nothing. His instinct cried out for him to flee. Instead, and not knowing to whom he spoke, he said: "What dost thou wish me to read?"

Silence greeted his query. After a moment or two, he regained his composure and again started to think he imagined the entire episode. He just sat there, numbed, against the cave's wall staring off in the distance musing over the moment's comparative quiet when again the wind blew itself into a fury around the small cave. Muhammad started to his feet but the tightening and strangulating again enveloped his body, forcing him back down. With his heart pounding in anticipation, he heard anew the voice that would change mankind for the better.

"Iqraa!" Charged the deep toned voice as it rumbled through the chamber.

62

Upon hearing the unearthly intonation, Muhammad shook his head. Motionless he sat, his breathing loud and irregular, feeling utterly alone. After a few seconds he calmed down. He only heard the wind and sighed, releasing his apprehensions. Then without warning, the voice again commanded, "Iqraa!"

As the unseen talons seized and constricted about Muhammad's frame, the roar of blood rushing to his head awakened and cleared away the obscurity shrouding his inner conscious. He called out with joy: "What dost thou wish me to recite?"

Minutes passed in absolute silence. The wind seemed to have stopped blowing, appearing like it hadn't blustered at all. Muhammad waited, his mind fully illuminating with Divine Light. An instant later the cavern flooded with heavenly radiance and the Holy messenger Angel Gabriel manifested holding an open silken scroll. Muhammad vocalized the consecrated Words etched in his mind when Adam was still amidst water and clay.(1)

"In the name of Allah, The Beneficent, The Merciful."

"Read thou! In the name of thy Lord Who created. He created man from a clot! Recite, and thy Lord is the Most Honorable. Who taught (to write) with the Pen, taught man what he knew not!"(2)

Dazed, Muhammad stared out the cave's entrance. He kept repeating the Holy Writ over and over. Next, he became aware that the stillness and serenity of the mountains had returned. He glanced around, seeking the angelic Emissary but Gabriel was nowhere to be seen. He sprang to his feet, seized with purpose and hastened out the now seemingly confining cave.

Flinging out his arms for balance, the Chosen One heedlessly plowed down the mount's rugged slope, stopping now and then to keep from tumbling. Midway in his descent he stopped to regain his breath when he unexpectedly heard a voice calling.

"Muhammad... Muhammad."

He began to feel by degrees the tingling onset of presentment as he straightened up. A thin sheen of perspiration gleamed off his face as he scanned the immediate vicinity. The mountain's shrubs swayed with the wind.   No sound issued from the night's insects or the small creatures usually scurrying about in survival. It appeared as if all life had suddenly sought the safety of shelter, fleeing some unknown presence. He looked to the mountain top. There, poised in a billowing luminescent robe, hovered the magnificent apparition of Angel Gabriel. In a voice full of authority, the heavenly host spoke.

"Oh, Muhammad! Verily thou art the Apostle of Allah and I am His Angel Gabriel.(3) By His Decree thou wilt guide humanity unto the Right Path, the Path of Truth."

Muhammad stood transfixed, swallowing reflexively for air as if a paralysis gripped his nervous system. Gaining control of his vocal cords, he gasped involuntarily, the horizon in all directions filled with a modicum of Gabriel's iridescent wing. He could not behold the majestic configuration of the angel's feathered limb, let alone see the seraphic form in its entirety. Benevolent and enchanting, Muhammad was lost in wonderment.

Al-Amin stumbled back into a projection of rock, feeling nothing. He was unaware of Gabriel's disappearance and remained oblivious of the night's passing, his mind teeming with thoughts and ideas.

Far to the East the faint light of dawn edged the skyline as the Prophet's consciousness returned to his surroundings. It surprised him to see the stars twinkling out. Exhausted, cold and shivering, he departed for home.

Meanwhile, Khadijah had sent the children to bed. Then owing to Muhammad's habits she herself retired, anticipating his eminent return. As time dragged into the early morning hours some mysterious instinct triggered her internal alarm. She rose feeling terribly frightened, sensing Muhammad's experience. Not knowing how to cope or respond, she stared out toward the mountains for the better part of an hour before forcing herself to act. With trembling hands she dressed herself and stood near the window hoping to see Muhammad suddenly appear out of the gloom. Finally at dawn's first light, she reluctantly admitted to herself that something might have befallen Muhammad.

Decided on a course of action, she quickly crossed the length of the house to Maysara and Zayd's room. She rapped her knuckles sharply against the door's framework, chiding herself mentally for not acting sooner.

"Maysara? Zayd?" Khadijah called out in a voice full of worry. "It is I, Khadijah. May I speak with thee?"

"Of course, of course!" Answered a groggy voice.

In a fluster, Khadijah began to relate her concerns and intuitive feelings but their blank looks of incomprehension caused her to switch tactics. She came right to the point and asked them to ride out to Cave Hira and check on Muhammad. Before they could depart, she heard the courtyard gate creak open and the fast firm footfalls characteristic of Muhammad's step. Anxiously she hurried to the door, almost snapping the wooden handle in her excitement to open it. Relief flooded her face as Muhammad walked toward her. Preoccupied, spent and ashen, he looked into her eyes and asked for a blanket. It was then the condition of his appearance registered in her mind.

Khadijah, Zayd and Maysara, all looked at one another in concern. None could ever recall having seen Muhammad in such a state of dishevelment, and while he sat mesmerized in thought nobody wanted to interrupt to ask what had happened.

"Maysara, please bring a clean blanket and warm water. Zayd, the children will be waking shortly, please prepare their meals and keep them occupied whilst I attend Muhammad," Khadijah said in one breath.

She knew something of importance had occurred but refrained from questioning him even though her curiosity screamed for answers. Biting her lip, she waited for Muhammad to explain.

"Please assist me up the stairs," asked Muhammad tiredly.

Without replying she helped him rise and walked him on up to their room where he fell heavily upon the bed.

"Cover me, please," Muhammad asked.

Khadijah covered and tucked the blanket's edges in around him. She sat down besides him biding her time, knowing he'd tell her in his own time. Never hadst he been so distracted before, she thought while examining his facial expressions. The whole time her thirst for answers increased with each passing minute. Finally she rose and stepped to the window hoping the diversion would suppress her inquisitiveness. She wondered again for the umpteenth time just what had happened.

Returning to his side, she took his hot dry hand in hers. In spite of the day's rising heat she felt chills crawling up her spine as she regarded Muhammad. He lay there motionless, staring at the ceiling. At the last, unable to bear the curiosity burning in her mind any longer, she cleared her throat softly and said, "My husband, can thou tell me what hath befallen thee? Never have I seen thee so absorbed."

Muhammad shook his head as if shaking off invisible restraints that imprisoned his mind. He drew himself up to a sitting position and put into words his experience.

There was a long moment of silence in which Muhammad observed Khadijah's every expression, looking for signs of belief or disbelief. But Khadijah returned his gaze tenderly, her features softening noticeably.

She thought: always hath he come unto me to discuss matters, never being deceitful or embellishing the truth. She said, "Verily, thou art blessed. Thy inner life is true and pure, and thy outer life kind and gentle. Ever loyal art thou to kin and hospitable unto strangers. No thought of harm or mischief ever stained thy mind nor word ever passed thy lips that was not true. Indeed thou art the Chosen one, for thou hast been always ready in the service of Allah.(4) Aye my husband, thou hast shouldered man's burdens unceasingly."

Muhammad laid back down, relief washing over him. He felt assured, alleviated, by Khadijah's support and encouragement. Comforted, he fell into a restful sleep.

Khadijah quietly retreated from the room and went about informing each member of the household that there was to be no unnecessary noise while Muhammad slept.

A short while later, Ali and the girls went outside, Zayd and Maysara parted for the square on errands, and Khadijah was left alone. With no one or anything to distract her thoughts, she started pondering the implications of what Muhammad had disclosed. She felt overwhelmed and unprepared, she couldn't perceive the coming consequences. With her mind in a jumble of thoughts, the heat became oppressively heavy on her flesh. She wandered about the house, shuffling her feet in their passage, thinking what she could do. Minutes passed, the heat worsened, she went to the window seeking air, a breeze, anything to cool herself. In the background she heard the pigeons cooing softly under the eaves, the sparrows chirping madly, frightened by the playing children, the grunts and snorts of passing animals, the distant barking of dogs, but the sounds of nature held no peace this day. Suddenly she pushed away from the window, urgently feeling the need to consult with her cousin Waraqah who was known for being knowledgeable about Holy Scripture.

As she approached the perimeter of her cousin's house, Waraqah's keen sense of hearing distinguished her gait from the differing steps of countless others passing by. Pleased to have her visiting, he rose, favor spreading across his face and opened the door just as she was about to knock. He stood in the open doorway, silhouetted by the sun's light streaming through the windows behind him. His old sagacious face creased in a toothless smile as he greeted her.

"Cousin, thou art looking well. Even without thy sight thou art still a handsome man," said Khadijah.

Waraqah wasn't sure but he thought he detected an edge of uneasiness in her voice. "Ah, my dear, dear Khadijah, it is only thee whom knowest how to bring the sun's warmth into an old man's heart," he returned while putting forth his hand to lead her to the table.

His hand pawed the air until she clasped his outstretched hand.

"What troubleth thee?" Asked Waraqah in concern, sensing her anxiety.

She immediately started conversing about trivial things. But Waraqah interrupted upon hearing the tenseness in her voice.

"My dear cousin, even though I am sightless, I can still perceive that thou art troubled. Thou knowest wilt I help thee in anyway I can."

Khadijah fell silent thinking where and how to begin. After a moment she took a deep breath and timorously recounted Muhammad's experience in its entirety. She was surprised to see his judicious old face fill with elation.

He said excitedly, "Oh, Khadijah, for more than thirty years have I kept abreast of the reports in regards to Muhammad. Since his childhood didst I believe a uniqueness about him. And now with thy account, Allah in His matchless wisdom hath bestowed the Great Truth upon Muhammad which came to His prophets in times past. Most surely is he the Prophet foretold by Prophet Jesus, peace and blessings be upon him. Saith thou unto Muhammad to stand fast for his right arm will be tested, and fear not for Allah in His mercy will guide him." Waraqah leaned back against his chair, trying to visualize Muhammad's blessed event.

Khadijah, having her thoughts confirmed, bid her leave and quickly departed. Exhilarated, she rushed home to find Muhammad still sleeping. She pulled up a chair and sat next to the bed, content to just watch him. He looked so peaceful, even the crow's feet around his eyes had smoothed themselves out when all of a sudden he opened his eyes and sat up.

Muhammad came wide awake feeling alive, rejuvenated, all his aches and pains gone. Khadijah told him of her conversation with Waraqah but he was thinking of something else entirely.

"Wouldst thou become a Muslim," asked Muhammad abruptly.

She stopped in mid-sentence, her brows arching in curiosity. "Muslim? What is a Muslim?" She returned.

Without the slightest pause, he replied: "A Muslim is one who chooses to acknowledge the Creator as One Being and submits his will to Him, the One God."

Khadijah at once declared her belief, and the Holy Mission began.

In other lands, the Emperor Phocus disgusted the Empire. Heraclius, a Roman Governor of a province in Africa, sent his son, also called Heraclius, to Constantinople to depose the tyrant and assume the reins of power. Young Heraclius, as Emperor of the Eastern Roman Empire was immediately beset with problems, inheriting a national war with the Persian Empire.(5)

CHAPTER TEN

Days later, Muhammad saw Waraqah in the Ka'bah and Khadijah's conversation flashed through his mind. "Waraqah, old friend. Didst thou wish to speak with me?"

"Oh, Prophet of Allah, I only wished for thee to relate thy blessed event." Waraqah reciprocated.

Muhammad took the old blind man to the quietest corner where he explained first hand his experience in Cave Hira. Waraqah listened attentively, his face changing expression several times. When Muhammad finished, he said: "Oh, Muhammad, unto thee hath the Decree of Allah come like unto those before you. Thou knowest what must be done. Remain firm for the kafirun will mock and belittle thee for thy beliefs, and attempt mischief, or expel and even fight thee. If Allah so willeth that should I live to behold such a thing, thou mayest rely I wilt do all in my power to aid thee." He, then, felt for Muhammad's shoulders. Gripping with a strength that surprised Muhammad, he embraced and kissed his cheeks.

Muhammad felt a little disconcerted from Waraqah's ominous predictions of violence. He cast his eyes about, surveying the multitude of hideous idols surrounded by a rough, tough and vicious people. He knew they were twisted by ignorance, error, superstition and perversity, for they gluttonized themselves in orgies of debasement and drunkenness. Their virtues and loyalties pointed toward offense, conflict, falseness and misrepresentation which went against reason and nature. He shook his head disgustedly as if warding away the evilness that permeated the Ka'bah's chamber.

In Cave Hira late that afternoon, Muhammad sat oblivious to the chill advancing with the sun's setting. He stared out over Mekkah, focusing his sight on the Ka'bah as he communed with himself. The day's fiery close seemed appropriate as a maelstrom of questions and thoughts inundated his mind. What was it all leading to? I am not a soothsayer foretelling passing events! Truth and reality of unity are gone from their minds. Who will join me to obey Allah's Will and Law? Who is fit to be the bearers of His Light? Verily, canst it not be men besot with words and mysteries or men whom politics have perverted, nor men whose propriety has ended in iniquity who speak of love and justice but exercise selfishness amongst their brethren. The medley of subject matter offered no solutions but he knew deep within his heart the answers would come.

Returning home late that evening an occasional bark marked his passage as he walked through the city. Finding his house darkened, he quietly unlatched the courtyard gate, opening it wide enough to slip through. Creeping in soundlessly, he traversed under the eaves, ascended the stone steps and eased into the bedroom he shared with Khadijah. He stood along side the bed and gazed compassionately with tired eyes upon his wife's moonlit face thinking how she befriended him when he had no worldly resources, trusted him, believed in him, yea a perfect woman.(1) Standing there, he radiated waves of affection like the moon diffusing its beams. As if sensing his presence, Khadijah murmured faintly but the words were filled with somnolence. Not wanting to awaken her with the erratic movements of climbing into bed, he withdrew from the room and slept downstairs.

Khadijah awoke to the pale light of dawn and sleepily looked around expectantly for Muhammad. Seeing his wrap, she knew Muhammad once again slept in the sitting room to keep from disturbing her. Briefly, she stared out the window at the lightening sky thinking loving thoughts. She rose from bed, passed the children's room, they were sound asleep. Going downstairs, she put water to heat and checked on Muhammad. Beholding him with deep fondness, the sight of his face soothed her. She thought he looked exhausted, drawn out and cold. Leaving for an instant, she returned carrying a thick blanket with which to cover him.

Muhammad stirred, wearily meeting her eyes and smiled endearingly. "In every respect thou art a vision of loveliness. Have I become a burden unto thee," he asked suddenly.

"Nay, my husband. Thou hath never been a burden," she returned, her voice a balm of tenderness. She saw his hand snake out from under the blanket, reaching for hers. Taking his hand, she encased it with both of hers.

Muhammad sighed contentedly and disengaged his hand from hers. Still looking at her, he said: "Wouldst thou awaken me shortly before noon?"

Khadijah nodded her agreement and left to rouse the children. Then had to shush them before answering their questions. Ali immediately asked after Muhammad and the girls followed suit. Zayd and Maysara also woke, stirred by the youngsters. After breakfast Khadijah sent the adolescents out, Zayd and Maysara discussed with her the talk of the city. Hours elapsed as they talked in great detail the latest accounts.

Spent from hours of play, the youngsters watched Maysara and Zayd depart. Ali, however, was intrigued over events the past few days and suggested by mime food to little Fa'timah, who in turn spread the idea among her sisters. As the notion developed they hungrily ran into the house.

"Where is Muhammad," asked Ali as the girls went for refreshments.

Khadijah thought before answering, a look of tenderness blooming over her face, hast thou grown much these past years. Yea little one, thou wilt no doubt carry on the legacy of truth. For none wilt ever know Muhammad's ways better than thee.

"He is sleeping," she replied. Then had to admonish the children not to snack as she was making the noon meal. After lunch, the youngsters returned outdoors. Preparing a platter of delicacies, she woke Muhammad.

Finished with the meal, Muhammad thanked his wife and walked toward the window looking out into the courtyard. He saw his daughters running in circles, playing. He thought: Fa'timah thou art the gentlest. Then seeing all was in order, he turned to face his wife. "Khadijah," he said, "whilst the younger ones amuse themselves let us go to the back of the house." They withdrew to the quietest part where the Splendor of all prophets began to praise the One God and offer worship.

Ali, driven by thirst, ran indoors to quench his need. Instantly he halted in mid-stride, the house was curiously quiet. With a sense of mystery governing his actions, he stepped carefully, easing around corners. He froze in place, the sound of Muhammad's voice beautifully expressing prayer utterly fascinated him. Never had he heard such enunciation of praise before. Noiselessly he crept forward to investigate the melodious adoration. He came upon Muhammad and Khadijah standing reverently, intoning words of homage. He glanced around, saw no idols and wondered. He waited until they finished, then asked: "Unto whom wert thou praying?"

"Unto Allah, the One God," said Muhammad. "Come, wilt I tell thee of my experience with Allah's Archangel Gabriel." Khadijah watched Ali's expression while Muhammad explained. She felt as if the young boy suddenly grew in stature, an awareness filling his features.

Muhammad ended and asked, "Wouldst thou like to become Muslim?"

Surprised by Muhammad's question, Ali thought a moment before answering: "May I speak with my father before deciding?"

"As ye wish, Ali."

That night Ali's mind was in turmoil, he couldn't sleep. Tense, he tossed and turned thinking of the import Muhammad's words conveyed, whether he should ask his father or not, or was it a matter of his own right to believe in One God. Into the early hours of morning he thought before succumbing to slumber. A few hours later, Ali's eyes fluttered open. His mind made up, he rushed downstairs hoping to catch Muhammad before he left for the day.

"Oh, Muhammad," said Ali immediately upon seeing him. "There is no need to ask my father's permission. I believe with thee in One God."

Soon afterwards Zayd and Maysara, having heard Muhammad speak of submission to God, and their unshakable faith in his integrity, accepted the old religion of belief in One God with their declaration. The two eldest girls, Ruqayyah and Zaynab, declared their belief while Umm Kulthum and the toddler Fa'timah wondered over the new excitement germinating throughout the household.

One day, Abu Talib and his son Ja'far were approaching Muhammad's home when near the courtyard they heard the sound of voices rhythmically praising God. Talib halted, grabbing hold of his son's arm. He raised his finger to his lips in signal for quiet and together they listened. The words are unique and beautifully chanted, thought Talib. He faced Ja'far: "Son, go and join thy cousin in prayer." Without a moments hesitation Ja'far opened the gate and treaded softly to join the small group in prayer.

Talib followed and stood in the rear near the wall. He watched in silence as they reverently stood, bowed and prostrated. He was convinced, Muhammad was indeed the Prophet and Messenger promised by Allah.

Muhammad completed the prayer. Ja'far stepped forward and professed his belief in the One God, and another Muslim was added to the association of Believers. After hugs and congratulations the adults moved indoors. The youngsters remained in the courtyard to pick up where they left off.

Talib spoke with Muhammad, but felt no need to question him about his business. His honesty, integrity and probity, said volumes about his intentions.

Early next morning, before dawn's first light, Khadijah abruptly awakened. Muhammad was breathing heavily, a dry wind escaping from deep within his lungs. Thinking him ill she was about to rise and light the oil lamp when the moon came out from behind the clouds. Aided by the grayish light she watched him toss and turn, perspiration freely flowing from his forehead. Her mind raced in worry when he suddenly began to mumble.

"Oh, thou covered under thy mantle! Arise and warn! And thy Lord, magnify! And thy raiment, purify! And every kind of abomination, shun it! And bestow not favors that thou mayest receive them back increased..."(2)

Khadijah knew it was no illness, dream or delusion. She understood, rejoiced, and tried to comfort him but he was unmindful of her ministrations.

Muhammad's eyes fluttered open, his respiration evened out. He started blinking as he focused his vision upon Khadijah's face. Disregarding the strain and stress of an experience rare to mortal men, he cast aside the bed covers, intending to rise. Reflexively Khadijah's arm straightened in restraint.

"Thou needest thy rest, my husband," said Khadijah imploringly.

Time for rest and sleep is gone. Must I speak with the people!" Muhammad returned while smoothly evading his wife's arm.

CHAPTER ELEVEN

A span of time had now elapsed since the Holy Apostle Muhammad had
+ seen or heard from Angel Gabriel. Tormented by the lack of communication with God's ministering Spirit, he trekked into the mountains, seeking the solitude and solace of Cave Hira. Sitting near the entrance, he reclined against the cavern's uneven surface to meditate. Abstractedly he admired the vivid hues of sunset.

"Nay!" Muhammad blurted into the wind as Gabriel's taciturnity intruded his thoughts. "Wouldst not Allah forsake me, but guide me as He wisheth! O' Lord of the Worlds, Thou knowest better than I, Thy slave's needs, and unto Thee alone seek I refuge..." At nightfall he descended the mount and made his way home.

Wending through the wilderness the skies were unusually clear with bright stars, illumining the path before him. The night air was crisp, cool and invigorating. It was then that God allowed a small portion of the mind's veil to peel back and reveal several Surahs of sacred Scripture.

Commencing with the Holy Name of God, Muhammad's concerns and restlessness vanished. The Divine Words were stippled with celestial light upon the ethereal tissue of his mind. He felt dazed as he attempted to focus on the common sights of man. Was I not forsaken, he thought jubilantly. Nay, am I but promised and commanded!

Hearing the creaking gate, Khadijah hastily made her way towards one of the windows facing the courtyard. Recognizing her husband's tread, she instead pivoted for the door. She opened the door and smiled until the room's candle light fell upon Muhammad's approaching figure. Immediately she saw the look of enlightenment which had filled his face sometime back. She cried out to Zayd excitedly, "Bring food and a flagon of water for Muhammad."

Sounding fatigued, al-Amin started speaking as soon as he crossed the threshold. In trance-like state he reiterated, word for word, the Message revealed by God, through His Angel Gabriel.

"In the name of Allah, The Beneficent, The Merciful."

"By the Noonday! By the Night when it darkened! Hath forsaken not thee thy Lord, nor hath He been displeased! And verily the end is better for thee than the beginning! And soon will give thee thy Lord that thou shall be well pleased!'

'What! Found He not thee an orphan, and sheltered (thee)? And found thee in loss (and immediately) guided thee, and found thee in need, and made thee independent! So, unto an orphan oppress not!

And as to the beggar, chide him not! And as to the bounties of thy Lord, thou announce."(1)

Ali, the next day, ran to inform his father that Muhammad had received another revelation, and together they returned to Muhammad's house.

The Prophet and Talib spoke. Muhammad expounded the excellence of true submission when he suddenly became motionless, his body stiff, breathing heavily. Sweat poured down his face. Alarmed, Talib cried out for help.

Everyone in the household and out in the courtyard momentarily froze at the sound of Talib's voice, then came running. Zayd, Khadijah, Maysara and the youngsters, stopped in their tracks upon seeing Muhammad's condition. Unknown to all, except Khadijah, the signs exhibited while undergoing Divine revelation, she asked everyone to remain calm and quiet as possible. She explained that Muhammad was in no danger and that he was in contact with the Unseen.

An apprehensive hush settled over the household. Khadijah, lest the young ones disturb Muhammad, sent them back outdoors. Ali crept around like a phantom wearing a white suffering face. Even Talib seemed to have forgotten his surroundings as he stared, awe and wonder filling his own features.

Khadijah, after tending to the girls, returned carrying several small towels. She sat next to Muhammad and began to wipe away the dripping perspiration from his face.

Talib in the meantime, kept a careful eye on Muhammad, thinking all the while his nephew's countenance shone with a bliss he'd never before seen. Some minutes later Muhammad abruptly sat up and looked around the room as if to make certain of his whereabouts. Beholding the worried faces of his loved ones, he assured them he was okay. Then looking to his wife, he cleared his throat and recited the Message. "In the name of Allah, The Beneficent, The Merciful.'

'Nun (Noon) by the Pen and by what they write, thou by the grace of thy Lord, art not mad. And verily there is for thee a recompense unending. And most certainly thou standest on sublime morality. So thou wilt see and they wilt see, which of you is demented. Verily thy Lord! He knowest best of him who is astray from His way, and He knowest best of those guided aright. So yield thou not to the beliers! Wish they that thou shouldst be pliant so they (too) would be pliant. And yield thou not unto any despicable swearer, defamer going about with slander, vehement hinderer of good, uncontrolled transgressor, sunk deep in sin, cruelly violent, besides all that, baseborn, just because possesses he wealth and sons; when unto him are recited Our signs, saith he: 'Stories of yore'; We will brand him on the snout!'

'Verily, for the pious ones with their Lord are Gardens of bliss. What! Shall We then make the Muslims like unto the guilty ones? What is the matter with you? How judge ye? Or have ye a scripture wherein ye read? Verily, therein is for you what ye choose? Or have ye a sworn covenant from Us tending to the Day of Judgment that ye shall surely have whatever ye judge? Ask them which of them will guarantee that! Or have they any 'Partners' (to Us)? Then let them bring their partners if they be truthful!"

"On the Day that the shin shall be laid bare, (i.e., befalleth an affliction), and they shall be called upon to prostrate in obeisance, but they shall not be able. Casting down their looks, shall cover them abasement, and indeed they had been called upon to prostrate in obeisance, while yet they were whole (healthy).'

'So leave Me and him who belieth this announcement, We will lead them on (to ruin) by steps from whence they know not and yet respite them; for My device is firm. Or askest thou from them recompense that they are burdened with a load of debt? Or with them is the knowledge of the unseen that they write (it) down? So wait thou patiently for the judgment of thy Lord! Be not thou like unto the Companion of the fish, when cried he when he was confined.

Had not a bounty from his Lord reached him, he would certainly have been cast forth on the naked shore while in disgrace. Then chose him his Lord and made him of the righteous ones. And those who disbelieve would almost smite thee with their eyes when they hear the Reminder, and say they: 'Verily he is mad.' And it is naught but a Reminder unto the worlds (the whole Mankind)."(2)

When Muhammad stopped, Talib exclaimed: "Al-Hamdu lillah! At the last we have our own religion."

Uncle," began the Holy Apostle, "submission unto Allah is not for one tribe or people. It is the Truth for all mankind; to whom turneth unto Allah, it is a Message of glad tidings of His Mercy. And if they do not turn to Him, it is a warning against sin and the inevitable punishment. The Gospel of Unity is the true cure for evil."(3)

Days later, while Muhammad was enroute to the square to seek out certain individuals, he encountered an acquaintance, Abu Bakr ibn Quhafah along the way. As they talked and walked Muhammad thought the years had been kind to Bakr. He was well-off and influential in Mekkah and surrounding areas. Abu Bakr likewise regarded his friend as they walked. He admired Muhammad, thinking him the most upright man he'd ever known. He also speculated that the majority of Banu Quraysh foolish and narrow minded. Subtly he examined the Chosen One through his peripheral vision and saw an undefined determination. He wondered if what he'd been hearing the past months were true. "Oh, Muhammad, wouldst thou tell me what thou hast been preaching?" Bakr asked abruptly. Muhammad stopped in mid-stride, instantly recalling everything he knew of his associate. He looked straight into his eyes and began relating his experience with Angel Gabriel. He recited several passages of the Qur'an, ending some minutes later. The two men just stared at one another thinking their own thoughts. Then to Muhammad's delight, Abu Bakr accepted what he'd heard and declared his belief in the Oneness of God.

CHAPTER TWELVE

With time's passage angel Gabriel continued to disclose God's Holy Writ. Muhammad knew the Message was no mere esoteric doctrine to be grasped by a few in contemplation.(1) He kept spreading the Word while maintaining his visits to those in need: giving solace; food; and, spiritual strength. And more often then not, found himself returning to the mountain cave for solitude and prayer.

After a particularly grueling day, he sat in Cave Hira thinking of the circumstances which brought him to the small cavern. As his mind flashed back over the years, he felt the onset of heavenly visitation. Then heard the deep voice of God's Messenger.

"In the name of Allah, The Beneficent, The Merciful."

"When the sun is folded, and when the stars darken, and when the mountains are removed (as scattered dust), and when the Ishaar (she-camel) shall be abandon, and when the wild beasts are herded together, and when the oceans are caused to boil and burn, and when souls shall be reunited (with their bodies), and when the female baby buried (alive) shall be asked for what sin was she put to death, and when the Books shall be unfolded, and when the Heaven shall be removed, and when the Hell shall be made to blaze, and when the Garden is brought nigh, every soul shall know what it hath presented.'

'I swear by the planets, the running and the gliding ones, and (by) the night when it endeth, and (by) the dawn when it brightened, verily it (the Qur'an) is the word of an Apostle, the most Honored. Gifted with Mighty Power, Honored in the presence of the Lord of the ARSH (Universe).'

'The Obeyed One (by all creation) and above all the Trustworthy. And (o' ye people!) your Companion (Muhammad) is not gone mad. And indeed he saw him (Gabriel) on the clear horizon. And he (the Apostle) is not avid about the unseen, nor is it the word of the Cursed Satan.'

'Whither then go ye? It (Qur'an) is naught but a Reminder unto (all) the worlds, unto him of you who willeth to go straight. And ye willeth not save that willeth Allah, the Lord of the worlds.'(2)

'Hallow thou the name of thy Lord, The Most High, He Who createth and fashioneth (all things), and He Who planned and guideth them, and He Who bringeth forth the herbage, then reduceth it to dusty stubble.'

'We make thee to read so that thou shouldst not forget save what willeth Allah, verily He knoweth the declared and what is hidden. And We shall ease (thy way) unto an ease (for thee), and thou go on reminding for it profiteth (mankind) reminding it. He that feareth (God) will mind the warning, and will avoid it the most reprobate one, who shall be committed to great fire, then he shall die not therein nor shall he live (in it). Indeed he (alone) succeedeth who purifieth himself, and remembereth the Name of his Lord and (regularly) prayeth.'

'Nay! Prefer ye the life of this world, although the hereafter is better and more lasting. Verily, this is in the scriptures earlier, the Scriptures of Abraham and Moses."(3)

As suddenly as the Revelations strain began, the veil was lifted from the Chosen one's eyes, and his soul for a moment was filled with Divine ecstasy.(4)

Taxed from the visitation, Muhammad wearily looked out over the city for several moments before taking his leave. Scaling down the mountain's side, he wondered at the lateness of hour. It seemed to him that the darkness appeared tenfold dark and the solitude tenfold empty. (5) Lost in thought, he made his way home.

The following day, while the Prophet's family was ending their morning meal, Muhammad began to recount his experience from the previous night.

Ali, who had the responsibility of transcription, colored and made haste for papyri, ink pot and bone, admonishing himself for not being prepared. As soon as he returned and seated himself, he started transcribing.

Muhammad completed the account and looked over to see Khadijah focusing her attention on him. He gazed at her for an instant, then glanced at Zayd who had a look of amazement on his face. Ali was busily writing. Next, he recalled the memory of the sublime joy he felt while in harmony with the Infinite. He thought: must I declare with an unfaltering voice the Unity of Allah and the Brotherhood of all mankind amongst a people steeped in ignorance, without cohesion or union... He never finished his thought, for the pangs of hunger suddenly invaded.

Meanwhile, Ali ended and hypnotically regarded the Divinely Inspired Text. He thought: Muhammad is indeed Allah's Prophet, for no man could humanly possible put together such words in beautiful harmony.

Khadijah likewise thought, except her thinking reflected the maturity of her years. Indeed, hath he risen to great spiritual heights. A perfect example for mankind to emulate. She knew with certitude he'd overcome the invidiousness that was sure to come from contemporaries. Closing her eyes, she bowed her head slightly and murmured, "Oh, Allah, Thou art The Knower of all things. Protect Thy Servant."

Close to three years had passed since the Holy Prophet received the first revelation. All the while, he continued making his rounds of consoling the oppressed, comforting the sick, helping the poor, and edifying God's Message.

Ali, ever at Muhammad's side, grew with Islam's growth during his most sensitive years. His psychological composition molded along the lines of Islamic teachings. Over the years he had grown to be a virile and energetic young man. Personable, strong, stocky, and somewhat on the short side, the first signs of fuzzy hairs were appearing on his chin. Beyond his physical appearance, however, was a personality of unique nature with a brilliant mind. He was quick-witted with powers of penetration into problems and a demeanor suggesting a maturity far superior to his age.

One evening as Muhammad returned from the poorer section of Mekkah, he noticed the stillness of night increase in intensity and looked about reflexively. Time surreally passed as his feet mechanically carried him forward through the city's twisting streets and alleyways. He thought he was trembling but then realized the ground was vibrating in a slow crescendo of power. Hearing no rumbling or crashing sounds, he affixed his mind upon the Lord of the worlds.

In the depths of his mind a soft white glow began to illuminate the furthest recesses. He directed his inner vision, focusing on the growing incandescence until it exploded into a brilliant swirling nimbus. As sweat beaded over his face, he closed his hands into fists until his knuckles whitened and the tendons of his arms visibly rose. The perspiration started dripping off his face, vice-like pincers enclosed about his breast, an explosion seemingly burst in his chest. He knew not of the world around him but heard the deep clear voice of Angel Gabriel ringing out.

"In the name of Allah, The Beneficent, The Merciful.

"And for thy Lord (endure every hardship) in patience! For when the Trumpet is beaten (sounded), that shall be the Day of distress (for those who disbelieve), unto the disbelievers (it shall be) any thing other than ease!

"Leave Me (to deal with) him whom I created alone! And unto whom I granted wealth in abundance, and sons abiding in his presence, and unto whom I made (life) adjustably smooth! Yet desireth he that I should further add! Never, for unto Our signs he was a foe! Soon will I make him afflicted of a severe punishment.

"Verily, he thought and determined, but may he be ruined how he determined. Again may he be ruined how he determined! Then looked he around, then frowned he and scowled! Then turned he his back and swelled in pride! Then said he: 'This is naught but sorcery from old! This is naught but the word of a human being!' Soon will I cast him into hell! And what will make him realize what hell is? It leaveth not nor it spareth (aught), it shrivelleth a human body!

"Above it (guardians) are nineteen. We have made not the guardians of the fire other than angels, and We have made not the number save as a trial for those who disbelieve, that certain may be those who have been given the Book, and may increase those who believe in (their) faith, and may doubt not those who have been given the Book and the believers, and that say those in whose hearts is a distress and the disbelievers: 'What meaneth God by this similitude?' Thus doth Allah alloweth to stray whomsoever He willeth, and guideth He whom He willeth, and knoweth not (any one) the hosts of Allah save He Himself; and this is naught but a reminder unto mankind.

"Nay! By the moon and by the night when it retreateth, and by the morn when it brighteneth! Verily it (the Hell) is one of the grievous woes! A warning (it is) unto mankind! Unto him among you who desireth to go forward (in goodness) or to remain behind, every soul, for what it earned is held in pledge! Save the people of the Right hand. In gardens shall they be, asking each other about the guilty ones: 'What hath brought you into the hell?' They shall say: 'We were not of those who offered the regular prayers (to Allah)! And we used not to feed the poor, and used we to talk vanities with the vain talkers, and used we to belie the Day of Judgment, till came upon us the Certainty (death)!

"So, shall avail them not the intercession of the intercessors! What hath happened then that they turn aside from the warning, as if they were asses affrighted, fleeing from a lion. Nay, but willeth every one of them that he may be given (the heavenly Book) in open pages spread out. Nay, but they fear not the hereafter. Nay! Verily it is a Reminder! So whosoever willeth may mind it, and they will mind it not unless Allah willeth; worthy is He to be feared and worthy is He from which to seek refuge."(6)

The dazzling light vanished and Muhammad languidly returned to the world of time, circumstance, and sense. Tired, but exultant, he continued on to share his encounter with Khadijah.

During the night Muhammad twisted and turned. His mind raced with ideas. Gabriel revealed another Surah and directed him to warn his relatives of Hashim, and openly reveal his sacred mission. Subconsciously, he organized his thoughts and prepared for the day that would surely demonstrate he was a Servant of the Lord.

He awoke with a yearning to fill God's Will, the fervor enkindling his passions to broadcast the Word. He would show and lead them in the true faith, guiding them to the Promised Reward, and seek their assistance against the Disbelievers .

At breakfast he immediately put into effect the first order of business. "Ali, after thou hast eaten set off unto each member of our clan and invite them to sup with us this evening. Upon thy return, follow these instructions for the night's meal."

As the day wore on there was an air of growing anticipation. Ali prepared an unusually small meal of bread, meat and milk. He wanted so much to question it's size but held his tongue. Muhammad, observing Ali's and the household's curious expressions kept his counsel and meditated until the arrival of his guests.

"What is the occasion," they all asked upon seeing the Prince of Peace.

He answered them alike: "After dinner will I explain all unto you."

Before the meal even began the crowd of forty men started grumbling as they espied the small bowls containing their meal, which wouldn't suffice for one man, let alone a multitude. Muhammad raised his arms for quiet. The group fell silent. He looked upon the food then blessed it with the name of God.

Ali began serving the dinner until the last man was served.

Throughout the meal the level of noise from such a large gathering was surprisingly subdued. However, the guests could not help but examine Muhammad and wonder.

Then, when the last person pushed his bowl away Muhammad stood and cleared his throat. "Have I requested thy presence because I wish to speak with thee about submission unto One God, and my plans to re-establish the Way in Mekkah. Using the Truth which Allah has given me to give unto mankind, intend I to bring as many people possible into the fold of Allah's Religion. Who-"

Abu Lahab rudely interrupted before Muhammad could complete his delivery. Sharp tongued and loving his position of authority, he vehemently opposed the ideal of submission to One God. Using the stunned silence, he began to claim the Holy Scripture a product of sorcery until the gathering dispersed.

Although Muhammad was disappointed with the evening's outcome, he never let the incident stop him. He again asked Ali to invite their relatives and make the same preparations of the night before. Once more the assembly behaved in the same manner. For a third time, the Holy Prophet renewed his requests and Ali carried them out.(7)

As soon as the meal was consumed, Muhammad immediately stood and addressed his guests. He said with authority: "Oh, sons of Abdul Mut'talib!" Then turned and faced Abu Lahab squarely, who withered noticeably. "I know not any one amongst our people whom bringeth a thing better than I. Allah hath dispatched me unto all His creatures and hath especially sent me unto you. Saith Allah: 'And warn thou thy relatives of nearest kin.'(8) Call I unto you to make an affirmation which is light on thy tongue but weighty in the scales of Allah. By it thou wilt be master of Arab and foreigner, by it wilt nations fall and submit unto you, and thou wilt enter heaven and escape the Hell-Fire. It is the testifying that there is no god but Allah and that I am His Apostle.(9)

"Know ye all that I am the Apostle of Allah to warn you of Him, and to warn you of an approaching doom. I am the bearer of glad tidings of the abode of eternal bliss to those who believe in the Only True God and in my ministry. Allah did not send any apostle of His but He sent along with him his Heir and Khalif. Who is there amongst ye who would be a Vazier to me and my Heir and Khalif, and join me in the task of the ministry?"(10)

It was quiet, only the birds could be heard warbling sleepily. Every one sat motionless except the few who were either scowling or looking at one another in disbelief. Then, with no warning or indication, the silence was suddenly ripped apart, shattering every ones thoughts. An adolescent voice, bold, firm, with a tone of defiance emphasizing its sincerity, exclaimed from the rear.

"I am here for thee, O' Apostle of Allah!" All turned toward the source of the voice and to their surprise it was Ali.

Some of the guests began to laugh derisively, thinking it absurd to see Ali, a mere boy of no more than fourteen years of age declaring his stand so pugnaciously. What they could not comprehend was the heart stirring spirit of faith in One God and how it fortified the Believers with courage to stand in the face of adversity.

Muhammad bade Ali to take his seat and reiterated the question. Complete silence answered his question. He scanned their faces, measuring the impact. Some faces changed into looks of disapproval, mockery, anger, and utter disbelief. A few even felt insulted, thinking he was asking too much of them. After all, they thought, how could they stop worshipping their gods or leave their ways of life just to start all over again. Not only that, they were called to follow someone who wasn't even the leader of Quraysh.

Ali jumped to his feet and affirmed his position.

Muhammad looked kindly at his charge and asked him to sit down. Undaunted by his kinsmen expressions, he said: "Which of ye amongst you will uphold me, so that he becomes My Brother, My Deputy, and the One to succeed me?"

While the clan members thought up excuses not to commit themselves to God, it was Ali who responded. "Wilt I help thee in this matter, O' Apostle of Allah!"

Muhammad summoned Ali to his side and situated him for all to see. He moistened his finger with saliva and rubbed it across Ali's lips, then embraced him, kissing both cheeks. Raising Ali's hand with his own, the Prophet of God commanded: "Know ye all! Verily, this is My Brother, My Successor, and the Executor of my will. Therefore, listen unto him and obey."(11)

"Oh, Abu Talib, thou hast better heed thy son Ali, for he hath been placed in authority over thee." Heckled one of the guests. Only a few laughed.

The night's events, however, generated discussion about the One God and the renewal of an old way to live as the gathering departed for their homes.

Some days later, shortly after the noon hour when the square was most apt to be crowded, al-Amin led Khadijah and Ali towards God's ancient House of worship where he would lead them in prayer.

The merchants gawked and gossiped with shoppers as they strolled from booth to booth. Atif, a local trader, shattered the air of wild speculation with a bellow across the marketplace: "Abbas! Abbas!" He started thumping his foot importantly, waiting for Muhammad's uncle to arrive.

"Abbas, my friend," Atif began with presence of mind, "doth thou knowest of this submission unto One God, which the city is going on about?"

Abbas studied Atif with cautious regard for several moments before replying. "Atif... Muhammad, the son of Abdullah, believeth not in gods or many in one. Believeth he in only One God. And as thou can see, few art Believers as yet."(12) Atif and Abbas continued to speak, dismissing the world around them.

Muhammad ended the prayer and turned to address the oglers, "Allah, The Beneficent, is The Creator and Nourisher of the Universe and besides Him there is none even equal unto Him. The One God is Merciful unto every life. He and none else wilt respond to prayer, and if thy prayer is to be heard, shouldst it be only unto Him and none else, for it wilt be in vain as Jesus, alaihis salaam, refers to.([13]) Man is assured, Allah The Lord-Nourisher, is Protector of not any one tribe, clan or nation, but of all the Universe. Verily, there is a Day of Requital when justice in it's fullness wilt be meted out and every weight of goodness wilt be rewarded and every weight of evil wilt be punished.(14) No one can pay for another's wrong-doing as Allah Almighty revealed unto Moses, alaihis salaam.(15) This Way of life, of faith and constancy, is not new, it is a Way taught by Allah's prophets of yore. And if ye be blind or thinkest to thrust off the truth, runneth ye foolishly unto death..."

Many of the listeners amusedly rejected the declarations and some even mocked his virtue. Others thought him mad or wanted material gain. However, those enlightened but yet undecided invariably remarked: "Seest we the truth of what saith thou, but if we abandon the ways passed down unto us, wilt we be deprived of our land." To which Muhammad always answered, "Thy land? The sanctuary of this Holy land and city is secure owing to Allah's Grace and if thou wouldst obey His Word, wilt ye be strengthened not weakened!"(16)

Russal, never forgetting how Muhammad stared him down, watched with curbed hostility as the Prophet exhorted God's Word. He imagined a variety of ways to harm the Chosen one, but lacking the character to brave his fears he instead ran for the protection of others.

"Oh, Abu Lahab," started the evil one before inflating himself with self-importance. "Doth thou knowest what Muhammad is up to in the marketplace?"

Lahab ignored Russal, brushing past him to investigate the matter for himself. Once in the square he learned more than he cared to, leaving him with impotent rage. Grinding his teeth as he stewed in his own juices, he looked for allies. Surrounding himself, he initiated a course tread by Disbelievers of old. He maligned Muhammad, implying his ultimate aim was wealth, twisted God's Word, and ended with blasphemies against the Creator for Muhammad's Prophethood.

Abu Jahl nodded as if a witness attesting to the truth of Lahab's words, then added in a voice meant for the hardest core against Islam, "I am uneasy about this new religion which is finding a way amongst the people and undermining our authority. In fact, am I afraid. Canst I not think of a thing more ominous or damaging unto our station than the threatening changes Muhammad bringeth. Of course, I think not this new trend will seriously take root and become a religion of distinction. But the tendency is there in the minds of those with nothing to turn to."

A wicked glint filled Abu Sufyan's eyes while he waited for Jahl to finish. He said, "Can I perceive what thou meanest very clearly. There is much in what thou saith, Jahl. Lately, hath there been much talk of this very thing amongst the tribes. There are many who believe that given a free hand we could crush this new Way by making examples of those who follow the teachings of Muhammad."

Evil smiles spread all around the group of men listening to the matrix of a plan that would embroil the Disbelievers in strife for years to come. Russal, ever at the beck and call of his masters, licked his lips wolfishly when Jahl motioned Umar to his side. Russal tilted his head as if to hear what Jahl whispered into Umar's ear but Umar stomped off and he followed in his shadow.

Russal, self-importantly, strutted behind Umar until reaching a booth where an elderly man bargained for goods. Umar who had seen the man visiting al-Arqam's house whenever Muhammad held lectures, caught the man unaware and violently threw him to the ground. Russal immediately set upon the stunned victim while Umar shrieked

Muhammad's teachings were nothing but falsehoods and the gods had instructed him to punish those who strived against them.

It was a pitiful scene: Russal cackled monstrously as he kicked. Umar's hulking body shook with rage as he stood screaming down at the man. There was little the old man could do but protect himself and endure the beating.

War had now officially been declared on the Muslims. Lahab, Jahl, Sufyan, Walid ibn Mughayrah, As ibn Wa'il, Aqibah ibn Abi Ma'ayyat, and the like of their ilk became self-appointed leaders against Islam. They wanted no change, for their livelihood depended heavily on idol worship which was now being threatened.

As a result, this unholy alliance began the systematic persecution of Muslims. Yet, following a series of beatings, the Disbelievers were unable to halt or impede the Truth's momentum. Such was the strength and forcefulness of God's pure truth that kinsman turned against kinsman. Even though Islam's adherents were still relatively few in number, their solidarity amid evil's hand was something to behold and their strength of unity began to gain the admiration of many non-believers.

CHAPTER THIRTEEN

From the time of Muhammad's first revelation, news of his Prophethood had slowly spread in an ever widening circle. The influential Arabs, many from his own tribe, having known him through business ventures and life's daily activities thought it impossible that a man not taught in human wisdom could deliver the Message of Truth. And in their ignorance they attributed the Message's power to magic and sorcery. Muhammad spoke of higher things than they knew, and acted from motives purer and nobler than they could understand.(1) So they began complaining to Abu Talib, claiming Muhammad was disrupting the order of things. Some went as far as accusing him of being mad and out of his senses. The fact of the matter was that they resented his rising prominence and ability to draw people away from their opinionated views.

Talib heard their complaints diplomatically, promising he'd speak with Muhammad. However, each time he thought or initiated his step towards his nephew's house the knowledge of Muhammad's integrity stayed him and he refrained from interfering. It was only when the denunciations abnormally increased that he began to distrust the affluent. Skeptical about their impulsive conclusions, he grew very cautious in allowing himself to believe in men whom he knew all his life. He thought: there seems to be a collective effort to reduce Muhammad's teachings to invention. He who seldom permitted his emotions to become involved with anything, suddenly found himself in turmoil. Al-Mustafa was right, he reflected, mankind tended to covetousness. It saved one from concerning himself with the higher aspects of life. And of course the rich and influential seized the advantage of man's natural trend in nature, electing to subject rather than elevate. The old religion of worship to One God had now been replaced by the worship of dinars. The growth of virtues and dignity preached by prophets of old had been lessened to the growth of one's power and man's humiliation by pressing him into subservience. The more he thought, Abu Talib perceived that it was indeed a plot to undermine Muhammad's reputation, and upon further study he began to see by whom and why. Yea, they cried: "There must be order for the sake of profits."

Arriving before the usual throng of people crowding the square, Muhammad stopped and scrutinized the merchants and traders as they prepared for the day's business. He started strolling among them and the individuals milling about, telling all of One God and that he'd shortly explain more at the Ka'bah's steps. He knew that somehow he must fulfill his mission to proclaim and promulgate the Oneness of God. As he walked through the marketplace he considered a variety of ways to commence his task when unbidden came a memory of long ago in which a poet had captured his audience's attention. He remembered the many different nuances the bard used to hold his audience and decided to employ the same tactics. Realizing he could no longer stand by silently while men killed their souls with false worship, he scanned the square once more before going over to the Ka'bah.

Muhammad found a small group of about ten people assembled on the Ka'bah's steps looking impatient. Ten art better than nine, he thought. Climbing to the top of the stairs, he looked over his small audience. He winced involuntarily as he recognized several faces in the background, suspecting Russal and Abu Jahl's meddling that influenced many of the trouble-makers which constantly plagued him. Whitherest I go Abu Jahl and Russal art there… Their own breast do they hold in spite, he thought grimly. He cleared his throat, immediately attracting their attention.

"Oh, ye men," began Muhammad, "doth thou not see that all things created follows a course which never changes? Man through arrogance or lack of knowledge advocates the existence of several gods but this is not so. There is Only One God and He hath no partners. Hence, I call ye to serve Him and Him alone. Thou-"

Abu Jahl, who'd been singing and clapping in front of the god Yaghuth, abruptly ended his appeal and heckled out from across the Ka'bah's chamber, cutting Muhammad off. "One God? What is this thou speakest of?"

"Submission and obedience unto-" said the Prophet before Jahl again interrupted.

"Submission and obedience unto whom? Thee? Thou art nothing but a man, not a god!" Abu Jahl blasted. His remarks eliciting but few taunts and jeers.

After Muhammad faced his small crowd to continue his explanation he suddenly jerked his head around and stared icily into Jahl's eyes. His look silenced the scoffers and wiped the smirk off Abu Jahl's face. As the hush descended over the Ka'bah, Muhammad's audience of a few had now increased to over twenty, twenty-five men, all trying to crowd the Ka'bah's steps.

He began again: "Oh, ye men! I am sent unto you as a Messenger of Allah, Whom belongeth all dominion of the heavens and all about thee. There is no god but Allah, He Who bequeathed existence and He Who delivereth death. Evil and Good cannot remain-" said Muhammad before being interrupted again.

"Then why are the wicked allowed to flourish?" Umar vociferated, hoping to confound God's Holy Prophet. Muhammad answered, "It may be that the very appearance of flourishment is part of the punishment. Allah in His Limitless Wisdom may punish the wicked by granting respite and provisioning worldly things, which abets them into transgression. Whereupon they are finally seized and caught by the Wrath suddenly and utterly."(2)

Abu Sufyan, one of the leaders in the opposition to Islam, grew incensed by Muhammad's inspired answer. He cried out insolently: "Art thou then the one sendeth Allah as Messenger?" He turned around importantly, seeking acknowledgment for his scythe-like superciliousness, then added: "Hath Muhammad invented a falsehood or has a spirit taken hold of his mind?"

There were few snickers. For the most part, many looked as if they were deep in thought.

Muhammad was irritated by the interruptions and started to ask for silence. Instead, he held his tongue and smiled knowingly: several more people, drawn by the diatribe's tension made him think with irony that the Disbelievers interference had only served to help him spread the Message.

Pleased over the crowd's size, now around forty people, and his largest yet, he started again. "To Evil and Good, canst there not be a mutual conclusion, and there is no authority the unjust can produce for their false imaginings. Will they in shame realize this on Judgment Day, when all illusions will vanish and they discover that time for repentance has past. The good man should bide his time, never losing patience, even when things go against him.(3) One's actions should reflect Allah's Will and Law. The Inventor of all things forsaketh not the struggling soul that turns unto Him.

"Now heed well Allah's Word, revealed unto me by His angel Gabriel. "In the name of Allah, The Beneficent, The Merciful. Verily, for the pious ones with their Lord are the Gardens of bliss. What! Shall We then make the Muslims like unto the guilty ones? What is the matter with you? How judge ye? Or have ye a scripture wherein ye read? Verily, therein is for you what ye choose? Or have ye a sworn covenant from Us tending to the Day of Judgment that ye shall have whatever ye judge? Ask them which of them will guarantee that! Or have they any 'Partners' (unto God)? Then let them bring their partners if they be truthful.'"(4)

A quiet fascination blanketed over the crowd. Muhammad waited for the scoffers, but they were unusually silent. A Christian suddenly cried out, excitement affecting his voice: "Verily, thou art the Spirit of Truth prophet Jesus spoke of! And verily, we have not a covenant unto Judgment Day, for Holy Jesus said: he could not reveal all of Allah's Truth!"(5) Slowly, others began to ask questions.

Jahl, Lahab and his wife Jamilah, and many others, stomped off in anger after seeing the crowd's enthusiasm.

Attracted to the Ka'bah by the sound of raised voices, Uthman ibn Affan, Abu Bakr and his cousin Mistah, stopped what they were doing and looked over toward God's House of worship. Abu Bakr asked Mistah to take his children, Asma'a and Abdullah, home while he and Uthman spoke with Muhammad.

"Oh, al-Amin, in this new Way of life that Abu Bakr has been telling me about, doth thou speak as the Messenger and Prophet of Allah," asked Uthman.

"By His Grace hath He selected me to warn mankind. And this, my friend, is no new way of life or religion. Didst not Abraham and his son Isma'il, alaihimus salaam, restore the Ka'bah long ago and establish it's rites and usages? Verily, they did! And they were Muslims who bowed their wills unto Allah in submission, and joined not the others with the One God in worship."

More than a few people in hearing range murmured, nodding their heads in agreement.

"This Way inviteth all people unto truth. And false are the people who corrupt Allah's Truth, or hinder men from coming unto Him."(6)

Far in the background several rich and influential tribal elders of Quraysh, Kin'ana, Mudar and Bakr, wanted to question the Apostle. But thinking it beneath their station to inquire while he spoke amidst the gathering of lowly people, they instead sent servants carrying messages to send the poor away.

Muhammad watched the various bondsmen leave their masters and weave through the crowd. He stopped and listened to each in turn, then looked over to their masters. He said in a loud voice, "In the name of Allah, The Beneficent, and The Merciful. Nay, refuse I to send away anyone sincerely seeking truth. Indeed, doth man transgress all bounds."

"Nay! Verily man is wont to rebel as he deemeth himself needless! Verily unto thy Lord (alone) is the return! Hast thou seen the man who forbiddeth a servant when he prayeth? Hast thou seen if he were rightly guided? Or enjoined piety? Hast thou seen if he belieth the Truth and turneth (his) back? Knowest he not that Allah seeth? Nay! (Let him beware!) if he desireth not, We shall surely drag him by the forelock! A forelock, lying, sinful! Then let him summon his fellows in council. We too will summon the Angels of the Hell (to punish). Nay! Heed him not! Prostrate thou in obeisance (unto thy Lord) and draw thyself near (unto Him)!"(7)

As Muhammad watched the servants scurry back to their masters, he turned to face his audience. "This Way of peace and submission unto the One God will not condone wrongdoing or the art of priest-craft or of private judgment in matters outside the home."

At the Prophet's last statement the crowd of men near Abu Jahl hissed and booed, then started ridiculing him for talking nonsense. It was too much for Muhammad. Discouraged, but not daunted, he left the Ka'bah amid a chorus of sarcastic laughter. He started for home but changed his mind and turned toward the mountains where he could contemplate the day's events without distraction.

Over the weeks hardly a day passed without a Muslim or two being ridiculed. The Disbelievers could only watch helplessly as their control over the Mekkans slipped away by degrees. Their arguments and abuse were of no help in overcoming the magnetism of undistorted truth. Though the greater number of Muslims were poor, their new faith had changed them into a strong dynamic group able to withstand the fulminating brutality with valor and courage beyond belief. And despite the malevolence the Muslims steadily grew in number.

In time the opposition began to view the Believers in a new light, a growing power to be taken seriously. Daily, with increasing enmity, they witnessed the crowds becoming larger as they trekked through the city toward al-Arqam's home to listen and learn about Islam.

CHAPTER FOURTEEN

During the many sessions Muhammad spent indoctrinating the crowds of men, women, and young people, one of the most frequently asked questions was, "How do we know the Message thou bringest is from Allah?"

Inspired and guided by the Knower of all things, Muhammad invariably answered, "The truth I bring is made manifest through Allah's Revelations. None can produce a one like unto them. Indeed, if there is any one other than Allah Who can inspire the Truth in such abundance, produce ye then thine evidence. Or is it that thy skepticism is nothing but rationalization against thine own conscience?"

Today, like before, he replied as usual then stopped addressing the crowd after that particular question. He scanned the faces expecting more questions but his reply always silenced the doubters. After a minute or so he continued, "The Message of Allah, is unto thee a guide that is sure to those who seek His Light. But those who belie faith are blind: their hearts are hardened and sealed. Woe unto the hypocrites, self-deceived and deceiving others, with mockery on their lips, and mischief in their hearts.(1) The insincere man who thinks he can get the best of both worlds by compromising with good and evil only increases the disease of his heart, because he is not true unto himself. Even the good which filleth the ear of corn or lendeth fragrance unto the rose also lendeth strength unto the thorn or addeth strength unto the poison of the deadly nightshade."(2)

Muhammad suddenly abbreviated his delivery, occupied with defeating the evil forces about the area. He watched the crowd depart considering the rise of animosity towards him and the followers of God's Word. He cocked an eyebrow thinking: Nay, the kafirun wilt not be persuaded to give up their ways! It is not I who deceive them, it is they who deceive themselves. They, with no experience by which to judge man's wisdom or folly, are but children guided by superstition. They use not their skills of reason to perceive the Lord. Nay, elect they to deny the real Truth and Power which created man from a mere clot. Do they not understand disbelief is ignorance? Nature, existence, our bodies, all function according to Allah's Will and Law. His train of thought vanished as quick as it came and he was struck with an idea detailing a plan of action that would take his Charge to all at once instead of the small groups attending his lectures.

Early next morning; Ali, per Muhammad's instructions, rode forth throughout the city heralding: "Oh, ye people, al-Amin summons all to Mount Safa at the sun's zenith."

Muhammad, from his home's panoramic view overlooking the small hills of Safa and Marwah, watched the city's inhabitants arrive.

They came alone, in pairs, and in groups until the area facing Mount Safa filled with humanity. "Al-Hamdu lillah!" The Prophet exclaimed. "Yea, it appeareth as if the entire city hath heeded the call."

With a quarter hour left before the sun peaked, he set out to propagate the Message. As he made his way through the city, it was unusually quiet. It was strange: he felt exhilarated; intoxicated with the spirit of Truth. Reaching the area, a Muslim far to his right, bellowed: "Prophet Muhammad approacheth!" The foregathering parted to let him pass. He climbed to the mount's top and proclaimed in a booming voice that pealed out over the assemblage: "Oh, ye people!" He repeated himself a few more times to quiet the crowd but nothing worked. He, then, just sat down to wait for them to settle.

The crowd, however, kept growing and it's curiosity soon turned to confusion as Muhammad just sat there. He noticed their restlessness developing in pockets throughout the mass of people, but decided to allow the tension to build a while longer. Then, before the agitation could encompass the crowd, he stood and the multitude fell silent.

The sight was awesome, for his figure standing atop the mount with the sun blazing in all it's majesty behind him fired their imaginations to perceive his appearance exceeding man's normal dimensions.

Muhammad raised his arms, jerking them back and forth to emphasize the importance of his tidings. In a firm voice, seemingly louder than before, he heralded out over the expanse of faces: "Oh, Quraysh! I forewarn ye to fear thy Lord's punishment. Save thyselves from the Fire.(3) My mission is from Allah Most High, The Exalted. I cannot chose, but obey. He has charged me to deliver His Message, and if I were to disobey Him, wouldst I myself incur His Wrath, and no one could save me. From every kind of trouble and difficulty, my only refuge is in Him. Must I proclaim His Message: otherwise I am false unto the mission He has entrusted me with.(4) My position is the same as that of the sentry protecting his people from danger of enemies.(5) If I told you there were a legion of men armed with weapons behind this hill, waiting to attack thee, wouldst thou believe me?"

Many in the crowd nervously looked around while others cried, "Yea," which was followed by a host of voices saying: "Al-Amin has never been known to lie," making some all the more nervous. Surprise and something akin to fear filled many a face, others turned ugly with scorn.

As Prophet Muhammad spoke of the higher things directing mankind, Abu Lahab gathered the other leaders against Islam in the rear of the assemblage where they heatedly discussed the latest turn of events. Al-Mustafa, all the while, kept his eyes on them, expecting some sort of trouble. So when Abu Lahab, Jahl, Aqibab, and several others, began to brusquely edge their way through the crowed, to reach the area directly in front of him, he pronounced: "There are no gods save Allah, He is The One and Only God!"

Abu Lahab savagely knotted his hands into fists and grimaced devilishly. His dun gray eyebrows arched upwards giving his already wicked looking face a sinister appearance. He ran his hands through his hair distractedly, then shriekingly shouted in rage: "Art thou mad? Perdition unto thee this very day! Was it for this that thou summoned us here?"

A shocked, death-like silence descended over the crowd. Everybody was stunned that Lahab would speak in such a way as to disrespect his own kinsman in public. Then to spite the truth of God's Message, Lahab barked out: "If there is to be a punishment for our sins, let it come at once!"

The realization of just how deep his uncle's hatred ran sank in as Muhammad stared at Lahab's retreating back. He felt a wave of ruefulness wash over him. He thought of how his uncle had grown maliciously hostile to him over the past few years and how it seemed he pleasured in being cruel, even in the most unimportant matters. He was demonical, despicable, past all understanding. Then comprehension penetrated his reverie: Lahab was naturally evil and black-hearted; adamantly against the pure and simplest human feelings, insolently scorning the emotions of others. This explained his indifference to family concerns, for there was no humanity, compassion, conscience or remorse in him.

Muhammad tried desperately to suppress his thoughts as unworthy to his natural devotion to family and his sense of fairness. One thought, however, kept intruding: why doth Lahab hate me so? Everyone else seemed to regard his uncle with respect, even though fear was the motivating factor behind it. Shocked and shaken, he replied before his uncle passed out of his voice's range: "The decree of Allah will inevitably come to pass; when cometh it, wilt thou wish it were delayed; how foolish of thee to cut off thy last hope of forgiveness."(6)

Following the exchange with Abu Lahab, Muhammad suddenly became still. Everyone stared open-mouthed as he underwent a series of dramatic changes. He began to breath deeply and heavily, his chest heaving in and out. Sweat started to pour from his forehead, making a noticeable stain in his tunic. His eyes rolled up, fixing toward the heavens. His behavior provoked startled gasps, others began whispering in excitement, and all wondered what he was envisioning. A moment later, the only evidence of Muhammad's Divine Revelation was the dampened tunic around his neck and the Message which seared their ears.

"In the name of Allah, The Beneficent, The Merciful."

"May perish both the hands of Abu Lahab, may perish (he himself). Shall avail him not his wealth not what he earneth. Soon shall he burn in the flaming fire, and his wife, the bearer of the firewood. Upon her neck shall be a halter of twisted rope."(7)

The Revelation went as fast as it came. Muhammad swiftly scanned the area for Lahab, but it was to late, he was already leaving the crowd's fringes for the square. Meantime, at the mention of Abu Lahab and his wife, people in the crowd turned to one another, nodding to accent their agreement. The majority, more than a little pleased, were also set at rest: Umm Jamilah, Lahab's wife and Abu Sufyan's sister, was just as bad tempered and wicked as her husband and brother. All knew she collected thorny twigs the day long and bound them with date palm fibers, strewing them about the path Muhammad took to and fro from the mountains.(8)

Gradually people quit the area, their minds alive with God's Revelation: feeling peculiar sensations and asking themselves many questions. The Prophet and his family departed surrounded by men and women questioning him about Islam.

That evening, Muhammad forewent his dinner and walked the courtyard, deep in contemplation while the family supped. After Zayd and Maysara began their nightly constitution, he made his way inside through the candle lit house until finding Khadijah. Upon seeing her, he inquired: "Art thou distressed over the things thou hath heard of late about me?"

Khadijah was momentarily taken by surprise with the question, then smiling at him, she flushed with color thinking it ironical. "Indeed not my husband, these past fifteen years hast thou grown wiser, even as life's hardships inflicted its blows. And thy strength, it hath inspired a respect amongst those whom feel adverse to thee."

Muhammad sighed wearily and the two retired for the night.

During the following months, the city's antagonism towards the Muslims and Muhammad increased. Threats and abuses intensified, causing much distress to the Prophet of Islam. Despised and rejected, the poor and some slaves constantly lived in a state of insecurity; fearing for life and limb; the safety of sons and daughters. In addition to the mounting problems, they had to contend with the pagans who took it upon themselves to prevent them from worshipping near the Ka'bah. And some of the more influential in Mekkah, in order to dishonor and make ridicule of the thickening Qur'an, divided what had been revealed into small parts and twisted it's truth, slandering both God's Testament and His Prophet.

94

Muhammad, however, disregarded the insults and abuses and continually sought solutions in curbing the hostility. Met with derision, he frequently journeyed to the mountains where he'd spend the night in Cave Hira asking God for guidance. He'd consume hours calling for Gabriel but silence, more than not, answered his petition. And by dawn, exhausted and not knowing the full extent of God's Charge, he'd feel frustrated in his efforts. Each time he returned home a little more disheartened. His only consolation was that he knew God would not forsake him, and Khadijah who steadfastly remained graciously tactful with understanding.

CHAPTER FIFTEEN

The self-appointed leaders against Islam were growing frustrated in their efforts to halt the spread of God's Religion. The teachings of Islam espoused made fools of them and their challenges, setting off bells of alarm throughout the assemblies of infidelity. Unsure of exactly how to contest the matter, they approached Abu Talib, the silent champion of Islam.

Talib listened to the Disbelievers, growing angrier with each passing minute. They talked long and hard trying to convince him that Muhammad had gone too far and that he should talk some sense into him. But he knew Muhammad was on the Right path. Would I not ever betray my nephew, he thought while they effusively belittled Muhammad.

During a break in the berating, Abu Sufyan interjected chillingly: "If thou canst stop not Muhammad as his guardian, then at the least permit us the freedom to dispense with him as we see fit."

Talib pivoted sharply toward Sufyan, and with a withering stare refused the request. He, then, argued with them to let Muhammad and Islam alone but they pressed and pressed hard, all to no avail.

Meanwhile, Muhammad continued full force in his Call to God's Way. By this time a good many Surahs had been revealed and Islamic knowledge was expanding rapidly. Almost daily it appeared the city was in confusion as Muslims and those wanting to know truth, trekked through the marketplace and up into the hilly section to al-Arqam's house to hear Muhammad's sermons.

The evil leadership of Disbelievers, thwarted in every endeavor to halt Islam's dissemination again consulted with Abu Talib. Following much of the same arguments during their first meeting, Lahab attempted an appeal to Talib's renowned sense of fairness at the meet's conclusion.

"We are simply saying that Muhammad has no right nor authority to impose this new religion onto the rest of us. And inasmuch as thou art leader of Quraysh it is thy duty to end his meddlesome activities."

Talib looked upon him pitifully and replied, "Oh, Abu Lahab, Muhammad forces not upon a body to embrace Islam. Truth needeth not support and his authority is from the One God, the Lord of the worlds."

Several days after the encounter with the infidels Talib departed for al-Arqam's home, intending to speak with his nephew about the Disbelievers' anger. He arrived and was surprised by the huge throng of people vying to enter al-Arqam's courtyard. Using his authority he edged his way into the walled enclosure. People were shoulder to shoulder sitting on the running ledge along the walls, all with their attention concentrated on Muhammad. His son Ali sat to the Prophet's right transcribing. Khadijah, the girls, the household, and Ja'far, formed an arc in front. Many others he knew and did not know sat in attendance, some writing and most listening. Deciding it better to wait before speaking to his nephew, he retreated to the rear.

A stranger next to him whispered: "The Holy Apostle of Allah just finished reciting one of His Messages and is about to start another.

"Of what ask they one another? Of the Great News, that which they therein differ. Verily, they shall soon come to know! Verily, verily, they shall soon come to know!"

"What! Made We not the earth a wide expanse and the mountains as bolts? And We created you in pairs, and cause your sleep a rest, and caused the night a covering, and caused the day for (your) seeking livelihood. And We have erected above you the seven strong ones, and We made therein a lamp burning, and send We down from the clouds water in torrents, that We may bring forth by it corn and herbs, and gardens of thick foliage."

"Verily the Day of Decision is a time appointed, the Day when the Trumpet shall be blown, and ye shall come forth in (huge) groups, and (they will find) the heaven opened, full of portals. And (they will find) the mountains set in motion, as if they are a mere vapor."

"Verily (they will find) the Hell in waiting, (being) for the transgressors the destination, to abide therein for ages. They shall taste not therein any coolness nor any drink, save boiling water and running pus, a recompense fitting (their evils)! Verily they looked not forward to their reckoning and belied Our Signs with a (persistent) falsification. And everything have We recorded in a Book. Taste ye then, and never will We increase for you aught but chastisement!"

"Verily for the pious ones is a great realization: Gardens enclosed and vine-yards; and mates, maidens beautiful; and a cup full. They shall hear not therein vain words nor any falsehood, recompense from thy Lord, an award according to the reckoning. The Lord of the heavens and the earth and whatever is between them two, The Beneficent God, they shall possess not from Him the right of addressing."

"On the day whereon shall stand the spirit and the angels arrayed, they shall speak not save he whom The Beneficent God giveth leave, who spoke (only) the truth. That is the day certain, whoso then desireth, may take refuge unto his Lord. Verily have We warned you of a chastisement nigh at hand, the day when man shall see what have sent before his two hands, and when the Disbeliever shall say: 'Oh, would that I were dust!'"(1)

Muhammad stopped and fielded the questions.

"Oh, Prophet, what is the seven strong ones?"

"The firmaments."

Wahshi, slave of Zubayr ibn Mut'im, acting under Abu Lahab'd orders to disrupt, cried out sarcastically from the rear. "Oh, Allah, if this indeed is Thy truth then rain down a shower of stones or deliver a grievous penalty as a sign unto us."

Every face in the courtyard either contorted with anger or disgust before twisting around towards the offending speaker. Ali, his brother Ja'far, the first to jump to their feet, were quickly followed by others, all ready to bodily eject the Disbeliever from the premises.

Muhammad, abhorring violence, extended his arm until it reached Ali's shoulder, thereby restraining him and the others. He, then, looked in the direction everyone faced. "The Reckoner punisheth in His own good time and not according to the foolish and frivolous taunts of kafirun."(2) The Holy Prophet glanced around the crowd expecting more taunts. Wahshi, suddenly lacking the false courage his masters instilled, fell silent and tried to camouflage himself amid the collection of humanity. A few tense moments passed before another called out his question.

"Oh, Apostle, what meaneth Allah: 'Of what ask they one another? Of the Great News, that which they therein differ?'"

Muhammad tarried, waiting for the assembly's complete attention. "Saith some it is my Prophethood about which they differ. Unto many I am the Apostle of Allah, unto others I am a sorcerer or mad. Saith some it is the Day of Judgment or the Noble Qur'an. The Noble Qur'an, the Resurrection, my Prophethood, are all great news unto man. Man, however, notwithstanding his belief in the articles of faith, still disputes. Faileth he to realize the fact that Allah, may He be Exalted, is ever represented by one who is closest unto Him by his absolute submission." Gesturing for Ali to stand at his side, Muhammad said: "The Great News is Ali.(3) He was the first in the House of Hashim to believe in Allah and His Apostle, and the first to support the Cause of Allah." With no more questions, the Prophet continued.

"There are duties that arise from our spiritual nature and relation to Allah. He hath created us, infusing into us the talent to employ knowledge and foresight, moreover, bestowed He our wit and instinct, which He made responsive unto our requirements. His Signs are lessons unto us. All in all, man's duties are sacred and whilst we are in this world of senses, those duties are by no means apart from what we owe ourselves and our brethren."

"Man can only behold up to the horizon. Allah needeth not us, it is us who need Him. Our hopes, happiness and success, depend entirely upon His Grace. The greatest reward man can envision is conceived in terms of this life, but giveth Allah not only these but a thing greater than the mind's capacity to imagine: the Hereafter!"

Pausing to catch his breath, he then and there became transfixed, in full attention to the High and beyond. He was out of contact with his surroundings. Perspiring copiously, his breathing grew labored, his color paled, and his eyes fixed as if in union with something only he could see.

Those recognizing the signs of Disclosure grew excited and immediately began to clear the courtyard. Abu Talib, Ja'far, and Ali, who had been recording the Prophet's sayings, stood and encircled Muhammad, anxiously awaiting for him to reveal God's Holy Message.

Muhammad's eyes abruptly cleared. There was no mistaking the light of revelation radiating out from his eyes.

"In the name of Allah, The Beneficent, The Merciful." He started. "Engageth you (your) vying in exuberance, until ye come to the graves. Nay! Soon shall ye know (your folly)! Nay! Nay! Soon shall ye know (your folly)! Nay! Would that ye knew it with the certitude nature. (That) ye shall certainly see the hell. Then, ye shall certainly see it with the vision of certitude. Then shall ye be questioned on that day, about the bounties (ye enjoined)."(4)

"Woe unto every slander, defamer! Who amasseth wealth and hoardeth it. Deemeth he that his wealth will make him live for ever. Nay! Verily, he shall be flung into 'HUTAMA'! And what maketh thee know what the 'HUTAMA' is? It is the fire Allah hath kindled, which shall mount above the hearts. It shall be upon them, closed over, in columns outstretched."(5)

"What! Hast thou not seen how thy Lord dealt with the fellows of the Elephant? Didst He not cause their device to err, and sent He down upon them birds in flocks, pelting them with stones of baked clay. Thus rendered them like straw, eaten up (by cattle)."(6)

"For the union of the Quraysh, their union during their journey in the winter and the summer; so let them worship the Lord of this House, He Who fed them against hunger and secured them against fear."(7)

"What! Hast thou seen him who belieth the Final Judgment? That is he who repelleth the orphan, and urgeth not others to feed the poor. Woe unto those praying ones, who are heedless of their prayer, who do (a good deed only) to be seen. And (also) withhold alms."(8)

"Say thou (O' Our Apostle Muhammad!): "Oh, ye who disbelieve! I worship not what ye worship! Nor worship ye Whom I worship! Nor shall I worship whom ye worship and nor will worship ye Whom I worship. Unto ye be your religion and unto me my religion.'"(9)

Muhammad ended the recitation of Revelations and was besieged with questions. He pointed towards a young man whom he watched select a place in front.

"Oh, Prophet Muhammad, can thou explain our 'Vying in exuberance?'"

"It is total indulgence for wealth, which defiles one's spiritual nature and corrupts the morals of an individual. It consumes the time of one's life, leaving no time to seek the higher purpose. This life is the illusion, for all things material are left behind. It is the moral and spiritual acquisition which follows one."(10)

Another young man, with confusion all over his face asked about the Elephant.

Al-Amin smiled, thinking the miraculous event would send home the majestic power of God. He knew the account, but requested Abu Talib to give the report: his father, Abdul Mut'talib, was a major participant in the historical milestone.

Talib turned to face the collection of people, thinking of his father, the premier sheikh of Quraysh.

"Doth it refer to an event before many of ye were born and occurred during the year of our beloved Prophet's birth. It is about the Providential Protection of Allah's first House, the Holy Ka'bah.

"At the time, Yemen was under the rule of Abraha, the Christian Viceroy from Abyssinia. Abraha, a wrathful man intoxicated with power subjugated and dispossessed the Jewish Himyarite rulers.

"Having established his dominance over Yemen, he built a church at San'aa hoping to make it the center of trade and a place of pilgrimage. But Mekkah and the Ka'bah had that distinction from time immemorial. Thus, fired with religious zealotry, he mobilized a huge army of men and elephants, and made for this city.

"Upon reaching the outskirts his men seized seven-hundred camels belonging to my father. Abraha, then, delivered by courier his charge: he came to destroy the Ka'bah. My father returned the courier with a message of his own: expressing a desire to meet the tyrant in person. An audience was granted, wherein my father complained about the theft of his animals and requested their return. Abraha laughed arrogantly and retorted, 'What? I have come to destroy thy place of worship, the House of thy God, and ye instead of pleading to save God's House, thou speaketh of thy camels?' 'Look,' said my father, 'the camels belong to me and I, as their owner, have come for them. The Ka'bah belongeth to Allah and it is His concern as owner, to save it or leave it in thine hands.'

"Stunned by my father's reply, Abraha numbly restored the camels and allowed him to return to the city. Thus knowing Allah would not permit the destruction of His House, he prayed: 'Lord, I hope not against them save Thee. Lord, withdraw Thou therefore Thy protection for them. Verily, he who is the enemy of this House, is Thine enemy. Verily they have not defeated Thy forces,' then advised the citizens to take refuge in the mountains.

"Abraha observed the people fleeing and became wroth, and ordered his army to attack. By an act of Allah, when they entered Mekkah, a cloud of tiny birds appeared and began dropping small stones on the invading force. To the man, save Abraha, the soldiers fell dead and crumbled like eaten fodder. Abraha beat a path to Abyssinia, unaware that one of the tiny birds trailed after him. He approached his king and related what happened. Like most men, the king found his report incredulous and asked: 'What kind of fowl could do such a thing?' Abraha raised his eyes to the sky and pointed to a small bird, whereupon the bird dropped it's stone and the oppressor of Yemen fell lifeless."(11)

Talib concluded the chronicle of As'haabul Feel, (those accompanied with elephants). There were no more questions and he departed with the others, forgetting his reason for coming to see Muhammad.

Banu Quraysh and the other lesser tribes conspiring against Islam, realized their tactics were failing miserably and only served to increase Muslim unity. Out of desperation, the leaders again asked to meet with Abu Talib. After an hour of platitudes and the rehashing of old arguments, Abu Jahl cut to the quick and voiced their ultimatum. "Stop Muhammad or war amongst the tribes may erupt!" His demeanor implying they were going to initiate a good deal of killing to accomplish their aim.

A tinge of color ran under Talib's leathery cheeks, his face tightening. He felt a ripple of hatred stir within as he thought with revulsion of their ultimatum. Forcing something like a smile, he said, "Wilt I speak with Muhammad about thy concerns."

Worried and torn between his desire to protect his nephew and his duty to Quraysh, he, at meeting's end promptly departed for Muhammad's home. Pausing at the courtyard's threshold, he regarded Muhammad for several long minutes as he sat near the potted palms deep in meditation. Forcing back the uneasy thoughts of war, he gravely approached his nephew. He said in a voice conveying the situation's seriousness, "Muhammad, have I just spoken with Abu Jahl and his confidants, and they are in an ill-tempered mood about thy teachings. They didst threaten war and murder no less! Now, I am in great difficulty, so pray I thou wilt get us both out of this terrible entanglement." Nervous thoughts flashed through al-Amin's mind. He thought of all the Muslims and their sufferings, Khadijah's support and her enthusiasm, Ali's youthful exuberance, Allah's promise and the life of decency He was ordering for mankind. He gazed deeply into his uncle's eyes, feeling unbound love and gratitude. Understanding Talib's predicament, he responded, voice full of resolve: "By Allah, O' uncle, even if they put the sun on my right and the moon on my left; in order for me to forsake my charge, never wilt I do so! Wilt I go on and on until Allah maketh the Truth a matter of course or I die in the effort!"

As Muhammad spoke, Talib could feel his nephew's tremendous internal energy emanating and unshakable determination to deliver God's Message, no matter the consequence. In silence they faced each other. He thought: such boldness of spirit thou hath. Indeed, thou art a man with contempt for the wrongdoers. Suddenly feeling an overabundance of pride that he was the Prophet's uncle, a smile of assurance began to spread itself across his face. He felt changed, gone were the thoughts of compromise he had ten minutes earlier. Full of optimism, his response came without reservation, "Teach then what thou loveth. By Allah, wilt I never be amongst those who doubt His Word or thy intentions for mankind. And wilt I not abandon thee."

Days later, Muhammad's words of unflinching resolution kept singing in Talib's heart. He made his decision, and gathered those of the Hashim and Mut'talib clans who were sympathetic to Islam. He recounted his meeting with the Disbelievers and their ultimatum. He ended his account with Muhammad's defiant answer, and watched them look at each other with awe on their faces.

In less than a week, the Comforter's rejoinder to the Qurayshie ultimatum spread throughout Mekkah. People talked of the One God, His Apostle, and the Message of Truth. The Disbelievers on the other hand, were desperately trying to find a way to stop Muhammad. Clutching at straws, they presented Abu Talib with an obsequious young man, saying: "Take thou this strong, handsome youth into thy house and after all is said and done, uphold not Muhammad anymore."

As old as Talib was, he felt a compulsion to strike out as the abominable offer effervesced his liver: causing bile to rise in his throat. Instead, he exploded with indignation: "What animals you are! Hast thou no sense of decency! What ye propose is a disservice unto humanity and an insult unto me. Furthermore, hast thou overstepped the bounds!" Finally angered to the point where he could not think, he turned and stormed away.

CHAPTER SIXTEEN

Five years had now passed since Muhammad became the Messenger of God. The number of Muslims had increased greatly. Their unity, service to orphans, the poor, their struggle in liberating slaves, the standing up for the rights of women, was an operation of humanitarianism never before witnessed. And as the Truth started exposing the Disbelievers weaknesses, more and more people were attracted to Islam's ideals and intrigued by the Way that made all men equal started changing their beliefs to follow the Word of God.

The Disbelievers, failing to stop the growing wave of people entering Mekkah seeking truth and too fearful to harass or brutalize Muslims belonging to influential clans, sought out the more weaker and defenseless Believers. Using torture, threats, bribery and inducements, they spared no one whom their agents caught alone.

Meantime, Muhammad's two eldest daughters had married. Zaynab, the eldest of the girls, wed Abu Lahab's son L'As after he embraced Islam. Raqayyah, wed Uthman ibn Affan, who was influenced by Abu Bakr to embrace the faith. A wealthy merchant, he used his power and influence to further the Cause of Islam.

Umm Kulthum, already the tallest of the four girls, was now maturing into womanhood, while Fa'timah, the youngest, was petite, charming and delicate, with an intelligent face. She had her mother's lively doe-like eyes and a mass of coal black hair. Naturally vivacious and of even temperament, she was bouncier than all her sisters. No one knew of her fondness for Ali or her unhesitating loyalty to him. However, her mother at times suspected as much.

Ali passing through adolescence, was growing into a strong muscular man. His voice had changed, deepening into a low bass whose timbre commanded attention whenever he spoke. During his years with Muhammad, he spent the most part of his waking hours in studious thought and learning Islam directly from God's Prophet. He saw first hand the abuse and torture dealt out to Muslims, and though he was never harmed physically or harassed, he was nevertheless pained to see the brutality. It anguished him to watch Muhammad's attempts to create an atmosphere of goodwill with Disbelievers who received his approaches with mockery and insults. In the end, he developed a feeling of great revulsion toward the Disbelievers and came of age detesting their ways.

One blistering hot day, a trade caravan traveling from Abyssinia unexpectedly arrived in Mekkah. The Mekkanese, surprised that merchants and tradesmen would journey during the summer's hottest month, turned out in force once they set up their booths and stalls.

Abu Jahl, while inquiring about some wares inadvertently discovered that one of the merchant's slaves was asking about Islam. The fact of there being knowledge of Islam so far away as Abyssinia infuriated him. Forgetting his business, he started interrogating the different dealers about who owned the slave. Uncovering what he wanted to know, he hurriedly departed for the home of his cohorts.

"What!" Screamed Abu Lahab in rage when Jahl told him and the others.

Following an intense period of argument in which several suggestions were discarded as unreasonable, they decided to call upon the services of Umar and Russal, instructing them to bring back the slave's owner.

The merchant, Umayyah ibn Khalaf, intimidated by Umar's size and rough appearance along with Russal's vehemence, reluctantly trailed them to where the polytheistic leaders waited.

"Doth thou own a slave named Bilal?" Abu Sufyan demanded of the terrified merchant.

"A-aye my lords," he readily admitted.

Confirming their beliefs, the infidels threatened the peddler in no uncertain terms that his wares and goods would be seized if he did not force his slave into publicly denouncing Islam.

Fearing the loss of his merchandise, and undergoing waves of vulnerability, ibn Khalaf returned with Umar and Russal to the caravansary where Bilal tended the animals. He was determined to use any means necessary to compel his slave into repudiating Islam's tenets. As he led the way, he thought of the Qurayshies and their underlings. Notwithstanding the possibility of confiscation, he dreaded the one called Russal and the actions he might take the most. He thought: their kind were never leaders of men, only parasites feeding off the misery of others. He shook away the feelings of trepidation with a silent shudder as they neared his campsite.

Bilal watched his master and the strangers approach. He knew instinctively that something was terribly wrong by the way they carried themselves. Suddenly his sense of foreboding made his skin crawl.

Ibn Khalaf marched purposely toward Bilal and confronted him about inquiring into Islam. He answered without a moments pause: "Master, submission unto Allah is the greatest Way of life that has come unto mankind and the Prophet Muhammad teaches that there is Only One God."

Sensing Umar and Russal's eyes boring into his back, ibn Khalaf sharply demanded that he denounce his faith. Bilal refused to do so. He, then, began screeching, cursing with the foulest of language, spittle flying from his mouth. Finally threatening Bilal with bodily harm if he did not change his mind. Bilal withstood the berating and remained steadfast, firm in his belief with absolutely no compromise, much to his master's displeasure. Ibn Khalaf was now frightened over the risk of losing his livelihood. Furiously he exploded in a rage of seething hostility and attacked Bilal brutally. Mercilessly he loosed a barrage of kicks, screaming repeatedly at the top of his lungs: "Denounce thy faith! Denounce thy faith!"

Despite the savagery of his master's wrath, Bilal resisted without surrendering. Frantic that Umar and Russal would return to tell of his failure to make his slave recant his belief, he grabbed the cut and bleeding Bilal by the hair and dragged him onto a small rocky knoll. Staking his limbs spread-eagle to the ground, he stood over him like some monstrous beast gasping for breath. A wicked gleam filled his eyes as something grotesque, beyond imagining, had risen from the depths of his hellish mind. Glancing back to the underlings as if seeking their approval, he set to work ripping away the scabrous crusts of drying blood from Bilal's wounds. Bilal screamed in agony and begged his master to stop. But ibn Khalaf continued, pitilessly and indifferent to his slave's tormented cries. It was his piercing shrieks that attracted people's attention from around the area, and word quickly spread that a slave inquiring about Islam was being tortured. Ibn Khalaf incessantly pressed Bilal to disclaim his belief in One God. Bilal maintained his convictions. Then, to the crowd's horror they watched ibn Khalaf use his tunic to pick up several large stones which were super-heated by the broiling sun. One by one he began placing them on Bilal's chest.

Between the pain from searing rocks and terrifying screams, Bilal managed to murmur something out. His master, seeing his lips move stopped the infliction and knelt down with a look of triumph filling his features. To his surprise and dismay he heard Bilal whispering: "God is One! God is One! God is One!"

All the while, Abu Bakr and Ali were in the square on errands for the Prophet when they heard word of another pauper suffering punishment for his belief in One God. Hurriedly, they went to the area and arrived as ibn Khalaf was placing another stone on Bilal's chest. They both stopped in their tracks as the scene's brutality numbed their senses.

Ali, nauseated by the event, involuntarily staggered back and nearly fell over his feet. He was appalled at the sight of the man tied to the ground, oozing life's substance from slowly encrusting wounds.

Bakr, a little more seasoned to life's barbarity, angrily stomped toward ibn Khalaf. Without ceremony he demanded in a voice more frightening than the merchant had fear of losing his goods that he be given the right to purchase Bilal's freedom.

Ali, without regard to the consequences of his actions pulled a small dagger from within the folds of his jalabiyyah and slit Bilal's bonds while Umar and Russal slithered away to inform their masters of Abu Bakr's intervention.

Once Umar and Russal reached Abu Lahab's dwelling where the Disbelievers gathered to await the plot's outcome, they both commenced to speak at the same time. Umar, resenting the scurrilous Russal's interference, turned on him with a withering stare that caused him to cower back and shut up in fear. Umar then related the failed plot's details.

Abu Jahl and Aqibah stalked from the house in a state of unleashed fury, looking for Muslims to vent their rage upon. Violently they shoved people aside as they made their way through the narrow streets and alleys. Jahl, recognizing Yassir and Sumayyah, a young Muslim couple, elbowed Aqibah and whispered something as he pointed the pair out.

Yassir and his wife, laughing and enjoying themselves as young couple in love do the world over, walked toward the infidels. Never suspecting for a moment that the existing danger to Muslims would actually befall them, they came abreast of the conspirators. Jahl suddenly screamed out an invective and cowardly attacked Sumayyah while Aqibah wrestled the stunned Yassir to the ground. In a volley of wicked punches and brutal kicks, Jahl in no time beat Sumayyah to the ground. The assault was so fierce and frenzied she went into shock. Aqibah released her weeping husband who immediately crawled over to his wife. Laboring for breath, bleeding and beaten, Yassir gently cradled his wife's head helplessly as her life drained away.

"Allahu Akbar," she mumbled out before dying.

Yassir was besides himself with grief. He looked up at their attackers and lamented: "In the name of Allah, why hast thou done this thing?"

Everyone witnessing the incident turned toward Jahl with disgust on their faces, waiting for his reply. The crowd, knowing his habit of thrusting his soul's blackness upon others who thought differently, regarded his actions repulsive and unjustified. Instead of answering, he spoke to Aqibah who then kicked the kneeling Yassir in the stomach, doubling him over in pain. He was dragged over to some nearby horses.

Gasping for air, Yassir fought back weakly, his strength no match for Aqibah. Realizing Aqibah's intentions, he began to struggle back valiantly. But the combined power of the two proved too much for him to overcome. They bound each of his limbs onto the horses' legs and whipped the animals until Yassir split in two.

News of Yassir and his wife's death spread like wild fire throughout Mekkah. When Muhammad heard he was jolted that the Disbelievers would go as far as manslaughter. He noted with alarm that Muslim persecution was on the increase and becoming deadly. In the same thought, he remembered his own experiences in the Ka'bah: he'd been praying when Abu Jahl came from behind and tried to strangle him. And the time while in prostration, someone had placed his foot at the nape of his neck, pinning him helplessly to the ground. By the Will of God, the man had a change of mind. Then there was Umm Jamilah, Lahab's wife, who did everything in her power to make his life miserable...

In the next gathering at al-Arqam's house the courtyard was densely packed, more then usual. It wasn't surprising considering the recent turn of events. The mood was somber and the air fermented with anxiety as all were feeling the violent deaths of Yassir and Sumayyah.

The Prophet, appearing drawn and strained, opened the meeting with his customary greetings: "As-salaamu alaikum."

"Wa alaikum as-salaam," returned the gathering.

"In the name of Allah, The Beneficent, The Merciful," began Muhammad. "Grievous are the burdens of sin which the transgressors will bear on their backs when they become aware of them.(1) Hath all mankind the nature of goodness created within them."

"Allah, by His Signs keepeth a constant reminder unto men of His Holy Names. Those who err scarce realize how slowly they fall into sin. Their respite has a term appointed, so fear not, the doom of evildoers must come and it may be on a sudden. So humbly draw nigh unto thy Lord, Allah The Creator of the Worlds. Declare ye His glory and rejoice in His service."(2)

"Now heed ye well the Message of The Aware, Well-Acquainted."

"Allah (it is Who) originateth the creation, then causeth it to return again, then unto Him shall ye all be returned. And on the Day when shall come the Hour (of Judgment), in despair shall be the guilty (ones). And there shall not be for them any intercessors from among their partner gods, and they shall be the deniers of their partners. And the Day when arriveth the Hour (of Judgment), on that Day shall (they) be separated from one another. As to those who believed and did good deeds, they shall be in the Garden, made happy. And as to those who disbelieved and belied Our signs and the meeting of the hereafter, these shall be brought over to the chastisement."

"So glory be to Allah when ye enter the evening and when ye enter the morning. And His (alone) is all praise in the heavens and the earth, at the sun's decline and when ye enter the noon. He bringeth forth the living from the dead and bringeth forth dead from the living, and giveth life to the earth after it's death, and thus shall ye (too) be brought forth (after ye are dead)."

"He setteth forth unto you a parable of yourselves. Have ye of those whom your right hands possess partners in what We have provided you for sustenance, so that in regard to it, ye are alike. Fear ye them as ye fear each other? Thus We make clear Our signs for a people who understand. Nay, those who are unjust follow their vain desires without any knowledge. Who can guide him whom Allah hath allowed to err? There shall not be for them any of the helpers."

"Then set thou thy face uprightly for (the right) religion, in natural devotion to the truth (following) the nature caused by Allah in which He hath made the people; no change can there be (by any one else) in the creation of Allah; this (uprightness) is the established religion; but most people know not. Turn ye back unto Him and fear His wrath and establish prayer and be not of the polytheists, of those who split up their religion and have become sects, every party rejoiceth in what is with them."

"And when afflicteth the people any harm call they upon their Lord turning unto Him, then when He causeth them a taste of mercy from unto Him; lo, some of them associate partners with their Lord. Let them be ungrateful for what We have given them, but enjoy ye (only for a while) for soon shall ye know. Or, have We sent down upon them any authority that it speaketh of what they associate with Him? And when We make people taste of mercy they rejoice in it, and if befalleth them an evil for what have already wrought their (own) hands; lo, they are in despair! What! See they not that Allah amplifieth the provision for whomsoever He willeth and straiteneth? Verily in this are signs for a people who believe."

"Then give thou to the near of kin his due, and to the needy, and the wayfarer; this is best for those who desire the pleasure of Allah, and these it is who are the successful ones. And what ye give out at interest, so that it may increase in the wealth of the people, but it increaseth not with Allah, and whatever ye give in charity desiring the pleasure of Allah, it is these that shall get manifold. Allah is He Who created you then provided you with sustenance, then He caused you to die, then bringeth you to life. Is there any of your associate gods who doeth aught of these things? Glory be to Him, and Exalted High is He, far above what they associate (with Him)."

"And indeed have We set forth for the people, in this Qur'an every kind of similitude; and if thou bringest unto them a sign, certainly will say those who disbelieve: 'Ye are naught but a false claimant.' Thus doth Allah set a seal on the hearts of those who know not.

Therefore be thou patient (for) verily the promise of Allah is True, and let not those who have no certainty hold thee in light estimation."(3)

Muhammad finished his delivery, his expression abruptly changing from the look of rapture to one of solemnity. Those who knew him recognized the transformation and erupted with questions. He eyed the crowd over, focusing his attention on a man whom he'd seen in the company of Disbelievers on more that one occasion. He pointed to him, saying: "Doth thou wish to speak?"

The man stood. The din fell. He asked, "Oh, Muhammad, if Allah is All-Powerful, why then doth He not force all peoples unto His Will?"(4)

Muhammad examined the man closely for some moments, scanning for any signs of mockery. Determining the man's sincerity in his quest for knowledge, he replied.

"Allah giveth unto people every opportunity of knowing and understanding things, but dost He not force them.(5) Had it been Allah's will and Plan to conscript people unto His Will, need He but say: 'Be', and it is. But His Will and Plan worketh in ways beyond our comprehension. Allah's Message is full of meaning, meant to instruct one's will so that it complieth to His Gracious purpose.(6) The Kafirun may scorn and mock Allah's Message of Truth and Righteousness, but soon wilt they behold the Power of His Word and realize the real significance of faith, which they oppose.(7) As it was then, unto the people of Noah, Abraham, Moses, alaihimus salaam, the Ad, Thamud, and the Companions of the Wood, so it is now. Those who enjoin evil and resist the truth accomplish their own destruction.(8) Nothing that the power of evil can do, will ever defeat the merciful Purpose of Allah."

(9) Turning to another, he indicated for the man to rise and speak.

The Disbelievers, ever in the habit of putting posers to Prophet Muhammad: questions they got from their cohorts; the Tritheists and Jews, which they thought he would be unable to answer, had their man ask about the floating Christian legend of the Seven Sleepers of Ephesus, hoping to discredit him. Muhammad not only told the man the main story but pointed out its current variations, then rebuked the man for disputing him about such details.(10)

Another Disbeliever, stumped by Muhammad's store of knowledge, sarcastically called out: "If all thou saith is true, then tell us when this final decision between right and wrong will come about."(11)

"If meaneth thou wilt put off thy repentance and reform then, it will be of no use: will it be too late for repentance, and no respite will be granted then; this is the respite, and thy chance,"(12) retorted

Muhammad a bit perturbed, suspecting the man's motives behind the question.

Glancing around, he waited for questions, none came. He ended the sermon with, "Allah's Signs are many, and so are His mysteries: yet each doth point to His Unity, Goodness, Power and Mercy. There are none like unto Him. His teachings are one, and men that asunder His standard Religion are but following their own lusts. Ungrateful are they to give part worship to others, when all worship, praise and glory are due unto Allah and Him alone.(13) Wilt Allah restore the balance in the End, for He didst create all things pure, and wilt He purge and purify, as He doth the world around us with the Winds. Destruction awaits those that break His Harmony and Law. Thus, let the righteous wait and endure with constancy, for evil is shaky, with no faith in itself and no roots, and is doomed to perish utterly."(14)

It was a critical and trying period for Muhammad and the Muslims. Daily, reports of some kind of torture to Islam's followers, reached the Prophet's ears. Troubled and at a loss on how to stop the fast escalating violence, he felt as if he were carrying an immense weight upon his shoulders. Frequently, the pain caused him to rise during the night and pace the courtyard until the reddish glow of dawn streaked the sky.

Weeks later, Muhammad's concerns still hadn't left him. One evening after the household retired, his feelings for the suffering Muslims surfaced. Restless, he rose from bed and started walking back and forth across the room. His hands clasped together in an unconscious gesture of inner suffering. He stopped near the room's window and gazed out until the onset of Divine Revealment took over his senses.

Suddenly aware of the breeze cooling his body, Muhammad turned to face Khadijah, whom he heard stirring. He saw her staring back at him.

"Khadijah," he said to her as she rose from bed. "I do not understand why the Kafirun want to keep people away from Allah, when draweth He all unto that which is good. For that path lieth the forgiveness of sins and the real prosperity. No kind or generous deed ever ruined anyone. Do not the Kafirun know the Qur'an has, step by step, confirmed the Law of Moses, and the Gospel of Prophet Jesus, alaihimus salaam. I have recounted to them the story of Pharaoh and Moses, and how Pharaoh relied upon his power and armies. Yet, no matter the strength of Pharaoh, Allah punished him and his forces, thus saving the Children of Israel. And as Moses warned the Egyptians, have I sounded the warning unto our people. But the Christians, Jews, and many of our own people resist the Path."

"My beloved, how is it possible for me to make life safe, without the persecution and torture of Muslims? When I meet those responsible, I wonder at the emptiness of their souls and if they can find nothing better to do than harass and slay men who wish only to serve Allah."

Khadijah felt a quivering pang within and could only nod her head sadly while Muhammad expressed his feelings. As he gave utterance to the community's concerns, that old familiar anguish began creeping over her. Her hands tightened on the night-covers, haunting memories of the past few years flashed through her mind. She thought of the many nights Muhammad had risen, troubled over the conditions Muslims were forced to live under.

She went to stand next to Muhammad and looked into his eyes. She said, "My husband, it is true all that thou saith, and I but wish I could answer thy questions. But trouble thyself not, for Allah will guide thee unto the right course and provide the answers thou seekest. Like the People of the Book, it is history repeating itself. Didst not the Jews reject and belie prophets of their own race who told them unpleasant truths? Their self-interest, prejudices, and dislike of any thing which runs counter to their habits, customs, or inclinations, are like our people whom oppose true faith. And they along with the Christians who mock thee, they should have learned from previous Revelations foretelling of thine arrival and welcomed thy teachings. Yet, they are blasphemous in their arrogance to claim all wisdom and knowledge of Allah is enclosed in their hearts.(15) Can they not set bounds to Allah's choice, for Allah is The Creator of all peoples.(16) So sadden thyself not my dearest, thou art not responsible for their transgressions, Allah will look unfavorably toward their pretended superiority."

With an hour or so before sunrise, they performed their dawn prayer and returned to bed where they fell into an easy slumber. Muhammad, soothed by Khadijah's understanding, slept peacefully for the first time in weeks.

Waking with a shiver, he found the huge room cool. The odors of cheese, compacted earth, warm wool and the gamey smell of animals invaded his senses. Drawing the blankets up to cover his and Khadijah's shoulders, he laid back for several minutes, staring at the ceiling thinking The All-Embracing, Comprehensive, had once again answered his questions.

Somehow aware of the rhythmic changes in Muhammad's breathing: from slumber to wakefulness, Khadiajh began to stir and awaken.

Muhammad watched her, marveling how she could be so in tune with her surroundings, for she invariably awakened soon after he did. As scenes of their life flashed through her mind, she was scrutinizing him with deep interest. The look gave him pause, then suddenly he smiled and spoke with a voice full of tenderness, "Khadijah, wouldst thou ask Ali to gather his materials for scribing? Whilst we slept, didst I receive Revelation." As an afterthought, added: "The affair of spreading His Word has not yet been won!" Instinctively, they both sensed the fight for human justice and decency which Islam embraced and propounded was still in it's infancy.

"Sometimes I think," said Khadijah, "that thou hath taken on too much. Never doth thou seem to have time to call thy own."

"For me," Muhammad started, "I am commanded only that I should serve the Lord of this city, Who hath made it sacred, and His are all things, and commanded I am that I should be of the Muslims (those who have submitted themselves to God), and that I should recite the Qur'an.(17) Work or even the business of earning a livelihood hath become not merely the source with which to enjoy Allah's Bounty, but reasons for existence in themselves and this is not as He intended."

Khadijah was silent. She was thinking of the stories she'd heard while at the bazaar. She was remembering when Muhammad first began his charge: the scoffers; mockers; malicious and bitter filled faces; the frightened faces of the poor seeking a better way of life; and, Abu Talib's unfailing intercession with the growing throng of Disbelievers.

Muhammad, however, misunderstood her silence. "Saith I unto thee, my wife," said Muhammad, resolve filling his voice. "That insha'a Allah, I will do all in my power to broadcast His Truth! Thou knowest the enemies, but nonetheless the Truth will win out and this Way of life will gain the support of those who hate their evil ways and everything that they do will be undone."

Later that day, as usual, Muhammad with Ali at his side was in the city's square teaching the Word of God. With the frustration lifted from his shoulders, Muhammad taught with an energy that attracted pedestrians by the dozens. Within the first hour, twenty-seven men and women declared their belief and joined the ranks of those following the exhortations of Prophet Jesus: "Ask, and it shall be given unto thee; seek, and ye shall find; knock, and it shall be opened unto thee."(18)

Abu Jahl was bristling with anger over the number of conversions. And when the last man stepped forward to declare his belief, he could no longer contain himself. He crossed the square and began to curse and insult the Prophet.

Russal, emboldened by his master's contempt, put on a brave face and let loose a string of invectives, directed at the new Muslims.

A ripple of apprehension spread through the crowd of listeners and Muslims. Muhammad, with a pained look, calmly stood his ground. An instant later his expression changed and he stared icily at Jahl.

Ali, fed up with all the abuse the Muslims and especially Muhammad had to suffer, started moving toward Jahl. He intended to do great bodily harm to teach once and for all that Muslims were not to be taken for granted. But before he could pounce one of the Companions saw the look of protectiveness in Ali's eyes and stepped between him and Jahl, forcibly restraining him from attacking.

"Ali," said the companion quickly, "it is not the time nor place to deal with the Kafirun. Let them act out their hatred. The Prophet will tell us when to fight back."

Abdullah Jad'an, a young handmaiden witnessing the event, saw Muhammad's uncle Hamzah entering the square's far side. She left the area, running to Hamzah and began recounting Abu Jahl's slanderous insults.

When Hamzah, boisterous and triumphant from a successful hunting trip, heard what happened he became livid with rage. Speaking to no one in particular but loud enough for those nearby to hear, he said: "Calleth Muhammad to believe in One God and nothing but filthy abuse doth he receive. What sense of decency is that?"

Those close by subtly retraced their steps in fear as vengeance filled and contorted Hamzah's face. Tremulously they took his measure as they watched him snatch the game from off his shoulders and violently throw it to the ground. Hamzah looked around, his posture tacitly daring any to raise an objection. None did, for he was a huge man respected for his use with weapons and no one felt brave enough to intervene or speak in Abu Jahl's behalf.

He rushed towards the Ka'bah where he'd seen Jahl cavorting with several of the leaders opposing the revival of God's Oneness. Roaring out his target's name, he struck him a vicious blow to the head, and delivered a blistering warning about any future abuse. Abu Jahl apologized and sheepishly retracted his remarks. Subsequently calming down, Hamzah went to find Muhammad. He decided to declare his belief in One God.

Meanwhile, Jahl's relatives wanted to take revenge for his thrashing. However, Jahl himself stopped them, fearing a great deal of trouble would ensue. Bruised and bleeding, he confessed the indecent treatment and foul language he used to insult Muhammad.

The attack on Jahl had been the first real act of retaliation against any one of the Disbelievers, let alone against one of the leaders. The other higher-ups, now frightened by the growing numbers and power the Apostle had at his command, turned to diplomacy hoping to avert any reprisals. They had no choice, realizing Islam's doctrine was revolutionizing their ways of life.

Abu Jahl was not one to let matters alone. Imagining Muhammad a practitioner of sorcery and poetry with some knowledge of the soothsayer's black arts, he believed the man of God materialistic with iniquitous aspirations. At the first gathering of Disbelievers, he said: "Must we send someone unto him who hath knowledge of the arts."

Ut'bah ibn Rabi'ah stood up, saying: "My tongue is persuasive and my familiarity with the arts is more than most. Will I convince him to stop his Call with promises of riches!"

"Oh, Muhammad," began Ut'bah oily, "art thou better than thy elders of Hashim? Didst they not condemn our gods! What indeed hath happened unto thee that thou rebuketh our deities and censure us worshipping them? If thou likest power, wilt we make thee the supreme Chief of all tribes. If thou desirest any woman, wilt we procure the most beautiful virgin of thy choice in the land. Or if thou likest wealth, wilt we present thee with so much gold that thou shalt be hailed as the richest man in the land. All these things art thine on condition that thou cease thy proclamation of One God, and create not diversity of opinion, nor decry the gods, our ideals, and the beliefs of our forefathers."(19)

Muhammad, having no selfish ambitions or dazzled by worldly power(20) grew so perturbed by the Disbeliever's impudence that he did not immediately respond. In silence he unwittingly stroked his beard. He thought: there is fear in their offers. Yea, I feel an undercurrent of violence too! He said, "I am neither concerned with wealth, station, nor sovereignty. Allah, The Self-Sufficient Master, has appointed me Prophet and bestowed unto mankind Holy Scripture, pure and undistorted. I am His Messenger and my charge is to warn man of Allah's absolute punishment and declare His recompense to the faithful.(21) In spite of His Signs and evidence of His goodness all around, men go about in Unfaith and mock at faith, but the End will bring them all to their knees."(22) Pausing, he put out his hand to touch Ut'bah's shoulder in friendly gesture. Ut'bah did not respond, a strange look suggesting hesitation and confusion appeared on his face. Then, all at once Muhammad's eyes fixed upon Ut'bah. He said in a voice accentuating his sincerity, "In the name of Allah, The Beneficent, and The Merciful."

"Ha Mim. A descent (Revelation) from The Beneficent, The Most Merciful (God): a Book, fully expounded are its verses, a Qur'an in Arabic, for a people who know, a Bearer of glad tidings and a Warner, but turn away most of them and hearken not. And say they: 'Our hearts are under coverings from that which thou inviteth us, and in our ears is heaviness, and between us and thee hangeth a veil, so act thou (as thou thinkest right): verily we too act (as we do).' Say thou (O' Our Apostle Muhammad!): 'I am only a man like you; it is revealed unto me that your God is One God, be ye then in attention straight unto Him, and seek ye His forgiveness; and woe unto those who associate others with Allah,' those who give not the poor-rate, and they in the Hereafter too are disbelievers. Verily, those who believe and do good, for them shall be recompense ceaseless."

"Say thou: 'What! Do ye indeed disbelieve in Him Who created the earth in two days(periods), and set ye up unto Him equals? That is the Lord of (all) the worlds.' And hath made therein mountains high from above its surface; and He blessed therein, and planned therein its foods, in four days (periods): alike for the seekers. Then He applied Himself unto the heaven, which was yet only a smoke, so said He unto it and unto the earth: 'Come ye two, willing or reluctant;' said the two: 'We do come willingly.' And He made the seven heavens in two days (periods), and revealed in every heaven His Will; and adorned We the lower heavens with lights (of the brilliant stars), and made it guarded (with angels); that is the decree of The All-Mighty, The All-Knowing. And if they turn away, then say: 'I warn you of thunderbolt (of a destructive punishment) (which afflicted the people) of Ad and Thamood.'"(23)

Ut'bah interrupted, pleading with Muhammad to stop his recital. He was experiencing an inner turmoil, feeling a fear spread over his body. He started trembling as the Truth penetrated the dome of corruption he lived under. He was so shaken by what he heard he knew it was senseless to continue with the offers he was instructed to give.

Muhammad did not stop. Instead, he became uncompromising, relentless in his drive to deliver the Truth. He added, "Have I fulfilled my responsibility. If thou but follow my counsel thou wilt attain blessings and deliverance, but if ye reject truth, will I nonetheless be steadfast until Allah, Most Wise, sanctioneth between me and thee."(24)

Ut'bah departed for his home deep in thought, forsaking the Disbelievers awaiting his return. Dreading to relay his information he kept imagining the scene that would take place when he told them Muhammad's reaction. He was convinced their offers of bribery were a waste of time, realizing that no matter the overture Muhammad would never be influenced by riches or position: he was undeterred by fear, the mockery of cynics, or the indifference of others.(25)

Suspecting Ut'bah of having deserted them, the leaders went to his house and maliciously accused him of succumbing to Muhammad's influence.

Ut'bah rebutted sharply; "How can thou reproach me with such a thing? I am a man of means and need not any thing! I spoke with Muhammad who in reply to all ye suggested, recited from the Qur'an, which was neither sorcery, soothsaying, nor poetry. I beseeched him to stop and he did, and I departed lest the thunderbolt from heaven destroy us all."

Abu Sufyan roared in rage: "Ye! Of all people shouldst have known that Muhammad used his charm!" Little did he know that what charmed Ut'bah was not Muhammad but the magnificence of God's Message. Unable to articulate his anger, he exploded with violence and recklessly hurled a small burning oil lamp at Ut'bah who easily side stepped out of the way. The lamp struck Russal, who'd been smirking over Ut'bah's failure, full force atop the head and spilled it's contents and caught fire.

CHAPTER SEVENTEEN

Close to six years had now passed and Mekkah's conditions were tense and unbearable. Evil had erected barricades for itself: it had eyes, but refused to see; it had ears, but refused to hear; it had intelligence, but it blocked up it's channels of understanding.(1) Even now, after numerous attempts to destroy or weaken the Word, new and treacherous plots were constantly being concocted.

Muhammad, comforted and guided by God, was directed to forgive the injuries, insults, and persecution, to continue to declare the Faith that was in him, and not only to declare it but to act up to it in all his dealings with friends and foes alike, to pay no mind to the ignorant fools who raised doubts or difficulties, hurled taunts or reproaches, or devised plots to defeat the truth: they were to be ignored and passed by, not to be engaged in fights and fruitless controversies, or conciliated by compromises.(2)

The Prophet, however, out of love and compassion for his fellow man, especially the Muslims, decided he would raise the subject of an exodus to Abyssinia. He'd heard through word of mouth that the king was kind and fair-minded to all men whatever their choice of religion.

Word quickly filtered through the Muslim community that the Prophet had come up with a solution to ease the difficulties of living in Mekkah. Thus, for a time spirits were high and the never ending persecution had little, if any effect upon the Muslims as a whole.

On the day they were to discuss the Prophet's proposal, the community of Muslims packed into Muhammad's courtyard, filling it to capacity. Talking of little else, they speculated about the answer to their plight.

Muhammad watched from inside the house as groups of men, women, and their small ones, arrive and immediately fell into discussion. When the tension started mounting, he exited the house and stepped onto a bench where he raised his arms for quiet. But the moment's anxiety gripped the gathering. He loudly cleared his throat several times before the crowd's concerns settled enough for him to speak. He gazed out over their heads, seeing the trepidation in their eyes. He thought to himself of the barrenness of man's heart to worship man-crafted things and his need to subjugate others.

"As-salaamu alaikum," hailed Muhammad.

"Wa alaikum as-salaam," returned the crowd.

"Allah is not unacquainted with the existence of folly and wickedness, and many other things besides that which knoweth not any mortal. However, can one behold little glimpses of His Plan upon reflection, and ye can be sure that He will not be late in calling one to account."(3)

"The seeing and the blind are not alike, nor are those blessed with Faith and those without. The former seeketh Allah, and attains peace and blessedness in their hearts, and a final Home of rest. The latter walk the path of crookedness and their end is terrible. If Allah in His Wisdom delayeth retribution, it is for a time. His promise faileth not: will it come to pass in His own good time."(4)

"His creation is subject unto His Law and Plan, so is man's life in every particular and at every moment, awake or asleep.(5) Suppose it were proper to worship other gods: Mammon, Self, or the invented deities set as idols. Yet of what benefit would that be?(6) Doth thou thinkest a mere cross or image will be able to help or intercede for thee with Him? Nay, not at all. All power is in Allah, The Exalted, and Most Wise."

"Right and Wrong, Good and Evil, are incompatible with one another. It is true that in men there may be various degrees of good and evil mixed together, and we have to tolerate men as our fellow creatures with all their faults and shortcomings. But this doth not mean that we can worship Allah and Mammon together. Wrong is the negation of right as light is of darkness.(7) Allah's Truth cometh unto man in revelation and in nature. Yet he must strangely resist Faith, and ask to see the signs of His power rather than the signs of His Mercy!(8) It is His Message that has led mankind from the depths of darkness into light. It came to every age and nation in it's own language. The prophets were doubted, insulted, threatened and persecuted along with the Believers. Hence, it is Evil that will be wiped out from His creation when He willeth. Allah's Truth is a goodly tree, firmly established on it's roots, stretching it's branches high and wide, and bearing fruit at all times.(9) His Truth maketh all things clear, and wilt He guard it. But His signs are not for those who mock: who fail to see the majesty, beauty, order and harmony, blazoned in His creation, and His goodness to all His creatures."(10)

"Man's origin was from dust; lowly, but was his rank raised above that of other creatures by the Fashioner, the Giver of Forms. No power has Evil over those sincere souls who worship Allah and seek His Way.(11) In all ages wicked men have tried to plot against Allah's Way, but succeeded not and were covered with shame in ways unexpected.(12) Allah's Truth may come in stages, but it giveth strength, guidance and glad tidings, and shouldst be held fast when once received. Be not like those who get puffed up with pride in worldly goods and scorn the truth. Enjoy the good things of Allah's Bounty, but render ye thanks unto Allah and obey His Law.(13) For it is He that has bestowed man with favors innumerable, The Source of all things."

Observing a great number of arms flagging for attention, Muhammad stopped his delivery and fell silent. Like a streak of lightening flashing across the heavens, he marveled inwardly at Allah's Mercy. Guided by inspiration, he had exhorted words that made them overcome the fear they were feeling, giving them strength and determination. Then intuition struck, he thought: wilt this Way of life take the place of differing religions throughout the world in generations to come as man became aware of the love and guidance Allah's Way accorded unto all seeking peace and harmony. I do swear, everything doth declare the Glory of Allah! He praised silently before his train of thought was interrupted.

An elder Muslim, unable to contain the sentiment welling up within him, shouted from the rear: "Oh, Prophet of Allah, thy words doth bring peace unto my breast. But, there are those of declining years, and the infirmed whom have no sons with which to stand and protect them from the infidels."

"Have I thought long and hard over this matter, ever beseeching Allah for direction. The kafirun, out of their mind's sterility, behold only greed and oppression as a means to gain this life's goodly things. With their irreverence for Allah and nature they forsake the Hereafter where real life commences but Allah forsaketh not the transgressors, and for them is a chastisement most grievous. Speak they falsely upon the slightest provocation, seeking to turn others from the True Path. And till our Lord willeth them to account, enjoin I unto those longing to depart the city, journey ye to Abyssinia where king Negus reigns. The king is a fair and goodly man who will permit the freedom to worship and praise Allah in safety."

Immediately upon Muhammad's response, a roar of voices blasted apart the congregation's tenseness. There were cries pledging fealty, intermingled with shouts of "Ahad," and "Allahu Akbar." Even the old and infirmed took up the cries. No one wanted to leave God's Messenger and Prophet, their love for the Lord's Way overwhelmed their fear of torture and abuse. But Muhammad knew Islam's enemies would continue to stretch forth their hands against the defenseless. So he raised his arms for quiet and waited for the crowd's excitation to subside. Then again advised egress to Abyssinia and appointed Ja'far, son of Abu Talib, as leader for those wanting to depart for the new land.

With the level of oppression already insufferable for many, the emigration began next morning. Anxious to exit the city before the Disbelievers could uncover Muhammad's strategy, no more than three Muslims left in any one group. In their haste to flee undetected, they were forced by necessity to abandon their non-believing relatives, friends, belongings and familiar surroundings. Stealthily threading their way through the winding streets and narrow alleyways, they encountered but few people and met up on the outskirts of Mekkah.

Next day, the sudden absence of certain men and women, many of them prominent with positions of authority caused the Disbelievers to panic, thinking a major plot against them. Then, when they learned the Muslims had taken flight, their panic turned to anger. They could or did not want to believe that Muhammad had outwitted them.

Realizing the Light of Islam would now spread abroad which would make their evil designs all the more difficult, they wanted to react. But Muhammad's stratagem had in a sense rendered them powerless: for the remaining Muslims had sons and kinsmen for protection. So, feeling as if the city's inhabitants were ridiculing them behind their backs, they felt the need to reestablish their imagined lost control.

They summoned Ut'bah and Amr ibn A'as, along with several other trusted minions, and instructed them to act as emissaries for Banu Quraysh to king Negus. As an inducement for the king they took pouches filled with gold dinar, gems and costly gifts, hoping they could persuade the king to force the Muslims back to Mekkah for crimes of heresy.

King Negus' court welcomed Ut'bah and his clique of richly dressed cohorts with open arms. After one of the king's retainers formally introduced Ut'bah and his entourage to the court, the infidels promptly set out to sway the king with flattery and gifts. The king, wise to the ways of man, abruptly raised his hand for silence.

"Why didst thou come from afar to pay homage unto me," the king bluntly asked Ut'bah.

Ut'bah was totally caught off guard. Stammering, he replied: "H-have we j-journeyed to entreat thee to compel the Muhammadans return to Mekkah for their unanswered crimes."

"Muhammadans? What pray tell are Muhammadans," asked the king.

"Oh, king, they are followers of a man named Muhammad ibn Abdullah. This man spreadeth dissension amongst our peoples and speaketh ill of thy god, Jesus, and now he hath sent his shi'a into thy lands to sow the seeds of free-thinking in order to cause Christianity it's downfall."

Amr ibn A'as added more lies about Islam and the Muslims. He even went as far as telling the king in so many words that his ruination was about to occur if the Muslims were not returned with dispatch.

The king arched his brows in surprise and demanded an explanation.

"Is not money the ways and means of Christianity, O' king," asked Ut'bah rhetorically. "If these Muhammadans are allowed to turn thy subjects away from thy gods, how can the priests obtain the wherewithal to continue it's patronage?"

"Indeed," blurted out the king, "what thou saith is cause for alarm. Return on the morrow and thou wilt know our decision."

As soon as Ut'bah and his group departed; the king, disconcerted by the Mekkans intimations, commanded a small detachment of guards to Axum with orders to bring back the Muhammadans' leader.

At day's end, Ja'far and several others were surrounded by guards as they were ushered in before the king who wasted no time with amenities.

"Art thou a Muhammadan?" Negus demanded.

"Oh, king," said Ja'far, "I am a Muslim not a Muhammadan. That is an epithet of the ignorant, applied by those who seek to depreciate the One God's Holy Message."

"Explain thyself," interjected the king.

"Through connivance, the Disbelievers of Mekkah wish us to be known only as followers of the Holy Prophet Muhammad, when in truth he but teacheth the Oneness of God and to follow His Will."

"From man's creation upon the earth has he bowed down to Allah. But over the ages he has twisted the Lord's Word to suit his own purpose. The Jews claimed Allah for themselves and Allah's way-"

"Allah's Way? Speak ye of this before thou goest further," interrupted Negus.

"Allah's Way is peace, obedience, and submission to His Law," answered Ja'far. Then seeing as how his explanation appeased the king, he continued. "Unlike Jesus, alaihis salaam, who brought Allah's Truth only for the lost sheep of Israel,(14) Islam is not an exclusive doctrine, it is a Message unto all peoples. But the Jews wanted to keep back knowledge of Allah's Revelations, and frequently read into them what they wanted or at best used their own conjectures.(15) Had they but looked into their own Books honestly and sincerely, they would have found proof in them that shows the Message is true and from Allah.(16) Their racial arrogance has made them adverse toward the reception of truth when a servant of Allah, not of their own race bringeth forth His Guidance."(17)

"Muhammad, the Chosen One, whom we knowest to be truthful and honest, called us to Allah. He teacheth us not to ascribe partners unto Allah, nor to worship man's invention of idols. Enjoineth he upon us to speak plainly and truthfully, to be true unto our trusts, to be merciful, to speak kindly of womenfolk, to regard the rights of others, and to consume not the wealth of orphans. He chargeth us to eschew vices and abstain from evil, to offer prayers, to render regular charity and to fast for spiritual strength."(18)

"For this reason are we persecuted by the Jews, Chris-" he suddenly stopped, apprehensive to speak out against Christianity. Moments passed in uneasy silence, but the truth compelled him to continue. "Christians, and our own people as well. However, many, but not all of Christianity take the poor's coin for their own coffers. They enjoin and condone the worship of idols, images, crosses, and of prophet Jesus, alaihis salaam."

"In God's Way, idolatry is an abomination against the One God. Didst He not Command: thou shalt have no other gods before Me, and thou shalt not make unto thee ANY graven image, or ANY likeness thereof that IS in heaven above, or that IS in the earth beneath, or that IS in the water under the earth. And thou shalt not bow down thyself to them, nor serve them.(19) Then, to add to their abominations, saith they: Jesus, alaihis salaam, is the 'son' of Allah. Jesus, alaihis salaam, himself rejects this claim.(20) Furthermore, does not thy Book call Adam, Jacob (Israel), David, alaihimus salaam, and others (21) the sons of Allah? Allah, far is He from what they say, Himself, clearly maketh it known that 'He is not a man'(22) to beget offspring. This saying, 'Son of Allah', has willfully been misconstrued by the Father of Lies and unknowingly or deliberately conveyed to corrupt the straight way to Allah. For the 'Sons of Allah' are those who follow the course of Allah.(23) No doubt these men of Allah never claimed divinity for themselves and prophet Jesus, alaihis salaam, saith specifically that he hath no divinity."(24)

"Thus oppressed and brutalized beyond tolerance, some of us fled our country hoping thou wouldst protect us from the oppression."

King Negus was thoroughly impressed with the Muslim's courage to speak the truth, despite his circumstances. He was intrigued by the renewal of the Message and wondered at Islam's capability to endow a man with such resoluteness. He, then, eyed the well-used leaves embodying the Qur'an Ja'far constantly carried about his person. And as the Truth's attraction overcame ingrained beliefs, he said: "Read thou from thy leaves."

"Aye, my lord. But in the tongue which God's Revelations were revealed it is called Qur'an which means to read, to recite, and to proclaim."

"In the name of Allah, The Beneficent, The Merciful," started Ja'far, himself excited by the prospect of the king's conversion.

"Kaf. Ha. Ya. Ain. Sad. (This is) a mention of the mercy of thy Lord unto His servant Zachariah. When called he unto his Lord (with) prayer in low voice.

Said he: "Oh, my Lord! Verily my bones are weakened and my head doth glisten with gray hoariness, but never am I in my prayer unto Thee, O' my Lord, been unblessed! And verily I fear my kindred (what they will do) after me, and my wife is barren, so grant me from Thyself an heir who shall inherit me and inherit from the family of Jacob. And make him O' my Lord, one with whom Thou art well pleased!'"

"(The Lord responded to the prayer saying): "Oh, Zachariah! Verily We give thee the glad tidings of a son, his name shall be Yahya (John), and We gave not to any one before (him) that name.'"

"Said he: "Oh, my Lord! How can there be for me a son while my wife is barren and indeed I have reached of the old age the extreme infirmity.'"

"Said He (the Lord): 'So shall it be.' Thy Lord saith: 'Easy is it to Me, for indeed have I created thee aforetime, when thou wert nothing!'"

"Said he: "Oh, my Lord! Vouchsafe me a sign!'"

"He (God) said: 'Thy sign is that thou speaketh not to the people for three nights, though sound (in health)!'"

"Then he went out unto his people and made signs unto them (with his hands) that they should glorify (God) morning and evening."

"(The Lord said unto Zachariah's son): "Oh, Yahya! Hold thou the Book fast!' And We granted him wisdom (apostleship) while yet a child. And compassion as from Us and purity, and a pious one was he, and duteous unto his parents, and neither insolent (nor) disobedient. Peace be on him the day he was born, and the day he dieth, and the day he is raised (once again) to life."

"And mention in the Book (Qur'an) about Mary (also) when she withdrew herself from her family (in the house) eastward. Then she took a veil (to cover herself) from them; then sent We unto her Our Spirit, then he (the Spirit) appeared unto her as a man sound (in form)."

"Said she: 'Verily I fly for refuge in The Beneficent (God) from thee, (be gone from me) if thou art God-fearing."

"Said he: 'I am only a messenger (Angel) of thy Lord, so that I give to thee a son purified.'"

"Said she: 'How can there be unto me a son while hath not touched me (any) man and nor was I unchaste!'"

"Said he: 'So shall it be; thy Lord saith, it is easy for Me, and that We will make him a Sign (miracle of Ours) unto the people and a Mercy from Us, it is a matter (already) decreed.'"

"So she conceived him and retired with him (pregnant) (away from her people) to a remote place. The throes (of childbirth) forced her to betake herself unto the trunk of a palm tree. She said: 'Oh! Had I died ere this and had been lost in oblivion totally forgotten!'"

"Then (a voice) called out unto her from beneath her: 'Grieve not thou, verily thy Lord hath caused from beneath thee, (to flow) a stream! And shake towards thee the trunk of the palm tree, it will drop on thee dates fresh (and) ripe. Then eat and drink and refresh the eye. And if thou seest any man, say: Verily I have vowed unto The Beneficent (God) a fast so never shall I speak today unto any man.'"

"And she came with him (baby Jesus) unto her people carrying him. Said they: "Oh, Mary! Indeed thou hath come with an unusual thing! O' sister of Aaron, thy father was not a bad man, nor was thy mother an unchaste woman!' But she pointed unto him. They said: 'How can we speak unto one who is (yet) a child in the cradle?' He (Jesus miraculously) said: 'Verily I am a servant of Allah; He hath made me blessed wherever I be and He hath enjoined on me prayer and poor-rate so long as I live. And (to be) duteous to my mother, and He hath not made me insolent unblessed! And peace be on me the day I was born, and the day I die, and the day I am raised alive!'"

"This is Jesus, the son of Mary; (this is) a statement of the truth about which they dispute. It beseemeth not Allah that He should take unto Himself a son, glory be to Him; when a matter is decreed, He only saith unto it 'Be' and it is. And verily Allah is my Lord and your Lord, so worship (only) Him, this is the right way."(25)

Ending, Ja'far looked up to face the king wondering if he had gone too far. The king, surrounded by his court, sat lost in thought with tears spilling from his eyes.

One of the clergymen near the king was scowling with rage. He feared the loss of revenue if the king embraced Islam. Unable to control his decorum, he vented his anger: "Oh, king, thou must condemn these Muslims, for they exhort blasphemy against our Lord Jesus!"

Ja'far's mouth fell agape. His countenance appeared incredulous as he turned toward the king. Noticing his displeasure, he started to respond to the indictment when the king, anticipating his defense raised his hand, palm out at Ja'far, and spoke sharply to the priest.

"Silence priest! Can one hear the Qur'an's words and those which were revealed to Jesus are from the same source. Ja'far, blest be thou and blest be the Prophet Muhammad!" Facing the priest, he said: "Fret and fume as thou please, for I am convinced Jesus was as the Qur'an says." Then turning to Ja'far, he said: "Tell me, can ye answer his accusation?"

"Oh, king, if one wouldest forthrightly weigh the Books he cannot but discern the wisdom and behold the effort to alter Allah's Word, or the clergy's endeavor to change it's scope and significance. Perfect is His Truth. Men of God show their qualities in their private counsels, in their sociability with one another as much as in public ministry,(26) and dispute not vainly about things which they know not. Why shouldst man not believe in One God or the Hereafter?"

"In thy Book, O' king, doth it not say Jesus, alaihis salaam, was crucified at Golgotha and left to die?(27) In another part of thy Book, it saith that Jesus, alaihis salaam, was killed and THEN hung on a tree.(28) And in another part, there is another version involving a different locale,(29) which provides a third rendering, distinct in aspect. To forsake argument, "tree" is accepted as being symbolic for a cross. However, one cannot rightly dismiss the stark discrepancy in reports: 'murdered and then hung' is decisively at odds with 'left to die on'. These varying accounts, aside from numerous others, burdens the truth seeker with confusion and Allah is not the Author of confusion.(30) Allah doth not inspire His servants to record confusion, inconsistencies or contradictions. Belief in Allah is to believe He is a Perfect God, and this alone validates thy Books were not Divinely Inspired, which is also confirmed by the writers themselves."(31)

"Now, O' king, put aside that which thou hath been led to believe and look beyond the arrogance of a people attempting to undermine a Prophet of God not of their own race or liking. We as well as the clergy must pass through the lure of temptation. But Allah Most Gracious, will save us if we accept Him, His truth and do right. Wickedness and transgression may have its respite, but most assuredly will it run into its own destruction. Hence, we must not dishonor Allah by holding monstrous ideas of Him.(32) And saith we Muslims as to the Prophet Jesus, alaihis salaam, what the Holy Apostle has taught us to say: he was the Servant of Allah."(33)

The priest was fuming with rage and stared icily at Ja'far. Speechlessly he worked his mouth, feeling exposed by the retort.

Negus turned his back to him, thereby dismissing his views and opinions, and spoke to Ja'far with kindness. "I assure thee, O' Ja'far, thy community of Muslims may remain under my sovereignty with full protection, for wilt I never surrender ye unto them."

The following day when the Mekkan envoy returned the Abyssinian monarch gave back their gifts, telling them: "Canst I not allow thee to take back the Muslims refugees. They are free to live and worship in my land as they please, and if ye speak ill of Ja'far and his party I will punish thee."

Back in Mekkah, Umar, opinionated, arrogant, and a strong supporter in the opposition against Islam, felt a sense of betrayal upon discovering the Muslims flight to Abyssinia. Angered and upset, it never occurred to him that they had fled to avoid persecution. Instead, he started to brood over the years since Muhammad received the Call. Deciding Muhammad was at the root of all his ills, his anger turned to fury. Intending to do away with the Prophet, he set out for the area Muhammad habitually occupied while lecturing. Along the way he encountered his friend Na'eem ibn Abdullah.

Na'eem, Umar's friend of long years, saw the murderous intent on his face as he rounded the Ka'bah. Old and wise, he had an inkling of the events about to unfold. He sliced through the throng, cutting Umar off before he reached his destination.

"Oh, Umar," said Na'eem, uneasiness inflecting his salutation. "Where doth thou goest in such haste and anger, my friend?"

"Na'eem?" Umar abstractedly returned. "Na'eem, I go to slay Muhammad. For thou knowest well enough he has brought an element of discord into the city with his teachings. Thus, with his death will I bring peace back amongst our people."

"Umar, thou hast known me for a camel's age, and if thou wilt allow me the liberty to offer thee a piece of advice before thou slayest Muhammad for his beliefs, will I tell you a thing."

"Speak ye then," Umar gruffly spouted out.

"Look unto thy kindred before thou condemnest another." Na'eem's timely disclosure totally took Umar by surprise, stunning him into indecision.

"Who?" Umar mumbled out as his mind screamed for an answer. With the new current of thought driving his earlier thoughts of slaying the Prophet into the realm of forgetfulness, his deadly intentions of manslaughter melted away and a rankling feeling seized him. Without so much as a word he spun on his heels and headed home.

Sullenly, he focused his mind on his kin's actions, half-heartedly refusing to give credence to the old man's insinuations. But as he dwelled on the possibility things suddenly started falling into place which he had considered odd before: the abrupt cessation of conversation whenever he entered the room where his sister happened to be speaking. Furthermore, he thought, there was an absence of any idols except in and around his sleeping area.

Minutes later he arrived. Having in mind to stop whomever of his kin's involvement with Islam, if Na'eem's report proved true. As he passed through the main room of the house he heard an unfamiliar voice coming from the house's after-part. Stopping to listen, he became curious by the tenor's voice harmoniously praising God with such sincerity. So intent was he listening that he mindlessly edged closer and crashed into a small table. The orator, at the collision's sound instantly terminated his delivery and hid himself. No longer able to eavesdrop, Umar boldly stepped into the room and demanded: "What did I hear?"

His sister Fatima, seeing the black look on his face, defiantly answered: "Nothing that thou wouldst be interested in hearing!"

Umar erupted with violence, charged the room's length and snatched his brother-in-law Sa'id by the hair. Thrusting him at arms reach, he held him there while doubling up his free hand into a fist to swing. Fatima, fearing for her husband against Umar's rage, jumped in between, bent on halting the attack. But before Umar could pull back he struck his sister full in the face, crumpling her onto the floor in a heap.

Sa'id, shocked, stared at Umar in disbelief.

Umar realized he'd struck his sister and immediately became remorseful. Feeling ashamed, all his anger drained away as he stooped to help his sister up off the floor. She on the other hand grew strengthened. Bleeding severely from a large cut opened up over her eye, she pushed away Umar's extended arm and said: "Aye! Aye, my brother, I am a Muslim!"

Emotions were quite high and the mental turmoil Umar experienced since Na'eem's intimation left him in a state of deep confusion. For peace of mind he needed to know and understand the how and why of his sister and all Muslims were so fearless. Umar asked, "What causeth thou thy courage, is it thy faith?"

Fatima regarded her brother while sopping blood from her face. "Khabbah," she called. "Come forth, no harm will befall thee."

Khabbah hesitantly peeped out from a cubbyhole used for storage, his wrinkled old face pale with fright. Trembling, his knees popped with each step forward.

"Wouldst thou please read from thy leaves, for Umar," Fatima requested.

"In the name of Allah, The Beneficent, The Merciful."

"Ta. Ha."

"(O' Our Apostle Muhammad!) Sent We not down the Qur'an unto thee that thou distressest thyself! Save it is a Reminder unto him who feareth (God). It is a Missive (communication sent down) from Him Who created the earth and the heavens on high."

"The Beneficent (God) on the Arsh is firm. His is what is in the heavens and what is in the earth and what is between them two and what is beneath the lowest of the low below the earth. And if thou utter aloud (or in whisper), verily (alike) knoweth He (all that is) secret and (whatever is) yet more hidden. Allah, there is no god but He, His are (all) The Best Names."

"From it (the earth) We created you, and into it will We return you, and out of it will We bring you forth for a second time."

"So be thou patient with what they say, and glorify thy Lord by praising Him ere the rising of the sun and ere the setting of it, and in some hours of the night also do glorify (Him), and during parts of the day, that thou mayest achieve the pleasure (of thy Lord). And strain not thine eyes unto that which We have provided (different) parties of them, (of) the splendor of the life of this world, so that We may try them in it, for the provision of thy Lord is better and more abiding. And enjoin prayer on thy followers, and adhere thou steadily unto it. We ask thee not for subsistence, and the (success of the) Hereafter is for the guarding (against evil)."

"And say they: 'Why doth he not bring unto us a sign from his Lord.' What! Hath not there come unto them the clear evidence which were in the former scriptures? And had We destroyed them with a chastisement before him (The Apostle Muhammad) certainly would they have said: "Oh, our Lord! Why didst Thou not send unto us an apostle, for then would we have followed Thy signs ere that we were (thus) humbled and disgraced."'

"Say thou (O' Our Apostle Muhammad!): 'Every one (of us) is awaiting, so do ye (also) wait. Then soon ye will come to know who have been the followers of the even way and who hath been the guided aright.'"(34)

Umar just stood there staring blankly, reflecting over what he'd heard. His heart softened. He felt an overpowering urge pressing him to seek out the Messenger of God and declare his belief in the One God.

Sa'id, Fatima and Khabbah, had watched in fascination as his earlier black looks transformed into expressions of enlightenment and understanding. They knew, as others had discovered, that once anyone sincerely reflecting over God's Message, His Word would annul the falsehoods of those belying the truth.

"This Faith," said Umar suddenly, "is not just a religion but the undistorted truth. The One god, Allah, hath truly revealed this Qur'an: for no other Book ringeth so true. The people have associated others with Allah in godhead, but this Faith teacheth to praise and worship the One God not the created. Can I see this Way is only for those who sincerely seek the truth."

"Many people do not believe, but it is because they are not ready to accept the truth and the reality of His Word. I was a kafir because I did not know better, and I ask thee to forgive me my faults. I know now we are all Muslims in the scheme of life, following His Law willingly or unwillingly. Al-Hamdu lillah, He Who raised the veil from my breast!"

At their smiles he abruptly turned without so much as a word and departed in search of Muhammad. Feeling the power of God's message, he felt an inner peace he never knew existed. He walked the streets semi-dazed, questioning pedestrians the Prophet's whereabouts. Told he was at al-Arqam's teaching the Word, he changed directions and made haste for Mekkah's hilly section. As he neared the home Muhammad used for indoctrination sessions, one of the Muslims perched atop the wall enclosing the yard, called out, alarm accentuating his cry, "Umar is approaching!"

There was a sudden hush, a hush of apprehension. A feeling of impending trouble swept through scores of Muslims and the uncertain attending the Prophet's inculcation. Even Muhammad fell silent and watched.

At the open gate, Umar asked permission to enter, causing a few raised brows. Granted admittance, tension mounted with his every step as he skirted around the crowd. Facing Muhammad, he took a deep breath and to everyone's surprise, declared his belief in the Oneness of God. He, then, entreated the Prophet's leave to take a place among the Muslims. Whispers erupted everywhere until Muhammad raised his hands for quiet. He continued on where he left off.

"...the life of this world is but empty, but what is serious is the life to come in the Hereafter. Allah's truth is not balked by frivolous objections, insults, or persecution. The wicked will be cut off to the last remnant,(35) their falsity is not due to want of knowledge, but to perversity and selfishness. They twist what they see, hear, and learn, and their deceptions will, before the Seat of Judgment, become clear in their own eye.(36) All other religions or creeds in the world have attempted their best to bring down Allah, The Most High, to man to reform and make him god-minded. But this Way offers guidance unto man in order that he may rise and get near The Creator, as near to Him as one's efforts can take him."(37)

Umar, in his eagerness to absorb all he could, called out the instant Muhammad stopped speaking. "Oh, Prophet, why doth Allah allow evil and transgression to exist in the world? Canst He not destroy it?"

"He can, but none knoweth His Mighty Plan. Allah in His infinite compassion and Mercy, giveth opportunity to repent and petition forgiveness. Bestoweth he unto us Truth and Guidance so that we may use our wills to show our worthiness to be in His Garden. The wicked, He will deal with them in His own way. It is not for us to complain, but to stand steadfast on the Right Path and accord unto Him all praise." Answering a few more questions, he gestured for quiet. Feeling a subtle change which he couldn't put his finger on, he stepped down from the bench and began to lead the gathering in prayer.

Muhammad closed the service, rose and turned to wish peace, but was unable to voice his intention. He froze in place and time, perspiration flowed from his hairline: the Blessed Word of God revealed itself from beneath the layers of his mind. Moments later, his eyes sharpened, the perspiration stopped, he cleared his throat and recited the Holy Scripture.

"In the name of Allah, The Beneficent, The Merciful."

"Ya Seen. By Qur'an (The Word of) the All-Wise. Verily, thou (O' Muhammad!) art of the apostles (sent by Us), on the straight path sent down of The All-Mighty, The All-Merciful. So that thou mayest warn a people whose fathers were not warned, and who therefore are heedless (of the truth)."

"Indeed the Word hath been proved true of most of them, and wherefore they believe not. Verily, We have put chains round their necks, and these reach up to their chins, and their heads are forced up stiffed. And We have to set before them a barrier and behind them a barrier, and We covered them over, so that they see not. And alike is it unto them if thou warneth them not, for they will not believe."

"Verily thou canst warn only him who abideth by the Reminder and feareth The Beneficent (God) unseen, so bear thou unto him the glad tidings of forgiveness and an honorable recompense. Verily We, (and) We (alone) give life unto the dead, and We write down what they have sent before them and (even) their footprints (which they leave behind them): and everything have We confined into a Manifesting Imam (Guide).

"And set forth unto them the instance of the people of a town when came unto it (Our) Apostles. When sent We unto them two (of Our apostles) they belied them both, then We strengthened (the two) with a third (one from Us) and said they (unto the people): 'Verily we are unto you the apostles (from God).' They said: 'Ye are not but men like unto us, nor hath sent down The Beneficent (God) any thing, ye only utter a lie!' They said: 'Our Lord knoweth that we are verily unto you the apostles. And on us is nothing but a clear deliverance (of the Message).' Said they: 'Verily we augur ill from you, if ye desist not, we will certainly stone you, and there shall afflict you from us a painful torment.' They said: 'Your augury of ill is with yourselves; what, when ye are admonished (deem ye ill of it)?' Nay! Ye are people transgressing (exceedingly).' And came from the farthest part of the city a man running and said: "Oh, my people! Follow ye (these) the apostles (of God). Follow ye those who ask you not any recompense, and they are guided aright. And why should not I worship only Him Who brought me into being? And unto Whom ye shall all be returned.

"What! Shall I take besides Him any gods, if (God) The Beneficent willeth to afflict me with harm, their intercession shall not avail me aught, and neither can they deliver me. Verily, I in which case shall be in manifest error. Verily, I believe in your Lord, so hear me!' It was said (unto him): 'Enter thou, the Garden!' Said he: 'Oh, would that my people had known, of that for which my Lord hath forgiven me and hath made me of the honored ones.' We sent not down upon his people any hosts from heaven, nor were We (in need) to send (any such hosts). It was nothing but one terrible cry, and lo, they were (like ashes) extinct. Alas, for (My) servants! There cometh not unto them an apostle but they mock at him. What! See they not how many of the generations We did destroy before them? They will return not unto them. And assuredly all, gathered together, shall be brought before Us."

"And a sign unto them is the dead earth; We give life to it and bring We forth from it grain of which they eat. And make We therein gardens of date palms and grape vines, and cause We to flow therein springs that they may eat of its fruits, and make it not their hands. What! Will they not then be grateful?"

"Hallowed is He Who created pairs (of) all things, of what grows by the earth, of their selves and of what they know not. And a sign unto them is the night, We draw forth from it the day; and lo, they are in the dark. And the sun travelleth unto a resting place fixed for it that is the decree of The All-Mighty, The All-Knowing. And the moon, We have fixed for it stages till it returneth to be bent like an old palm branch. It is not for the sun that it should overtake the moon, nor can the night outstrip the day, and each rotate on in (it's peculiar) sphere."

"And a sign unto them is that We bear their offspring in the laden Ark, and that We have created for them (the other conveyances) like it, on which ride they. And if We only will, We can drown them, then there shall not be any one to help them, nor shall they be rescued. And when it is said unto them: 'Guard ye against what is before you and what is behind you, that ye be treated with mercy.'"

"And there cometh not unto them any sign from the signs of their Lord but from it turn they away. And when it is said unto them: 'Spend ye of what Allah hath provided you with the sustenance,' say those who disbelieve unto those who believe, 'What! Shall we feed him, if Allah willeth, He could feed?' Ye are not but in a manifest error. And say they: 'When will this promise come to pass, if ye be truthful?' They wait not but for a single (terrible) cry which will seize them while they wrangle with one another. Then shall they not be able to make a bequest, nor shall they be able to return unto their families."(38)

Muhammad stopped to sip water from a nearby skin. The pause was all it took before a barrage of questions came. He murmured: "Verily, saith Allah the truth." Nodding towards the most frantic, he held his hands aloft for quiet.

Abu Bakr, urged by Umar, said: "Oh, Prophet, what meaneth Allah by, 'And everything We have confined into a manifesting Imam', doth it mean in a clear Book of evidence like the Torah given to Moses?"

"Nay."

"Is it the Evangel given unto Prophet Jesus?" Abu Bakr questioned again.

"Nay, it is-" was all Muhammad could say before Abu Bakr cut him off with another query.

"Is it the Noble Qur'an?"

"Nay," returned the Apostle of God while raising his arms to stifle further interruption. He turned towards Ali, motioning him over to his side. "Verily this (Ali) is that Imam (Guide) in whom Allah, The Most Wise, hath contained the knowledge of every thing." Muhammad, then shifted his sight from the two and addressed the assemblage. "Oh, group of men! There is no branch of knowledge which Allah, The Protector, did not bestow unto me that I have not conveyed unto Ali. Verily, Allah hath contained in me knowledge and I have contained it in Ali."(39)

Muhammad stopped and took the crowd's measure, allowing them to assimilate the significance of God's legislative Will. He thought: for too long hath man been deluded by false imaginings of unconditional escape from his wrongdoing through vicarious atonement in return for believing in man made gods and goddesses. Verily Allah hath sent me to render a death blow unto man's inventions and misrepresentations which giveth the illusion that he can act with impunity and not be held accountable.(40) Suddenly he said, "Oh, ye who believe! Bend thy ear and hearken unto The Reckoner. 'Say thou (O' Our Apostle Muhammad!): Of your associates is there any one who can guide unto truth? Say thou! It is Allah alone Who guideth unto truth. Is then He Who guideth unto truth more worthy to be followed or he who himself goeth not aright unless he is guided? What then hath befallen you? How (ill) ye judge.(41) What! Is he who goeth along groveling on his face better guided, or he who walketh upright upon the straight path?(42) What! Do people imagine that they will be left off on (their) saying: 'We believe?' And they will not be tried?"(43)

The Prophet wound up his sermon and once again assessed the gathering's response, all but the stubborn manifested signs of understanding. He was about to ask for questions when an individual called out from the rear.

"Of whom speaketh Allah, 'He sent two apostles then strengthened them with a third?"

"It concerns the Prophet Jesus, alaihis salaam, who had sent two disciples unto the city's environs to preach. When approached they the people, a shepherd inquired as to who they were. One of the two replied that they were messengers from Jesus, alaihis salaam, the

Apostle of Allah, and were sent to invite people to the true faith: submission unto Allah. The shepherd then asked if they had any signs to prove they were really from the Prophet of Nazareth. (44) Again, one of the two answered saying that they, by Allah's leave, could cure the sick, restore sight unto the blind, and heal lepers. The shepherd immediately informed them of his son who lay very ill and could not be cured by any of the healers. He petitioned their help. The disciples prayed unto Allah and by His leave cured the boy. Grateful, the shepherd heeded the Call and embraced the faith of submission unto Allah. However, the king who was an idol worshipper heard of the disciples good acts and had them imprisoned. Jesus, alaihis salaam, upon hearing the fate of his messengers then sent Simon, the third disciple."(45)

CHAPTER EIGHTEEN

Abu Sufyan was the first to learn of Umar's turn about. Thinking it a clever ploy, he smiled smugly and approached Umar at first chance. He started questioning him about Muhammad's weaknesses, but instead of the usual camaraderie he expected, Umar fumed and glared icily, making him stop in mid-sentence.

Guided by Qur'an, Umar saw through his one time confederate and reined in his anger. He raised his hand, cutting Sufyan off. He said, "Oh, Abu Sufyan, canst I not judge thee as I once judged others but I can relate unto thee the truth. What thinkest thou of Prophet Muhammad is indeed a manifest error. Our knowledge of Allah has come from Jews and Christians. The Jews, though they teach the Unity, pursue after false gods, and the Christians invented the Trinity.(1) Priest worship, the worship of saints and idols, are abominations in the Lord's sight. The mere notion of a separate order of priesthood to stand between Allah and man, and claim the exclusive repository of His Message, decrieth His Goodness and Grace.(2) As I didst, worshippers of idols and or of deities other than Allah may pretend that they are symbols in which to get nearer to Allah,(3) they as thy self are on the path of falsehood. Thus, if thou repent not thine ways be thou assured, the Subduer wilt judge thee on the Day of Judgment."

Taken aback by the intensity of Umar's sincerity, Sufyan could only stare with open-mouth disbelief. He worked his mouth several times attempting to retort but by the time he found his voice, Umar had already turned his back to walk away.

He received Umar's harangue as a personal attack and glanced about in anger, thinking that whatever happened he would never forget Umar's disclosure. Feeling his face color, he cursed sharply and condemned the Prophet in the silence which had been complete since Umar walked away. He wouldn't even condescend to acknowledge the salutations of others passing by. With his anger mounting into rage, his brows knotted hideously, his face became pinched and desperate, his hands clenched involuntarily. Then, flinging up his head in an exaggerated attitude of calm, he departed the square to inform his counterparts.

As Sufyan cynically told the other leaders of Umar's conversion, a deeper fear began to instill itself in their hearts. Thwarted in all their attempts to curtail the teachings of Islam, and now the unsettling news of their staunchest supporter's change of belief, left them entangled in a web of recriminations.

Abu Lahab, with his quick and angry impatience, screamed: "Now is not the time for accusations! We must plan ahead, foresee the time to come and devise our stratagems in accordance."

Russal, who had been nicknamed al-Taghut: the evil one, was lurking in the background and saw an opportunity to gain favor. He rubbed his sparsely covered pate absently, remembering the oil lamp which scarred and made him look bald. He stepped forward cautiously, and wily said: "Aye my lord, with thy wisdom can we end the threat of this message once and for all. For the Muslims have no authority to keep us from our gods. The Ka'bah is ours too! It is our right to worship what we please."

Russal was once again Lahab's pet. That he or the other leaders still did not accept him as an equal was of no concern to him. He was content just to bask in their approbation. Lahab was strangely pleased and looked upon Russal with satisfaction as his anger smoldered out.

Ut'bah listened and was astonished. The evil one's technique to mollify was stuff and nonsense. He glanced around the room surreptitiously, observing their enthusiastic nods of assent. Suppressing a smirk at their naivete, he knew that the truth of God's Way would continue to spread in spite of their malevolence or ill-conceived schemes. Also, he knew that in time, Muhammad would be recognized as the Holy Prophet and Messenger of God, for he not only preached the Brotherhood of all men and Oneness of God, but encouraged one to cast away the yokes of desires and traditions of handed down religions which became corrupted with time. Yet, as he realized the truth, he refused to abandon his ancestral beliefs.

Meanwhile, Na'eem's account of Umar's intentions to slay the Prophet, and now his stand on Islam, set the city afire with wild speculation. Some believed Umar to be paying lip service and would eventually deliver a crushing, if not mortal blow, against the still budding Faith. Muslims rejoiced in that another powerful enemy had been enlightened and entered the Brotherhood of man. Nevertheless, apprehensions grew as the denunciation of polytheism spread and the numbers to embrace the Message increased.

As a new wave of antipathy swept over Mekkah, victimizing aged and defenseless Muslims, a second migration of eighty men and their families departed for the safety of Abyssinia.

Shortly following the Muslims second flight, Muhammad was besieged with escalating problems of the destitute unable to escape the infidels' rage. He felt the overpowering need for solitude to contemplate the next direction. Thus, returning to the Mountain of Light which Cave Hira was now called, he sat and stared into the valley below, mesmerized by the faint lights of flickering candle and oil lamps.

Sadly, he compared the wicked Children of Israel who had higher chances in the realms of heaven. But, again and again, after numerous warnings, many resisted him as the Jews resisted their prophets and rejected God's Signs. And like the Holy Book of Israel, twisted and distorted, the Disbelievers try to falsify the Qur'an and turn their backs on truth. If only the unrighteous couldst see the consequence of their deeds, they would see the terrible Penalty: that all their power is in Allah's Hands,(4) not in that of idols, crosses, or images.

The familiar sensations and effects associated with Divine Revelation punctuated his last thought and transported his consciousness across the bounds of rationalistic thought into a dimension where few men have gone. In spite of the night's darkness and absence of capacity, it's splendor pulsated with all consuming radiance, furiously palpitating with the spark of celestial vitality. Yet, as soothing as the heavenly corporeality engulfing his cerebration was, his primordial instinct tingled as his mind enlarged to take in the swirling world of dazzling reality. Only the cave's bumpy protrusions against his back and his heart's wild pounding kept him in touch with the existence of life. Then, the deep voice of angel Gabriel telepathically rolled through the corridors of his mind.

"In the name of Allah, The Beneficent, The Merciful."

"Ta. Seen. These are the verses of the Qur'an, and the Book maketh the truth manifesting, a guidance and glad tidings unto the Believers, who establish prayer and give the poor-rate, and of the Hereafter, they are sure."

"Verily, those who believe not in the Hereafter, We have made their deeds fair-seeming unto them, so they wander bewildered. These are those for whom shall be a grievous chastisement, and they in the Hereafter, who shall be the greatest losers. Verily thou (O' Our Apostle Muhammad!) receivest the Qur'an from The All-Wise, All-Knowing."

"Say: 'All praise be (only) to Allah, and peace be on his servants whom He hath chosen.' What! Is Allah better, or what they join (with Him)?"

"Is not He Who created the heavens and the earth, and sent down for you water from heaven; then caused We to grow by it gardens beautiful; it was not in your power that ye grow the trees thereof. What! Is there any god with Allah? Nay, they are a people who (yet) find equals (unto Him)!"

"Is not He Who made the earth a resting place, and made in it rivers, and made on it mountains, and caused between two seas a barrier; is there any god with Allah? Nay, most of them know not!"

"Is not He Who answereth the distressed one when he calleth Him, and removeth the distress and maketh you the successors in the earth; is there any god with Allah? (Nay!) Little it is what ye reflect."

"Is not He Who guideth you in the darkness of the land and the sea, and Who sendeth the winds as the bearers of the good news of His Mercy? Is there any god with Allah? Exalted High is Allah above what they associate (with Him)."

"Is not He Who originates the creation, then reproduces it, and Who provideth for you sustenance from the heaven and the earth? Is there any god with Allah? Say: 'Bring ye your proof, if ye be truthful.'"

"Say: 'None (either) in the heavens or in the earth knoweth the unseen save Allah; and they perceive not when they shall be raised.' Nay, hath reached them the knowledge about the Hereafter; nay, they are in doubt about it; nay, they are blind unto it."

"And on the Day when We will collect from every people a party from those who belied Our signs, then will they be formed into groups. Till they come before Allah (Who will) say, 'Belied ye My signs while ye comprehended them not in your knowledge? Or what is it ye were doing? And the word shall come to pass on them for they were unjust, and they shall speak not."

"What! See they not that We have made the night that they may rest therein, and the day with light (to see); verily, in this are signs for the people who believe."

"And the Day when there shall be blown the Trumpet, and those in the heavens and those in the earth shall be terrorized, save him whom Allah willeth, and all shall come unto Him abased. And thou wilt see the mountains which thinkest thou firm, solid, pass away the passing of the clouds. It is the work of Allah Who hath made everything firm; verily He is All-Aware of what (all) ye do."

"Whosoever bringeth good, for him shall be better than it and they, of the terror of the Day, be secure. And whosoever bringeth evil, these shall be cast down on their faces, in the (Hell) fire; ye shall be recompensed for aught save what ye were doing."

"(Say thou unto them O' Our Apostle Muhammad!) I am commanded only that I should serve the Lord of this city, Who hath made it sacred, and His are all things, and commanded I am that I should be of the Muslims (those who have submitted themselves to God), and that I should recite the Qur'an: so whosoever is guided aright for his (own self), and whosoever goeth astray, then thou say: 'I am only of the warners.' And say thou, 'All praise is Allah's. Soon will He show you His signs that ye shall recognize them;' and thy Lord is not heedless of what all ye do."(5)

With an abruptness which left Muhammad disoriented, Gabriel's voice vanished from the tenuous abyss of his mind. He lay against the cave's wall curled in the fetal position, regaining his senses. The glowing sunrise with it's raw grandeur, boisterous mountain winds, verdant colors, the cave's shelter and warmth, had no effect on his awareness as he shivered uncontrollably. Then, when the sun's temperature and brightness obliterated the smothering haze of obscurity, he wiped the perspiration which had condensed into a layer of chilly moisture from his forehead and shook the droplets from his beard. Exuberantly he thought of God's Way, how the Qur'an taught harmony, and always, as the need arose the answers came like the fruit of the soul's own yearning, to enlighten with profound spiritual truths and ordain for them laws by which all could live in society lives of purity, goodness, and peace.(6) Yea! Civilization required an ordered society, governed not by capriciousness, but by the Law of One Who knoweth and is All-Wise. "Allahu Akbar," he suddenly intoned in praise before rising to depart.

CHAPTER NINETEEN

In Najran, adjacent to Yemen, a predominately Christian settlement 1100 miles south of Mekkah, the Christians were spending their days talking of Islam and it's ideals. Yet, there were those who disputed hotly, clinging to the belief that God needed partners; holding that Prophet Jesus was God incarnate or the Son of God, and going as far as to worship his mother Mary as the mother of God.

During the last council of elders, there were those who felt Islam was not a new religion but a renewal of the true belief in Allah, The One God. To them, the appeal was both easy and intelligible: the natural evolution of religion must be under the necessity of civilization's growth and sophistication; their own Bible foretells of the Arab nation's rise;(1) Prophet Muhammad's advent (2); Luke's disclosure that the New Testament is hearsay;(3) Paul's lying about the Apostle Jesus' imminent return;(4) his (Paul's) assertion that the New Testament is his gospel;(5) and, Jesus himself saying that pardon for sins come from Allah, not him.(6)

An elderly Christian, trying to inspire those refusing to seek after truth, said: "Did not Allah's Prophet Isaiah, say: Hearken, O' heavens, and give ear, O' earth: for the Lord hath spoken, I have nourished and brought up children, (Israel) and they have rebelled against Me. The ox knoweth his owner and the ass it's master's crib, BUT Israel dost not know, My people do not consider. Alas, sinful nation, a people laden with iniquity, a seed of evil doers, children who are corrupters! Thou hast forsaken the Lord, thou hast provoked the Holy One of Israel unto anger, thou hast turned away backward. Why shouldst ye be stricken any more? You will revolt more and more. The whole head is sick, and the whole heart is faint.(7) For Jerusalem is ruined, and Judah is fallen, because their tongue and their doings ARE against the Lord, to provoke the eyes of His glory.(8) And saith Allah: ...Behold the former things have come to pass, and new things I declare; before they spring forth I tell you of them. Sing unto Me a new song and My praise from the ends of the earth, ye that go down to the sea, and all that is therein; the isles, and the inhabitants thereof. Let the wilderness and the cities lift up THEIR VOICE, the villages THAT Ke'dar* ¹doth inhabit: let the inhabitants of the rock sing, let them shout from the top of the mountains.(9) I have a long time held My peace, I have been still AND restrained Myself. NOW I will cry like a travailing woman; I will destroy and devour at once. I will make waste mountains and hills, and dry up all their vegetation; I will make the rivers islands,

---

¹ * Ke'dar, 2nd son of Prophet Isma'il, the Patriarch of the Arabs.

and I will dry up the pools. And I will bring the blind by a way that they knewest not; I will lead them in paths that they have not known. I will make darkness light before them, and crooked things straight. These things will I do for THEM, and not forsake THEM. They shall be turned back, they shall be greatly ashamed that trust in graven images that say to the molded images, ye ARE our gods. (10) ...Therefore I have profaned the princes of the sanctuary, and have given Ja'cob to the curse, and Israel to reproaches."(11)

A younger Christian, following the only way he'd been taught, angrily interjected: "Nay! Nay this Muhammad is but a poet! Poets can invent things and say them in beautiful words!"(12)

His friend interposed in a show of support: "What we should like to behold are miracles like the prophets of old performed!"(13)

The elder returned sharply, "If such miracles as thou readeth, failed to convince Disbelievers of yore what chance is there that Disbelievers will believe now? Miracles may come but they are not cures for disbelief.(14) Let us read the Book with sincerity and understanding in our breasts and wilt we behold all of Allah's prophets prostrated and submitted to Allah as this man Muhammad dost. Even prophet Jesus, alaihis salaam, fell upon the ground in submission to offer prayer unto Allah.(15) Thus, if he were Allah or Allah incarnate, sound reasoning telleth one to question why wouldst he prostrate? Nay, it is we whom have been misled. In our own Book it is clearly written that Holy Jesus, alaihis salaam, is Allah's Servant (16) and a prophet.(17) And Jesus, alaihis salaam, saith of himself that he is only a prophet."(18)

"Out of ignorance and desire to believe in Allah we Christians have followed the ways taught unto us by a people to arrogant too prostrate in submission unto Allah, or even acknowledge that The Prophet would come form the Isma'ilites. Indeed, with true enlightenment one becometh aware that our Book has been tampered with. Moses, Jeremiah and Jesus, alaihimus salaam, foretell of this very thing.(19) And the belief I once held that Prophet Jesus, alaihis salaam, was Allah is preposterous now that Truth reacheth us undistorted through Allah's Holy Apostle Muhammad. We shouldst embrace the Old Way as the renewed Message of the One God. Bear thou in mind it is foretold of one coming with Truth unto all the nations. So let us understand it rightly and send a delegation unto Mekkah to learn first hand, and not be swayed by those who rely on corrupted texts."

At the end of the elder's retort the council severed into two groups. The Skeptics and Disbelievers, calling the seekers after truth; fools, and the Prophet of God a sorcerer. The Believers only shook their heads in sadness.

Several weeks later a fact finding commission of twenty Christian elders arrived in Mekkah to seek out the Holy Prophet. Upon entering the city's square they were immediately drawn toward a huge crowd of people. Dismounting their animals, they penned them and edged their way through the throng of onlookers where they found the Holy Apostle lecturing about God's Way.

Muhammad had seen the group of strangers approaching and meld into the crowd while he spoke. "...look at all of Allah's creation, contemplate it's unity of design and benevolence of purpose. Death must and will come unto all, but life and faith are not objects of ridicule. The Truth will outlast all mockery, it is Allah Who calleth because careth He for thee, and on His Judgment Seat, He will weigh each act, each thought, each motive, great or small, with perfect justice.(20) No good deed is fruitless, so work ye for righteousness whilst there is yet time: for with the Hour of a day inevitable, the door will be closed to repentance. No false gods of fancy can help.(21) Will ye not then take warning from the dreadful consequences of evil clearly proclaimed? Come ye all, seek for worship the One True God, and strive in His service, and reject not His Blessed Message."

"I close as I greeted thee, as-salaamu alaikum."

"Wa alaikum as-salaam," returned three quarters of the crowd then fragmented into several directions: some departing for their homes, others continuing on with their business.

Alone with his companions, Muhammad watched curiously as the group of Christians converged towards him. Ali and several others, their backs to the men from Najran, saw Muhammad's expression and turned in unison. They poised themselves as if ready for what may come. But Muhammad having observed their postures, gently said: "Welcome the wayfarers into our midst."

Acting as spokesman, the eldest Christian started the conversation. "Oh, Muhammad, we are of Banu Harith from Najran. We come in peace to hear Thee speak on the message. The few words we heard have much wisdom and we wish to learn more. We recognize in the Way Thou speakest of the reasoning and natural development of Allah's Revelations as given in earlier ages."(22)

Pleased, Muhammad recited portions of the latest revealed Surah, "In the name of Allah, The Beneficent, and The Merciful."

"The likeness of those who take to themselves guardians besides Allah, is the likeness of the spider that maketh for itself a house; but verily the frailest of all houses is the house of the spider; if they but know (this). Verily, Allah knoweth whatever thing they call upon besides Him and He is The All-Mighty, All-Wise. And these similitudes We do set forth unto people, but understand them none but the learned (ones). Allah created the heavens and the earth with truth; verily in this there is a sign for the Believers."

"Recite thou (O' Our Apostle Muhammad!) that which hath been revealed unto thee of the Book and establish prayer; verily prayer restraineth (one) from filth and evil; and certainly the remembrance of Allah is the greatest (duty of the Believers); and Allah knoweth what ye do."

"And dispute not with the people of the Book save what is best, except those of them who act unjustly, and say ye (unto the people): 'Believe we in that which hath been sent down unto us and sent down unto you, and our God and your God is One, and we unto Him do submit."

"And thus have We sent down unto thee the Book (The Qur'an); and those whom We have given the Book (scriptures given to Moses and Jesus) believe in it; and of these there are those who believe in it; and dispute not against Our signs but the disbelievers. And thou didst not recite any book before it (The Qur'an) and thou didst not transcribe one with that right hand of thine, for then would have doubted those who utter falsehood."

"Nay! It (Qur'an) is the clear signs in the breast of those who have been granted the knowledge;* and dispute not against Our signs except the unjust (ones). And say they: 'Why hath not been sent down upon him the signs from the Lord?' Say thou (O' Our Apostle Muhammad!): 'The signs are with Allah (alone); and I am only a plain warner.'"

"What! Is it not enough for them that We have sent down unto thee the Book which is recited unto them? Verily in this there is mercy and a reminder for a people who believe."

"Say thou (O' Our Apostle Muhammad!): 'Sufficient is Allah as a witness between me and you; He knoweth what is in the heavens and the earth; and those who believe in the falsehood and disbelieve in Allah; these it is who are the losers."

"And they challenge (ask) thee to hasten on the chastisement; and had not the term been decreed, the chastisement would certainly have come unto them; and certainly it will come unto them suddenly while they perceive not. And they challenge thee to hasten on the chastisement, and verily the Hell will encompass the Disbelievers."

"On the Day when shall cover them the chastisement, from above them, and from beneath their feet; and shall say He, 'Taste ye what ye were doing.'"

"Oh, My servants who believe! Verily My earth is vast, therefore

---

* Prophet Muhammad said, "I am the City of Knowledge and Ali is its gate."

Me alone should ye worship! Every soul shall taste of death, then unto Us (only) ye shall (all) be returned. And those who believe and do good, certainly will We lodge them in the exalted places in the gardens beneath which flow rivers, they shall abide therein; how excellent is the recompense of those who act (aright), those who are steadfast and on their Lord do they rely."

"And how many a moving creature that doth not carry it's sustenance; Allah sustaineth it and yourselves; and He is The All-Hearing, The All-Knowing. And if thou ask them: 'Who created the heavens and the earth and made subservient the sun and the moon?' Certainly they will say: 'Allah!' Whence are they then turned away?"

"Allah (it is Who) maketh abundant the sustenance for whomsoever He willeth of His servants, and (similarly) He causeth it to be straightened for him (whomsoever He willeth); verily Allah is Well-Cognizant of all things. And if thou ask them, 'Who sendeth down from heaven the water, and giveth life unto the earth after it's death?' Certainly they will say: 'Allah!' Say, 'All praise is His.' Nay! Most of them understand not."

"And nothing is this life of the world but a vain sport and play; and verily the abode of the Hereafter, is certainly the life: if they but know. And when embark they on ships, call they upon Allah sincerely vowing worship (only) unto Him, and when He bringeth them safe to land, behold, they associate (others with Him), let them thank not for what We have given them, and let them enjoy; but soon shall they know."

"What! See they not that We have established a Sacred Precinct Secure, while people are ravaged all around them? Will they yet believe in the falsehood and in the bounty of Allah disbelieve? And who is more unjust than he who forgeth a lie against Allah, or belieth the truth when it hath come unto him? Is not in the Hell the abode for the disbelievers? And those who strive hard in Us, certainly will We guide them in Our ways; and verily Allah is (always) with those who do good."(23)

Muhammad's elocution had the entire group of Christians exploding with questions at the Surah's end: their enthusiasm overriding each others zeal to learn more. He smiled with pleasure at their spontaneity. "Allahu Akbar," he praised aloud, he thought: never didst I think in my resolve to bring some stability and peace into the harsh and tormented life of the oppressed, that the Mission could award such sensations of satisfaction. "Al-Hamdu lillah," he said and in the time it took to raise his arms for quiet, his expression varied minutely as he realized the kafirun were so limited in thought. And now they will become even more uncompromising in their attacks once

143

word reached their ears of Najran's men accepting Islam. "Masha'a Allah," he said and began responding to their inquiries.

For more than two hours the Christians occupied the square's corner with Muhammad answering their questions in depth. And, at the last, they were so impressed with Islam and it's doctrine, they knew deep within their hearts that the religion of submission to God was the True Faith. They found in Islam, by way of Qur'an, the Right Way and the fulfillment of their own teachings. Hence, all twenty declared their belief in Allah, the One God, and became Muslims.

The new Muslims, graciously accepting Muhammad's hospitality, spent the next few days camped in his courtyard. There, under his tutelage, they studied the Way and familiarized themselves with the purification process in preparation to prayer while they waited for a complete transcription of the Qur'an.

Muhammad, who was unschooled in the knowledge of pen-craft, took every precaution in safeguarding the Message against personal interpretation by having the transcribers read back what they had written. Several times, Abu Sa'd al-Khudri, one of the Prophet's youngest Companions assigned the task of transcribing the Revelations, had to amend his transcription when the written material deviated from the exactness of Angel Gabriel's words. Consequently, at the end of his third night, under the oil lamps glow, the young man completed his duplication. The following morning as the Najranians prepared for departure, Muslims from all over Mekkah turned out to bid farewell. Muhammad promised them that if any more Revelations were revealed they would be written down, verified for accuracy, and delivered by courier.

The conversion of Najran's men had infuriated the infidels to no end to say the least. Of course their narrow minded opinions and beliefs were colored by the fact of their failures to put an end to Islam. And with it's rising success corroding away the very foundation of their power structure, they began to doubt themselves and their reasons for opposing Islam.

One day while the enemies of Islam were gathered, Jahl, Sufyan and others, voiced their doubts. "For what real reason are we so cruel to the Muslims? Why do the Muslims numbers keep increasing? How can they stand so bravely in the face of trouble and tortuous abuse? Why is our every effort to stop the way Muhammad teacheth a vain attempt?"

Abu Lahab, disregarding their self-serving reproaches, stiffened. His temples pounded with fury and bitterness, causing his brows to pull together in contemptuous observation. A tight smile spread itself into a savage thin line across his face, his eyes ablaze with hatred as the anger fermented in his veins. "Nay! On the contrary," he began resentfully. "Those accursed Najranians were seduced by Muhammad's charms. The situation may seem hopeless but I will not forgo the campaign against him, and if ye value thy livelihood thou wilt continue the struggle!"

Striking at the heart of their deep rooted interests, the Disbelievers readily forgot their misgivings and renewed covenants to maintain their antagonistic activities.

Some evenings later while Muhammad preached at al-Arqam's home, three of the Disbelievers, through independent decision had decided to secretly investigate why their endeavors to stop Islam came to naught. Fearing reprisals if discovered, they dressed in old tattered garments with deep hoods as a means of avoiding detection. Under the night's darkness they furtively circumnavigated the direct streets until reaching al-Arqam's house.

Arriving by different paths at different times, the infidels found places to ensconce themselves on the crowd's fringes, all the while hoping they wouldn't be recognized. Long, agonizing minutes passed as the crowd settled in. Much to their relief, it appeared that not one of the hundreds present paid them any mind. They listened closely as the Prophet recited several Surah's and couldn't help but be impressed by God's Message, and the discussions that followed. But, The Watchful, had hardened their hearts with rebellion and they rejected His Truth.

Muhammad raised his arms to end the questions. He said, "It is time for prayer."

The crowd's sudden activity took the masquerading Disbelievers completely by surprise. People began arranging themselves on their knees, in closed ranks, women moved to the rear to prevent distractions while one communed with God. Others performed the ritual of ablution.

At a loss at what to do, and the threat of exposure constantly in their minds, the doubters followed everyone else's movement. They inched themselves near the rear ranks and imitated the men around them.

At the conclusion, the crowd broke position and embraced each other. Some, grouped to converse and others departed. The infidels believing their deception duped all, skulked out. It was then they literally bumped into one another.

Embarrassed, they stuttered out excuses all at once, claiming curiosity. The next night, imaging the other would never dare show up, they approximated their clandestine approaches to Muhammad's assembly place once more. On the third night they were caught, by each other again. They swore an oath never to return and the matter was never mentioned. However, The One God neutralized their callused hearts with flickering sparks of Truth in which He used their unwitting utterances as a catalyst to actuate the spark of interest in others.

In the days that followed, Lahab was the first to notice the subtle changes in the three men. At first, he thought of confronting them individually but reconsidered, opting to expose them in front of the other leaders.

Afterwards, in an effort to show their opinions and views hadn't changed, the three men heightened their energies and aggression against Islam. Daily, Muslims were persecuted: attacked with physical violence, others suffered ridicule and imprecations. It was a painful time once more for the Believers, especially Muhammad.

He wouldn't blame anyone for the distress he felt. He never used a harsh word against them, nor lost his temper. He wouldn't force his way, nor compel Islam onto any; instead, his heart opened out towards people, caring much about the abasement of his brethren to the servitude of idolaters.

His patience and tolerance in tribulation's face exceeded beyond the bounds of normal men's capacities. Ever persevering, his poise, his composure, and readiness to extend an arm for the benefit of his fellow man, his example set a precedent of behavior equaled only by God's chosen before him. He, of course was under constant scrutiny by his enemies who were on the lookout for weaknesses they could exploit.

With no faults to profit by, Qurayshie leaders initiated a propaganda crusade against Islam. The four sacred months were close at hand and it was the long established custom in which feuding was forbidden. They figured with Ukadh's arrival, the yearly gathering would best serve their aims to check Islam's call. Turning to the frivolous mind of Nadr ibn al-Harith, a noted poet. They engaged him to compose prevarications about the Message, hoping his fame would turn the curious away.

Accusing Muhammad of necromancy and soothsaying, Nadr commenced to spout his fabrications upon the arriving hordes. The scheme, however, regarded as infallible, only served to inflame the curiosity of those hearing the spurious poetry: the infidels unwittingly became one of the means of aiding the Prophet in bringing the Message to all.

Khalid ibn Walid, his inner spark generating an interest he couldn't contain, fled the square after seeing the huge reception Muhammad received after one of Nadr's poems. Absentmindedly he circled the plaza's arches until he came to rest on the other side of the wall where al-Amin taught God's Word. He squatted down against the wall not more than ten feet away from where the Prophet spoke.

"…all people who have faith have the right to listen unto Allah's Word and receive His Mercy, whether they are publicans or sinners, low caste or of superior stations.(24) Truth is for all peoples, yet to be worthy of the service of the One True God, we must love and serve His creatures. The parents who cherished us in childhood deserve our humble reverence and service: next come the rights of kinsmen, those in need, and wayfaring strangers: unto each according to his need."(25)

"There is none like unto Allah. Exalted beyond measure is He. All creation declareth His glory. His Revelation is Truth, but beyond comprehension unto those who believe not in the Hereafter.(26) Arrogance, jealousy, spite and hatred, was the Evil One's fall, so let it not be the cause of your fall. Man hath been given preeminence above much of Allah's creation and oweth higher responsibilities. He should give thanks for Allah's mercies and remember the Day of Account."(27)

"True knowledge is with Allah alone. We are not to dispute on matters of conjecture, but rely on the truth that cometh from Allah. As in the Parable: the man who pileth up his riches and is puffed up with this world's goods, despising those otherwise endowed, will come to an evil end, for his hopes were not built on Allah."(28)

"What hath been revealed in Qur'an, giveth straight directions to make our lives straight: to ward us against Evil and guide us unto Good everlasting. Allah worketh wonders beyond our fathoming: how belief is a sure refuge in ways we know not.(29) Allah will provide, so fulfill thy trusts for orphans and deal with all in the strictest probity. Pry not into evil from curiosity,(30) for not the scheming of Evil, and it's followers, will deflect Allah's Plan in the least. Thus, be ye of sincere heart and seek His true Guidance; for truth will last and falsehood will perish.(31) And know ye that Allah's Wrath when kindled is a terrible thing. So rejoice and give praise that He forebeareth and forgiveth."(32)

Khalid sat and listened, absorbed in the Message's meaning. He had been maliciously expecting some ostentatious display of rhetoric, but the spark of belief ignited into slow burning embers. He set out leaden footed, trying to combat the incorruptible white heat threatening to overcome a life of irreverence.

His mind in confusion twice confounded, he considered the different paths open to him, postulating their ends. If I embark upon the wrong path wouldst it be folly manifest! But which is the Right Path? Should I just slip away from Mekkah like a thief in the night? By the gods, this is the sort of decision that changeth a man's destiny!

Grudgingly conceding that he couldn't make up his mind, he felt the sting of inadequacy to meet the demands of his life's choices wash over him. Previously convinced, if only subconsciously, that he had an easy command over his life, he saw his life in a flash of clarity as the denied faults dissolved the layers of imagined ability. His self-esteem had made him insensible to life's realities and to justify his coldness and impotence, he defined his apathy and emasculated powers of analysis to mean a wise disassociation from man's difficulties. And, now at the point of proving his mettle, he used his unresolved misery as an excuse to flee the city and his inner convictions.

Meanwhile, Muhammad's session lasted well into the afternoon. Well received, a good many non-Mekkans hungering after truth, welcomed and embraced Islam. And at the gathering's end, Muhammad walked among the crowd feeling a great deal of satisfaction. He thought: the Message in Abyssinia, Najran, and now when the new Muslims returned to their homes they would carry the Message to Arabia's furthest parts and beyond.

CHAPTER TWENTY

In Abu Jahl's gargantuan hilltop house, the Disbelievers were once again in council. Bickering amongst themselves, they discussed their inability to influence the Ukadh's masses and past failures to halt Islam's progression. They knew well their points of arguments, and the persecution did nothing but bond the Muslims in belief.

Jahl was straining to control his temper as his own angry defiance surfaced. He thought it incredible that in a little over six years, the Way had not only survived but was now spreading it's teachings into distant lands. And as the realization set in, his anxiety shook his heart with fear. Fear made disgusting mealy mouthed men, his thought continued, we cannot back down like common beggars!

For a moment he forgot the others' presence, his contempt for Muhammad growing fiercely by the second. He glanced around furtively. Then, exclaimed in a sudden quickening of hatred, "Saith I unto thee, there is no use in counter changing blame. I am an enemy to Muhammad and will oppose him till my death. Yea, let us then enlist the aid of others and together we can put an end to him!"

In a move born of desperation, the leaders hatched a plot that promised to be successful. Pooling their resources, they summoned the hardest core against Islam and gave instruction. Russal, Akhnas, Suraqah ibn Malik, Shaybah ibn Rabi'ah, Aswad ibn Abd Yaghus, As ibn Wai'l, and Uqbah ibn Abi Mu'it, would at Ukadh's end scour the city for the most hardened men and hire them on as guards.

In the meantime, Mansur ibn Akramah drew up a document declaring: all forms of commerce and business with the shi'a of Muhammad is a criminal offense; association with them is prohibited; matrimonial alliances with Muslims is banned; and, the opposition of Islam needs must be supported in all circumstances. The entries were endorsed by Mekkah's grand council of Disbelievers and would be enforced as legal decree.

At the appointed date the declaration was hung within the Ka'bah. Simultaneously throughout Mekkah the guards began gathering up Muslims of the Hashim and Mut'talib clans. The economic blockade and confinement began.

Abu Talib, Muhammad, and many others who wanted to stay with the Holy Prophet, led the way to a fairly spacious valley, away from the environment of idolaters. Situated between the mountains, the Believers erected tents, lean-tos, and built pens for their livestock. The guards, stationed at strategic points across the mountain tops watched with indifference. The smaller children, unaware of the ordeal to come, amused themselves in the valley's expanse until their playing took them near the invisible barrier separating them from freedom.

Under orders to prevent any members of the clans and their children from leaving the area or engaging in contact with those outside their confines, the mercenaries lined the heights with long bows, ready to strike down any who might escape and to discourage visitors. Two of the sentries, eager to blood-let, let loose a volley of arrows upon the unsuspecting children. Frightened, they ran screaming for the safety of their parents.

Following the harrowing experience the valley filled with sounds of wailing children. Muhammad grimaced and thought: a portent of things to come? Yet, as the children's lamentations rippled through his soul, his duty to God remained uppermost. He asked Ali to gather every man, woman and youngster of reason for prayer.

Completing the prayer, he turned to face the assembly. Searchingly he looked, seeing the looks of displacement. He felt an old familiar stirring: like their mettle were being tested. He thought: surely I think not these thoughts alone!

"Oh, my people!" Muhammad said resolutely. "In the sight of Allah all men are equal. That is the task before us: to give man hope even in the face of ill-will. To assure him of the Hereafter and that only with the Lord, Most High, is there a better life. We must keep our resolve to show the kafirun and non-believers that Allah forsaketh not His servants. So heed ye well and mark His Word."

"In the name of Allah, The Beneficent, The Merciful."

"Hallowed is He in Whose hand is the Kingdom (of the heaven and earth), and He, over all things is All-Powerful, Who created death and life that He may try you (to prove) which of you is best in deeds; He is The Ever-Prevalent, The Oft-Forgiving, Who created the seven heavens layer above layer; thou seest not in the creation of The Beneficent (God) any defect or incongruity. Then look thou again; seest thou any gap? Then repeat thou (thy) gaze again and again, thy gaze shall return unto thee dulled, being wearied."

"Indeed have We adorned the lower heaven with lamps (the stars), and We have made them (as) missiles to repulse away the satans, and We have prepared for them the chastisement of the flaming fire."

"And for those who disbelieve in their Lord is the chastisement of the Hell, and evil is the destination. When they shall be flung into it, they shall hear it's roaring as it boileth up, as it would burst with rage; whenever a group is flung into it, it's keepers shall ask them: 'Came not there unto you a warner?'"

"They shall say: 'Yea! Indeed a warner did come unto us, but we belied (him) and said we: Allah hath sent not down aught, ye are in naught but a vast delusion!' And they shall say: 'Had we but hearkened (unto them) or pondered (over what they said), we would not have been amidst the fellows in the flaming fire. So shall they confess their sins, but far will be (from mercy) the fellows in blazing fire."

"Verily, those who fear their Lord in secret, for them shall be forgiveness and a great recompense. And conceal ye your word or declare it; verily, He is The Knower of whatsoever is in the breasts (hearts). What! Knoweth not He that created? And He is The Subtle, The All-Aware."

"Say thou: 'He is The Beneficent (God)! Believe we in Him and on Him (alone) do we rely; so ye shall come to know who it is that is in manifest straying."(1)

At Prophet Muhammad's first indication of ending, his Companion Zayd shot his arm into the air and waved for attention. Acknowledged, he said: "Oh, Apostle of Allah, I am not as knowledgeable as the others and my question is of two parts. One, whilst thou recited the Holy Message didst thou use a term I have never before heard nor do I understand it's meaning. And two, why do our Christian brethren say Allah's Kingdom is to come?"

"What is it thou doth not understand, old friend?"

"M-missiles," returned the coloring Zayd.

Al-Mustafa took a few seconds to gather his thoughts. "The physical world in which we live is made up of seven regions called the seven heavens. The heaven containing the earth with all the celestial bodies and galaxies, from the nearest to the farthest is contained in the lowest heaven."(2)

"The wonderful beauty and symmetry, and bliss of the upper heavens, are denied unto evil forces. These regions are reserved only for the godly, who are rewarded for their piety and struggles against temptations. Hence, Allah The Exalted, hath protected the eternal abode of Believers with flaming missiles or stars."

"As to thy second question, the church established by the pagan Emperor Constantine of Rome, in the name of Jesus, alaihis salaam, teacheth it's followers to believe: 'Our Father which art in heaven, Hallowed be Thy name. Thy Kingdom come. Thy will be done in earth, as IT IS in heaven.' (3) The Christian prayer marketh their mistaken belief that Allah, The Praiseworthy, is only in heaven and not in the earth or elsewhere. Their prayer saith that the Kingdom of Allah's Authority is limited to heaven and extends not beyond that: for His Authority is yet to come. It is blasphemous to believe that some one else other than Allah, The Eternal Owner of Sovereignty, holdeth authority in the earth. Thus, to neutralize the confusion, Allah The Most Merciful, hath revealed the Truth: to educate human minds against the imaginary and conjectural dogmas about the existence of others in Godhead. Man is now informed as he was in the past, 'I am the Lord: that IS My name: and My glory will I not give to another, neither My praise to graven images.' (4) There is none but One and Only One, Who owneth the Authority Supreme over the Universe and adoration in any sense and gratitude in any way is due only unto Him. Far be such about Allah, the Omnipresent and Omnipotent Lord, Who owneth the exclusive Authority over every part and particle, known and yet unknown, of the visible and invisible worlds."(5)

A voice called from the rear: "Oh, Prophet, those who enter the Garden - will they weep for their loved ones?"

"Nay," answered Muhammad, "in perfect felicity of the righteous all such feelings will be blotted out. The hearts and minds will be so purified that all past rancor, jealousy, or sense of injury, will be obliterated. The true Brotherhood will be realized there. Each will face the other with joy and confidence, there will be no sense of toil or weariness, and Bliss will last forever."(6) Hamzah, Bilal, Hamid and a score of others raised their hands to be called upon. Muhammad, pleased to see such an avid interest answered their questions to the last man and woman.

Muhammad's calmness in the hour of seemingly disaster, inspired all around him. The earlier looks of displacement were now looks of determination as they broke up to continue on with their business of settling in. Before retiring to his tent for the evening, Muhammad toured their encampment, encouraging the besieged to remain steadfast in prayer and patience. At each tent the question was asked, "How long are we to stay here?" He responded: "Know I not Allah's Designs or Plans, but here in this almost treeless expanse will our wills be molded and purged of false motives. Here will we dwell amongst one another, sharing joys and sorrows, and building a unity of Brotherhood no evil can undo. So fret not the Ways of Allah, The Most Wise, He will surely guide us."

That night, Muhammad, after long conversations with Khadijah, Ali, and his daughters, fell into an exhausted sleep. Within minutes he started tossing and turning, his subconscious stirring into heightened activity. The familiar sensations of Divine revelation awakened him momentarily before entering the rapture.

Meantime, Umar, Abu Bakr, and other Muslims not included in the siege were growing frustrated by the lack of communication. The best of them encouraged level headedness and patience.

In the following weeks the full impact of their forced captivity was kept at bay with the struggle of setting a routine, compatible to all. Each family had the task of assigning chores to coincide with the overall plan of survival. Boys pooled the camp's feed and portioned it out to the animals. Girls helped the women with cooking, mending and child care. The men devised ways of communicating with the outside and insured their families care. Muhammad, besides his own obligations helped the others in all areas while continuing the teaching of Islam.

After nearly a month of settling in the captives again met for the weekly assembly: time for prayer and the best social intercourse. Muhammad reviewed the community's spiritual life, offered advice, exhorted the wisdom of living piously, and recited the latest revelations. Immediately afterwards the hands raised, each trying to catch the Prophet's eye. Muhammad called on Maysara.

"Oh, Prophet, what is the Zodiacal?"

"The canopy of heaven above marketh the sun's path through the heavens year after year, and the moon's and planets limit of wandering, which have been divided into twelve divisions called Signs of the Zodiac. Each marketh the sun's path whereby we can mark off the seasons. Then, there are other wondrous facts of the heavens, some of which effect our physical life on this earth. The highest lessons we can draw from them are spiritual."(7)

Recognized, Abu L'as asked: "Why was Abraham in fear when the angels approached him to give glad tidings, O' Messenger?"

"When the angels arrived, Abraham, alaihis salaam, had by that time passed through the fire of persecution in the Mesopotamian valleys and left the ancestral idolatry of Ur of the Chaldees. Then, tried by Nimrod, he triumphed over the indignities,(8) and made his home in Canaan.(9) However, he remained alert and weary to Nimrod's treachery. Thus, when the three angels, in man's form, refused to partake in the sumptuous meal of roasted meat, he became alarmed. With feelings of hesitation and fear in his mind, he thought they were agents of Nimrod until they explained they were messengers of Allah and didst not eat but had come with glad tidings."

Muhammad, then, saw Samurah ibn Jundab and Sa'ad ibn Ubadah, two of his other scribes, squirm for attention. Smiling, he called out to Ubadah, "Sa'ad, old friend, see I the question on thy face but knowest not the words. What wouldst thou like to know?"

"My thirst for knowledge and understanding compels me to ask which cities were destroyed that thou spoke of in the last Surah?"

"Ah, a good example of Allah's Wrath. Those cities, Sodom and Gomorrah were given to unspeakable abominations, addicted to unnatural acts. So when news of three handsome young men, who were angels, entered the city to speak with Allah's prophet they in their wickedness became inflamed with lust. Thus, the term appointed overtook them and both cities were utterly laid to waste."

Turning toward another, Muhammad saw Usd al-Ghabah suddenly jump to his feet and start signaling for attention. Usually reserved, Usd's frenzied actions incited the assembly into laughter.

With the mirth crinkling the corners of his eyes, the Prophet nodded at Usd.

"Oh, Muhammad, who are the Companions of the Wood?"

"They were of the Madyan peoples, to whom Shu'ayb, alaihis salaam, was chosen as Prophet. He spoke unto them, teaching Allah's Word, but the people refused to heed. Thus, the people were destroyed for their wrongdoing."

One of the last men to embrace Islam before their internment, asked: "Oh, Prophet of The Most Praiseworthy, of whom doth thou speak that divided Scripture?"

"They are the People of the Book, whom Allah and history have shown to be Jews and Christians, who were in origin a sect of Jews themselves.(10) The original Scripture, in it's purity came from Allah but was lost, distorted, or rejected.(11) And over centuries of Jewish racial pride, they took out of what they remembered and what suited them(12) and used their own writings as the Message of Allah which had no Divine Authority.(13) And instead of adhering to the Books of Revelation and seeking to do the Will of Allah, they pursued after all sorts of occult knowledge(14) and divided Scripture into three parts: Torah, the law; Nebiim, the prophets; and Kethubim, the Writings."(15)

Remembering that several Muslims had not shown up for the prayer, Muhammad added: "Jihad meaneth not only battle but also the struggle to strive in Allah's Cause. We must contend against the Jinns and kafirun that constantly plague us. More than not, they attempt to wedge their black hearted ways into our souls, using the cleverest methods to keep us from building a strong community. Do not think for a moment you can outsmart the Father of Lies or his minions. Call upon Allah for strength against Evil."

"Allah giveth each man or woman the freedom of choice in matters of belief. His Truth is like His rope unto mankind, it is there to grasp or reject. Once the rope is grasped, there is no room for one to use personal fancy or conjectures."

"Salat is one of the articles of Faith. The spiritual significance of public prayer is more than we can know..."

As the Holy Prophet spoke something unseen started generating itself throughout the crowd: a sense of joy without the undercurrent of fear. People began turning towards one another as if to verify the abstruse permeation each felt. Even Muhammad stopped to glance around.

"Al-Hamdu lillah," al-Mustafa suddenly voiced, overcome with feelings of unity.

The Muslims returned the praise, vocalizing their homage for several minutes. Muhammad had to raise his hands for quiet, then continued on with another Surah.

Ali, knowing Muhammad's nuances better than any when he was about to end his delivery, stood and addressed the Prophet before any could call his attention. "Oh, Apostle of Allah, so all may know, of whom wert thou speaking when thou mentioned Witnesses will stand forth on the Day?"

"On that Day, the Day of Judgment, the Book of each man's deeds and motives will be placed wide open and the Prophets and teachers of Truth will bear witness to the fact that they preached and warned men. And Allah, knowing every fact and circumstance, will give due weight unto all things, great or small, and upon the evidence will with absolute justice pronounce judgment."

With no more questions, Muhammad bid the crowd peace. Starting for his tent, his cousin Ja'far's countenance flashed in his mind. He turned back toward the group of scribes who habitually gathered after his lectures.

It was Muhammad's idea to use the coming freedom that came with Ukadh, to secretly send couriers to Najran and Abyssinia with Qur'an's latest revelations.

On eve of the four sacred months start, the armed guards abandoned their posts. Their absence wasn't noticed until the next day at dawn when Ali started gathering the men and women for prayer. As Believers began turning out of their tents, the news of their captors' withdrawal spread throughout the encampment. More than once Muhammad had to raise his arms for silence in order to commence prayer. The sudden realization of freedom after months of forced captivity had the gathering in rare excitement. Muhammad could not blame their distractedness: for he too felt the overpowering yearning to escape the monotonous valley. Finally, after about ten minutes of animated loquaciousness they one by one adjusted to their new situation and settled down.

At prayer's end, and free to move about as they pleased, they lost no time in contacting relatives and friends. The occasion, the influx of people from all over Arabia and surrounding countries for the annual Ukadh, made leaving all the more exhilarating.

Abu Ubaydah ibn Harith, chosen for the most secret mission of delivering Qur'an's to Najran and Axum in Abyssinia, visited with friends before his departure. He let it be known that in a fortnight he would be leaving for Yathrib, thereby insuring no suspicion as to his task.

Khadijah, Maysara, Zayd and the girls, returned to their hilltop home. Muhammad and Ali went to the city's square where Muhammad earnestly began the propagation of God's Way.

To all who knew him it seemed as if the past eight months had no effect on him. In fact, to their surprise, his energy and enthusiasm attracted a good number of people who were otherwise engaged in the business of bargain hunting. And by the time they left to continue on where they had left off, six or seven had declared their belief and joined the ranks of Believers.

Abu Lahab who had become one of the most inveterate enemies of Islam was near madness in his fury over the success of Muhammad's ability to enfold people with Islam. In his anger, spittle flew from his lips as he raged against his cohorts and all things holy. Finally, he ended his tirade with the Prophet's condemnation.

Several Disbelievers, frightened by the intensity of Lahab's raving and fearing the power of his influence, fled Mekkah to disassociate themselves with the evil tyrant's schemes. It was some three days later before Abu Jahl summoned up the courage to face and inform the Qurayshies of the desertions in their rebellion against submitting to God.

Lahab exploded violently when he heard. He cursed, screamed and knocked things over. Of the Disbelievers witnessing his outburst, except the hardest core, thought it was a telling fact about their efforts to halt Islam.

As a result of the subterfuge, a mistrust between leaders and their underlings developed as the rope of slavery to evil twisted and coiled itself about their necks.

After releasing his ire, Lahab thought: instead of outright bribery he could persuade Muhammad to acquiesce to his demands using guile. Yea, wilt I subtly suggest the promise of greatness with an abundance of wealth to come.

Early next morning, forsaking his usually flamboyant attire, he carefully donned garments of conservative dress and left his home. He silently congratulated himself for his craftiness and selected a position to wait where Muhammad was sure to pass on his way to the square. He tucked himself between the buildings and cooled his heels until the Prophet appeared.

A short time later, Muhammad, along with his family, were smiling and enjoying the freedom of unrestricted movement as they came through the narrow streets on their way to the bazaar.

Abu Lahab emerged from the shadowed recess and started walking toward them. Khadijah and the girls' hearts chilled upon seeing him. Ali jumped to the forefront, ready for any possibilities. Muhammad, instantly alert, surveyed the area for any trickery. Lahab couldn't help but notice the situation's tension and raised his hands, palms out in a gesture of peace.

"Oh, Muhammad, have I come in truce. Wouldst thou allow me to speak with thee in private," said Lahab, all the while keeping his eyes on Ali.

Before replying Muhammad reached out and gently squeezed Ali's shoulder, giving him an unspoken assurance. Then said: "Ali, take the womenfolk onto the marketplace." Reluctantly, Ali led his cousins and Khadijah away. Once alone, Abu Lahab smiled insincerely and initiated the conversation. "Muhammad, the light of thy teachings has entered my heart and now I worship Allah alone."

Muhammad's eyes chilled, freezing with crystal-like reserve which cut Lahab off before he could add any thing further. He picked up on his uncle's use of the word "thy" which dripped of sarcasm, and saw through the thinly disguised veneer of self-righteousness. When he spoke his tone remained neutral, curbed, and cold and without the slightest inflection of the pity he felt for his uncle. He said straightforwardly, "Woe unto those who persecute the truth! Doth thou dare to proclaim belief when thy breast is engorged with mischief? Thou hath not the will to divest thyself of false worship on account of thy interests."

"I, being a messenger of Allah do not and canst not possibly desire to follow thy false ways. You and thy confederates, as custodians of the false worship, have not the will to give up thy ways of worship.(16) I, having been given the truth canst not enjoin falsehoods; ye, having vested interests, will not abandon them. For thy ways the responsibility is thine, for my ways the responsibility is mine. I have rehearsed unto thee the truth."

"Thy schemes, threats and opposition, are but in vain: for the truth will overcome and prevail in the end.(17) So take thou heed of the Day of Account, for Mighty eyes behold all that men do and they will answer for it when the Judgment cometh. Hence, be thou warned: learn from the Message of Allah, The Beneficent God." Muhammad turned on his heels and left his uncle standing alone.

Lahab was flushing with color, angered as he stared malevolently after Muhammad. He worked his vocal cords, wanting to retort smartly but the sound issuing from his throat was no more than a paltry squeak which seemed high pitched and womanish. Embarrassed, his blood began to boil. He seethed with hatred as he eyed Muhammad walk toward the square, indifferent to the shame he felt. Upon regaining his composure, he thanked the gods, Uzza, Lat and Manat, for permitting no one to witness his nephew's stinging rebuke and his inability to respond. And now, more than ever before his desire to crush the Prophet of Islam became an all consuming passion.

Covertly, he began to trail after Muhammad, spying from around any thing or person that could afford some semblance of concealment. He observed, made mental notes of everyone Muhammad came into contact with. Then, as the Prophet moved onto another, he approached telling them Muhammad was a spreader of lies and not to heed his words. Some, he bribed with dirhams but as before his actions only fired their curiosity.

CHAPTER TWENTY-ONE

The pagans of Banu Quraysh and other lesser tribes, including Jews and Christians, in their efforts to recruit men of power and influence to join their war of words against the truth, had their minions posted throughout the city. Their orders were to speak with every man of means about stopping Islam.

Al-Burah ibn Azib, one of many visitors contacted, agreed to learn more and was told whom to see in the city for additional information. He went along more out of curiosity than any real desire to join the opposition: for he had some knowledge of the Muslim plight in Mekkah, being from Axum.

He met with the Disbelievers, heard their arguments against Islam, and thought their case outright ridiculous. Previously, he had believed the stories he heard of abuse and persecution to be mere exaggerations until his meeting. Shocked by the planned barbarity in store for the Muslims at Ukadh's end, he felt morally obligated as a Christian to search out the Prophet and relay his information.

Wondering how best to tell the Holy one of God the distressing news, or if he'd be believed, he wandered through the streets and alleyways aimlessly, his mind in turmoil. After a short while he came to the conclusion that no matter his reservations he had to relate his knowledge.

Azib entered Mekkah's square and found the bazaar at it's height of activity. Carts, litters, beasts of burden, women with market-baskets or water jugs balanced atop their heads wove through the artisans, consumers and slaves. People were swarming around gaming tables, booths and stalls, as tradesmen, merchants, food hawkers, and charm and idol fashioners, shouted to be heard above the other, all vying for customers. A herd of sheep and it's shepherd plowed through the throngs of people, leaving waves of human chaos. He couldn't help but notice a score of women, immodestly garbed in shimmering fabrics of all colors alluring to one's senses. They had painted faces, kohl shadowed eyes, and paraded around shamelessly in a wantonly manner as they kept in step with the musical notes of various instruments. There was drunken revelry, running and screaming children, amidst snorting and spitting camels, braying asses and whinnying horses. Smells of exotic oils, incense, spices, food and animals, compounded by visuals, harried his sense of morality.

In his somber mood, Azib thought of the riotous scenes described in Jewish scriptural writings as he tread a path through the mass of humanity searching for Muhammad. On the square's far side, he noticed a crowd of people listening to someone only by their decorum. Investigating, he discovered the Prophet Muhammad in their midst sermonizing.

Thinking better of just barging his way through and relating his news, Azib slowly edged his way in until he was quite close. Nearly an hour passed when he realized the crowd's size wasn't decreasing but burgeoning by the numbers. In his impatience to warn the Islamic leader, he started shifting his weight from foot to foot, glancing around restlessly as he waited.

Muhammad had watched the meticulously dressed stranger work his way through the throng of listeners. But when the man began his nervous dance, he instinctively knew there was more on his mind than learning Islam. Intrigued, he scrutinized the crowd for hostile faces but there were no signs of danger or enmity filled faces. He continued a while longer then concluded the day's teaching with "As-salaamu alaikum." From his elevated position Muhammad watched the crowd disperse, breaking into small groups as they carried on Islam's logic, all the while never losing sight of the stranger.

Azib saw his opportunity and started gesturing excitedly toward the Prophet. Muhammad took a quick look around and then approached warily.

"Peace be unto thee, friend," greeted Muhammad. "Is there some way I can be of assistance unto thee? Thou doth seem to be in a difficulty."

"Oh, Prophet," replied Azib as he surveyed the area for any Disbelievers. "I have knowledge of an evil plot afoot which is to be set in motion at fair's end. It is against the Muslims of the Hashim and Mut'talib clans."

"Come, join me in my home where we can talk of this matter more privately," returned al-Mustafa.

Azib's news created an emptiness the like of which Muhammad hadn't felt since his mother's death. Several days later, after al-Burah ibn Azib's unveiling the infidels plan, he still could not rid himself of the deep concern gripping his soul. Finally, knowing he could not put off telling the elders any longer, he called out to where Ali and Fa'timah sat under the now grown palms, discussing Islam, life, and the new items the Ukadh brought. He said: "Daughter, permit me a few moments time with the young man at thy side."

The two looked at one another, Ali beaming in sheer delight, Fa'timah colored perceptively and answered with feigned exasperation, "Oh, father!"

As Ali crossed the courtyard, Muhammad thought: What a fine young man hath he become. Strong of mind, firm in belief, and molded in character by the Qur'an...

"Doth thou wish to speak with me," asked Ali cutting off Muhammad's thoughts before he could finish.

Muhammad told Ali the news ibn Azib had brought, then asked him to summon several individuals for the evening meal.

That evening the usual gaiety and chatter were missing from the dinner table. Family and guests, detecting Muhammad's gloomy mood, refrained from normal conversation. Apprehensively, they waited for him to speak of the reasons for their sudden summons. But it wasn't until after the servants cleared away the table that he spoke.

"My friends, it has recently come to my attention a matter of the gravest concern. It appeareth the kafirun in their war against Islam are again employing guards to keep the Hashim and Mut'talib clans isolated as they didst last year. There-"

Umar angrily jumped to his feet and nearly shouted in his passion, "Give me the command, O' Prophet, and shall I gather a small force to remove the heads of those infidels!"

Several of the younger men present, including three elders, nodded their heads in agreement. Even some of the women, frail creatures that they are, wanted to join their men in arms. But Muhammad took exception to Umar's remarks and made a motion with his hands to cut him off.

"Knoweth I how thou feeleth," announced Muhammad, "but to fight now would be from human motives and the gaining of personal ends. Engaging our enemies from such motives is wrong at any time. When the command is issued by Allah, will we fight but it shall be in the Cause of Allah."

A heated discussion followed Muhammad's remarks as the animosity for their enemies inflamed with indignation. Irritated that the men didn't listen, Muhammad raised his arms and sharply demanded silence. He said in a voice underlining his authority, "It is not the time to bear arms! The Most Courageous, Subtle, has His Own Designs for us all and it is not our place to question His time. So go ye out amongst thy brethren and warn them to prepare for another siege after Ukadh." His added comments put an end to their arguments. And as they departed for their homes the thought uppermost in their minds was that it was indeed a sad day. Nevertheless, the following morning they set out to inform the Muslim community.

Many of them upon hearing the news of their planned re-internment wanted to take up arms and fight the ungodly for the right to remain in their homes. Fortunately there were more Muslims seeing the wisdom of Muhammad's counsel and stopped their brethren from acting rashly, therein preventing a premature offensive.

A week prior to Ukadh's termination, Muhammad and the elders had assigned individuals the responsibility of having the

Muslims ready. Others were given the task of erecting tents at their old camp site. And before week's end, Muslims of the Hashim and Mut'talib clans, along with their shi'a, were settled back in the valley.

The Disbelievers were not expecting the Muslim mobilization and felt like fools for disbursing huge sums of money to extra guards hired for rounding up the Believers. Then adding insult to injury which made matters worse and hardened their hearts all the more, the guards whose services would not now be needed turned to drink with their small windfall. They started boasting with gall biting levity, telling all who would listen how ridiculous the Muslims made the high and mighty leaders against Islam look.

The Ukadh ended a day before Muhammad received several new Revelations which would in months to come, strengthen the three hundred plus Mekkan Muslims during their ordeal. The Chosen One had the sun setting behind him when he addressed the assembly. He said: "Oh, ye Muslims, the best of peoples. Allah in His Mercy has revealed yet another Message to soothe our troubled hearts. And in His Wisdom showeth man's folly, ingratitude, and confirmeth the grievous chastisement awaiting those who have no belief. So take ye heart, the Lord dost not forsake His servants. He is The Knower of all things, secret and hidden."

"In the name of Allah, The Beneficent, The Merciful."

"Ha. Meem. Ain. Seen. Qaf."

"Thus doth reveal unto thee as (did He) unto those before thee, Allah, The All-Mighty, The All-Wise. His is whatever is in the heavens and whatever is in the earth, and He is The Highest, The Greatest."

"Nigh it is (that) the heavens cleave asunder from above (for the very awe of His glory), while the angels are (there) celebrating the praise of their Lord and seeking forgiveness for those in the earth; be it known that verily, Allah, He (alone) is The Oft-Forgiving, The Most Merciful. And those who take aught besides Allah as their guardians, Allah watcheth over them, and thou art not over them a guardian. And thus have We revealed unto thee (O' Our Apostle Muhammad!) an Arabic Qur'an, that thou mayest warn the Mother City (Mekkah) and those around it, and thou warn of the Day of Gathering together (the Resurrection), wherein (there) is no doubt; a party shall be in the Garden (of Paradise) and a party (shall be) in the burning (Hell) fire."

"And had Allah (so) pleased certainly would He have made them a single people, but admitteth He whosoever He willeth into His mercy; and the unjust, for them shall not be any guardian or a helper. Or have they taken besides Him, guardians? Allah, He is The Guardian, and He giveth life unto the dead, and He is over all things powerful."

"He (God) hath prescribed for you the religion what He ordained unto Noah and that which revealed We unto thee and what ordained We unto Abraham and Moses and Jesus, that: 'Establish ye the religion and be ye not divided therein;' hard is it to the disbelievers what thou callest them unto; Allah chooseth unto Himself whosoever He willeth, and guideth He unto Himself whosoever turneth (to Him). Nor were they divided until after had come unto them the knowledge, out of rivalry between themselves; and had not the word gone forth from thy Lord (respiting them) to a fixed time, certainly, the affair had been decided between them; and verily those who were made the heirs to the Book after them are certainly in disquieting doubt about it."

"For this then invite on thou (unto the truth) and be thou steadfast (on the Right way) as thou art commanded; and follow thou not their vain desires, and say thou (O' Our Apostle Muhammad!): 'Believe I in what Allah hath sent down of the Book; and I have been commanded to do justice between you; Allah is our Lord and your Lord; for us (is the responsibility) of our deeds, and for you your deeds; no contention (need there be) between us and you; Allah will gather us together; and unto Him is the ultimate return.'"

"Or for them are any partners (of God) who have prescribed for them any religion which Allah doth not sanction? And had it not been for the word of decision (to await until the Day of Reckoning), the decision would certainly have been made between them; and verily the unjust, for them shall be a painful chastisement. (On that Day) thou wilt see the unjust alarmed for what they have earned, and (the chastisement for) it shall befall them; and those who believe and do good deeds shall be in the meadows of the Garden; for them shall be whatever they please with their Lord; that is the greatest grace."

"That is of which giveth Allah the glad tidings unto His servants who believe and do good deeds; say thou (O' Our Apostle Muhammad!): 'I demand not of you any recompense for it (the toils of the Apostleship) save the love of (my) relatives;' and whosoever earneth good, We increase for him good therein, verily Allah is Oft-Forgiving, The Most Grateful (One)."

"He it is Who accepteth repentance from His servants, and forgiveth the sins, and knoweth He whatever ye do, and He respondeth to those who believe and do good deeds, and increaseth unto them of His grace; and the disbelievers, for them shall be a severe chastisement."

"The way (to blame) is against those who do injustice unto the people and transgress in the earth unjustly; these, for them shall be a painful chastisement. And indeed whosoever remaineth patient and forgiveth, verily this is an act of great resolution."

"Respond ye unto your Lord ere cometh the Day from Allah for which there is no averting; for you shall not be any refuge on the Day, and nor for you will it be to make any denial."(1)

"Are there any with questions before I continue?" Muhammad asked.

A flurry of arms went reaching for the sky. The Prophet eyed the crowd sifting, his sight rested upon Abdullah. He smiled with delight, thinking: even the young soon forget the troubles of the day when they reach out for the Word. He particularly liked the boy for his habit of writing everything down whenever he spoke.

"Young Abdullah, hath thou a question?"

"Oh, Prophet, have I noted at the beginning of some Surahs, saith thou certain letters. Wilt thou explain those letters?"

"Askest thou a good question. These are symbolic letters encoding divinely sealed secrets known only to Allah, The Majestic, myself, and those whom He purifies. If Allah willeth, it may be that in the fullness of spiritual development and understanding, one will know their meaning. Interpretation of these letters by anybody other than myself or those whom Allah Himself hath purified and blessed, is forbidden."

"Oh, Prophet," started Nafisah at Muhammad's nod, "which city is the Mother of Cities and wilt thou warn people in other lands?"

"In ancient times peoples of the earth worshipped Allah, The Most High, wherever they could: for there were no common places in which to gather for worship, except in Bakkah. Thus, Allah, The Ever-Living, appointed Abraham and his son Isma'il, alaihimus salaam, to restore the purity of His House which had been taken over by idolaters. They cleansed the Ka'bah of it's paganism, and established religious rites. The City was renamed Mekkah and peoples from all over, as they do today, came to worship. Also, the glad tidings and warning, will reach all people as falsehood cannot win over truth. So worry not thou, O' Nafisah, thy kinfolk will receive the Message."

An elderly man asked, "Oh, Apostle of Allah, who are the heirs to the Book?"

"It is about those who were given Scripture. If one could place side by side all the Scriptures as they were revealed, man would see that all the Apostles of Allah taught the same basic principles of Islam: the unity of Allah and righteous living. But people were arrogant and rebellious, and created doubts and indifference in the truth which had been conveyed to them through Allah's Apostles.(2) Each came for their people, and the followers named the Way taught after it's teacher. The Apostle Jesus, alaihis salaam, left the world prophesying the Spirit of Truth would give the Whole Truth.(3) Thus, Allah, the One God, now revealeth the Whole Truth and He Himself hath Decreed the Way."

As Muhammad signaled his uncle Hamzah to ask his question, a young boy's voice suddenly rang out from somewhere in the rear: "A rider is coming!"

All the while, guards from their vantage points along the ridges had observed a lone rider long before their prisoners in the valley. Some notched their arrows while others just watched, for none knew what to do. Their instructions were to keep the Muslims from leaving the area, and before they could decide what to do, Abu Ubaydah ibn Harth was dismounting within the camp. He led his mount to where the horses were kept, found an ewer of water and performed the rites of ablution and joined the congregation.

Muhammad silently thanked Allah for Abu Ubaydah's safe return and began the prayer. A short while later, upon completion of their devotions, he bid the crowd peace and anxiously returned to his tent to await Abu Ubayda's report. Al-Mustafa immediately embraced him as soon as he crossed the tent's threshold. Muhammad was the first to speak, "My friend, have I prayed for thy safety and counted the days for thy return. Yea, doth it bring much joy to behold thy smiling face again! Tell me, what news hath thou of my cousin Ja'far and our brethren in Axum?"

Smiling broadly, Abu Ubaydah's greeting was just as warm. He said, "There is so much news I find it difficult where to commence. Thy kinsman Ja'far, he is well and is a fine man of uncompromising principles, and has taken a wife who hast born him two strong sons. Thou shouldst have seen the look upon his face when I presented him with all the latest revelations. His eyes lit up like the sun coming from behind darkened clouds. He took possession of the leaves and immediately set scribes to work making exact replicas. Uthman and thy daughter Ruqayyah are well and send thee their love. The others are well also, and the community of Muslims has grown to over five-hundred men and women, and Islam is spreading to neighboring cities."

"People are hungry for the truth. I believe they are weary of paying the Christian priests for a place in the Garden, even king Negus asked for a Qur'an."

"Following a day's rest, I exchanged mounts and returned by way of Najran. Well received was I, and again it was like the sun coming out from behind darkened clouds when I delivered the Qur'an. They questioned after thee most solicitously and asked of our plight. They were very concerned. I could not tell them of the re-internment for I didst not know. A day's rest there, then I returned straight away..." The report continued on for another thirty minutes or so before he took his leave.

At the end of their second year of siege, the Muslims were still most patient and enduring in spite of the tremendous hardships, suffering and deaths. Muhammad had continued receiving revelations which strengthened the Believers in their faith and never did the besieged people weaken or show the slightest sign of compromise. Qurayshie leaders and other Disbelievers saw themselves as failing once again.

Meantime, the warners could not stop themselves from telling people about the nightly cries of hungry children filling the valley. Guilt, slowly began preying on the Mekkanese as stories of Muslim ill-treatment spread in an ever widening circle, causing a reversal of sentiment against the oppressors.

The siege lifted during the Holy months and Muhammad once again wasted no time in spreading God's Message. Every day of the Ukadh he taught and preached Truth, converting many more Mekkans and non-Mekkans into the true Way of life. And before the ending of the annual gathering, Muhammad asked his kinfolk to return back to the valley as word of their re-imprisonment circulated.

Following a few months after their return, the region entered it's second year of drought. And with the scarcity of life restoring rain, the area succumbed to famine which the infidels attributed to Muhammad's preaching against their gods.(4)

The great number of Believers forced to live outside the city with no chance of vying for the goods they needed to survive were reduced to eating the boiled hides of animals. And as the nearly foodless weeks passed into months, starvation started clamping it's ugly claws on Muslim stomachs. Mainly the old and very young died miserable deaths, others became skeletal in appearance. Khadijah's weight fell to less than a hundred pounds. Abu Talib, once a robust man, had now weighed just over a hundred and forty pounds. Yet, in spite of all the misery and privations suffered, the Muslims maintained their enthusiasm for Islam and refused to submit to arbitration where their beliefs were concerned.

A number of guards, having more compassion than others, began to publicly proclaim the siege unjust and unbecoming of Quraysh to impose their oppression upon a people warranting no such action. Their stories recounting the children's mewling cries as the pangs of hunger gnawed their insides, and the gruesome descriptions of emaciation worked again to soften many hearts. And God, never forsaking His servants in their time of testing, instilled among the humane the desire to smuggle food to His servants, thereby preventing Muslim mass starvation.

It was during the third year of the Believers incarceration that the Najranians began to rehear rumors of the Muslim situation. The

Christian men of Najran, in keeping with the Disbelievers, thought they deserved no less. However, the small Islamic community, concerned over their brethren's predicament called a council of elders and discussed for hours whether or not they should send a man to Mekkah to investigate. At meeting's end they decided fifty men could make the journey just as fast as one.

All fifty men, strong and rugged from desert life, rode with an unspoken urgency toward Mekkah. And what would have normally taken over a month of traveling time, took much less. As they rode into the city, their bearing, one of trained soldiers, caused a stir among the Mekkans.

Salim, acting as spokesman, questioned the first Mekkan crossing his path. "Ye there! Where can I find the Holy Prophet Muhammad?"

"Why? Art ye the shi'a of Muhammad," answered the man haughtily.

"Take thou heed of thy tongue and be not impertinent. For the Muslims are our brethren," retorted Salim sharply.

The man, taking a good look past Salim noticed the horsemen's stern looks and reined in his flippancy. He said, intimidation now inflecting his tone: "I implore thy pardon, lord. He, along with all the Muslims of the Hashim and Mut'talib clans are isolated under authority of Quraysh in a valley ringed with mountains on the city's far side."

"For what cause are they being held," charged Salim.

"Know I not, for that thou wilt have to read the document posted in the Ka'bah."

Salim, nettled over having his fears confirmed, dismissed the man with a wave of his hand. Penning their mounts, they made their way toward the Ka'bah.

Along the way, many Mekkans were feeling threatened and started blathering about the cruelty and unjust treatment the Muslims had been undergoing for years.

Zuhair ibn Umayya, a distant relative to Muhammad, Hisham ibn Amr, Salim and his men, along with scores of Mekkans were growing combative with each story and commenced to voice their opinions about the Qurayshies and other tribal leaders to people in the streets.

Roused by the rhetoric, others became overwhelmed with feelings of guilt and fell in behind Zuhair, Hisham, and the Najranians. United in purpose, the crowd marched for the Ka'bah. With emotions running at fever pitch, Salim stopped atop the Ka'bah's steps and beckoned Zuhair and Hisham next to him. Zuhair raised his arms for quiet.

"People of Mekkah, the siege inflicted upon the Muslims is not only senseless but brutal to say the least…"

While Zuhair spoke, Salim's men suspecting a group of well-dressed men as having part in the proclamation's order, delivered sidelong looks, making it clear to the suspected Disbelievers observing them that they could not make any objections without running the risk of violence.

"…is not Muhammad, his family, and many others in the valley, of Banu Quraysh? How can ye deal so unreasonably with thine own kin? Before he could add further indictment, the multitude roared out in acquiescence.

"Free Muhammad and the Muslims!" "Rip the publication to shreds!" And numerous other shouts were yelled out passionately. Surging forward, the crowd pressed the Najranians into the Ka'bah where they witnessed Zuhair and Hisham ripping the termite eaten document to pieces.

News of the Nis get rid of the hard tabs?ajranians inciting the Mekkans into defiance reached infidel leaders just as a horde of citizens and Muslims from Najran were arriving at the valley's entrance where Muhammad and the others were being held.

Abu Lahab, upon hearing the news, stepped to the window and stared in the valley's direction. Seeing the rising cloud of dust he swore a vile curse in the name of a man shaped god, then spun around to face his cohorts. Twisting his mouth into a snarl, he glared at the men surrounding him. He said, "Once more the gods have favored those accursed Muslims and before the tide turneth completely against us we must approach Muhammad with a proposition he cannot refuse."

Meanwhile, back in the Muslim encampment cries of alarm were sounded as the huge cloud of dust raised by the people coming to free them put everyone on alert.

"Women and children to the rear," bellowed Muhammad out over the din of frightened voices, then stepped forward to make his stand against the oncoming horde. His Successor, Ali, took his position next to the Prophet.

Up on the mountain tops, the guards were frightened by the mass of horsemen and people rushing in their direction. In fear they hastily deserted their posts.

Muhammad, recognizing Zuhair leading the scores of riders and hundreds of people, turned around and told those near him to spread the word that there was nothing to fear.

Zuhair, smiling from ear to ear, reined in his mount amid a cloud of dust. Jumping from his horse, he embraced Muhammad and exchanged greetings while the throng from Mekkah ran past them towards their kinfolk and friends. There were cries of joy and within minutes excitement was running wildly throughout the camp as news of their freedom spread.

Muhammad, before their new found freedom, had been waiting for mid-afternoon prayers to recite the Message received the night before. But caught up in the moment, it took him half an hour longer to start. He had excused himself from the men around him and asked Ali to gather the people to hear God's Word.

Less than a half hour later there were over four hundred and fifty people clustered in front of the Prophet's tent. A nervous tension settled over the crowd as Muslim and skeptic alike waited to hear Muhammad speak.

"Oh' ye people," began Muhammad, "last night Allah's Inspiration came unto me with yet another Message. It is because Allah is the Friend of the Friendless and the Help of the helpless that He heareth all sincere prayers.(5) Revealeth He how worldly pride and power are now humbled in the dust by resisting truth. The Disbelievers cannot fully realize what a tremendous thing it is that Allah is their Lord and Cherisher as He is The Lord and Cherisher of the Whole Universe.(6) Allah giveth every chance unto His creatures, however rebellious, to submit their wills. Some are thus reclaimed unto the path and some remain obdurate and learn not, until at the last: Judgment seizeth them with a mighty onslaught.(7) So, as I say the Lord's Words, know ye that His mercy and Grace protects the Truth."

"In the name of Allah, The Beneficent, The Merciful."

"Ha. Meem."

"By the Manifesting Book (Qur'an), verily We sent it down on a Blessed Night. Verily We have ever been warning. Therein are made distinct all wise affairs, (becoming) a command from unto Us; verily, We are the senders (of mercy and peace). A mercy from thy Lord; verily, He is The All-Hearing, The All-Knowing, the Lord of the heavens and the earth and whatever is between them two, if ye be sure in faith. There is no god but He; He giveth life and causeth death; your Lord and the Lord of your fathers of yore. Yet they are sporting in doubt."

"So await thou the day when the heaven shall give out a smoke clearly visible, enveloping the people; this will be painful chastisement."

"(They will say): "Oh, our Lord! Remove from us the torment; verily we are believers!""

"How shall they be admonished when there came unto them an apostle making (the truth) manifest, (and yet) turned they their backs unto him and said: '(He is) tutored (by others), a mad man.'"

"Verily, the tree of Zaqqum,(growing at the bottom of Hell), shall be the food of the sinful, like the molten brass; shall it boil in (their) bellies, like the boiling of hot water." "(There will be a cry saying):

'Seize ye him, then drag ye him down into the midst of Hell, then pour on his head of the torment of the boiling water.' (It will be said again): 'Taste thou; verily thou was forsooth the mighty, the honorable; verily this is what ye did dispute about.'"

"Verily, the pious ones will be in a secure place, in gardens and springs, attired in fine silk and in rich brocade, (sitting) face to face. So shall it be, and We will unite them with fair ones; with wide, lovely eyes. They shall call therein for every (kind of) fruit, (being) in security. They shall taste not death therein save the first death, and He will save them from the chastisement of the hell, a grace from thy Lord; this is the great achievement."

"So have We made it (Qur'an) easy in thy tongue that they may be admonished. Therefore wait thou: verily they (too) are waiting."(8)

At the Surah's end, Muhammad scanned the array of faces, expecting questions. But an unusual hush had draped over the crowd as everyone stared back apprehensively. The Message, mainly about Banu Quraysh, cut deep into the hearts of many, for it's implications inspired fear with it's ominous warning.

Ali finally raised his hand and broke the spell gripping the conclave. Acknowledged, he stood and asked if he could address the people. Given permission, he faced the congregation and said: "Oh, ye people, this Surah Prophet Muhammad has just recited affects me profoundly as it does a good number of ye. Most of ye know I am of the Mut'talib clan which is of Quraysh, but it's import has a wider meaning that is for all men to heed. And to those wanting in faith, turn unto Allah that ye mayest not suffer His Wrath when it cometh. Verily, for the righteous are Gardens of Bliss in the Hereafter."

"Jazaa Kalaah, Ali," said Muhammad, then added, "thy words were most appropriate."

When Ali ended, Muhammad was not surprised by the absence of raised hands as they thought of Allah's Justice. So with no more questions, he said: "As-salaamu alaikum," then sat down to watch the assembly disperse with an air of jubilation.

Salim, left standing with his men, asked them to standby. He approached Muhammad, "Oh, Prophet, is there anything I or my men can help with?"

Muhammad's mind, without his knowing or control, withdrew from the calm where within it's own depths he found refuge. Raising his eyes to meet Salim's, he said: "Ah Salim, thee and thy men have been of great service, may Allah bless thee. There are a goodly number of old and infirm whom can use the strong backs of thy men to assist with the return to Mekkah." The Najranians, having heard the Prophet's wishes, turned and left as one before Salim could ask. Left alone with Muhammad, Salim asked permission to join him which he graciously welcomed. Squatting down across from Islam's intrepid leader, Salim began relating the events which led him and his men to the valley.

Later that evening, with over three quarters of the camp already having departed, Ut'bah arrived to relay the Disbelievers' message.

Hamid, the first to see him, lowered his hand unto his dagger's hilt and challenged him about his business.

"I come in peace with a message for Muhammad," said Ut'bah, a bit unmanned by the young man's gestures.

Suspicious, Hamid unsheathed the wicked looking dirk several inches before recalling the Qur'an's admonition about those seeking peace. Squinting his eyes, he scrutinized the dusky terrain behind Ut'bah. Seeing no movement, he brusquely said: "Oh, Ut'bah, if at thy tongue's root lieth deceit be thou assured wilt I separate it from thy mouth." Then taking another glance around, he added: "Follow me. Wilt I escort thee to the Prophet." He led Ut'bah to the far side of what remained of the camp, near an area where numerous small boulders had amassed after rolling down the mountains.

There atop the largest rock they saw Muhammad silhouetted by the glowing light cast from the crimson mound of burning coals. No sound issued save the whispering breeze, the popping brushwood and twigs crackling in the small fire Muhammad built to ward off the desert's chill.

Hamid raised his hand, silently indicating for Ut'bah to halt, and called in a voice full of apology: "Oh, Prophet." Hearing no response, he turned and whispered to Ut'bah to remain where he was. He stepped toward Muhammad tentatively and again repeated his call. Once again there was no answer. Wondering if he might be intruding upon the Prophet's meditation, tremors of hesitation gripped his body as he began to circle around so he could approach from the front of Muhammad's position. Treading his way through the rocks, he suddenly stopped just out of Muhammad's line of sight. He could see that his eyes were riveted somewhere on the darkening horizon, he thought: never have I seen him so transfixed. Deciding to call once more before telling Ut'bah that Muhammad could not be disturbed, he took another step when the Holy Apostle spoke out.

"Hamid! Why art thou lurking about and where is thy companion?"

Hamid nearly jumped out of his skin at the suddenness of Muhammad's voice and stammered out: "Pro-Prophet Muhammad, pardon my intrusion but moments ago Ut'bah ibn Rabi'ah rode into camp. Saith he that he bringeth a message from the Qurayshie leaders. Hence, I brought him here and hailed thee but hearing no reply I started around to approach from thy front when thou spoke."

Muhammad turned in the direction he'd last heard two sets of footsteps and peered into the gloom. As if mesmerized, he just stared then said: "Ut'bah come forward." After Ut'bah made his appearance, he asked Hamid to leave.

As soon as they were alone Ut'bah said: "Oh, Muhammad, I am but a messenger of Quraysh bringing tidings of their wish to meet with thee."

"Tell the leaders of Quraysh I will come to them when all the Muslims and their belongings are in their homes."

Alone once more, Muhammad's gaze went back to the darkening heavens. His mind started drifting back over the years of hardships endured by Islam's followers. The siege, lack of food, exposure to the elements, and the rugged living conditions which had left many of the elderly in worse health than the year before. His uncle Talib, now nearing eighty, was weak, frail, but still full of spirit. Khadijah, his beloved wife, who out of compassion frequently forewent her meager food rations in order to supplement the crying children's diet, and now she too was badly malnourished. Suddenly Muhammad's feelings intensified, the supple veins in his neck enlarged and throbbed, his eyes glared with determination, pupils retracting into pinpoints, and his hands involuntarily clenched. He thought: we must persevere at all costs; from the falsehood mongers; the exploiters; the haters; the fools; and, the kafirun. Yea, they must be made to realize there is more to life than wealth and property!

A few weeks prior to the Ukadh's commencement, the Muslims were all settled back in the city.

CHAPTER TWENTY-TWO

The wind, blowing hard from the south western end of the Arabian peninsula was as arid as the barren plains of Egypt. Relentlessly it blew, leaving Khalid ibn Walid's face dry and gritty. He stood in contemplation, a goat skin water bag half raised to his mouth, in the desert west of Mekkah, wavering between belief in Islam and the beliefs of his forefathers. He thought: will Lahab always hate Muhammad; it is something more than the Way of Allah, his hatred is of many years, years filled with jealousies. He shook his head and turned towards the city, narrowing his eyes into a squint as if he could see it's citizens in the distance. I know not, may it be that men fear the new and must create opposition to fight against whatever they fear losing? It was then and there that he decided to visit Muhammad and discover for himself what Islam was all about.

Some days following Muhammad's return into the city, he awoke from a restless night of tossing and turning after deciding to visit the Disbelievers as he pledged to Ut'bah. Lately, the strain of anxiety caused by the constant harassment and aggression against Muslims, particularly the old and powerless, began to take it's toll. Knowing what had to be done, his heart started to pound in anticipation as he groggily slipped out from beneath the bed covers. He stood and listened but heard nothing save the drumming of his heart. He trudged toward the balcony overlooking the courtyard where he became cognizant of the sounds emitted from an awakening city, in the ashy light of dawn. Next, tilting his head to hear better, he noticed a slight rattling coming from downstairs in the now unusually quiet house. An odd sensation flashed through his mind and his heart renewed it's pounding. He experienced a foreboding unlike anything he ever felt before. Shrugging his shoulders as if suddenly chilled, he attempted to shake off the ominous aura of dread surrounding him. Descending to the house's lower level, he found Khadijah preparing the morning meal. He halted in mid-stride, the weight of gloom encroaching it's way back from oblivion. He could not see his wife's vitality or her exuberance for life any longer. Thin, frail, her once luxurious black hair was now infused with gray. Her eyes had sunk into her skull and the shadows were more pronounced. He thought: the most honorable of women, she has sacrificed so much and...

Sensing Muhammad's presence, Khadijah turned around and broke Muhammad's line of thought when she smiled.

"Khadijah," he said, "have I been considering that the Muslims should depart from Mekkah sometime soon. What saith thou?"

"Muhammad," she returned, her voice came out strained and raspy. She smiled as if in apology, then continued. "Thou knowest best, my husband."

He found her efforts to simply speak unbearably heartening and quickly replied, sparing her, "I must speak with Talib before I speak with the kafirun." He left the cooking area thinking The Most Merciful would soon call her into the Hereafter.

After the morning meal Muhammad departed, still unable to rid himself of the pessimism threatening to overwhelm him. The advancing heaviness seemingly spread to his limbs, his step becoming that of an old man. He stopped just after a short distance from the courtyard gate and looked back towards the house feeling a disquieting alarm. Concentrating upon the almost tangible feelings of apprehension, he said, as tears rolled down from the corners of his eyes: "Fi-amaan Allah, Ta'aala", and continued on to his uncle's home.

At Abu Talib's house his poignant sense of perception instantly gave warning. As he walked through the house his sense of premonition struck full force. He saw no one, the rooms were still and empty. Approaching his uncle's room he heard muffled sobs and his bodeful feelings returned with an intensity that made him tremble involuntarily. He stepped soundlessly towards the arched doorway, fear clutching at his innards. Abruptly, memories of his uncle's struggle to cope with the siege invaded upon the anxiety inundating him. Stopping at the threshold, he hesitated a moment recalling one of Talib's stanzas: "Thou hast guided me and knewest I thou art the truthful and I bear witness thou hast uttered the truth, and from before been the trustworthy one. Indeed know I that the religion of Muhammad is the best of the religions in the world."(1) He moved aside the curtain draping the entrance and peered into the room.

Hearing the soft swish of curtain, faces twisted around to see Muhammad standing there. He first saw the tear stained faces of his kinsmen, then several of the Disbelievers, and finally his sight fell on the lifeless body of Abu Talib. Muhammad remained where he stood, under the arch. Before the first tears of sorrow spilled from his eyes he flashed over his childhood years in his uncle's home.

Ibn Abbas watched painfully as Muhammad's countenance filled with grief. Deciding his brother's last words would help ease the suffering he approached him and related Abu Talib's will. "Oh, Muhammad, near the time of death Talib said unto us: 'I advise ye about thy kinsman Muhammad, because he is the trusted one of Quraysh and the truthful one of all Arabia. Possesseth he all the virtues and hath brought thee the religion of the One God, which hath been received by the breasts, but the tongues have chosen to deny it on account of fear of mockery. I can see that the weak and helpless of our land hath gotten up to support and believe in Muhammad, and hath he risen to help them break Qurayshie ranks. Hath he humiliated the chiefs and hath made the weak strong and given unto them standing. O' my kinsmen! Become thou the friends and supporters of his faith. Whoever followeth him enjoyeth prosperity. If death had given unto me more time, wouldst I have defended him from all dangers.'(2) Then as he was about to breathe his last, saw I his lips moving slowly. Couldst I not hear, thus moved I nearer to him and he uttered out the kalimat, the words of belief thou hast commanded one to declare.'"(3)

Muhammad thought: Indeed! Thou art like the Believer who hid his faith from Pharaoh. As he began to pray for his uncle's soul others started the preparations for burial.

The Disbelievers, after paying their respects, stopped Muhammad on his way out and started in with subtle offers of bribery to abandon the Call.

Muhammad's anguished mind cleared. And when he failed to react they tried persuading him which finally ended with thinly veiled threats. In his usual calm manner he listened to all they had to say, then to their surprise he asked: "Wouldst thou like dominion of all Arabia and rule other countries as well?"

"What!" Abu Jahl exclaimed incredulously.

Muhammad glanced at each of the Disbelievers, then looked Jahl straight in the eye. He said: "Say, there is no god but Allah and Muhammad is His Messenger."

Abu Sufyan, all the while taking heed of the conversation's direction, quickly interjected with comments belittling Islam's followers before any of the leaders could delve into the Prophet's notions.

Following Sufyan's long winded tirade Muhammad replied frigidly. "Be that as it may, my duty unto Allah, the One God, is by far greater than any loyalty thou canst purchase with wealth and promises! So, remember this day, the day of tragedy thou hast caused. There are no excuses for cruelty, it is a most despicable thing a man can do unto his brother."

Neither the Prophet nor the Disbelievers could see any forthcoming change in the other. And as the silence lengthened, the infidels started calling to mind the years of hatred thrust upon the Muslims. The tension mounted with each passing minute, becoming like a slowly rising barrier, penning them in.

Abu Jahl, always so adept in frustrating situations, now fumed mutely. Sufyan glared at Muhammad with dark, threatening eyes, attempting to instill terror but the Prophet reciprocated the stare with a steady gaze which made him turn away.

Feeling Abu Lahab's eyes burning into him, Muhammad turned to face his uncle. He was shocked but not alarmed, and showing no outward sign from the malignant look from which all sanity and reason had vanished, he watched Lahab's expression suddenly change as his breathing accelerated.

"Curse thee, Muhammad!" Lahab blasted out with measured fury, his voice full of venom.

Muhammad's mind blanked momentarily. He became oblivious to everything except the overpowering malice exuding from his uncle's eyes. He stepped up to his uncle until they were within an arms length of each other.

"Heed my words well, Abu Lahab," Muhammad said forcefully. "I too have something to say. Was I a fool to consider thee or the others might change thy evil and blasphemous ways. Seest I now that none of you will amend thy ways unless Allah willeth it to be so. Thus, want I nothing of thy evilness or falsehood. But be assured will I express and declare unto the people without need of priests or priest-craft; without miracles save those that occur with Allah's leave, without mystery, save those mysteries which unfold themselves in the growing inner experience of man and his perception of Allah.(4) I will explain to them that selfish pride of birth, the massing of power and wealth, the slaughter of female infants, the orgies of gambling and drunkenness, the frauds of impious temples with their idols and priests, the feuds and arrogance of tribes and races,(5) are all wrong. If willeth Allah, I will fight wholeheartedly to bring an end to thy power until all know that Life and Truth come from Allah, The Most High." Speaking his mind, he felt an alleviation such as one feels after being unburdened of heavy weights atop the shoulders. With nothing more to be said he spun on his heels and left the premises.

With the close of Muhammad's unexpected harangue, a tense silence fell over the room. Russal began to feel waves of alarm after Muhammad's departure and absently started using his fingers to comb through his scraggly beard in nervous apprehension. And knowing his masters would presently vent their anger he scurried from the area unobserved.

Lahab, Sufyan and Jahl, suffering the sting of humiliation more than the others broke the uneasy calm by bursting into uncontrollable rage. Almost in concert they started shouting obscenities at one another, then turned on their underlings, blaming them for their repeated failures to stop Islam. When of a sudden, Lahab ceased his ranting in mid-sentence and sharply raised his hand, demanding silence. His eyes turned vicious as his facial features came ablaze with demonical malevolence. Barely able to suppress the mounting violence within, his face acquired a devilish cast and the dark virulent eyes seemed to suggest something more invidious. In a voice becoming increasingly vile with mordacity, he dismissed their parasitic followers and spent the rest of the day cloistered with his peers. For hours they discussed new strategies, going over every detail. He wanted to know about Islam, Muslim habits, even the kind of foods they ate. Of course Jahl and Sufyan could not answer all his questions but he was nevertheless surprised at how much they did answer under his intimidating interrogation. Finally, the scant amount of knowledge Lahab accumulated led to the formation of new plans against Islam, and the closing admonition, "We must put a stop to this sorcerer!"

Following Talib's death, Muhammad instead of mourning, ardently continued to proclaim the Word of God. Several more Divinely Inspired Surahs were revealed. The Prophet's Companions, relentlessly searched out the city and neighboring townships for those seeking after truth.

After a long day in Mekkah's poor section, Muhammad asked Ali to return home and tell Khadijah not to expect him for the evening meal. He watched Ali until he turned onto another street. Retracing his steps past the impoverished section, he headed toward the mountains. Ever since meeting with the Disbelievers he'd been feeling the need for contemplation and reflection. And only in the Mountain of Light could he find the kind of peace he needed.

He entered the cave, immediately feeling an air of timelessness and tranquility. A sense of well-being flooded over him as he positioned his body to look out across the haze and smoke filled city. "Ignorants!" He vehemently expressed aloud as he thought of the infidels. He knew Abu Lahab and the other Disbelievers were tortured with unreasonable fears, but fear of what? Allah's religion didst not demand poverty, only to share a small portion of the bounty He bestowed. If they had any passion at all it was the passion for power. The intuition struck him for no discernable reason until his mind traversed back through the intricate maze of memories when the words leaped out with startling clarity: never be afraid for a scared man will never be in peace.

Suddenly overwhelmed with an earnestness, not for himself but for Islam, he wanted the world to know the beautiful truth of God's Religion and the peace one could harvest from it's precepts. Raising his sight in humble reverence toward the heavens to praise God, he noticed the sun's position and realized it was time for prayer. Rising to brush the dust from his clothes, he made himself as clean as possible then focused his thoughts upon The All-Mighty to purify his mind of any thoughts other than of the One God.

He made it home just as the sun's glow was fading into darkness. Crossing the courtyard, he stopped himself from opening the front door. Instead, he stood listening to the sounds within: Ali narrating stories; his daughter's laughter; Zayd's deep voice as he spoke with Maysara. Then wondering why he hadn't heard Khadijah, he opened the door and entered.

All conversation ceased the moment the door opened as everyone turned to greet Muhammad. He in turn returned their salutations and asked his wife's whereabouts. But before any could respond Umm Kulthum giggled and rolled her eyes sideways, indicating the back of the house where her mother habitually retired to await Muhammad and escape the summer's night heat.

Khadijah, upon hearing the sound of Muhammad's voice stopped reading the Qur'an and looked toward the doorway expectantly. When he appeared in the opening she smiled and thought: his beard; once of the deepest black was now streaked with gray as it fell in long waves over his breast; his face, what could be seen was tanned with dark serious eyes.

Muhammad greeted her warmly and affectionately which ended her reminiscence. He asked after the household's welfare as he took a seat in one of the stiff backed chairs.

"All is well," Khadijah replied as she rose from her seat. She suggested some refreshments to which Muhammad quickly agreed. She returned shortly with a small platter full of dates, nuts, and a goblet of juice. She resumed her seat.

"Thought I of thee all the way home from Cave Hira," said Muhammad. He did not need to elaborate fully or precisely to gain her comprehension. He thought: she seemed to understand with a minimum of words or an exchanged glance. Have we understood one another since the day of our marriage. Turning the cool goblet in his hands, he said, almost inaudibly: "I thank you, my beloved wife." He sighed and shifted his vision from her to take in the room's surroundings.

"I understand not these kafirun, why they like to control, to force their wills upon others. Even on animals!" Muhammad remarked. He sighed again, exhaling deeply, and stood up, his face clouding as he started pacing back and forth across the room. He felt disgust for those who received perverted pleasure from imposing their wills on others.

Khadijah said, after recognizing the agitated expressions crossing his face: "My husband, Allah's Ways are shrouded in ways we know not. Besides, thou shouldst not be troubled by their faithlessness and iniquities. Didst not thou say unto me, 'There villainy unwittingly served Allah's Cause by attracting attention to His Message?'"

"Ah," intoned Muhammad, "you are right my wife." He returned to his seat and sat down with deliberate hesitation. "It all cometh down to the fight against evil, the fight against those who see property and possessions as the only reason for living." Pausing momentarily to wet his lips, his brows drew together as the thought of Khadijah's weakening condition flashed through his mind. "Yea, wilt Allah's Message prevail."

Late that night Muhammad was in that ghostly region between slumber and wakefulness, where segments of one's dream drift into conscious thought then melt away, dissolving into kaleidoscopic images when his subconscious pulsated with the familiar tingling sensation of Divine Occupation.

"Oh, Muhammad," began the beatific voice of angel Gabriel, "trouble not thy mind with things thou knowest not. For all Creation is created for just ends, and Falsehood is but straying from the Path.(6) What the ignorant say is of no account, truth carrieth it's own vindication: follow it firmly. There are fine gradations in the Kingdom of Allah: thus strive for the best. All will come right in good time, so persevere with patient firmness of purpose. Justice that seems to tarry cometh really on swiftest foot but sure…"(7)

Khadijah awoke to the sound of Muhammad's slurred words as he spoke in response to God's seraphic spirit. Even before twisting around to confirm her thoughts, she knew he was undergoing Divine Disclosure. She rose from bed and crept out of the room. Returning minutes later, she had a small earthen vessel filled with cool water and fresh linen. As not to disturb him, she carefully slid a chair next to the bed. Not knowing how long the manifestation would last, she sat there watching, waiting, and wiping the perspiration dripping off his face. All the years of strain vanished as she fixed her mind on him. The only remnants of her ordeal were her once beautiful eyes, which had sunk into her skull, leaving dark shadows, and the under weight frame of her body.

In the meantime, Muhammad started repeating aloud the Revelation as it showed itself upon his mind: "In the name of Allah, The Beneficent, The Merciful."

"Ha. Meem."

"The descent (Revelation) of the Book is from Allah, The All-Mighty, All-Knowing, The Forgiver of sin, The Acceptor of repentance, The Severe to chastise, The Lord of bounty; there is no god but He; unto Him is the ultimate end of the (life) journey (of everything)."

"Dispute not about the signs of Allah save those who disbelieve, so (O' Our Apostle Muhammad!) let not their going to and fro in the cities deceive thee! Did belie the people of Noah before them and the parties after them, and did scheme every people against their apostle that they may seize him and they disputed by the falsehood that they might by it render into naught the truth, so I did seize them; and how (terrible) was then My retribution? And thus did prove true the sentence (the Word) of thy Lord against those who did disbelieve that they are the inmates of the Fire."

"Those who bear the Arsh and those around it celebrate the praise of their Lord and believe in Him and seek forgiveness for those who believe in Him (saying): "Oh, our Lord! Thou comprehendeth all things in (Thy) mercy and knowledge, therefore forgive Thou those who turn (unto Thee) and follow Thy way, and save them from the torment of the Hell: O' our Lord! Admit them into the ever-blissful gardens which Thou hast promised unto them and those who do good from their fathers, and their wives, and their children; for Thou art The All-Mighty, The All-Wise! And keep from them evil, and whomsoever keepest Thou from evil, this day indeed Thou hast bestowed mercy on him, and that is a Mighty Achievement.'"

"Verily, those who disbelieve, unto them shall a voice cry: 'Certainly, Allah's hatred (of you) is greater than your hatred of yourselves when ye were called upon unto the faith and ye did disbelieve!'"

"They shall say: "Oh, our Lord! Twice didst Thou cause us to die, and twice didst Thou give us life, and (now) we do confess our sins: is there then a away to get out (of this)?'"

"This (hath befallen you) for when Allah alone was called upon, ye did disbelieve, and when associates were assigned unto Him, ye believed; and (all) authority is Allah's, The Highest, The Greatest. He it is Who showeth you His signs and sendeth down for you from the heaven sustenance; but payeth not heed save he who turneth (unto Him). So call ye upon Allah, devoting religion exclusively unto Him, though averse be the disbelievers."

"The Exalter of the ranks, the Lord of Arsh; causeth forth He the spirit at His own behest on whomsoever He willeth of His servants, that he may warn of the day of meeting, (of) the Day when they shall come forth (from their graves), when naught about them shall be hidden from Allah. (A voice shall ask): 'Whose is the kingdom this day? (It is) Allah's, The One, The Subduer (absolute)!'"

"This day shall every soul be recompensed for what it hath earned; no injustice (shall be done on the Day); verily Allah is quick in reckoning. And warn them, then, of the approaching Day, when hearts shall rise up to their throats choking; for the unjust there shall not be any sincere friend nor an intercessor who shall prevail."

"He (God) knoweth the deceit (treacherous look) of the eye, and what the breasts conceal. And Allah judgeth with truth; and those whom they call upon besides Him can judge not any thing; verily Allah is The All-Hearing, The All-Seeing."

"And said he who hath believed: "Oh, my people! The life of this world is only (a passing) enjoyment, and verily, the Hereafter is the abode to last. Whosoever shall have wrought an evil shall not be recompensed but the like of it, and whosoever shall have wrought good, whether a male or female, and he (or she) be a believers, these shall enter the Garden, wherein they shall be provided with sustenance without measure.'"

""Oh, my people! How is it that I invite you unto salvation and ye call me unto fire? Ye call on me that I should disbelieve in Allah and associate with Him that I have no knowledge of, and I invite you unto The All-Mighty, and The Oft-Forgiving (Lord). No doubt is there that what ye call me unto, hath no right to be invoked in this world nor in the hereafter, and our return is unto Allah, and that the extravagants shall be the inmates of the (Hell) Fire. And ye shall remember what I say unto you, and I entrust my affair unto Allah: verily, Allah seeth well (His) servants.'"

"Verily, We do help Our apostles and those who believe, in the life of this world and on the day when shall stand forth the witnesses. The day when shall benefit not the unjust their excuses, and for them shall be the curse, and for them shall be the evil abode (in Hell). So be thou patient; verily, the promise of Allah is true; and seek protection for thy (followers) shortcomings, and celebrate the praise of thy Lord in the evening and the morning."

"Verily, those who dispute about the signs of Allah without any authority having come unto them, naught is there in their breast but (a vain desire) to become great, which they shall attain not; therefore seek (thou) refuge in Allah, verily He is The All-Hearing, The All-Seeing."

"Surely, the creation of the heavens and the earth is greater than the creation of people, but most people know not. Not equal are the blind and the seeing, nor those who believe and do good and the doers of evil (are equal); little is it that ye reflect."

"Verily, the Hour (of Reckoning) is to come, there is no doubt therein, but most people believe not. And saith your Lord: 'Call ye unto Me, I will answer you;' verily those who are arrogant to serve Me, shall soon enter Hell, disgraced."(8)

Khadijah had not been aware of the time passing, nor of dawn's pale wash streaming in through the curtained window's sides when she sensed, rather than felt, Muhammad begin to stir underneath the cool compress. She turned to replace the towel and noticed the light of day had broken. Reapplying a fresh compress, she thought: only a few moments ago had it been the dead of night.

Flat on his back, Muhammad slowly reentered the world of awareness. He opened his eyes and saw Khadijah leaning over him, pressing something cool upon his forehead. Love and tenderness overwhelmed him as he regarded her: even in her weakened condition she maketh time to watch over me. "Jazaa kalaah," he said aloud. Smiling warmly, he rose from bed saying: "My dear, Gabriel hath revealed another Message from Allah. But first let us prepare to offer salat, then will I tell you what was revealed."

At prayer's end, Khadijah asked: "Wouldst thou like me to wake Ali to transcribe the Message?"

"Nay my wife, take thy ease, will I awaken Ali to pen the Word."

During the past week people from the interior, the hills, and surrounding countries, had been arriving in Mekkah for the annual gathering of Ukadh. And much to the Disbelievers displeasure, the question most often asked was, "Where can one learn of Muhammad's teachings?"

Aside from Khadijah's poor health, it was time of great fulfillment for Muhammad. Daily, he taught and recited the Divine Message fourteen out of every twenty-four hours and still the people sought him out, either to ask questions or to declare their belief. The Qurayshies and other tribal leaders, meanwhile, were besides themselves with anger: for it seemed that everywhere they went the topic under discussion was Islam or the new Prophet of God.

Across the city up in the hilly section, Lahab was waking. It was well after sunrise when he rose from bed in search of a servant to prepare his breakfast. He shuffled lazily through the house, going from room to room, when of a sudden he froze in place. Off to his left, near the cooking area, two kitchen maids were deep in conversation discussing the number of people converting to God's Religion. Instantly angered, he burst into the room and screamed a variety of invectives. He finally ended his tirade by threatening them with the whip if they even so much as mentioned religion or Muhammad's name again. Then, ordered them to summon the other leaders of the opposition.

Jahl, Sufyan, and several other influential leaders arrived within the hour. As a group they entered the hall leading to Lahab's drawing room. Lahab heard their voices, and already livid with rage, stood up to face them as they made their way toward him. Malevolently, he stood gnarling his fists, eyes narrowing into slits, his face rigid in a grotesque mask of evil.

"We must end this talk of the Old Way and Muhammad now!" Abu Lahab bellowed out with seething fury. Following a short period in which he cursed God's Messenger, he finally suggested with malice aforethought that thieves and murderers be employed to single out Muslims for torture.

The next day, a Syrian, engaged because of his reputation for brutality and blood-thirstiness, departed Lahab's house with a purse full of silver dinars. He was a particularly cruel man: not so tall as powerfully built and when he loosened the silken cord of his greasy burnoose, one saw a walnut colored, bearded face; an intense violent looking face with scar tissue over the protruding ridges above his eyes; a bulbous nose; and, a wolfish smile that seemingly appeared at once sneering and beastly. Used to intimidating those around him, he defiantly set out for the marketplace in search of a victim.

On the way he came across a small kiosk where the men sat cross-legged, cajoling, bargaining, or purchasing outright a skin of nabeez; a fermented date juice, while prostitutes, beggars, and soothsayers vied for their attention. He decided to celebrate his good fortune at easy money. Several hours later, drunk, he started boasting of what he'd do to the first Muslim he encountered. His bravado not only called attention to himself but attracted two others hired for the same purpose. After a while, all three: Shaybah ibn Uthman; Zubayr; and the Syrian, left the booth with mayhem on their minds.

As they drunkenly wove their way through the city's narrow streets, a group of young toughs followed in their wake, lusting after the promise of violence. Doggedly, the men eyed everyone crossing their paths until one of the youth's treading on their heels called out: "To the right come three Muslims."

Unaware of the imminent danger approaching, Ammar, the orphaned adolescent son of Yassir and Sumayyah who were murdered for their beliefs, was coming from the square accompanied by Khabbab and Abu Fukayhah: two elder Muslims that had more or less adopted Ammar.

The cutthroats, allowing the Muslims to pass unhindered, fell in behind them as their following did behind them. At once, the Syrian initiated the conversation, ridiculing Islam while his cronies simultaneously curse the Prophet. But when the disparaging remarks produced no reactions other than effecting the Muslims to quicken their steps, they closed the gap between them. The Syrian viciously cuffed Ammar, propelling him into the dirt. The other two rogues, then, stepped in front of Ammar's friends to stop them from aiding the sprawled out youngster. The Syrian turned to join his partners and they began shoving the older Muslims back and forth in between them.

"Let us be!" Fukayhah angrily voiced.

"We wish no quarrel with thee," said Khabbab.

Ammar picked himself up. He thought of his parents' death, and in defiance of the danger, faced the three infidels squarely. He said: "We are peaceful men of Allah, and thou hath not cause to molest us."

At his statement, the ignominious men erupted with contemptuous laughter at Ammar calling himself a man. The Syrian looked down at the pugnacious youngster facing him and replied scornfully: "We need not reason to deal with the likes of ye. Why doth thou not call upon thy God to send unto us a grievous chastisement as Muhammad is fond of saying?"

As they renewed their laughter, Fukayhah and Khabbab took advantage to collect Ammar and retrace their steps in escape. But before they could take more than a few steps, Zubayr snatched Khabbab by the back of his robe and swung him to the ground where he started to kick him about the body. The Syrian did the same to Fukayhah, except he delivered a blow to his ribcage which doubled him over and then kneed him in the face that flipped him over onto his back. Shaybah, meantime, had seized Ammar by the hair and punched him full in the face until he dropped in insensibility, then turned to join his confederates. The sound of blows upon their bodies was so sickening, that all but the morbid turned away in disgust. Even the blood lusting youngsters turned away.

Ammar, regaining his senses somewhat, looked toward the fray and saw his friends being assaulted: both were curled in fetal positions, grunting with each blow while gasping for breath. Without thinking of his own safety, he rose shakily and charged Zubayr from the rear. He vaulted onto Zubayr's back and impotently begun to struggle with him. Zubayr's eyes opened wide in fright, thinking other Muslims had come to the rescue. Then realizing his assailant's ineffectiveness, he twisted around, grabbed Ammar off his back and slammed him up against a nearby wall where the youngster slid down the wall, laboring for air.

The Syrian and Shaybah, distracted by the commotion, spun around to look. "Art thou the grievous punishment?" Shaybah gasped out.

In that moment of respite, Fukayhah recalled a verse on one of the leaves compiling the Qur'an: "...and (those) who, when afflicteth them any great wrong, they get helped by themselves."(9) And knowing no blame would befall him in the sight of God, suddenly sprang to his feet, roaring: "Allahu Akbar," and catapulted into Zubayr, knocking him into the wall which stunned him into inactivity. Then whirled around and attacked the surprised Shaybah.

At the same time, Khabbab, following his friend's example, launched himself at the Syrian. The counterattack, carried out with such fierceness, completely overwhelmed the men into nonresistance. Sore, bruised, and bloody, Fukayhah and Khabbab helped Ammar to his feet and left the area.

Word of the Disbelievers' beating rapidly spread throughout the city and with each telling, the number of Muslims involved grew. By the time enemy leaders learned of the incident, some twenty Muslims had waylaid the three men who were out only to enjoy themselves at the bazaar.

Lahab was infuriated over the reports regarding his men. He sent couriers through the region, some as far as sixty miles away, with messages to Qurayshie allies requesting the chiefs to present themselves for a council at his house within three days time.

As expected, before the time limit expired, the ruling heads or their representatives of Banus Bakr, Khuza'ah, Makhzum, Thaqif, Hawazin, Sulaym, Zahrah, Khaywan, Kalb, Hudhayl, Malik, Madh'hij, the Jewish Kin'anah and branches, the Christian Tagh'ab and Bahra with their branches, arrived. It was a meeting such as never before seen. The leaders milled about waiting for the council to convene. One time rivals imagined the caucus a prelude to war. Rumors were running unchecked until, on the day of the third afternoon.

Abu Umayyah, another leader recently enticed into federating his clan with the opposition, summoned the tribal and clan chiefs into Lahab's antechamber. Entering the spacious inner sanctum, they were at once impressed by the room's opulent ornamentation. Low ebony tables set with platters of meats, fruits and nuts, were placed in a circle and ringed with bright colored cushions. Spaced at regular intervals were golden finger bowls filled with fragrant water. Matching decanters, reeking of aromatic wines and amber hued candelabrum adorned the table. The walls were veiled with intricately designed Hindu tapestries depicting lascivious scenes of their mythical gods, Siva and Shiva, others blazoned landscapes of nymphs, satyrs and fauns, obscenely engaged in acts of carnality. And standing in the far corner on raised bases were three huge idols: Wadd, in the shape of a man represented manly power; Yaghuth, shaped in the figure of a lion personified strength; and Nasr, shaped in the likeness of an eagle symbolized insight.

Once the men seated themselves among the cushions, Lahab rose and stood importantly, raising his arms for quiet. When the hubbub of excited whispers and murmuring subsided into silence, he opened the conclave with magnanimous salutations, mentioning each tribe and clan by name. He, then, delivered with unaccustomed eloquence the advantageous reward of allying their tribes against the rebellious teachings of Islam. And ended with the uncalled for brutal attack committed upon his men by twenty Muslims. The highly exaggerated episode so inflamed their passions, the newly formed Confederation enacted arbitrary ordinances to step up endeavors countering the Islamic wave, in spite of the prohibition of all types of violence during the four holy months.

Khalid was just attaining Mekkah's outskirts when he recognized his two friends, Budayl ibn Warqa and Ikramah, Abu Jahl's son, riding towards him. They were leaving the city on their way to Nakhlah, a small town about ten miles away.

"Look! Cometh ibn Walid," Ikramah exclaimed as he pointed.

Budayl raised his hand above his brows to block the sun's brightness. He said skeptically: "Art thou certain?"

"Aye, who but Khalid can sit a mount like that?" Ikramah returned.

Khalid, having learned his horsemanship at an early age, was legendary for his skills among the Arabs. In a dashing display of mastery, he dismounted and waited for his friends while his horse pranced to and fro.

Amid embraces and warm greetings, Budayl asked good-naturedly: "Whither hath thou been ye old scoundrel?"

"Was I," was all Khalid managed to say before Ikramah cut him off.

"It matters not," Ikramah interjected with an air of celebration. "Our friend hath returned in fine health. Hence, it is cause enough to up end the skin and drink from the fruit of the vine."

Consequently, the untimely appearance of Budayl and Ikramah disengaged Khalid's mind from discovering the truth about Islam.

CHAPTER TWENTY-THREE

During the ten years of Prophet Muhammad's Divine Mission, the truth of Islam had converted a multitude of people away from Paganism and the Trinity's reinvention. In Mekkah alone there were hundreds of Muslims. And along with the numbers came political power.

The Confederation, unable to stem Islam's tide washing over Mekkah, nevertheless continued their reign of terror and torture of Muslims. The latest to suffer at their hands was the attack on Sa'd ibn Abi Waqqas, which caused an uproar as Muslims cried out for retaliation.

He, and Sa'd al-Khudri who escaped unscathed, were returning from the marketplace when Uthman ibn Talhah suddenly stepped out from around a building and kicked Sa'd in the abdomen. As he fell moaning in pain, Uthman's friends, Micros ibn Hafts al-Achieve, Amr ibn al-As, and Walid ibn Ut'bah, joined the attack. Horribly beaten, Sa'd was then bound, his hands tied to his feet behind his back. The Disbelievers then placed a rope around his neck and dragged him through the streets. Left for dead, he managed to crawl away to a place of safety where he was eventually found hours later.

The assault had so enraged the Muslim community that a group of young men, wanting to exact revenge against the infidels for all their evilness, converged on Muhammad's home to ask for counsel.

Muhammad, seeing the height of their emotions, first calmed them down then sent for the elders. Twenty minutes later his sitting room was packed with the learned men and men of fighting age. Knowing the concerns, he reiterated the Qur'an's verses which he suspected some of the men may have used to base their grounds for retaliatory action.

Umar, thinking the opportunity for reciprocity had been mandated, excitedly began signaling for attention the moment Muhammad ended his delivery.

"Umar," called Muhammad.

"Can we now seek out the Disbelievers and fight them as ordained by Allah?" His question introduced a stillness into the room, causing tensions to mount. The warriors among them thought: at long last we can avenge the wrongs inflicted upon us.

Muhammad felt the abrupt change in atmosphere and noticed the only movements were heads nodding in agreement. He took several long moments to carefully weigh and consider the consequences his response would bring.

"Oh, ye who believe," began Muhammad, "of late, Allah in His mercy has indeed given unto us the right to right the wrongs inflicted upon us. But we must not seek a compensation greater than the injury done unto us.(1) Verily, in the past many of us have been subjected to persecution and unspeakable tortures. However, I fear if we were to redress the oppression against us now, the community bent on revenge(2) would exceed the bounds ordained by Allah, Who is Most Wise." He paused a moment to scrutinize reactions, then continued: "We are not a people cowed down or terrorized into submission.(3) The fact of our being here and learning the Great Truth attests to that. One's own defense, insofar as Allah's Law permitteth, is lawful and no blame wilt thou suffer. We must not seek out the transgressor to slake the thirst for vengeance, but to follow better ways leading to the reform of the offender or his reconciliation.(4) Forgiveness, however, is best for it reaps the higher reward in the Hereafter."

Muhammad's annotation into the problem seemed to have resolved the question at issue, for the air lost it's voltaic charge. There were a few who grumbled over the disinclination to wage war, but upon reflection saw the wisdom of the Prophet's words.

One evening six weeks later; Khadijah who rarely if ever, complained and told Muhammad that she could not prepare the evening meal because she lacked the strength. Muhammad eyed her critically, discerning more than her words communicated. Considering neither time nor age in relation to himself, he analyzed in an instant her depleting energy, the lost flesh, the bouts of sicknesses, and reaching the only conclusion possible, he realized the Angel of Death was drawing near. Abandoning all desire for sustenance, he asked Fa'timah to make the household's meal and retired to the bedroom where he spent the time near his wife's side. That night he was awakened by the flailing arms of his wife. He rose, lit an oil lamp, and tried to comfort her. Khadijah, in the throes of difficult breathing was becoming weaker and paler as he watched, then ceased to breathe.

At the moment of her passing Muhammad thought the house eerily quiet: the night's sounds seemed to have faded into a deep and echoless void. The moonlit room and it's air seemingly grew chillier, spectral and still. He glanced about the room where he had spent the last twenty-five years with his beloved Khadijah. Hours passed unnoticed as he sat there reminiscing the years of their lives. Then, when the slate colored light of dawn penetrated into the room, a gray bar of light fell across Khadijah's lifeless face. With each second her features became clearer until he saw her complexion. It was then her death assaulted his senses. He just sat there dazed and numbed. Once or twice he tried calling out to Maysara but the sound came out dull and pitiful. He started to call again but changed his mind and instead said the last rites and prayed for her soul.

Ali, the first to enter the bedroom after hearing Muhammad's prayers, stopped a few steps past the threshold. It was immediately apparent that Khadijah had passed on. His heart accelerated, pounding in anguish, and he began to weep.

Seconds later, Fa'timah, Umm Kulthum, Maysara and Zayd, rushed into the room. Fa'timah let out a loud mournful cry, tears gushing from her eyes. Her lips moved but her throat constricted in a spasm of grief. She seemed to shrink while mindlessly backing away until colliding with the wall where she crumpled in commiseration. Umm Kulthum covered her face with her hands, giving herself up to complete distress. Zayd and Maysara were simultaneously stunned into disbelief. They looked at one another, not only feeling the sorrow of losing someone dear to them but felt a deep compassion for Muhammad. Mechanically, they walked over to him and placed their trembling hands upon the Prophet's shoulders in condolence.

The pain tore away at Maysara with heart wrenching agony. He stood there next to Muhammad, frozen in sorrow long after Zayd departed to summon members of the clan. Around midmorning he pulled himself away from Muhammad's side who remained deep in grief.

Ali, Umm Kulthum, and Fa'timah, in the midst of their bereavement had taken places around the death bed where they remained subdued and listless until the elders sent them from the room.

Muhammad asked to be alone and silently watched through eyes filled with tears his loved ones vacate the room. He began to tremble as his inner anguish surfaced and pulsated into a tangible feeling of discomfort. Suddenly, he bent over and kissed his wife's cooling forehead and began preparing her body for burial. Finished, he intoned: "Allahu Akbar, Allahu Akbar, Allahu Akbar, Allahu Akbar. I bear witness that there is no god but Allah, Thou art alone without partners. O' Allah, this woman is Thy servant, daughter of Thy man and woman slave. Hath she come unto Thee, and Thou art the best resting place. O' Allah, I know nothing about her save what is good and Thou knowest more about her than I. O' Allah, increase her good deeds and forgive her faults. Bestow Thy mercy on her, and place her near Thyself in the Highest Station and be Thou Guardian for her family forever. Bestow Thy mercy, O' Most Merciful of those who show mercy." He turned and left, going to what had been Khadijah's favorite room. There he remained and prayed until the body was taken for internment the next day.

The day was bleak, overcast with huge rain laden cumulus clouds stretching from the Red Sea to the distant horizon. The grave, a raw ugly wound in the earth. Muhammad stood along side the open pit staring down into the black gash that contained his wife's shroud-covered body. He looked as gray as the heavens.

Zaynab, Umm Kulthum, Fa'timah, Jahsh and Umm Hani, weeping and disconsolate, stood to one side of Muhammad. Maysara, Zayd, Ali, Hamzah, Abbas, and Abu L'as, stood on the other. Surrounding them were friends of the family. After a few prayers consigning her to God's care, she was interned in the same valley in which they were incarcerated during their three year siege.

Once Muhammad had adequately recovered from his grief, the Mission pushed on. The infidels, with more than ten years invested persecuting the Muslims and opposing Islam, had created an air of doubt among themselves rather than one of enthusiastic support. Their arguments, designed to challenge Muhammad's authority and the Qur'an's authenticity had non-Muslims questioning their own ways of life and worship. However, there still remained an element of hard core Disbelievers in control of the city who refused to believe in the defeat that was slowly usurping their hold over the populace. Also, since Abu Talib's demise and Lahab's subsequent rise in the Qurayshie hierarchy, tensions had escalated into new levels of hostilities which exempted no one.

Ayyub, a transient from Ta'if, lured with promises of financial reward, fell in with Quraysh. He was of the same ilk as Russal, and like him, he started using every opportunity to retard Islam's growth. One afternoon he saw the Prophet walking alone through the narrow alleyways. He quickly scanned the vicinity searching for any who might try to provide aid. Satisfied there were none to help, he without reason or provocation began hurling refuse at Muhammad as he passed by.

Muhammad, who was returning home from his morning's visit to the Shi'b quarter, found himself suddenly hemmed in by a large throng of men and beasts. Absently he listened to the men and women speaking in strange languages, cameleers screaming to their herders contending with their struggling herds. The pace slowed and he started entertaining the notion of venturing beyond Mekkah's precincts to teach true submission to God. He decided then and there to seek out new avenues. High in spirits, he cut a path through the congestion and resumed his steady pace when something struck his back. Spinning around, he ducked and dodged as best as he could against the flying debris. He didn't say anything nor react with anger. Instead, he stood tall, full of dignity, and faced Ayyub. He stared him straight in the eye, brushed the rubbish from his clothes then turned to continue on his way.

When Fa'timah saw her father come through the courtyard gate covered with offal she burst into tears. It was too much for her to bear: her mother's death and now her father's ill-treatment. She ran to him, crying out: "Oh, father, how couldst they? How couldst they?

"Shed not tears, my daughter," responded Muhammad. "Allah will protect me."

Soothed and comforted by her father's words, Fa'timah tears dried up as she went to get him a basin of clean water and clean tunic.

Later that evening the household was subdued over the growing amount of incidents involving Muslims, let alone the Prophet. Hoping to change the mood, Muhammad informed them that he had decided to journey to Ta'if where he hoped to find a safe haven from the never ending persecution.

"Zayd," said Muhammad, "wouldst thou travel with me? May it be that together we can find a refuge for our brethren."

Zayd consented with no hesitation.

Muhammad, then, turned to his Chief Deputy and Successor. "Ali, thou art in charge here. So please Allah, The Exalted, on the morrow wilt Zayd and myself be leaving for Ta'if."

Early next morning the two rose and started off for Ta'if, a small city some sixty miles away. Along the way they stopped at Nakhlah where Muhammad at once began to proclaim the Message. Unfortunately, the town's response was no different than that of the Disbelievers back in Mekkah. Finally reaching Ta'if, they entered the city followed by a horde of children asking them their business.

"Zayd," said Muhammad, "tend to our lodgings whilst I seek out how we are to be received." Going into an edifice used for worship, Muhammad saw the humanistic shaped idol Lat dominating the chamber's interior. He should have known but nevertheless the disappointment spread across his face. As he watched the men and women supplicating and glorifying the grotesque caricature, he maneuvered through the idolaters until reaching a corner free of any idols.

"Oh, people of Ta'if," Muhammad said, then had to stop and clear his throat several times before he could get their attention. "Oh, people of Ta'if, I come unto thee to proclaim the One Truth, and bring glad tidings, and as a Warner to men. There is no god but He, Allah, The One and Only God. Commandeth He to eschew all evil, for man was not created without purpose of responsibility.(5) Man was evolved out of nothing and given insight and understanding. Allah showed him the Way, and if man doth willfully reject the Right, chooseth he but chains, yokes, and a Blazing fire for his own soul.(6) Never canst evil escape Allah's Order and Law: His angels are ever present to bring the wicked to their bearings and they ever strive and press forward to bring comfort and succor, and Allah's Mercy unto those who seek it.(7) And those who attain the Path of Righteousness, in full felicity and honor will they live in the Garden of Delights, and share in the Banquet, the Presence and Glory Divine!"(8)

"Can ye not see, O' men, the mighty works of Allah in the heavens and on earth? The darksome splendor of the Night with it's multitude of Stars. And the daylight splendor of the Sun? How the earth, with its spacious expanse, and it's mountains, yieldeth moisture and pasture, and feedeth and sustaineth men and cattle, through Allah's wise Providence? Transgress ye not then the bounds and earn not the fire or Punishment, but fear Allah and His Judgment.(9) With every breath of our life, cometh nearer and nearer the appointed Hour of Judgment where the proud and haughty will be brought low.(10) The Day of Account is an event Inevitable. Thus, is there-"

Muhammad was rudely cut off from saying any more by one of the town's leaders who had been listening more or less to humor the Prophet from Mekkah. He started asking scurrilous questions which caused a deal of laughter, then voiced disapproval for attempting to disrupt their way of life. And because of the interruption and biting remarks the people who were listening lost interest. They dispersed talking about the man from Mekkah who preached the existence of only One God and another life after death.

Falling short of his hopes to find refuge and a people receptive to God's Message, Muhammad left the temple preoccupied with thoughts of the Brotherhood. A moment later, he turned to Zayd who had joined him shortly after he began his delivery.

"Zayd," said Muhammad distractedly, "for now, the town's leaders have too strong of a hold over the people. But no matter, insha'a Allah wilt we try again." Zayd was only too happy to quit the area, for he didn't like the black looks he saw directed towards Muhammad.

The next two days brought more of the same. On the third day, under bidding of the town's chieftains, Muhammad and Zayd were attacked. Zayd was the first to recognize the coming trouble when he noticed the trouble-makers of the past two days gathering on the crowd's fringes. Becoming alarmed, he turned to Muhammad who at the time faced the opposite direction. He said: "Oh, Prophet, thinkest I it wouldst be best to leave this place at once!" Just as he ended his warning the first stone flew past. Startled, Muhammad stepped around to look and was struck with a rock. Zayd cried out something but his voice was drowned out amid the shouts. He grabbed the Prophet by his hand and fled the area.

The mob, not content with the injuries inflicted, let alone their escaping, gave chase, all the while hurling stones and invectives. The barrage of rocks were mainly striking Muhammad, yet a good portion had struck Zayd as well, leaving both men cut and bleeding in several places. With the pursuit continuing for more than a half mile, the mob soon became tired and ended the chase.

The Prophet and his Companion never once looked back to check the rabble's advance. They kept running and running until Muhammad faltered and collapsed from exhaustion. Zayd, mindless of his own injuries, dropped to the ground next to Muhammad. He cried out to God with tears of anguish spilling down his face, asking Him to curse Ta'if's leaders and it's Disbelievers. Then, having vented his anger, he noticed a low wall nearby and thought it would afford some protection should the infidels return. He collected Muhammad in his arms and carried him over the wall where he began to wipe away the dirt and blood from his mentor's cuts.

Shortly thereafter, al-Amin regained his strength much to Zayd's relief. Sitting up, he twisted around to look over the wall and twinged from the pain. Suddenly feeling the weight of dejection descend upon his shoulders, he turned back around and observed his Companion's face marred by lumps, bruises, and cuts. It caused him greater pain to see Zayd suffer so. He shifted his sight up to the heavens, raised his arms in petition and put into words his anguish.

"Oh, Lord! Unto Thee alone make I complaint of my helplessness, the paucity of my means and my insignificance before mankind. Thou art The Most Merciful of the merciful. Thou art the Lord of the helpless and weak, O' Lord of mine! Into whose hands hath Thou abandoned me, into the hands of an uncompromising enemy who wouldst impudently scowl at me, or unto the foe who hath been given control over my affairs? But if Thy Wrath doth not befall me, there is nothing for me to concern myself with. I seek protection in the Light of Thy Countenance, which illuminateth the heavens and dispelleth every darkness, and governeth all affairs in this world as well in the Hereafter. May it never be that I shouldst incur Thy Wrath, or that Thou shouldest be wrathful unto me. And there is no power or resource, but Thine alone."(11) Dropping his arms to his sides he closed his eyes and drifted off into an uneasy sleep.

Zayd, also, succumbed to fatigue and fell asleep.

Some yards away, Addas, a bondsman who had been tending his master's orchard, heard the beautifully intoned supplication. Intrigued, but fearing another trick by his owners to discover whether or not he'd stopped his belief in the One God, acted as if he hadn't heard and continued on with his duties. He waited for more than a quarter hour before he nonchalantly edged closer toward the wall. Seeing no one, he glanced about suspiciously and was about to dismiss the incident when the solemn litany echoed through his mind. Deciding to investigate further, he went up to the wall and saw two men who looked like they'd been trampled by horses, slumped against the wall sleeping. He turned and ran back to his master's house.

He returned minutes later bearing a skin full of freshly drawn water, strips of linen, and a bowl filled with fruits. Finding the strangers as he left them, he looked from one to the other then knelt down next to Muhammad because of his severity of wounds. While he ministered to Muhammad's injuries, he noticed him sweating profusely, as if in strenuous exertion. Thinking the injuries were more than superficial, he entreated God's help.

Zayd came awake with a start the moment he was touched, fearing another attack as his whereabouts registered in his mind. He edged back and looked around apprehensively.

"As-salaamu alaikum," said Addas. "There is no one to harm thee or thy companion."

"Wa alaikum salaam," Zayd returned.

Zayd saw the truth of his words and said: "May the blessings of Allah be upon thee and thine kindred for thy mercy. I am called Zayd ibn Harith." Then looking over to Muhammad, his eyes lit up with gratefulness, seeing the Prophet's dressed wounds. He added: "Will Allah look favorably on thee for thy kindness to His Holy Prophet. Doth thou not know of him? Muhammad, the son of Abdullah?"

Before Addas could answer, Muhammad opened his eyes which ended their conversation.

"Al-Hamdu lillah Rabb al Alamin," Zayd exclaimed. "Muhammad, this man came to our aid and attended unto our injuries."

"What art thou called," asked Muhammad.

"Addas," he returned. "I am a Christian from Nineveh, indentured to Ut'bah ibn Rabi'ah." Muhammad and Zayd looked at each other curiously at the mention of their enemy's name.

"By thy expressions, I assume he is an enemy unto you for thy beliefs. But worry thyselves not, for he and his sons are in Mekkah," Addas said while offering them a bowl of fruit. Muhammad, feeling better, took the proffered fruit and thanked Addas. Before eating, he said: "In the name of Allah, I ask Thou to bless this sustenance Thou hast provided from Thine Bounty." Then bit into the date.

"Is He the Only God thou callest upon, the God of Abraham?" Addas probed.

"Verily, Allah is The One God of all mankind. He is the Lord of Creation. And it is He Whom I call upon and no other, for there is no god but He." Excited by Muhammad's answer, Addas asked more, seeking the fulfillment Christianity lacked.

Seeing his enthusiasm, Muhammad said: "Oh, Addas, there is much to learn about the Incomparable, the Originator, but in what time we have will I explain to thee which thou seekest. Allah is One! Not the irrational hue and cry of three gods in one which the Bishop Athanasius of Alexandria propounds. Since the time of His first

194

Prophet, hath He sent them to guide, instruct, show the Way, and proclaim His Word. Not to drive people to do good, but to convey the Message of Truth, in all the ways of persuasion that are open unto them. If men perversely disobey that Message, they disobey not the prophet but disobey Allah.(12) He hath sent the truth unto many nations as a matter of sacred trust, commanding the Message to be broadcast and taught and made clear to all within reach. But priesthood at once erected barriers, claiming sole responsibility for the making public His Word. But worse, they tampered with the Truth, taking what was convenient and ignoring the rest(13) because they feared men rather than Allah."(14)

Addas continued to question Muhammad for over an hour and at the end of their discussion, he declared his belief, his allegiance, and joined the ranks of true Brotherhood.

Muhammad said: "It is pleasing to see another put aside his prejudice and enter Allah's Way of life. In answer to my prayer, The Possessor of Highest Reverence made it known unto me to distress not: for by the buffets of a world steeped in selfishness,(15) arrogance, or by man's persecution, He, (God), will deal with His enemies fittingly. (16) The Day of Account will surely come and man's conscious will bear witness against the evilness his own hands have sent forth. Thus, rely on Him alone and let not Allah's service be a matter of difficulty: do all thy duties in wholehearted remembrance of Him and ever seek His bountiful Grace."(17)

"Hence, hearken ye unto what hath been revealed, whilst I lay resting: for I am commanded to proclaim the Truth."

"In the name of Allah, The Beneficent, The Merciful."

"Say thou (O' Our Apostle Muhammad!), 'I only pray unto my Lord, and I associate not with Him any one.' Say thou, 'I own not for you any evil or good.' Say: 'Never can protect me against Allah any one, and never find I besides Him, any place of refuge.' Save a delivery (of the Message) from Allah, and His Messages; and whosoever disobeyeth Allah and His Apostle, verily, for him shall be the fire of Hell, they shall abide in it forever."

"Until when see they what they are promised, and then shall they know, who is weaker in helpers and fewer in number. Say: 'I know not whether that which ye are promised is nigh or if my Lord hath appointed for it a distant term. (He alone is) The Knower of the unseen, and nor doth He reveal His secrets unto any. Save unto that one of the apostles whom He chooseth, for verily He causeth a guard to march before him and after him.' That He may know that indeed they have delivered the Message of their Lord, and He encompasses (by His knowledge) all that is with them, and taketh account (God) of everything."(18)

"Hast thou a compilation of the Scripture with thee," asked Addas as soon as Muhammad finished rehearsing God's signs.

"Indeed, my brother. Hath His Word been transcribed precisely as it was revealed unto me. Insha'a Allah, the next time thou art in Mekkah thou wilt be given a complete transcription of what hath thus far been disclosed."

At that, Addas said with an air of newly found strength: "My friends, remain here whilst I fetch ye supplies for thy journey back to Mekkah. Canst I not replace thy mounts for I am a poor man, but by Allah wilt I restore the nourishment from His enemies to sustain thee back to the city."

The trip back was slow and uneventful after the hard-hearted and cruel reception of Ta'if.

CHAPTER TWENTY-FOUR

Once back in the city, Muhammad resolutely began to deliver the Holy Message. The Confederates, with ungodly Qurayshies directing tactics, never let up their inhumanity towards God's followers. And after another particularly brutal attack, the Holy Apostle of God lapsed into a state of impasse.

The Disbelievers latest act of aggression weighed so heavily on Muhammad's mind he began to review the adversity, the many appalling experiences, and tragedies of the past ten years. Unbeknownst to him, it was at this critical time that he would embark upon a journey of remarkable significance, rendering him a great deal of psychological comfort and asseverate the magnificence and glory of the Lord of the worlds.

It started the next day. Muhammad was returning from Cave Hira late in the evening when he decided to spend the night at his cousin Umm Hani's home. Answering the late night knock, Umm Hani welcomed the Chosen one in. Pleased, she began expatiating about her children, more for her own sake than that of her cousin's. Suddenly taking note of the drawn look in his eyes, she stopped her flow of words and asked: "Oh, Muhammad, is there anything I can do to ease the heaviness in thy heart?"

"Nay, I am just in need of some rest," he replied, not wanting to burden her with his problems.

Umm Hani raised her brows knowing better but held her tongue, and watched him leave the room to retire for the night.

During the night Muhammad started stirring in his sleep. He mumbled out his concerns then grew mute as perspiration began flowing from his head and the bands of Divine presence enclosed about his breast. In the center of his mind's unlimited capacity, the void silently exploded with illumination. His mind's eye involuntarily contracted against the splendor then sharpened to take in the phenomenon. Awed, he directed his second sight straight into the blazing luminosity. Mesmerized, his mouth unconsciously fell open as he stared in wonder. Next, he started blinking as fast as his eyes permitted while he watched particles of light coalesce into the majestic configurations of Angel Gabriel and a pearl colored stallion, resplendent with enormous wings.

Gabriel communicated directly with Muhammad's consciousness: "Come, O' Prophet Muhammad. Sit besides me, astride Buraaq. The Lord thy God hath decreed that thou be shown the grandeur and supremacy of His Works."

Muhammad felt as though he floated across the room onto Buraaq. He, through thought transference, asked: "Will not the others miss me?"

"Without the mantle of time or separation of space (1) the duration is of no consequence. Our journey will last less time than it takes to blink an eye," came the reply. Buraaq suddenly reared up on hind legs and soared heavenward. Muhammad involuntarily tensed.

"Have not fear, O' Prophet," the Archangel voicelessly intoned.

He relaxed and sat hypnotically as he underwent the marvels of flight. His bird's eye view witnessed what no mortal man had ever before seen. The landscape expanded with the increasing altitude until it curved out of sight in all directions. The sun, cresting over the distant horizon flooded the land in daylight. Yet, as they navigated through the celestial regions; night, with it's multitude of heavenly bodies encompassed them about. An instant later they were hovering over Mount Sinai where Prophet Moses received God's Commandments.(2)

"Oh, Muhammad, what thou beholdeth art the Signs of Allah revealed unto thee, so thou mayest make them clear unto men. From the most ancient of times didst thy Lord's prophets proclaim what He hath named taught thee. And here atop this Mount was the Law given unto Moses. Didst the Lord thy God tell Moses to exhort: thou shalt have no other before Me; thou shalt not make unto thee any graven image, or any likeness of ANYTHING that IS in the heaven above, or that IS in the earth beneath, or that IS in the water under the earth; and thou shalt not bow down thyself to them, nor serve them: for I the Lord thy God AM a jealous God...(3) Yet, the Law was violated by the very people who claimed to be it's custodians."(4) Buraaq, like a streak of light flashing across the heavens, winged his way to Jerusalem.

"Here atop the Mount of Moriah sitteth in ruins the Temple of Solomon,(5) and it's history is amongst the greater Signs. Solomon didst complete the building of the Temple a millennium before the arrival of Prophet Jesus. Then, a little over four centuries later, the Wrath of Allah was poured out unto the Jews(6) for their backsliding and arrogance. The Babylonians under Nebuchadnezzar penetrated Jewish lands,(7) destroyed their Temple and carried away the men and women into captivity.(8) There they remained under the iron fist of Babylon for sixty and six years. Afterwards, Cy'rus, the king of Persia, in his first year of reign issued a proclamation bestowing the Jews their freedom.(9) Returning, they started life afresh. And under Ezra and Nehemiah, they rebuilt the Temple, carried out various reforms, and fashioned a new Judaism.(10) Ezra, with no true text of the Law of Moses,(11) used the law promulgated by priests and scribes in the reign of Josiah(12) which came from Hezekiah's account of the Law, after combining two versions of sacred history, some one hundred years before Josiah. And then Ezra rewrote the Law again."

"Consequently, Israel in the course of time didst revert to transgressing against the Truth. Thus, Allah divested the Jews of His Grace. Hence, Antiochus Epiphanes, one of Alexander the Great's successors, usurped the seat of power from his brother in Syria and used his throne to subject the Jews. His follower Jason, seized position of high priest in the collapsing religious hierarchy and turned the Temple into a house of idolatry."

"Next amongst His Signs, the Romans made Antipater of the Idumaean dynasty, procurator of Judaea. His eldest son Phasaelus was made governor of Jerusalem, and Herod over Galilee. Five years later, Antipater was slain and the Jewish people placed under his son's governance. And within the year the brothers found themselves engaged in hostilities with Antigonus, the last of the Asmonaean line. Phasaelus was captured and Herod, with Roman support, routed Antigonus from Jerusalem. Herod, then, on a visit to Rome two years later was made king of Judaea. He returned to Jerusalem and the city began to thrive under his reign, until Antigonus again rose up against him. Herod retook command of the city and Antigonus was done away with. Thus, with no lineage to further Jewish fealty, being descended from Esau rather than of Ja'cob, he undertook the task of reconstructing the Temple, hoping to gain their loyalty. But his efforts were wasted, yet the city continued to prosper for a time."(13)

"The Jews, however, again manifested their flagrant irreverence for the Law in the time of Prophet Jesus. Hence, to show mankind the personality of Israel, Allah unleashed Titus, son of the Roman Emperor Vespasian, to destroy any credit or power garnered from their distinction. And the inevitable doom followed in the destruction of the Temple some seventy years after Prophet Jesus."(14)

Buraaq's ears suddenly straightened and the mighty equine gravitated toward the earth. Muhammad found himself standing in front of a large gathering of prophets leading them in prayer. At prayer's end, Muhammad was again atop Buraaq. Gabriel commanded the powerful stallion to soar. Buraaq's nostrils flared, emitting thunderous snorts, and with a forceful thrust of his wings ascended towards the uppermost regions of the heavens. Again, Muhammad marveled at the mysterious workings of the universe, wondering how from the light of day they could enter the darkness of night and now emerge into the ethereal light of the Kingdom of Heaven.

As they soared through the firmaments, Muhammad became witness to God's Glory. There were beautiful picturesque gardens, filled with the sound of bird song, all harmoniously in tune. Birds, rare and exotic, were feathered in colors spanning the spectrum. Verdant trees abounded everywhere, yielding luscious fruits the like of which he'd never seen before, others flourished with succulent red pomegranates, dates and other recognizable fruit. Flowers of every tint and shade grew from the richest beds of loam he'd ever seen, and permeated the gardens with an emanation of indescribable fragrances. The grass was of the greenest hue and so sumptuous it appeared to carpet the landscape. Sparkling water bubbled out of crystalline springs which flowed ever so melodiously as it nourished the herbary. Living souls, attired in luxurious vestments were everywhere, and as he passed through, the maidens with their big, beautiful eyes chastely restrained their glances.

Interpenetrating another garden, he observed a number of souls dressed in garments of fine silk, reclining on thrones of pure gold and encrusted with precious jewels. Instinctively he knew that these souls were foremost in faith, for only those could cast a countenance of such sagacity. There were prophets from ancient times and some from later eras, attended by youths of ever lasting wholesomeness bearing platters of fruits, the flesh of fowls, others carried goblets embellished with gems and filled with the elixirs of heaven. Their companions, equal in age, were undefiled and beautiful. Without warning the thought suddenly struck: this is the garden for those nearest to Allah!

Just then Buraaq slowed and came to a stop. It appeared as if they arrived at the edge of the universe. A feeling of dread infused itself in Muhammad's consciousness. Buraaq whinnied his aversion. Muhammad peered over the brink, down into the bowels of Hell.

Putrid black smoke and the mordant smell of burnt flesh filled his nostrils. Terrifying screams and cries of sufferance assailed his auscultation, inspiring raw fear to course through him. Swallowing his fright, he looked closer. There in the place of torment, amidst a blazing conflagration stood seven massive gates guarded by angels wielding huge flaming swords, and wearing the most uncompromising expressions. Their swords were fierce weapons as each emitted bluish sparks of fire. Their wings were not feathery as he thought but rather leathery looking.

Muhammad's commanding view over the infernal regions afforded him to see beyond the portals of Hell. In sort of a staging area, angels held flaming swords above their heads ready to smite. They were bellowing: "Enter ye the gates of Hell, to abide therein and wretched the abode of the arrogant!"(15) Other angels were seizing sinners by their forelocks and feet,(16) binding them together and casting them into constricted places.(17) Their cries answered with: "Call ye not this day for one death but call ye for death multiple!"(18) In another area, he saw sinners heavily chained with fetters, yoked about the neck and covered with liquid pitch, being consumed in fire as an angel retorted to their petitions of mercy: "This is the Hell which ye were promised, enter ye into it, for ye were disbelieving!"(19) Shifting his vision he came upon others mired in seething fetid mud with boiling water pouring over their heads, scalding their bodies while being told : "Taste ye the torment of the burning (Fire)!"(20) Looking elsewhere, others were bound to iron pillars amid incandescent pools of fire, choking, gasping as the fires of Hell seared their lungs. Their wailing rebutted with: "Taste ye the chastisement of the fire which ye used to belie!"(21) Again, he shifted his vision to see others being seized and dragged into the midst of blazing fires, given fluids the like of molten brass to drink. Their outcries sternly acknowledged with: "Taste ye then! And never will We increase for you aught but chastisement!"(22) Unable to bear any longer the sounds of their agonizing screams and the repetition of their punishments, he strained backwards, unaware of his legs pressing Buraaq's sides.

Buraaq reflexively moved back several steps.

Muhammad, his face drained of all color, sat long and silent while staring off into the void. After a time, he turned to face the ministering Spirit. Gabriel judiciously weighed Muhammad's state of mind, then issued a silent command to their winged mount.

Buraaq abruptly reared forcefully, forelegs pumping emptiness, great blasts of air discharging from his nostrils, and swiftly winged away, zooming toward the pinnacle of Heaven where the greatest of all honors awaited the Holy Apostle.

As they soared up into the loftiest realm of Heaven, the underlying Heavens were incomparable with the magnitude of grandeur in God's Kingdom. All at once, Muhammad began to feel inconceivable power emanating from it's zenith. He started trembling as tremors of fear rippled up and down his spine. His thoughts abandoned him as the Omnipotence of His Presence absorbed all energy.

Buraaq came to a halt with a gentle flutter of wings.

Lost in amazement, Muhammad, the Chosen, gazed upon the Light of the Worlds. It was a sight beyond description. He could only bask in the Radiance and Magnificence of The Eternal Blessedness.

As Muhammad returned to the world of time and space, he noticed a small caravan heading for Mekkah. Buraaq winged over it, low enough for him to take in it's detail. It was unusual, he thought, for he could not perceive it's significance. Suddenly Muhammad was wide awake, still in the grasp of Divine Bliss. He rose from bed and walked into the main room of the house.

A startled gasp burst forth from Umm Hani. Muhammad's eyes were shining abnormally bright and transmitting a palpable energy which she instantly felt. His whole look was one of unearthly occupation. She, recognizing the look of Divine enlightenment, immediately set about asking the others to leave the room, explaining Muhammad needed sometime to prepare himself for the day. When the last of the family members left the room, she asked excitedly: "Oh, Muhammad, hast thou received another Sign?"

He stared blankly at his cousin, unaware of her observation or question. With absence of mind he watched her lips move but the sound couldn't pierce the aura of rapture engulfing him. Consequently, she had to repeat her question several times before her inquiry sliced through to his reasoning.

He glanced around conscientiously, almost expecting Gabriel and Buraaq to be there behind him, then unconsciously wrinkled his nose as the memory of charred flesh momentarily assailed his nostrils. He regarded Umm Hani some time before responding to her question, then asked her to sit while he explained in detail his experience.

"Oh, cousin, truly is it miraculous but thou must not relate thy account lest ye be accused of madness," she pleaded when he finished, fearing trouble and disbelief his journey would create.

"Cousin," Muhammad said kindly. "Have I never hidden the truth; and now, more than before, I can bear witness to our Lord's promises."

Story of al-Amin's heavenly ascension swiftly spread throughout Mekkah. The Muslim community hailed it as a Sign, while a clan of Jews were calling it a mere figment of Muhammad's imagination: raising old arguments that Angel Gabriel was an enemy to man because Daniel feared him,(23) and would not be the one to take a man of God into the heavens. Furthermore, they reasoned, it took over a month's travel time to reach Jerusalem, let alone to other places. As a result of the controversy, the infidels took to laughter and ridicule whenever hearing the story.

Shortly thereafter, Abu Bakr, while on household errands in the square was drawn toward a group of people bursting with laughter. Stopping at the small gathering's outer edges, he gave ear. But upon hearing the ignoble rendition of Muhammad's journey, he angrily shoved past the audience, rebuffing scoffers as he went. He confronted the lyricist.

"Hear me O' Nadr," blasted Bakr, "in thy contemptible levity of verse, thou hast taken to idle tales instead of truth. If Muhammad, who is the Prophet and Messenger of Allah, saith he undertook the journey then it is so!" Forgetting his reasons for being in the marketplace, he spun around and departed for Muhammad's home, wanting to hear first hand the account of his experience.

He arrived to find Muhammad sitting in the courtyard, surrounded by Muslims listening to the story of his ascent through the heavens. Seating himself, it was only a matter of minutes before the sublime descriptions of heaven had him enthralled. But when Muhammad began narrating the ghastly scenes of Hell, his enchantment waxed into dread as the Underworld's horrifying punishments vividly came alive in his mind.

At the end of Muhammad's account, an awe inspired silence greeted his searching gaze as he scanned for those with questions. The queries came slow. People waited for the lurid pictures of Hell to dissolve before asking their questions. And then everyone wanted to know about the Gardens with all its different aspects. No one asked of Hell.

Bakr, knowing that Muhammad had never been to Jerusalem asked when his turn came to describe the city. He listened carefully, assimilating the details. Then, before the Messenger could finish, he rose to his feet, nearly stumbling as he stepped back in astonishment. He was staring at Muhammad incredulously. "By Allah." Exclaimed Bakr, "that is the very way Jerusalem is! O' Prophet, I seek thy forgiveness for my hesitation to believe wholeheartedly in thy journey."

In following days, discussion about Muhammad's mystical journey had found it's way into every quarter of the city. And in spite of Bakr's confirmation, there were many minds filled with skepticism. Qurayshie leaders, ever alert to discredit the Prophet, sent Ayyub to question him in regards to the caravan he said was on it's way to Mekkah. Russal was instructed to advance disbelief throughout the city.

Ayyub, sure that he would soon be acknowledged as the one responsible for proving Prophet Muhammad a charlatan, insolently traversed the square to where Muhammad taught Islam. He barged past the crowd and froze in his tracks.

Ali, the first to react, jumped to his feet ready to face any unexpected move. The other Companions encircled Muhammad and prepared themselves likewise. "What business has thou to interrupt Allah's Messenger whilst he speaks?!" Ali demanded harshly.

Ayyub suddenly lost his nerve as doubts flooded his mind. He timidly answered: "I-I wouldst only like to ask of the caravan Muhammad spoke of."

Muhammad quickly interjected, arresting the tension. "Ask ye what thou wilt."

Ayyub started questioning Muhammad in detail. But being wise to the Disbelievers methods of trickery, he answered in depth everything put to him, even going as far as to give the time of arrival, number of camels, and adding the description of a small brown dog covered with spots.

By week's end the unbelief and suspicions plying the city had the Confederacy believing they would at last succeed in destroying Islam and expose Muhammad for a perjurer. And augmenting Russal's efforts, they began gathering in the square to voice their opinions: "We are the leaders and merchants of Mekkah, and no word has come to us of a caravan." "Surely Muhammad is a fraud." "He uses his own words to create a religion."

Once again their contemptuous censure had buttressed the invisible barriers separating Truth from Falsehood, and people divided themselves as if into armed camps, each avowing their particular beliefs. As the days passed, tensions increased significantly: fights were erupting in every section of the city.

A week and some days later after the Prophet made his disclosure of the caravan, Hamid came running across the square towards the corner where Muhammad lectured shouting at the top of his lungs: "A caravan is coming! A caravan is coming!"

By the time the caravan reached Mekkah's outskirts, hundreds of people had turned out to witness whether Muhammad's words proved true or were the inventions of falsehood.

The dark spotted canine, drawn by odorous smells of different foods emanating from the city, had run ahead of the train. A hush of anticipation fell over the crowd as they watched the animal loping towards them.

"Allahu Akbar! It is as the Prophet foretold!" Shouted a lone Muslim excitedly. The faithful, roused by the cry, followed suit and even some of the pagans picked up the yell.

Suddenly there were feelings of approbation rolling through the city. The walls of doubt fell as quickly as they had risen. That evening hundreds flocked to hear the Comforter fulfill God's Word. Remember the Day (of Judgment) when We will summon every people with their Imam (leader); then whosoever is given his book in his right hand, these shall read their books (with pleasure), and they shall not be dealt with (even) a shred unjustly."

"And whosoever is blind in this (life), he shall in the Hereafter (also) be blind and gone further astray from the (Right) way."

"And verily they had well-nigh purposed to turn thee away from that which We have revealed unto thee, that thou shouldest forge against Us other than that, and then they would surely have taken thee as a friend. And if it was not that We had firmly established thee, thou wouldst surely had been nigh to incline unto them a little. In that case We would surely have caused thee to taste a double (torment) in this life and a double (torment) after death, (and) then thou wouldst not have found for thee against Us any helper."

"And verily well-nigh they purposed to tare these away from the land that they might drive thee out from it, but then, they would not have tarried (therein) after thee, but a little."

"This was Our way with those of Our apostles whom We did send before thee, and thou shalt find not in Our way any change..."(24)

"Oh, Prophet," someone called out the moment Muhammad ended.

Muhammad scanned the sea of faces, trying to pinpoint the speaker. A hand was raised. "What is thy question young man," asked the Prophet.

"Art thou not the Imam of all the people?"

"Aye, I am the Imam of the people whilst I am alive in this world; but after me the Imam will be Ali ibn Abi Talib, followed by his Divinely chosen issues. The people attached unto them will be safe and shall gain the knowledge for salvation, and those who go astray and disassociate themselves from them, will be lost. Of your associates is there any one who can guide unto truth?(25) It is Allah alone Who guideth unto truth; is then He Who guideth unto truth more worthy to be followed or he who himself goeth not aright unless he is guided? What then hath befallen you? How (ill) ye judge?"(26)

"As the stars are the source of guidance unto the wayfarer, the holy ones of my Ahlul Bayt, (the Twelve Holy Imams), are the source of guidance for the people. And as the stars will remain in the sky until the Day of Judgment, the earth will never be without a Divinely commissioned guide from my family..."(27)

Qurayshie leaders, suffering another defeat, nervously awaited the backlash of their lies. They knew, more than ever, their power structure, credibility and prestige, would fall under attack by the very people who supported them.

Far away to the north in Yathrib, the Message, Prophet Muhammad, and story of his journey into the heavens had become the main topic of conversation in and about the city. Daily there were heated arguments about Islam and its virtues, which frequently led to altercations. And as the city divided itself, a group of elders seeing the Islamic wisdom in Prophet Jesus, asked Abu Dhar al-Ghafari whom they knew to be a lover of truth, to seek out Muhammad and learn first hand the verity of Islam.

Upon evening, Abu Dhar, preferring travel during the night's coolness, excitedly began stowing supplies for his trek across the Hijaz. After the sun had well settled and amid a score of well-wishers, he felt honored at having been chosen above the others to discover

Islam's true tenets. Mounting up, he promised to return as quickly as possible.

With the rising sun diffusing dawn's grayish light, Abu Dhar reined in his mount to scan the terrain, searching for the oasis where he'd rest until the day's heat passed. Off in the distance, the patch of earth blossoming with greenery beckoned his exhausted body. He arrived a half hour later to find several nomads taking it easy under the palms. Thinking they might have news of the man being hailed as the Prophet, he dismounted, scattered fodder for his animal, then initiated the conversation.

"Salaam," said al-Ghafari, nodding at those present. "Ah, what a mercy that Allah, the One God, has furnished this spring for us in the middle of the desert."

"It is indeed so," replied the eldest man there. "Of late, have we heard much of Allah's mercies and His teachings through His Prophet Muhammad."

Becoming visibly excited, Abu Dhar's lassitude vanished. He said: "Was I hoping thou hadst news of this man. May I join thee for conversation?"

All through the day they discussed the renewal of God's message until the nomads noticed the sun's reddish hues setting in the horizon. Rising as one, they bid leave and started making preparations for departure. Abu Dhar, submitting to his fatigue reclined against a nearby palm and examined the beautifully colored sky. He thought: we spoke a great deal longer than I expected, just before succumbing to sleep.

Waking long after the stars had appeared, he lay there for nearly a quarter hour staring up at the canopy's different points of light, analyzing the information supplied by the nomads before rising to continue his journey. The details of Muhammad's ascension through the heavens, his accuracy in foretelling the caravan's arrival, and learning that many of his skeptics were now claiming him to be the Prophet of God intrigued him profoundly.

The trip was long and tedious. He kept his mind occupied pondering all he knew and learned about the message to lighten the monotony of travel. With that being so, before journey's end, he reached the conclusion that if what he'd heard was factual he would embrace the Faith and declare his fidelity to Islam's Canons.

Upon arrival in Mekkah, he straight away started making inquiries as to Muhammad's whereabouts. Directed to Ali, he spent a short time with him relating his business and purpose. Ali was convinced of his sincerity and led him to Muhammad. He introduced him, adding that he came representing the men of Yathrib to learn about God's message.

Abu Dhar listened attentively while Muhammad explained Islam's principles and recited various Surahs. He asked numerous questions, dissecting the answers. Finally, finding himself most impressed, he said: "Oh, Prophet of Allah, can I perceive the truth and wisdom of the Message. Fain wouldst I become a Muslim."

"Say thou then: 'Believe I in no deity except Allah, the One True God, and Muhammad is His Servant and Messenger,'" the Apostle returned.

Once repeating the affirmation of belief; he, in the same breath, praised Allah. All at once, he felt overcome with an exuberance he couldn't contain. He embraced Muhammad, bid farewell and rushed from the area toward the square. Forgetting his mount in the excitement, he made his way through the streets exclaiming: "Al-Hamdu lillah!"

Uqbah ibn Abi Mu'ayt, a Disbeliever standing near the square's entrance, was ogling a group of dancing girls salaciously gyrating when he heard the impassioned cries behind him. He spun around, instantly angry as he watched Abu Dhar happily expressing his sentiments. He called to two of his inebriated friends, Amr ibn al-As and Umayyah. He pointed out Abu Dhar with one hand while using the other to wave his friends over. Following a brief conference, they set about trailing him until he reached the Ka'bah where they fell upon him, screaming threats.

Abu Dhar, indifferent to the repeated warnings and in spite of the pushing and shoving between his antagonists, continued to vociferate his heartfelt feelings up to the moment when they started to beat him.

However, as God willed, Abbas along with Talhah ibn Ubayd, Abd ibn Arqat, and Arqam ibn Abi Arqam, were near the Ka'bah when they heard al-Ghafari's cries.

Abbas recognized Abu Dhar and swiftly stepped in, cutting short the beating before any serious injury occurred. Then, forcing friendliness into his voice, told the contentious infidels that the man they were assaulting belonged to a powerful tribe which would exact a dear price if he was hurt. It was enough to stop their assault.

Abu Dhar picked himself up off the ground. Wiping the trickling blood from his nose, he glanced around defiantly and resumed his broadcast. This time he urged the onlookers to renounce idolatry and convert to the Way God's prophets had taught from the beginning.

Abbas and his companions snapped their heads around to look at Abu Dhar, surprised to learn he was Muslim. Disbelievers were drawn to the scene and began moving as one group towards the man from Yathrib, intending to silence him. But, the Muslims as Brothers in Faith closed ranks till they stood shoulder to shoulder in front of their wronged Brother. Effecting a standoff, the antagonists commenced a tirade of denunciation and threats. The Believers remained unmoved, neither returning the abuse nor taking the offensive. Abu Dhar, all the while, bobbed between the wall of heads condemning the evils of living irreligiously. The confrontation lasted until other Believers arrived, forcing the infidels to back down.

Abu Dhar returned to Yathrib forgetting the beating he received at the hands of Disbelievers. He told the elders of everything he learned with an enthusiasm that simply amazed them. His transformation mystified and caused them doubts. Unsure of how to analyze his information, the elders held another council: deciding to send a small party of men to speak with Muhammad, reasoning that maybe Abu Dhar had somehow been duped.

CHAPTER TWENTY-FIVE

Coming up on the twelfth year of the Islamic mission, several events took place which gave genesis to seriously reconsider the Muslim position of remaining in Mekkah.

Another particularly brutal attack upon an elderly Muslim woman in front of her grandchildren left the Muslim community voicing their objections. Umm Muzaffar, along with her grandsons, were in the marketplace purchasing wares when Urwa ibn Zubayr, Russal and Aqibah, without justification assaulted her with a viciousness that nearly killed her.

A small party consisting of six men versed in Scripture, chosen for their incorruptibility and fairness, arrived from Yathrib to study Islam's precepts. And the homecoming of the Prophet's second eldest daughter Ruqayyah, her husband Uthman, and the widowed Sawdah bint Zama: her husband having died in Abyssinia.

With the never ending infliction of abuse, many Muslims feared to venture from their homes. Communication between Muslims and non-Muslims had all but ceased. Reports of the weak and aged Believers being set upon were reaching Muhammad on a regular basis. So when the Prophet met with the men from Yathrib who after a few days discourse embraced Islam, he had an inkling of where he'd take the Muslims.

One evening a short time after, as Muhammad returned from Cave Hira, he observed Sawdah huddled up against the city's walls trying to keep warm. He was immediately overcome with compassion and thought: she has never complained of her destitution and suffered much for her beliefs. I fear, he continued along the same line, she being well past the years of youth will have no chance at regaining her life. He decided then and there to wed and provide her with the security and comfort of a home.

"Sawdah, will I not allow thee to suffer any more indignities," said Muhammad benevolently. "Thou shalt stay with my daughter Zaynab and her husband Abu L'as until thou hast me as thy husband."

Meanwhile, back in Yathrib, the six newly converted men had arrived and were expounding Islam as enthusiastically as Abu Dhar had. The sudden influx of Truth to a people hungering after the Way accepted the Message and converted. They felt if there existed an Old and New Testament, then the natural outcome would be a Final Testament. Thus, yearning for additional enlightenment, word was sent to Muhammad asking that he meet a twelve man delegation at Aqaba.

The delegation, comprised of men representing Banus Aws and Khazraj, two of the largest tribes in Yathrib, met with Muhammad four weeks later on Aqaba's outskirts. From late morning till past sunset they discussed in detail God's teaching. And in the end, excited by the renewed Message, they all affirmed their belief in Allah, the One True God.

Muhammad was pleased with their acceptance and asked them to pledge to worship none but Allah, to not bear false witness, to not commit adultery, to not maraud or pillage, to not kill their children, and to obey him in all that was just.

Bara ibn Ma'rur, the first to speak, looked around at his companions and seeing nothing but nods of assent, said: "Oh, Prophet of the Ever-Lasting, the Enduring, we pledge unto thee to uphold all thy conditions." Then everyone attested to the qualifications.

Muhammad rejoined, "Upon my return to Mekkah will I send back Mus'ab ibn Umayr to help further thy guidance, for he is well versed in Shariah ."

After Muhammad's return to the city, he informed Mus'ab of his decision to send him to Yathrib. Mus'ab, that evening prepared for departure and left the following morning. Riding alone, he reached Yathrib in under two weeks time.

Asad, a young man who had been anxiously awaiting the Muslim from Mekkah, watched the stranger enter Bara's home. Unable to hold his curiosity in check, he paid a visit and learned the man was indeed the Muslim from Mekkah. He at once forgot his manners and invited Mus'ab to live in his house to which Mus'ab quickly agreed.

Over the ensuing weeks, Mus'ab enjoyed great success in converting people to Islam. Even the city's Jews and Christians who at first refused to believe that Prophet Jesus' prophecy had finally fulfilled itself, listened with open minds. In the end, they too could not deny the unimpeachable truth of Qur'anic teachings and declared their belief. His only obvious resistance came from some of the lessor tribal leaders who resented their exclusion from the twelve man delegation. But as the truth overcame their prejudices, they too converted. And within six months a large part of the city's population were claiming it an honor to have a Prophet of God who spoke their language, and took umbrage against any who disrespected Muhammad.

The news of events occurring in Yathrib had rapidly spread down the line of tribes until eventually reaching the Mekkan Disbelievers. They in turn urged their counterparts back in Yathrib to step up their struggle against the Muslims.

Muhammad had been considering their predicament when recent dispatches from Mus'ab about Islam's reception and encouraging prospects intruded upon his thoughts. He knew the troublesome situation of Mekkah would not improve, nor would the Message penetrate the hearts of those oppressing it's Believers. He realized many would-be converts were in abject fear of persecution to declare their belief and decided the time had come for mass migration, hoping his departure would at least take some of the pressure off those wanting to convert.

Thus, for the next two months riders streaked back and forth across the desert between Mekkah and Yathrib. The Yathribians were anxious to have Prophet Muhammad make his home in their city and facilitated his plans in every possible way. So, in order to prevent the Confederacy from discovering the imminent exodus, a secret meeting was scheduled to take place in Aqaba during the Ukadh which allowed the Chosen one sufficient time to prepare the Islamic community for emigration.

Days before the conclave, the seventy-three Yathribian Muslims were mentally laboring with the slow moving caravan of over five-hundred animals as it distended over the desert like some brown speckled serpent on it's way to Mekkah.

At the same time back in Mekkah, Abbas, who was to accompany Muhammad for Mina in the Valley of Aqaba left his home in secret. Stealthily, he traversed through the narrow serpentine streets and alleyways. More than once darting in and out of doorways to avoid detection by late night revelers.

Across the city, Muhammad began his vigil for his uncle. Straining his eyes for any movement or sound that would indicate Abbas' approach, he watched intently the direction his uncle would be coming from. He didn't fear for himself, but feared the retaliation by Disbelievers against the Muslims if their plans were discovered.

The minutes passed slowly until, accentuated by the moon's pale wash, Muhammad discerned a shadowy figure manifest itself as if by magic from the wall opposite his courtyard. He sighed in relief as he recognized his uncle's idiosyncrasies. They waited till midnight before making their way away from the hilltop residence.

Across the Hijaz, the Yathribian Muslims were unable to ride ahead for fear of exposing their purpose. They grew increasingly irksome with their dromedaries as they straggled their way through the shimmering dunes. On the tenth day of their journey and eve of the midnight rendezvous with Prophet Muhammad, the caravan reached Aqaba's outskirts. Hardly had the train's riders dismounted before the Muslims had their animals unburdened and tethered. Then wasting no time they rolled out their sleeping gear and feigned a weariness that convinced their fellow travelers of their exhaustion. Some hours later, several men empowered to speak for the various tribes of Yathrib silently splintered off from the sleeping caravansary, making haste for the prearranged location to meet with the Will of God.

The two parties met and introductions followed. Abbas was the first to speak out, his tone intimidating: "Oh, Khazrajites," he said while taking time to look each man in the face. "Ye have voiced thy support for Muhammad. So be ye aware that he is the most dignified person of his tribe. All Banu Hashim, whether they believe in the Message or not, are responsible for his defense. However, Muhammad now inclineth towards ye and desires to be amongst thee. If ye are of a certainty that you will abide by thy agreement and will protect him from every harm, we are prepared to let him go with you. However, if ye are not capable of defending him in difficulty you are free to leave and let him be amongst his kinsmen with great dignity and respect."

"By Allah!" Bara declared while rising to his feet. "Had there been anything in our hearts other than that which we have spoken with our tongues we wouldst have expressed it. Have we no other intention than sincere compliance with our agreement and sacrifice in the path of the Holy Apostle."

Muhammad interjected: "Take I this oath from thee that you will defend me in the same manner in which ye defend thy children and family members."

Bara added: "We are the children of campaign and battle and have been trained as warriors!" Upon Bara's last word, he pledged allegiance, followed by every man present.

Muhammad spent the remainder of the night questioning about Islam's reception and reciting Qur'an. Just before dawn, he promised he would depart Mekkah at an appropriate time and the gathering dispersed.(1)

In Mekkah, through the mindless prattle of children drawing water, Abu Umayyah inadvertently learned of the clandestine meeting at Aqaba hours after Muhammad and his uncle's return to the city. Thinking but a few minutes whether or not the children's gossip held any merit, he decided to contact the other leaders to discuss the possibility.

Within the hour the Disbelievers were at Lahab's house. They talked for some time debating the probability of likelihood. Most of them, however, in their arrogance found it difficult to believe the Yathribians would dare conspire against them. Lahab on the other hand, refused to leave any thing to chance and advised they ride out to interrogate the caravan's Captain.

Two miles out of Mekkah they encountered the caravan. Lahab raised his arm imperiously, palm facing the train's point man. "Summon thy Captain and be quick about it," he demanded harshly.

The point man regarded Lahab, glanced at the other riders who stared back. He determined these men were not to be fooled with and signaled the caravan's halt. Then without so much as a word he rode off in search of the Captain.

Moments later the Captain came riding up. Upon recognizing Mekkah's leaders, he submissively asked how he could be of service.

"Who were the men meeting with Muhammad," Lahab questioned without the courtesy of salutations.

"I know not of any such meeting, lord," answered the Captain obsequiously.

Abu Jahl, then, directed the Captain to send for the elders. They too, unaware of any meeting, categorically denied knowledge of such an event.

For the time being the infidels were convinced Umayyah's report was the mere coloring of children's stories. However, in the course of time Lahab began to suspect something which he couldn't put his finger on. He started noticing a subtle change among the Muslims. Frequently he observed them grouped together glancing about and begin talking, stopping whenever a non-Muslim approached. Finally, his mind made up, he called upon the Confederacy's leaders insisting they have their men press the aggression against the Believers and learn what was transpiring.

Through his Companions, Muhammad informed the Muslim community of plans for mass emigration to Yathrib. The Prophet decided after assessing the chances for success with the minimum amount of trouble, to maintain high visibility hoping to retard the Confederacy's suspicions while small parties of Muslims left the city.

During the Ukadh's last two months of hustle and bustle, the attacks had intensified. The Muslims, nevertheless remained calm and departed Mekkah in groups of three or four, forsaking their homes, non-believing relatives and businesses. And by Ukadh's end more than four fifths of the Muslims had left the city when the Disbelievers discovered Muhammad's plan. The information came to light when three women and an infant were leaving.

Russal happened to be leering at some women while they walked with their husbands when he recognized the three Muslim women. Thinking himself important since the Disbelievers reasserted their control, he converged and casually asked: "Where art thou off too?"

Two of the women ignored him completely. The woman with the child looked about apprehensively. Russal saw the fear on the young woman's face and closed in, snatching the infant from her arms. He, then, withdrew his dagger and put it to the baby's throat menacingly, saying: "Wilt I slit thy daughter's gullet if thou dost not tell me what it is ye Muslims are up to!"

The terror stricken women could not speak as they gasped in horror. They stared at the gleaming blade against the child's throat.

The mother, fearing for her baby's safety, began sobbing and reluctantly revealed the plan.

Abu Lahab exploded in rage when Russal informed him of Muhammad's stratagem. His anger spent, he ordered the trembling Russal to summon the other leaders for immediate council. As a result, several things emerged which frightened them: Muhammad would build a power base in Yathrib where they had little if any control. Furthermore, they feared that once he consolidated his power, he would take revenge by halting their caravans as the route crossed through Yathrib's province. The idea so terrified them that orders were dispatched to their underlings to stop the Muslims at all costs. Thus commenced a vicious campaign, extremely more violent than before. The old and weak were captured and imprisoned while others were tortured in the most gruesome manners.

To no avail did the Confederacy's efforts deter the Muslims, for the winds of freedom were blowing and the Faithful blew with them: away from the constant persecution. And after nearly four months of evacuation, there were only a handful of Muslim families left in Mekkah, save those taken prisoner, or the elderly who because of their advanced age decided to live out what remaining time they had in the city.

The godless leaders, realizing that there were less than forty Muslims left who could not be fallen upon without the likelihood of their clans taking retaliatory measures, fumed and clamored for action.

Abu Sufyan, surrounded by his counterparts, angrily articulated the Islamic movement with a brief synopsis: "By the gods, when Muhammad first proclaimed Revelation from Allah we mocked, taunted and laughed at him, but he increased in strength. Then, when he commenced to attract people with the Message, we ill-treated and tortured it's followers. Yet, they stood steadfast in belief and continued to grow in number in spite of our persecution. Thus, should Muhammad alight to Yathrib he will become a danger unto us. Therefore, we shouldst-"

Abu Lahab interrupted before Sufyan could defeat his evil designs, thinking the tone of his summary nothing but sackcloth and ashes. He exclaimed: "Enough of this drivel! Let us contrive a plan that will stop the Message in it's tracks."

Abu Jahl trembled with desire at the artfully voiced allusion to assassination. His eyes flashed diabolically as murderous thoughts filled his mind with Muhammad's decapitation. "Aye," he blurted out, "let us sever the head and surely the rest will die!"

Lahab smiled wickedly, knowing Jahl's thought process and called for a council of all tribal leaders opposing Islam.

Next day, after the sun's decline, fourteen chiefs representing the Confederacy met in Dar-ul Nadwa. The air was thick with suppressed violence as the conspirators discussed a variety of ways to murder God's Apostle. When all was said and done, no one tribe wanted the responsibility of killing the Prophet.

One of the elders became so disgusted with the group's recreant attitude, suggested a plan which all agreed to unanimously. He proposed that the fiercest killer from each tribe commit the manslaughter. The council, then, decided the assassins would gather near Muhammad's house at a designated time and simultaneously attack and slay the Prophet. Reasoning his kindred would back down from taking revenge against so many tribes.

The assassination was set to take place at dawn two days later. During the interval, the Confederates carried on as if triumphant, gloating over the coming demise of Islam. They smirked knowingly whenever they saw Muhammad, while he maintained his high visibility.

The assassins reviewed their plans step by step, synchronizing moves.

The day before Muhammad's planned execution, he happened to be in the square engaged in conversation with one of the more understanding merchants when his senses suddenly pulsated in alarm at the lack of animosity toward him. Imperceptibly he narrowed his eyes, scanning the area for danger. Observing no threatening signs, he nevertheless terminated his business and casually returned home to ponder his apprehensions.

Confused by the experience, he sought a meditative mood. He went out into the courtyard and sat near the potted palms which now towered above the surrounding walls. He remembered the first time he saw the palms, a fraction of their height now. He saw Khadijah, beautiful Khadijah, standing on the balcony, then the dream-like vision vanished and he snapped out of his reverie to wonder over the impressions received in the marketplace. An hour passed. He remained lost in thought, unable to decipher the enigmatic feelings. The answers eluded him. He implored the Lord of Majesty and Bounty for wisdom to understand his anxiety, when without warning the familiar sensations of Divine intervention assailed his body. Following the Revelation, Gabriel then interpreted Muhammad's anxieties and ended with instructions.

"Muhammad," Ali called from inside the house. Hearing no response, he stepped over to the window and called again.

Muhammad's eyes fluttered open at the sound of Ali's voice. Momentarily dazed, he looked around bewildered, then wiped away the perspiration and answered: "I am here, Ali."

"Come and sup, the women have prepared a delicious meal!" Ali returned.

After the meal, Sawdah, Umm Kulthum, Fa'timah, and Zayd's wife Zaynab, began to clear the table when Muhammad suddenly stopped them. He said: "Ah, the repast you gracious ladies made was most superb that this night we men will clean up."

Everyone looked at one another in surprise, then turned to stare at Muhammad, wondering if it was their time to leave the city.

"Zayd," said Muhammad, "take the women to the home of my uncle Abbas for safekeeping. Then go to Abu Bakr and say unto him, to take his wife, A'ishah, his son and liegeman, to my uncle's house for protection. When asketh he about his other daughter, say unto him to bring her here once his family has been secured. And Zayd, when thou hearest of my escape bring thy charges out of Mekkah and take them to Yathrib, for the kafirun will not pay thee any mind as they search for me."

The farewells were short and hurried. Muhammad turned to Ali and said: "Let us await the arrival of Bakr and Asma'a and after I instruct them, will I tell thee my plan."

Inwards of an hour, Bakr and his eldest daughter made their appearances, finding Ali nervously pacing the courtyard while Muhammad sat composed under the palms.

Following the greetings of peace, Muhammad wasted no time in coming straight to the point. He said without preamble: "Bakr, await me in thy house with Asma'a. If Allah willeth, wilt I be there on the morrow before dawn."

"As thou wisheth, O' Prophet," replied Abu Bakr.

"Asma'a, follow thy father and make up provisions for three days time, for myself and thy father, and have them ready for us after dark. Let no one know of this," added Muhammad for precaution's sake.

As Ali watched Bakr and Asma'a leave, Muhammad returned to his place under the palms where he stared at his cousin for some moments in deep regard. Drawn by the Prophet's introspection, he walked over to sit next to Muhammad and waited for him to speak.

Finally, he said: "Ali, have I been forewarned of a plot to slay me. The attempt is not to take place until tomorrow night, shortly before the new day begins. But I have a plan..."

Ali had nearly jumped to his feet in alarm after Muhammad revealed the plan. He pleaded with Muhammad to leave Mekkah immediately but it was to no avail. It took some time to allay Ali's concerns, for Muhammad at the last explained that he could not deviate from God's designs, which set his cousin's mind at ease. However, Ali kept glancing around suspiciously as if expecting the killers to appear at any moment. Ali, had without hesitation or shown the slightest sign of fear for his own safety, agreed whole heartedly to the plan. Yet, uppermost in his mind was Muhammad's means of escape. "Wilt thou be safe?" He asked, more to alleviate his worry than of actual fear.

Muhammad, all the while, had been observing Ali intently. His eyes watered and overcoming with parental affection, he embraced Ali. "Oh, Ali, never doth thou think of thyself even in the face of death. Hadst I not been instructed otherwise thou wouldst be the one escaping. So hold thou fast unto which is divinely Inspired for Allah forsaketh not His servants and fear not."

"Oh' Apostle of Allah, my life is of little account. But it is paramount that thou remaineth safe to re-teach the True Way and be the Warner for which thou wert commanded."

On the eve of Muhammad's appointment with death it appeared for all intents and purposes that he was upstairs in his candlelit room. In fact, it was Ali wearing the Prophet's mantle pacing the room, allowing the assassins to see 'the Prophet' doing what he so frequently did: pace the room. Muhammad, meantime, was downstairs waiting to make his escape once the shadows engulfed the city. He had donned a black cloak and watched to see if he could pinpoint the killers' positions.

There was no moon but the stars were exceptionally bright, casting a waxen light over Mekkah. Tensely Muhammad tarried, until, unexpectedly a cloud bank rolled in from the Red Sea. Finally satisfied he wouldn't be seen he silently slipped into the courtyard and made his way along side the house up to the junction where wall met house. He paused a moment to rest a heart pumping with adrenaline and palpitating so hard he thought it's sound could be heard. He scanned the area, no one could be seen moving but he knew his would-be killers were lurking about. He thought of his home of twenty-seven years, heard the neighing of frightened horses and snorting camels which filled him with nostalgia and regret. Minutes later he scaled the wall and made his escape to Abu Bakr's home. He had not gone far, when to his surprise and against his explicit instructions, he came across Bakr skulking in the shadows. Displeased by his disobedience, Muhammad held his tongue and sharply gestured him to follow.

Meanwhile, per Muhammad's instructions Ali lay in the Prophet's bed awaiting the attack. So powerful was the influence of what was to come, he couldn't stop his eyes from darting from the doorway to window to balcony every few seconds. After what seemed hours, but were in actuality only minutes, he realized there were yet hours till the assassins made their move. He let his mind drift: has Muhammad made it to safety? Why do the kafirun dread living righteously? Why? Then, deciding it best not to dwell on things he could not answer he pulled the bedcovers up over his head and soon fell asleep, in spite of the apprehensions he felt.

An hour before twilight, the assassins again rehearsed their strategy then separated to their assigned positions. They surrounded Muhammad's house with deadly menace, some with scimitars specially honed for the occasion, others wielded heavy battle axes or carried double edged falchions. Tremulously they waited, each thinking how he would kill the Prophet.

Finally when the horizon passed from night to darkest blue, a bird call shrilled out, shattering the early morning stillness and signaled the time for attack. With violently beating hearts the killers converged and cautiously penetrated the house from different points, eager to kill.

Ali suddenly woke to a darkened room, the candle long since burning out. A poignant sense of approaching malevolence permeated the room. He resisted the urge to leap from bed and attack his attackers. Instead, he pulled the covers back over his head and prepared himself to meet death. He strained his powers of hearing, his eardrums attuning themselves to the looming danger. He detected a sandal scuffle on the staircase.

The killers, making as little noise as possible climbed the stairs and froze when they heard the hardened leather scratch against the step. The air charged itself with increased electricity as they stretched their necks looking up the stairs, listening for signs of Muhammad's awakening. After a few seconds of absolute silence, they predaciously continued on and crept into the room. There in the semi-darkness they saw Muhammad's sleeping form under the covers. With glee, weapons were raised, poised to deliver the deadly bows when the clouds rolled past and bathed the room with ashy light which now brightened with every passing second. One of the assassins, filled with blood lust, wanted to see the Prophet's face as the assault ended his life. Waving his arm, he soundlessly gestured for them to wait until he wrenched the blanket aside. To their surprise it was Ali who stared back at them.

The shock on their faces was so obvious that Ali could see several of the would-be murderers veins pulsing at their temples in agitation. Speechlessly they gawked, weapons slowly lowering to their sides.

"Where is Muhammad?" Someone angrily shrieked out.

A long moment of silence elapsed before Ali retorted. "How wouldst I know! Ye were the watchers, not I!" His remarks fell like an iron hammer across their moods, making their failure all the more humiliating.

The conspirators, next, moved away from the bed toward the far corner of the room to prevent Ali from overhearing their discussion.

Ali watched quietly for the possibility of death still hung heavily over him. When, without any warning the situation exploded with each killer turning on the other. They started shouting, trying to affix blame for their incompetence.

Ali knew he had to make his escape before they shifted their frustrations to him. So steeling himself against an attack at any moment, he unobtrusively slid off the bed and walked out of the room.

Asma'a extinguished every candle and lamp in the house, expecting Muhammad and her father to arrive at any time. She paced nervously, fretting over her father violating the Prophet's orders. In the dark she walked to and fro until the pressure forced her to sit. She took a place next to the window and spied through the curtains. It made her jump when the door suddenly opened, for she had seen no one approach the house. Much to her relief she recognized their silhouettes and quickly rose to close the door behind them.

Abu Bakr uncovered the hearth and used an ember to light a small oil lamp while his daughter hastily started tacking the curtains down to prevent any light from escaping.

Muhammad ran his eyes over the room's interior, looking for the supplies he'd asked Asma'a to prepare. Seeing them stacked in the corner, he began to reveal the second part of his plan.

As it unfolded, Asma'a realized the Prophet and her father could no longer remain in Mekkah. She was overcome with emotion and began to weep while retrieving the food packs. She couldn't stop herself from thinking dire thoughts and abruptly dropped the packs and embraced her father. It only took a few minutes to reassure her but the tears fell once more as she watched them slip out and depart for Mount Thawr.

Some hours before the assassins struck, Muhammad and Bakr were just reaching Mount Thawr's base, five miles south of Mekkah. Burdened with packs laden with food and water they scaled it's heights in near total darkness, broken only by the occasional break in cloud cover. They climbed hard, heedless of the cuts and scrapes received from the many sharp protuberances of ancient volcanic rock to gain the small cavern concealed by shrubs in a ravine near the top. Hours later, they finally reached the gully and took refuge inside the cave. A cave which years ago, Muhammad discovered while searching for a place to ponder over life's difficulties. The situation grew tense as they sat in silence. Neither lit or even suggested a fire for fear of discovery, but when the quiet began to magnify itself to intolerable levels they started conversing in whispers to dispel the stillness.

On the morning, the Confederacy expected to hear of Muhammad's death and assembled at Abu Jahl's house. In anticipation they began to feast from a large table spread with fine foods and wines. They talked excitedly how things would now return to their ways: profits and servility. During their celebration, a knock resonated across the room, interrupting their boasting and revelry. An air of expectation filled the room as everyone fell silent.

Jahl stood drunkenly and announced: "Tidings of our triumph have arrived!"

Abu Lahab was the first to recognize the look of apprehension on the man's face as he passed through the doorway. Before the man could say anything, he harshly demanded: "What has happened?"

The would-be killer gulped in fear. He glanced about the room seeing the suddenly rigid faces staring back at him. He lowered his sight to the floor and stutteringly said: "D-do I-I know not my lords. En-entered we the house and ex-executed the plan as th-thou char-charged but the Pro-I mean Mu-Muhammad was not there."

Lahab convulsed with rage and overturned the food filled table. Coming around the mess, he snatched someone's scimitar and screamed: "You witless fool," before severing the man's head from his body. With his black heart hammering with renewed hatred, he bellowed for silence. "Listen, we must not waste time with accusations. Canst not Muhammad be far. Summon Abu Karz and offer a prize of one-hundred gold dinar for Muhammad's head! And tell all to search northward, towards Yathrib!"

Within hours the huge reward had thousands of Disbelievers out searching for the Prophet. They scoured the countryside, some going as far as thirty miles but Muhammad was nowhere to be found. Abu Karz, however, known for his skill at tracking took several men and headed in the opposite direction: toward Mount Thawr.

Meanwhile, Muhammad and Bakr had eventually fallen asleep after their long exhaustive climb. Awakening just as the sun passed it's zenith, they hungrily rummaged through their packs for food when sounds of sliding rocks reverberated off the cave's walls. Tensely they listened for approaching sounds as the cave's acoustics echoed louder, then the distinct sound of voices reached them.

Bakr gasped in panic, the odor of fear exuding from his pores.

Muhammad, blessed with the tranquility from God and strengthened with a host of angels,(2) stretched out his arm, resting it across Bakr's arm in a gesture of reassurance. He whispered sharply: "Fear not man, Allah will protect us!"

"But they will catch us and we are but two," exclaimed Bakr timidly.

"Nay," returned Muhammad and again reminded that God was with them.(3) He could not help but naturally compare and contrast the faith in God and courage of Ali with the faith and courage of Bakr.

Abu Karz, seeing the small opening where God's Apostle had entered ordered one of his men to investigate. Slipping and sliding back every two steps for every step forward, he eventually made his way to the aperture. He knelt to crawl through, but upon seeing a dove guarding her nest and a spider's web across the opening he reasoned no one could have entered without breaking the delicate threads of silk or frightening the dove away, and departed the area.

For the next two days and nights al-Mustafa and Bakr remained in the cave. Building neither fire nor venturing outside the protection of their sanctuary, they waited until the last part of the plan fulfilled itself.

On the third night, under cover of darkness, Bakr's son Abdullah and three mounts left the city to meet with his father and the Prophet. Asma'a, an hour past night fall mounted one of the two camels packed with staples and water. She partially circumvented Mekkah before turning onto an old beaten path leading to the mountainous range south of the city, where she'd rendezvous with Urayqit and Amr ibn Fuhayrah. During the time it took Asma'a and her party to reach Mount Thawr's base, Abdullah had scaled part way up the mountain to scan the moonlit terrain. Finally convinced of his solitary presence he piped out a dove's coo, waited a few seconds then piped out two more.

Reaching Thawr's base, Asma'a and the others stopped and looked back over their shoulders to see if they were followed. Satisfied no one trailed after them, they dismounted and hid their mounts alongside Abdullah's camels and waited.

Meantime, Abdullah's cooing was easily heard in the stillness. Muhammad and Bakr, their senses heightened since nightfall, sighed in relief upon recognizing the signal. Exiting the small cave's confines, they breathed deeply the cool mountain air and started down the mount. It surprised them because what took hours to climb now took less than half an hour to descend. They met with Abdullah, embraced, and continued on to the hidden mounts. When they saw Asma'a, Urayqit and Fuhayrah, all simultaneously voiced "Allahu Akbar." But Bakr's happiness immediately changed to concern upon seeing the discoloration about his daughter's face.

"Who has done this to thee," Bakr asked tenderly, his emotions threatening to drive him back into the city to deal with the offender.

"Abu Jahl struck me," she returned as she recalled the frightening moment. "I was the day ye escaped. The kafirun came to our house searching for the Prophet. Jahl burst into the room and demanded to know where he was. Said I unto him that I knewest not, then Ayyub seized me whilst Jahl struck me."

Concerned for her safety, Bakr asked Muhammad if his daughter could accompany them to Yathrib now instead of later, but before Muhammad could answer, she said, knowing she'd only slow them down: "Wilt I be all right now, father. Besides, the infidels are done with me."

"Worry not thyself, father," Abdullah added, "I will protect her, and soon, insha'a Allah, will lead our families to Yathrib."

PART THREE
HIJRA
(Flight of Prophet Muhammad)

CHAPTER TWENTY-SIX

At the Prophet's request, Urayqit, leading the four man train and six beasts, set out westward for a rarely used mountain pathway toward the Red Sea's coastal city of Asfan where they would then turn north and follow an even older path to Yathrib: a perilous journey in and of itself, let alone the danger of discovery.

Muhammad was saddened by the turn of events which forced him to leave the place of his birth. And as his party passed through Juhfa, The Most Merciful God disclosed through His Angel Gabriel: "Verily He Who hath ordained the Qur'an unto thee certainly bringeth thee back (to thy) home."(1)

All through the night's ascent, Urayqit who was a guide with more than forty years experience thought nothing of the treacherous climb. His only concerns were for the Prophet's safety.

Muhammad in his own right a veteran of travels, thought the narrow route, precarious curves and loose terrain would discourage all but the most hearty still searching. He traveled up the mountain without any of the fears associated with such a precipitous climb.

Abu Bakr and Fuhayrah, however, fared much worse. As if attuned to each other's brain waves, they continually thought of their vulnerability to rock slides, the sheer drops, and the possibility of detection. It was only through Muhammad's reassurances and constant reminder that they were under God's Protection that they were able to endure the ordeal.

At dawn's first light the tetrad was still ascending the heights when Urayqit glimpsed an opening in the mountain's side. Thinking it best, now that the sun was rising to take cover, he led the small procession to a concavity where they could conceal themselves and rest away the daylight hours.

During the next night's travel, they crossed over the summit and descended until arriving at Asfan's furthest habitation where the trail turned northward. Their destination now stretched over three-hundred miles along the Red Sea's rugged mountain ranges, and another seventy some miles inland.

With less than an hour's time before sunrise, Urayqit still wanted to put as much distance between themselves and Asfan in case word had reached it's people of the reward for Muhammad's head. He drove the column of beasts and men without letup up the new series of mountains. Finally, when the sun peaked over the horizon, they came to a plateau overgrown with stunted trees and shrubs. Constructing a makeshift camp, they built their first fire, ate heartily, slept half the day, then continued on.

Prior to gaining the uppermost heights where they'd be lost to sight, a lone rider on his way to Mekkah observed the cloud of dust trailing Muhammad's party. Curious as to why any train would be traveling the old hazardous mountain route he raised his hand to block out the sun's glare to study the ant-like figures. He thought it mysterious in light of the valley's safer thoroughfare. Shrugging his shoulders, he dismissed the eccentric Arabs and journeyed on.

Arriving in Mekkah a day and a half later, he came upon a mob of angry Mekkans discussing Muhammad's escape. Someone called out to him: "Stranger, hath thou seen any riders in route to Yathrib?"

Four figures climbing the heights instantly flashed across his mind. He said: "About a day and a half ago, on the old trail didst I see four men and six animals, more or less headed in that direction."

Suraqah ibn Malik immediately thought of the huge reward. He turned to those he'd been conversing with and said: "It canst not be Muhammad because nearly five days have passed. Surely with five days start wouldst he be more than a hundred to a hundred-twenty miles away! Besides, there are four men, not two." He kept on until he felt certain he had them convinced the stranger couldn't have seen Muhammad. Shortly afterwards, he was sure his scheme to keep any from searching the old road had succeeded and took his leave. He rushed home intoxicated by thoughts of wealth. Arming himself with his best weapons, he mounted his fastest horse and galloped away in pursuit.

Eventually attaining the uplands, he felt confident in his horsemanship and felt no misgivings as he commenced up the rock strewn heights at a spanking pace. Stopping further up, he scanned ahead to survey the winding trail, looking for signs of Muhammad's passage. Seeing nothing but rugged terrain and an erne soaring overhead, he slowed his steed to a gait. By dusk, his horse started stumbling in exhaustion and he had to halt for the night. Using a natural depression, he watered his mount as he kneaded it's knotting muscles, then let the animal browse among the mountain's sparse vegetation while he napped. Five hours later, he picked up the chase. He estimated that every mile Muhammad made he made four, and at the pace he was going he reasoned he'd overtake them the next afternoon or shortly thereafter.

Late noon the next day he rounded a bend and came upon a pile of droppings. Excitedly, he reined in his mount and dismounted. Handling the dung, he determined by it's moisture that his victim was no more than an hour or two ahead. Leaping onto his horse, a large eagle flying overhead shrieked out piercingly in territorial ownership. The horse reared wildly, frightened by the fowl's sudden screech.

Suraqah was caught off guard and fell from his mount, tumbling down into a small ravine.

Bruised and shaken, he climbed out and remounted. Angrily he kicked his horse's sides, demanding the spooked animal into a canter. Rounding another bend, the steed's hooves slid on the loose rubble and both rider and beast impacted the earth.

Suraqah landed on his side and rolled onto his unsheathed dagger. Bleeding from a punctured arm and battered with a face full of abrasions, he picked himself up cursing his horse all the while. He wrapped his arm, looked around with narrowed eyes, and again mounted to continue the hunt. Savagely he kicked his steed into a gallop.

The horse, with a chunk of flesh ripped from it's flank, whinnied in pain and accelerated to his master's desire. At full speed, the animal started covering ground when without warning it stopped dead in it's tracks.

Suraqah somersaulted over the horse's head and landed on his back against a small boulder. The spill robbed him of air and as he lay gasping for breath, he thought of the last time he'd been thrown from a horse. The thought unnerved him and along with his cuts, scrapes, contusions, and falling victim to his own weapon, he considered the mishaps a bad omen and decided to return to Mekkah.

Bakr, at Suraqah's last fall heard a human cry of pain followed by sounds of sliding rocks. Alarmed, he halted his camel and called for Muhammad to listen. Muhammad stopped, put his ear to the wind, then jumped to the ground and ran back towards the sounds.

"Oh, Prophet, go not back there, I beg of thee. I fear a trick," Bakr shouted with a voice full of pleading to Muhammad's retreating figure. The Prophet paid no mind, his only concern was that someone needed help.

Muhammad came around the bend and saw Suraqah's horse licking at it's flank. He cast his sight about and observed a man lying irregularly on the ground. The man was laboring for breath, bleeding from several gashes in his forehead, and had his arm pinned underneath his body amid a thickening pool of blood.

"Bakr! Abu Bakr! Bring the skin of water," bellowed Muhammad back over his shoulder towards his companions. Kneeling down, he gently raised the injured man's body to extract the mangled arm. He, then, ripped from his tunic a strip of material and began to wipe away the oozing blood obscuring the man's face when to his surprise the man spoke.

"Oh' Muhammad, leave me alone, for I deserve not thy attention for my unworthiness."

Recognizing Suraqah after cleansing away some of the blood, he suddenly became conscious of the various weapons. Nevertheless, compelled by compassion for his fellow man he continued his ministrations.

"Why doth thou bid me to leave thee," asked Muhammad, then added before he could reply: "Surely, art thou unable to tend unto thine injuries thyself. Suraqah, any who cries out in pain or laments for a better life is worthy of attention. For we are all Allah's creatures, and man has the inherent nature to aid and comfort one another."

"B-but thou dost not understand, camest I to slay thee for the reward offered by the Confederacy. However, didst I change my mind just before thou arrived."

"Then, there is no harm done," answered Muhammad. "So rest whilst I attend to thy wounds."

Muhammad and Bakr helped Suraqah to his feet and led him back towards the others. Muhammad decided then and there they'd better return to their night traveling, at least for another night.

"Fuhayrah, wilt thou gather the animals and spread out their feed," Muhammad asked, then faced the guide without waiting for an answer. He added: "Urayqit, wilt thou begin the evening meal whilst Bakr and I set camp."

After the meal, the men sat and talked in general while their food digested. When dusk neared Muhammad told them it was time to ride on. As the men began to strike camp, Suraqah watched Muhammad intently, surprised by his helping the others. Half an hour later, it was close to dark when he took the pro-offered reins from Fuhayrah. He stood and bent his knees but stopped just as he was about to leap onto his horse. He turned back to face Muhammad.

"Oh' Muhammad, wilt thou teach me God's Religion," asked Suraqah.

Near midnight, Urayqit, Bakr and Fuhayrah, began to ready themselves for departure. Suraqah looked across the dying embers into Muhammad's eyes, thinking of all he said on submitting to God. He tried desperately to suppress the maelstrom of pent-up emotions that he doggedly believed in. All at once, he let his head fall onto his chest as if he suddenly lost his neck and started to weep silently. He fell to his knees, begging for forgiveness.

"Suraqah, it is not I that thou needeth to ask forgiveness from, but ask Allah, The Most Merciful," said Muhammad sympathetically.

Urayqit himself felt for Suraqah but his main concern was for Muhammad as he urged him to mount up. Finally, Muhammad told Suraqah to search his heart where he would find the answers he needed. "As-salaamu alaikum," said Muhammad, then mounted his animal and followed the others.

Suraqah sat next to the dying fire watching the Prophet and his party ride off into the darkness towards Yathrib. He felt like his mind had been freed of superstitions and cleared of the Confederacy's influences. He felt wonderful. No longer did he feel the aches and pains of a few hours ago. He rose to his feet, feeling a new sense of purpose as he stepped to his animal: noticing his step seemed a little lighter.

Traveling the rest of the night until first light, Urayqit stopped the train to allow the animals several hours rest before continuing on. Everyone it seemed, except Muhammad, kept glancing back over their shoulders, scanning for pursuers.

Two and a half weeks later, Urayqit began their descent from the highlands, towards Quba'a, four miles southeast of Yathrib. He led their party to the encampment of his old friend, Umm Ma'bad who usually sat at her tent's flap waiting to aid the weary traveler.

Umm Ma'bad, upon seeing riders in the distance, stood and clapped her hands in delight, then turned to prepare refreshments. A short while later, she stepped from her tent and started waving the riders her way.

"As-salaamu alaikum," said Muhammad.

"Wa alaikum as-salaam," returned Umm Ma'bad.

Muhammad spoke for the others and gratefully accepted her hospitality, then thanked her for her kindness. Urayqit, then,formally introduced Muhammad, Fuhayrah and Bakr. Following the refreshments, they moved on to Quba'a where Muhammad decided to make camp and wait for his successor, Ali.

Bakr, who was tired of living in makeshift camps began to plead with the Prophet to go onto Yathrib but was cut short.

Muhammad said: "Ali has endangered his own life to deliver mine. He is my cousin, my brother, and I will not abandon this place until he joins me."(2)

Within an hour of their landing in Quba'a, Kulthum ibn Hadam, the Chief of Banu Awf, who had heard much of Muhammad and Islam, invited the Prophet and his party to share his dwelling until such time as they desired to leave.

The next day, a trade caravan on their way back to Yathrib, stopped in Quba'a to refresh themselves at the town's well. Zubayr ibn al-Awwam, through the hamlet's inhabitants, learned of the Prophet's presence and dropped what he was doing and notified the other Muslims. And together they all went to pay their respects and join him for prayer. Afterwards, they rejoined their caravan and headed for Yathrib where they spread word of Muhammad's imminent arrival.

That evening, the town's few Muslims and their brethren from Yathrib came in one group after another to welcome the Prophet.

Then, when the reddish glow of sunset colored the heavens, Muhammad asked all to prepare themselves for prayer. As they started forming the ranks, he thought, it was indeed a gratifying change from Mekkah's conditions to be among people not only seeking The Truth but being able to offer worship in peace.

On the morning of their third day in Quba'a, a young boy came charging from the well, shouting at the top of his lungs. "Oh, Prophet! O' Prophet, there is a man resting at the well who calls himself Ali."

"All praise is due unto Allah," Muhammad cried aloud. He spun on his heels and asked his host: "Kulthum, may I use thy mount?"

"It is thine for the taking, O' Prophet."

The day following Muhammad's flight from Mekkah Ali entered the market place and loudly declared: "Whoever has entrusted anything to Muhammad, the Apostle of Allah, shouldst seek counsel with me. He has made me his deputy to return all trusts and to pay all debts owed." Having satisfactorily fulfilled the responsibilities charged with, he began arrangements for the safe departure of Muhammad's family and any who wished to quit the city.

Many of the Disbelievers made their resentment known and exchanged hot words with Ali. He, however, would protect his wards and defend the honor of Islam with his life if need be. Turning to God's enemies, he issued challenge: "Whomsoever wisheth to be cut to pieces step forward." It was something in his bearing that made the agents of Quraysh back down and adopt a conciliatory attitude. Ali nevertheless took no chances and left the city on foot, hoping to draw attention away from the Prophet's family.

For nearly three weeks he crossed the desert's wide expanse. He traveled by night not only to escape the blazing heat but Islam's opponents as well. Finally reaching Quba'a, he was parched with thirst, half starved, dirty, and cadaverous in appearance. Collapsing in total exhaustion some thirty yards from the town well, he was awakened by the sound of children drawing water. He called to them, telling them who he was and asked where he could find the Prophet.

Muhammad came thundering up as Ali, with the children's help, was pulling himself up onto the stones surrounding the well. Leaping from the horse, he jubilantly exclaimed: "All praise and gratitude is due unto Allah, the Lord and Sustainer of the Worlds! He hath delivered thee from our enemies." He rushed toward Ali with tears of joy spilling down his cheeks, embracing him as if he hadn't seen him for years. "Praise be to Allah," he extolled, and drew water to wash away the desert's dust from Ali's face. As he commenced to cleanse the crust of dirt from Ali's feet, Ali suddenly felt self-conscious and cast his sight about watching the peoples faces as they arrived. Embarrassed by

Muhammad's ministrations, he said with a voice full of emotion; "Oh, my Prophet, it is not fitting for thee to bathe my feet."

"Ali, thou wouldst do no less for me. How then can I not do for thee what thou wouldest do for me?" Muhammad replied in gentle rebuke.

In spite of all that Muhammad had endured the past few weeks he awoke the next morning invigorated. And knowing his family would be arriving shortly, he spryly rose from his pallet and performed his devotions. Then, following a light breakfast he set out to find a level site where he could lay the foundation for a mosque dedicated solely to God. Surveying the terrain as he walked, he found what he looked for and started clearing away the rocks. Within minutes he was joined by others, and when the reason spread, people began to arrive by the scores to pitch in. They toiled ceaselessly until the sun passed it's zenith when Muhammad called a halt so they could offer salat.

Without a word of reminder, the Muslims started using clean sand for ablution in preparation to prayer. Lining up side by side, shoulder to shoulder, row after row, they stood silently and reverently, waiting for the Prophet to begin the prayer.

The non-Muslims watched with something akin to awe. Never before had they seen such a man as Muhammad who inspired one to use the limits of his ability for man's betterment or the Muslims move in unison like one solid body of humanity, all praising and glorifying the One God.

Afterwards, Muhammad picked up where he left off. He continued laboring until day's end, taking time out only to carry out his duties to God. At nightfall they had the site cleared for masons to begin working the next day.

Two days after Ali's arrival he had regained his strength sufficiently enough to assist with the mosque's construction. Muhammad, however, decided it was time to leave. He thanked Kulthum, appointed an elder to oversee the mosque's completion and he and the others departed for Yathrib.

Along the way Muslims from Yathrib joined the Prophet's party as they made their way. A short distance from the city, in the vale of Banu Salim, Muhammad stopped to offer salat and address the crowd.

"Al-Hamdu lillah, Whose help and guidance I seek and declare my absolute faith in Thee, O' Lord, and hold in abhorrence the kafirun.I declare that Thou art One and that I am Thy Messenger whom Thou hath blessed with guidance, light and wisdom, and has sent me unto the people at the time when the prophets had ceased to come and the people had forgotten the teachings of the preceding prophets and were led astray. Listen ye! The Day of Resurrection is at hand.

"Whosoever obeyeth Allah and His Prophet findeth righteousness and whosoever disobeyeth goeth astray beyond doubt, and is in error manifest. Admonish I ye to fear Allah. The best advice that a Muslim can give unto his brother is to observe piety and eschew that which Allah hath commanded ye to avoid. There is no better instruction than that, of piety and fear of Allah. These are the sources of strength and help in the next life. Thy relation with Allah, whether in the seen or unseen sphere of thy life shouldst be based on truth and fidelity and this goal can be best achieved when ye have no other end to pursue except that of seeking the pleasure of Allah. Such a course of life will allow one to get honor and distinction in this world and it will prove to be meed in the Hereafter, when man standeth badly in need of good deeds and wisheth that there had been a great distance separating him and his misdeeds. Cautioneth ye Allah with His Power and Authority, and this He doth because He is compassionate and merciful towards His servants. Allah is Truthful and fulfilleth His promise as saith He in Qur'an; 'My words canst not be changed, nor am I indeed unjust to My subjects.' Therefore, fear Him in this world and the world to come in the seen or unseen since he who feareth Allah, He will grant him redemption for his transgressions and dispense a great reward."

"Fear of Allah saveth man from His Wrath and His punishment. This will light the faces of people and uplift them on the Day of Judgment. Yea, fear Allah and walk on the path of virtue and piety. And do not show any slackness in obedience to Allah."

"Allah hath revealed the Book for thy instruction and hath made the Right Path clear for thy guidance so that Truth can be distinguished from falsehood. Just as Allah hath shown thee His good will, likewise thou shouldest obey Him earnestly. Look upon His enemy as thine and exert thy best for gaining His favor. Allah hath chosen for ye for Himself and hath given ye the name of Muslims. He hath decreed that those who are to be destroyed will be swept away and those who are to survive, after the Clear Signs have come to them, would live with insight and on the strength of evidence from Allah."

"No power is of any help except that of the Power of Allah. Therefore, keep Him in mind as much as ye can and live for the Hereafter. The man whose relation with Allah is founded on sincerity, He will help him against evil. None will be able to harm him. His command is supreme over all peoples. But people canst not command Him. Allah alone is Master of all men and men have no portion of His Lordship. Therefore, keep thy relation with Allah on the right footing. Do not bother about others, for He is the Greatest Protector. Allah is The Greatest and there is no Power but that of Him."(3)

Back in Mekkah, the Confederates were storming with anger. They realized Muhammad and all of Islam's adherents had vanished from the city, saving the ones held prisoner. It galled them, for neither their plans nor rewards were of any help except to unify the Muslims. And now with the majority of the Confederacy's leaders reconciled to having been outwitted, they started talking of Muhammad in terms of admiration. Everywhere they went, be it to the square, Ka'bah, or out socializing, they felt rankling humiliation of their failure through the stares of others.

Abu Lahab was unable to bear the condescending looks and restricted his movements to within his house. After a few days seclusion he thought of another plan that would, at the very least, redeem Qurayshie stature among the Mekkanese. Summoning his servant, he said contemptuously, "Secure my cloak and be quick about it or wilt I have thee lashed!"

He went onto the square and looked where Ayyub usually spent his time indulging in drink, imagining all the way the ridiculing laughter of his fruitless endeavors as he passed the marketplace's patrons. Suddenly seething with rage, he approached Ayyub as unobtrusively as possible.

Unaware of Lahab's proximity, Ayyub was drunkenly boasting among the customers that if he'd been in charge of things there'd be no Islam.

Already in a passion, Lahab's rage exploded in violence. He seized Ayyub by the hair, nearly snapping his neck, struck him across the face with the back of his closed fist, and slammed him onto the ground.

"You impudent son of a sow, how dare you! If I ever hear of thee speaking in such manner henceforth, wilt I hew off thy head and feed it to the dogs! Now get thyself up and fetch Abu Umayyah, Jahl, Sufyan and Aswad ibn Abi Yaghus, to my house."

The men entered Lahab's house apprehensively. Ayyub had conveyed in no uncertain terms Lahab's state of anger. As they walked through his dwelling, Jahl became perceptive to an ominous tension filling the house. He slowed his pace so the others could step ahead of him, hoping Lahab's indignation would befall them. But when he saw the man's face with eyes blazing in hatred, he knew Lahab's soul held a hideousness that surpassed any thing he'd seen before. He suddenly dreaded coming.

Over the years he'd known Lahab he came to believe the man a paragon of sensibleness. But, now as he watched the old withered, malignant face, he realized how wrong he was for Lahab was unbalanced.

Lahab paced agitatedly back and forth across the room in front of the men, expounding his newest plan. Periodically, while listening to their ideas and suggestions, he used a silken scarf to wipe away imaginary perspiration which confirmed Jahl's suspicions. Finally he stopped in front of them and banged his fist on the table to emphasize a point.

"Have we not a friend and supporter amongst the tribe of Ghanam, near Quba'a? Ah, see I by thy smiles ye know of whom I speak. We can dispatch a rider this very evening to Amr with sealed instructions.

Several days after the rider departed, a new fear set to work in the hearts of Disbelievers. It was like a gelatinous cancer sluggishly encrusting itself over their souls, eating away at any peace from having the city to themselves. They not only had to contend with the anxiety of interrupted trade but the imaginary attack by Muslims forces upon Mekkah.

CHAPTER TWENTY-SEVEN

Muhammad arrived in Yathrib surrounded by a huge crowd of people expressing affection and gratitude while others vied for attention. All wanted the honor of having him live in their home. Muhammad, not wanting to hurt anyone's feelings, raised his arms for quiet. He said: "This she-camel upon which I ride, let her wander until she stops and wherever it is will I be their guest."

Everyone seemed surprised by the suggestion but after a few seconds thoughts, murmurs of "What could be fairer," were heard throughout the crowd.

Muhammad let loose the reins. The camel looked right, left, at the crowd behind, then plodded forward. The gathering fell silent, watching the dromedary. One could feel some degree of suspense in the air. From one winding street to the next the beast trudged on; until, at the last she stopped.

A young girl giggled.

Muhammad stared with gentle amusement at the camel, for she came to rest in a rock strewn, debris filled lot. But the Prophet saw beyond the emptiness, envisioning a huge mosque with connecting area to reteach The Way, and a home with direct access to both structures. All at once he was overwhelmed with a feeling of excitement. He forgot those around him as he ran his gaze slowly over the site. He thought: Aye, a bow shot's length in each direction, plenty of room for the needs of the people. The throng behind waited expectantly for him to comment. But in lieu of a response, he raised his head toward the heavens, closed his eyes and silently praised God. Next, without moving or opening his eyes, he spoke with a voice full of gratitude.

"Ali, seek out the owner of this land and inquire about it's purchase."

"Oh, Prophet," interjected Mus'ab, "this lot belongeth to two orphans named Sahl and Suhayl who are under the guardianship of As'ad ibn Zurarah."

"Seeing that their guardian controls the land, perhaps he will offer it up for sale. Mus'ab, wilt thou take Ali to the guardian?" Muhammad returned.

"As ye wish, O' Prophet."

After the purchase, Muhammad started removing the accumulated rubbish and rocks. Seconds later, the crowd joined in and the lot was cleared in less than an hour. When Muhammad stood to brush away the dust, he was amazed that the number of people had increased from around a hundred and twenty to more than four-hundred, and more were coming by the minute. The excitement was running high, filling him with a powerful sense of home. He knew God's Way would surmount the infidels, the Jewish annoyance, and distorted tenets of the Church. What a difference, he thought, between now and a few weeks back. How wonderful to behold these people clamoring for truth. Then noting the sun's position, he walked to the property's outer boundary and performed Tayammum. The Muslims followed suit while non-believers watched with fascination.

As the Muslims formed themselves into ranks and settled down, Muhammad gazed out over the congregation. "Doth thou not see Allah's Mercy," asked Muhammad rhetorically, then bellowed: "Allahu Akbar," and turned to begin the prayer.

Subsequently, with the prayer ringing of well defined worship, Muhammad's discourse on righteous living and recital of several Surahs, a good number of Jews in attendance recognized the Message as the one proclaimed from the beginning of time to the teachings of Jesus. It so astonished them they sent a party of their scholars to interview Muhammad, certain he would bring Jesus' prophecies to fruition. They probed Muhammad for more than an hour, asking numerous questions to ascertain Islam's articles of faith before converting en masse.

The Christians and learned men present, as they watched the Jews, were saying amongst themselves: "Didst not Prophet Jesus express that more was to come when he said: 'I have yet many things to say unto ye, but thy ears canst not bear them yet', and that the Spirit of Truth will guide us unto all truth. (1) Holy Jesus saith himself he only came to fulfill the law (2) for Israel.(3) I know not of any man other than Muhammad who hath brought Law and judgment unto all the peoples." Also, they noted in Islam synonymous accounts of the Word in their Peshitta,* and acknowledged the Message as a further extension of their Book: reasoning, in light of Jesus' testimony, the advent of a Final Testament would logically follow. Their conversions came much like that of the Jews.

After all was said and done, skeptics departed ridiculing the Believers in One God and His Holy Apostle. The Yathribian Muslims who became known as the Ansar and Mekkan Muslims as Muhajirun, ended the day sitting around the Prophet discussing the fulfillment of God's Law and Qur'an, which had grown to more than seventy-five Surahs.

Muhammad on the other hand, advised and listened somewhat preoccupied as he concentrated his energies on solving the problems of displaced Muslims. It troubled him deeply to see them forced into

---

* Syriac version of the New Testament used by eastern Christians

living in makeshift shelters on the city's outer limits. As he inwardly communed=, the solution came without warning. Raising his arms, the crowd quieted down, and he introduced a concept that would strengthen their unity and forever set the standards of Brotherhood.

"Oh, ye who believe," began the Chosen one, "the Muhajirun amongst us have forsaken their homes, families and livelihoods, in the Cause of Allah. So ask I of the Ansari to invite their brethren into their homes until such time, insha'a Allah, they can build their own."

The Ansari at once agreed, happy to accommodate their Brothers and Sisters in faith. Muhammad, however, recognizing man's varying nature, had to rematch a score of Muslims to prevent quarreling that comes with incompatibility. Many of the Ansari, already having taken in as many as seven Muhajirun into their homes still vied for the honor of having the Prophet reside with them.

Upon establishment of the Brotherhood; Ali, with tears in his eyes, caught the Prophet's attention. "Oh, Prophet, thou hath organized the Brotherhood amongst the Muslims, but thou hast not me the Brother of anyone."

Muhammad replied; "Ali thou art my Brother in this world as well as the next world. By Allah Who hath appointed me to guide the peoples, delayed I the question of thy Brotherhood for the reason that I desired to become thy Brother when Brotherhood amongst all others hadst been completed. Thy position in relation to myself is similar to that of Aaron unto Moses, alaihimus salaam. Thou art my Brother, my Deputy, and my Successor." (4) The Prophet, then, as he had previously declared in Mekkah, again reiterated Ali's status and position in front of the Muslims and formally requested Ali to continue living with him and his family at Abu Ayyub al-Ansari's house, while waiting for the completion of his home.

Ali's inclusion not only confirmed the invisible bond between them but affirmed his designation of thirteen years earlier. The only other male to share the honor of living with the Prophet was a young Muslim boy named Anas who acted in the capacity of attendant.

As construction of the mosque, hall, and Muhammad's home, got underway things began to change for the better. Muhammad devoted his time to prayer, teaching Islam, and helping others. He continued to receive Divine Revelation. He was presented with a beautiful white mare called Duldul, and the city was renamed Madinah, (the city of the Prophet), to honor the Holy Apostle of God.

Following a night of heavenly communication, Muhammad woke to the sound of hungry fledglings chirping madly for their morning meal. Smiling in appreciation of God's Wonders, he rose to perform his devotions.

At prayer time that afternoon, he hailed the assembly with his usual salutations of peace and led them in prayer. Afterwards, he faced the gathering and spoke.

"Oh' ye who believe! There is no god but Allah, The One without partners or sons! He is The Self-Sufficient, The Wonderful Originator, and Acceptor of Repentance."

"In the name of Allah, The Beneficent, The Merciful."

"Indeed successful are the Believers, those who in their prayers are humble, and those who, from what is vain, keep (themselves) aloof, and those who act for purification, and those who guard their private parts, except from their wives or those whom their right hand possess for then verily they are not blamable. But whosoever seeketh beyond that, then, these are they the transgressors of the bounds. And those who keep well their trusts and (honor) their promises, and those who take care of (the regularity in) their prayers, these are they the heirs. (These are) those who inherit the Paradise; they shall abide therein."

"And verily they who are thrilled for fear of their Lord, and those who believe in the signs of their Lord, and those who associate not (anything) with their Lord, and those who give what they give (in charity) while their hearts thrilled for fear that unto their Lord they must return. These (are they who) hasten unto good things and they are the foremost to (attain) them."

"And task We not a soul but to the extent of its ability and with Us is a Book, it speaketh the truth, and they shall not be dealt with unjustly. Nay! Their hearts are in overwhelming ignorance about this, and they have other than this, deeds which they do, until seized We the luxurious ones of them with chastisement: Behold, cry they in supplication!"

"(It will be said unto them) 'Cry not this day for succor! Verily from Us ye shall not be helped! Indeed My signs were recited unto you, but ye used to turn back on your heels, puffed up with pride about (against) it (Qur'an) discoursing foolishly by night.'"

"What! Ponder they not over the Word (Qur'an) or hath that come unto them which came not unto their fathers of old? Or recognize they not their Apostle that they deny him? Or say they that there is mania in him (The Holy Prophet Muhammad)? Nay! He hath brought unto them the Truth, but most of them hate the Truth. And should the Truth follow their vain inclinations certainly will perish the heavens and the earth and all those who are therein. Nay! He hath brought them their Reminder, but from their Reminder they turn aside. Or is it that thou asketh them for a tribute? But the recompense of thy Lord is the Best, and He is The Best of the sustainers."

"And verily thou callest them unto the straight path; and verily those who believe not in the Hereafter are from the (Right) path, the deviators. And should We have mercy on them and (should) We relieve (them) of their distress, they would obstinately persist in their transgression, blindly wandering on. And indeed We seized them with a chastisement but they submitted not themselves unto their Lord, nor did they humble themselves (unto Him). Until when We did open upon them a door of severe chastisement; lo, they got into despair at it."

"He it is Who caused for you the hearing and the sight and hearts; (very) little it is what ye give thanks (unto Him). He it is Who multiplied you in the earth, and unto Him (only) ye shall be gathered. And He it is Who giveth life and (causeth) death, and (in) His (control) is the alternation of the night and the day; what, do ye not then understand? Nay! Say they the like of what said the ancients."

"They say: 'What! When we are dead and become dust and bones, shall we (even) then be raised? Certainly this have we been promised, we and (also) our fathers aforetime, but this is not but fables of the ancients.'"

"Say thou (O' Our Apostle Muhammad!): 'Whose is the earth; whoever is in it, if ye know?'"

"They will say: 'Allah's (God's).'"

"Say thou (then): 'Will ye not reflect?' Say thou: 'Who is the Lord of the seven heavens, and the Glorious Throne?'"

"They will say: '(that they are) Allah's.'"

"(then) Say thou: 'Will ye not then guard (yourselves against evil)?' Say thou: 'Who is it in Whose hand is the kingdom of all things and Who protecteth and is never protected, if ye do but know?'"

"They will say: 'In Allah's (hand).'" "(then) Say thou: 'From whence (then) are ye beguiled?'"

"Nay! We have brought unto them the Truth, and verily they are liars. Never did Allah take unto Him a son and never was there with Him any god: else would each god have certainly taken away what he had created, and some of them would certainly have overpowered others; far from the glory of Allah, be what they attribute (unto Him). (He is) the Knower (alike) of the seen and the unseen, so exalted is He, far above what they join (with Him)." (5)

"Those who disbelieve and hinder (others) from the Path of Allah, He shall render in vain their deeds. And those who believe and do good, and believe in what hath been sent down unto (Our Apostle) Muhammad, and (that) it is the truth from their Lord, He will remove from them their evils, and (shall) improve their state. That is because, those who disbelieve follow falsehood, and those who believe follow the truth from their Lord; thus doth Allah set forth unto the people their examples."

"Oh, ye who believe, if ye help (in the way of) Allah, He will also help you, and will set firm your feet. And those who disbelieve, stumbling (with destruction) shall be for them, and He shall render (all) their (good) deeds in vain. That is for they hated what Allah sent down, so shall He render null their deeds."

"What! Have they not traveled in the earth and seen how was the end of those before them? Allah brought destruction on them, and for the disbelievers shall be the like unto it. That is, for Allah is the Guardian of those who believe, and that the infidels, there shall not be any guardian for them."

"What! Is he who is on (the path of the) clear proofs from his Lord like unto him whom the evil of his work is made fair-seeming; and follow they their (own) vain desires?" (6)

Seven months after Prophet Muhammad's escape from Mekkah, his home, the mosque and hall, were ready for occupancy. And as the family prepared to relocate the air turned festive as hundreds of Muslim men, women and young people from all over Madinah and it's surrounding precincts arrived for the mosque's opening.

What an auspicious beginning, thought Muhammad as he took in the crowd's size. He voiced aloud: "Al-Hamdu lillah," then led them toward the House of worship. There were so many people, he ordered the removal of furnishings from the adjoining hall to make additional room for the crowd.

"As-salaamu alaikum wa Rahmatul-laah," Muhammad formally welcomed the gathering. Following their return, he commenced the prayer and ended with instructions on righteous living.

Before long, the freedom from anxiety, abuse and torture, served as a catalyst to propel the Muslims into deeper study and understanding of Islam. Moreover, in light of recent Revelations decreeing the right to combat evil, the Prophet lost no time in protecting the budding Islamic nation.

Muhammad knew the Confederacy would never let the Muslims live in peace after thirteen years invested in trying to destroy God's Way of life. So, guided by the mystic forces of the Unseen, he organized the Muslim community: teaching the ways of internal protection against Disbelievers and the art of defense against external enemies. Shortly afterwards, he secured the peace between two of Madinah's largest tribes who had been warring for years. Made treaties with Jewish and non-Muslim tribes for the mutual defense of one another's people. Traveled along the trade routes, visited the surrounding area, forged alliances with the Sa'ida, Jusham, Najjar, Awf, Nabit, and many other tribes. In the end, he established a city-state, giving it's population a written constitution; the first of it's kind ever in the world. Also, at this time, Abu Bakr presented his daughter A'isha's hand for marriage which the Prophet reluctantly agreed. He was reluctant to accept owning to her immaturity, but upon her father's persistence and second thought he relented and accommodated Bark's press, thinking that in time the youth would serve the growing number of young women embracing God's Way of life.

Consequently, as the message and ideas of Islam rippled out from Madinah people began realizing the falsity of priesthood, the deceptions of Christianity, the distortions of Jewish propagation, the insidiousness of idolatry, and started reverting to the old Way of life in huge numbers with their conversions to Islam.

Muhammad didn't wait for the infidels response, he seized the initiative and commenced to flex the Islamic muscle to serve notice that Muslims would no longer tolerate or submit to any form of persecution.

In a move which alarmed the Mekkan leaders, Muhammad sent out scouts in reconnaissance to root out information about any plans against the Believers. Over the course of time in his search he learned of their campaign to enlist men for an army, and their great fear of him stopping their caravans. He directed his scouts to patrol in force and make their presence known along the road from Mekkah to Syria. The Confederation felt intimidated and tried to show a sense of confidence they neither felt nor had with the continuation of their traffic to the northern provinces. They hoped to demonstrate that things were still under their control.

* * * * *

With the Islamic voice but a whisper in the conscious of humanity, and struggling against inbred beliefs of a people astray, world conditions were ripening for Islam's march on the heathenistic religions dominating civilization.

Following a succession of Persian victories which swept into Egypt, another Persian army was conquering Asia Minor and nearing the Byzantine seat of power at Constantinople. At the same time, vicious Avars were attacking from the opposite side. With Roman enemies enclosing on both sides, various Christian sects, Jews and Arabs, that had been persecuted as heretics joined the battle against the Romans.

Heraclius, in desperation conceived a brilliant plan. Knowing the Persians were weak in sea power, he left a detachment of soldiers to protect the city and under the shroud of darkness took his army to sea. Using his navy, he transported his army through the Aegean to the bay south of the Taurus Mountains. Attacking from the rear, he caught the Persians unawares and routed them. Then, hastening for the sea, his army returned to Constantinople and made a treaty with the Avars, using them to help keep the Persians at bay.(7)

Closed in on all sides by the ongoing state of war, the Persian Emperor Khasraw Parwiz and Emperor Heraclius paid little mind to the Peninsula of Arabia. Thus, as the empires battled for dominance, Arabian politics were left to the Arabs and Islam grew unhindered by world powers.

CHAPTER TWENTY-EIGHT

Close to two years had now passed since Muhammad's flight from the city of his birth. The Islamic city-state prospered and grown to encompass surrounding areas. A versifier from a passing caravan composed a chant, which became the Adhan. The mosque had undergone new construction to include several attaching apartments. Many believed the Persians to be overcoming the Roman Empire. And within Arabia's borders the winds of war were fast building: leading to the inevitable clash between Good and Evil.

Fa'timah reached marriageable age, which brought to the fore old customs. The well-born, thinking of pedigree and the influence such a marriage would bring, were covetous of marrying into the Prophet's family. The notables, one after the other, approached Muhammad with generous offers for his daughter's hand. All were rejected, for none could match her piety and faith. Then, Abu Bakr asked for her hand: he was denied. Umar followed, he too was refused. Next came Abdur Rahman, who made a huge dowry offer.

"No," said the Prophet; growing resentful that these men only wanted the prestige and honor, which would come with wedding Fa'timah. Muhammad was about to add further when he suddenly bent over and scooped up a handful of small stones. He said: "Here, take these to increase thy wealth!"

Abdur Rahman looked in his palm; his mouth fell open in awe: the stones had transformed into pure pearls and precious gems. Raising his gaze, he started to speak, but al-Mustafa cut him off.

"The question of marriage with Fa'timah will be at the Will of Allah, The Most Wise," said the Holy Prophet.

The unacceptable aspirants realized Fa'timah's future husband had to be of special character, possessing virtues on par with God's Apostle: faith; truthfulness; spiritual merit; and, moral excellence. Thus, to test Muhammad's declarations about Ali they went searching for him. Finding him at his garden, they suggested he ask for Fa'timah's hand; adding that such a union would give distinction.

Ali washed and prepared himself, donning his best attire. Finally ready, he stepped towards Muhammad's quarters, saying: "With the name of Allah, The Beneficent, The Merciful." He rounded the apartment, stopped and thought a moment, then turned and headed for the lady Umme Salema's residence.

At the knock, Muhammad asked his wife to answer the door, saying: "Go thou and open the door. Thou wilt find standing at thy door the one who loveth Allah and His Apostle and whom Allah and His Apostle love the most!" Umme Salema hurriedly answered the door.

"As-salaamu alaikum," greeted Ali and moved to sit before the mercy to all creatures with graceful humility. He lowered his vision to the floor, his demeanor all the while indicating someone with something on the mind. His hesitation and intent so obvious, al-Amin smiled warmly and took the initiative.

"What hath brought thee thither, O' Ali?" A reserved silence answered Muhammad's query. "Is it for the hand of Fa'timah, thou hast come asking?"

"Oh' Apostle of Allah, thou hast raised me as thine own son and now I need a home of my own."

The Holy Prophet smiled knowingly and asked: "Oh, Ali, hast thou anything to offer as dowry for Fa'timah?"

"Oh, Apostle of Allah, nothing which I own is hidden from thee. I have a horse, a camel, a coat of mail and a sword."

Muhammad returned: "The horse and sword thou needeth to fight for the defense of truth, the camel for the labor to earn thy sustenance, and the coat of mail thou needeth not, for Allah is thy Protector. Go thou and sell it."

Meantime, God's blessings came through His Angel Gabriel, for the two to be bonded in matrimony: "And He it is Who hath created man of water, and made him related in blood and in wedlock; and thy Lord is All-Powerful."([1]) Muhammad informed Fa'timah that Allah, The All-Knowing God, sanctioned the marriage, to which she ecstatically agreed.

Ali sold his coat of mail for five-hundred dirhams and returned to give the dowry.

"Oh' Ali, whom didst thou sell thy coat of mail to? Knowest thou who the Arab was?" Muhammad asked.

"Nay, O' Prophet of Allah."

"Lo! It was Allah's Messenger Angel Gabriel who purchased it from thee, and he has left it with me to be returned unto thee! Glad tidings unto thee, O' Ali! Allah, The Most High, has willed the wedding of Fa'timah with thee in heaven and I have been ordained to enact it on earth."(2)

The betrothal was set, and nuptial's followed two months later. Thereafter, the Holy Prophet started stopping in front of the newlyweds home every morning before the dawn prayer. He announced: "Oh, people of my household! Attend to salat. Allah desireth to keep every sort of uncleanliness away from thee, my Ahlul Bayt."(3)

Recent Revelations dealing with the aspects of every day living brought to light an underlying element of hypocrisy among those claiming belief. The Prophet, with hardly any time to call his own, was aware of the hypocrites trying to undermine Islam. He counseled Ali: instructing him how to combat the deceit, then warned the community against them. Spending his days indoctrinating new Muslims with God's Message, his nights were used for prayer, interpreting scout reports and developing strategies for defense.

At the same time, several Jewish tribes having had their hopes crushed of ever regaining their former power and prestige by the city's growing adherence to the laws ordained by God, started making public spectacles of swearing fealty to Islam while secretly meeting with leaders of the Mekkan Confederacy.

In Mekkah, the leaders in a show of force assembled together one of the largest caravan's ever seen in Arabia. Hoping to lure the harassing Muslims into a trap, they spread word that the caravan would be carrying an abundance of goods and wares. On the morning of it's departure, Abu Sufyan took command and replaced the drivers and traders with armed men. However, over the weeks traveling across the hot barren desert, nerves began to fray as the heat magnified their anxieties. It seemed, thought Sufyan, the nearer his train got to Madinah's stronghold of Muslims, his men started turning against one another while others simply vanish

As Sufyan came upon the familiar landmarks which quietly informed him they were within ten hours of Madinah, he felt his heartbeat accelerate with fear. In this part of the Hijaz, the desert with all it's characteristics was well known to him as the contours of his own face, but now it's appearance assumed menacing dimensions.

He called a halt to their advance, needing time to still his racing apprehensions and formulate new plans now that more than a quarter of his armed guards had taken to the wind. Dreading what the next day might bring, he summoned his trusted men to discuss ways of sneaking past the city with the least amount of trouble. Finally deciding to time their passage during the early morning hours, the caravan rested until sunset.

At Sufyan's signal to start the train, hesitation filled the hearts of everyone. Traveling in silence, each man thought of ways to escape the Muslims if attacked. A half hour before the gray light of dawn slivered the horizon, the caravan was just reaching Quba'a's outskirts. Word was transmitted down the line and men urged their beasts into a gallop.

Meanwhile, minutes prior to dawn, Bilal was in the uppermost part of the mosque preparing to make the Call to Prayer. Upon seeing the streaks of light showing itself in the distant horizon, he praised God and cupped his ears to convoke the assembly when he noticed in the distance a huge number of riders. Thinking the infidels were surrounding the city in preparation to attack, he bolted down the staircase in a state of terror.

"Muhammad! Muhammad!" Bilal yelled upon reaching the ground floor. "There is a great many riders south of the city!"

"Summon the men," returned Muhammad instantly, then bounded up the stairs to see for himself. After a minute or so, he realized that the riders were part of the great caravan he'd been hearing about. Deciding the time had come to show the Mekkanese that Muslims were now a force to be reckoned with, he quickly descended and encountered a group of arriving men.

"Ali, Dujanah, gather ye a force of two-hundred men to give chase. Ye other men, round up the mounts," Muhammad said in one breath.

By the time the men were assembled and ready to pursue the Disbelievers, the Prophet knew the caravan had distanced itself with at least six or seven miles, and stopped his men from pursuing. Knowing their enemies would have to pass the city on their return, he called for a council of elders, wanting the city's endorsement before instituting his plan of action.

That evening, elders representing Muslim, Christian and Jewish tribes, crowded into the learning hall. Young men of fighting age, with the exception of Ali who stood at Muhammad's right side, gathered in the doorways and windows.

Muhammad opened the meeting with a short prayer, followed with a detailed explanation of the situation. Thirty minutes later he asked for suggestions. At the end, it was unanimously agreed upon to send two scouts five miles out, northeast of the city where they'd camp and act as an early warning system. Muhammad wasn't sure but thought several Christian and Jewish elders offered their accordance with some reluctance. He thought: wilt I attend to them another day.

The lines were now drawn. Islam's opponents would yet feel the weight of a God-fearing people. The Muhajirun and Ansari awaited the caravan's return with rising apprehensions while the hypocrites sought to exploit Muslim anxieties with innuendo of defeat. Muhammad spent the time instructing the men on tactics and rules of warfare.

Weeks later, the Mekkan caravan departed Syria. All was well until the train came within three days ride of Madinah. Sufyan's primordial instincts came alive with alarm as he felt a sense of coming doom. He was convinced a horde of Muslims lay entrenched somewhere in the desert. For two days while the caravan progressed, the fear of battle nearly drove him to the point of panic. Then, in a moment of lucidity, he thought the Muslims would this time succeed in attacking. And dreading an encounter, he selected his best rider and swiftest mount to make haste on the old mountain path for Mekkah to inform the Confederates of the potential danger and his need for armed men. Stopping some ten, fifteen miles from the hidden scouts, he issued orders for his men to dismount and counseled with his captain about reconnoitering the area.

Stripping their mounts of everything which might jingle and give them away, Sufyan and his captain rode out. Zigzagging across miles of desert, they kept to hollows between the dunes. Finally coming to a rest, they stopped less than seventy-five yards from the Muslim sentinels. They crawled up the dune and peered over it's crest, looking for any sign which might indicate an army's presence. They were scanning the terrain when one of their mounts began to urinate just as the winds shifted direction towards the concealed spotters.

The scouts, startled by the reeking odor of urine drifting their way abruptly ceased all conversation. They both raised their heads and glanced around, narrowing their eyes suspiciously. They crept up the dune's side and ran their eyes over the desert. Seeing nothing but rolling waves of sand, they nevertheless continued their surveillance for the smell of urine was strong and signified the presence of others. After some minutes they both saw two heads pop up behind a distant dune. Abandoning all discretion, the scouts made haste for their mounts and sped for Madinah.

Abu Sufyan, still not seeing his expected horde of Muslims, whispered to his captain then dashed to another dune. Climbing to it's ridge, they scanned the area and observed two riders galloping away toward the city. Sufyan's face drained of color. He knew intuitively the horsemen were Muhammad's men and turned to his captain shouting shrilly: "Let us not tarry here any longer, for we have been discovered!"

The scouts, driven by hard pumping adrenaline, had lashed their horses into an all out run and reached the city's outskirts within a few minutes. Their flag waving approach alerted the citizens who in turn notified the Prophet.

A short time afterwards, over three-hundred Muslim warriors were assembled and moved out under Muhammad's command, roaring: "Allahu Akbar! Allahu Akbar!..."

Back where the caravan waited no one knew with any certainty how serious things were, only that their predicament seemed to be worsening with each passing minute.

Sufyan kept looking back over his shoulder in fear as he rode back to his men, expecting Muhammad's forces to suddenly appear coming over the dunes. Then upon seeing the caravan, he breathed a sigh of relief.

"Mount up! Mount up!" Sufyan screamed at the men. "The Muslims are coming! Make haste for the mountain path!" But some of the men, anticipating a stay of some time had unloaded their beasts and had to reload them, much to Sufyan's displeasure. Finally the train was ready to go. Sufyan glanced back in the city's direction and to his horror saw a huge cloud of dust rising in the horizon. Panicking, he rode the train's length whipping the beasts as he passed. Goods and more than a score of men were left behind as the animals bucked and raced away. He did manage to lead the caravan away before the Muslim force could engage them in battle.

The Islamic troops rode back into Madinah a little taller and full of confidence, for the Disbelievers flight was in itself a small victory. Muhammad knew it was only the beginning of a long dangerous road that would surely end with death. The phrase, "Allahu Akbar," became the rallying cry of the Islamic nation: reflecting their dependence on God, The Defender, The Witness.

Meantime, Sufyan's emissary who averaged over forty miles a day reached Mekkah nine days later. Some of the Mekkans, watching the fast approaching rider saw the man waving his tunic frantically. To them, it signified only one thing: danger. They in turn rushed to inform the townspeople.

Russal, one of those to hear first hand the rider's shouting and exaggerated account of Muhammad's forces blocking Sufyan's caravan, dreaded what he had to do. Mindlessly, he rubbed his sparsely covered pate nervously and headed toward the hilly section of the city to inform his master.

Once the Confederacy's leaders had been appraised of the caravan's situation, they screamed for the death of every Muslim.

Abu Jahl took his sharp tongue and fiery temper to the streets where he inflamed pagan passions with the lust for battle. Abu Umayyah and several men rode off to surrounding towns and started recruiting men, while the other leaders began fashioning plans.

Jahl, already having an eight-hundred man standing army, sent his soldiers through the streets to gather men and conscript those of fighting age who showed any sign of hesitation. By sunset of the second evening, Jahl had an army of one-thousand men ready for mobilization, all armed with various weapons: seven-hundred on camel-back, the remaining rode horseback. Feeling absolutely sure of victory, Jahl took command of the army. Sunrise the next morning he gave the order and the military force moved out. They rode toward Madinah until meeting with Sufyan and his train.

Sufyan saw the army in the distance and breathed a sigh of relief. He galloped over to the point man.

"Who is in authority," demanded Sufyan.

"Abu Jahl, lord," returned the man submissively.

"Well, where is he?"

"Rideth he in the rear, my lord."

Without another word, Sufyan rode off in search of Jahl, finding him as he rode up to investigate the disturbance. Sufyan first explained his reasons for the urgent dispatch, then told him that most of the merchandise had to be left near Madinah in order to make their escape. When news filtered back through the ranks that the danger had past, a feeling of pointlessness spread and the lust for war dissipated like heat on a cooling night. Sufyan sensed the changing mood and spoke to Jahl, but he refused to listen and insisted the army continue it's advance.

Next day, even Jahl could no longer dismiss the soldiers listlessness as they sluggishly plodded forward. Fearing a revolt, he consulted Sufyan. They decided that since man and beast needed a rest anyway, to make camp at Badr. At dusk, when the army stopped for the night, Jahl summoned his captains: informing them that upon reaching Badr's plains they could rest for three days time, at which point he would allow the celebration of their coming triumph. Hoping to bolster their flagging passions, he added that their victory would be hailed throughout Arabia and beyond, and they would be recognized for their boldness and feared for their valor. Most of the men however, cared not for reputation but relished the idea of dipping their cups.

The Muslims, through sources along the trade route, had been aware of the infidel army's movement almost immediately after it left Mekkah. Also, about the same time, Muhammad ascertained the Jewish tribe Qaynuqa's treachery against Islam. But owing to the oncoming army, he could not deal with them at the moment and he needed Ali at his side. He called another council, inviting Muslim elders only.

Once the private session came to order, it took less than a minute before the Prophet questioned the assembled men: "What is thy view of the approaching army?"

Abu Bakr stood immediately, he said: "The chiefs and war-like men of Quraysh have joined this army! Not all Qurayshies have expressed faith in Islam, nor have they fallen from the zenith of glory… into the abyss of degradation. Furthermore, we art not fully prepared!"(4)

Annoyed by the defeatest attitude, Muhammad angrily said: "Sit down!" He looked away and nodded towards Umar.

Umar rose and rephrased Bakr's concerns. He was also told to take his seat.(5)

Miqdad, without waiting for acknowledgment, stood and addressed Muhammad. "Oh, Holy Apostle of The Most High, pardon my eagerness. Our hearts are with thee, for thou acteth according to Allah's Will. By Allah! Shall I tell thee what Banu Israel told Moses, alaihis salaam, when he asked them to perform Jihad. Said they: "Oh, Moses, thou and thy Lord shouldest go and do Jihad and we shall sit here!' We, however, saith unto thee quite the reverse: let us Jihad under Allah's Providence and Blessings, we are with thee!"(6)

"Al-Hamdu lillah!" Muhammad exclaimed. He gestured to Sa'd ibn Ma'adh of the Ansari.

"Oh' Prophet of Allah, we have faith in thee and testified that the Message Thou bringeth is the true religion; and promised we to obey thee. We vow by Almighty Allah, Who hath appointed thee to the prophetic mission that if thou goeth into the sea, we shall follow suit with none lagging behind. We are not at all afraid to face the enemy. It is that we may render services and make sacrifices in this regard which may brighten thy eyes; in obedience unto Allah's command, thou mayest send us unto any place thou deemeth!"(7)

Sa'd and Miqdad's words so pleased Muhammad that he came upon his decision instantly. "We shall take the fight to them! Allahu Akbar!"

"Allahu Akbar!" Roared back the council. They dispersed and raised the call to arms.

A force of three-hundred thirteen men assembled. For the most part, the men were physically fit. Yet, they were inexperienced and ill-equipped for the battle to come. Less than half were appropriately armed, sharing seventy camels and two horses. Nevertheless, they began the fifty mile trek to Badr, shouting: "Allahu Akbar."

Numerically the odds against them were near four to one, counting the men from Sufyan's caravan. The Believers, however, were led by God's Servant and were prepared to lay down their lives in defense of Islam.

It was the Holiest of months: Ramadhan. The weather, cold and dreary as the soldiers of God marched with steady resounding steps. They took turns riding the animals and quickly established a regular procedure. At sunset of their second day out they reached Badr's plains and found the pagan army.

Muhammad ordered the small Islamic force to halt and make camp, a little more than four bow shots length away from their enemies. He spoke with Ali, while scanning the darkening terrain: assessing the situation. Judging by campfires and level of noise, he estimated over a thousand men. He thought with disquiet: no doubt they are fully equipped with the latest accouterments of war. Regardless, he stood atop a rise overlooking the plains: planning and mapping his strategy.

Ali, naturally gifted with an eye for the obvious, carried out Muhammad's instructions to the minutest detail and improvised in areas unspoken of. He designated a crew to erect a command tent for the Prophet and then started assigning priorities in fortification.

All evening long men stepped in and out of the command post, until Muhammad requested time alone. The Prophet knew the importance of this battle and those near the command center could hear the anxiety in his voice as he supplicated.

"Oh' Allah, this Quraysh has come with all it's arrogance and boastfulness trying to discredit Thy Apostle. Allah, I ask Thee to humiliate them tomorrow. Allah, if this Muslim band will perish, Thou shall not be worshipped!"(8)

Across field, pagans had watched the Muslims approach and grew exultant over their size. They laughed, scorned it's largeness, and continued to drink in celebration. Feelings of an easy victory took over their senses and over a hundred infidels closed the distance to within a bow shot: hurling stones and taunting their opponents ragged appearance.

Abu Jahl's brows suddenly wrinkled into an angry gnarl. He turned and glared at Sufyan with fiery eyes. He said, voice full of hatred: "How dare these Muslims oppose my army! By the gods, on the morrow wilt I crush them underfoot!"

"Jahl," Sufyan responded, taking pains to keep his facial features relaxed to mask his apprehensions, "would I advise thee to order the men to rest now, for the morrow bringeth battle and it would be presumptuous to underestimate Muslim bravery."

"Sufyan!" Jahl retorted, an edge of irritation in his voice. "Do we not outnumber them greatly and have the foremost warriors in all Arabia?" He turned and walked away without waiting for an answer.

Under thickening cloud cover, a gloom quickly filled the land with an eerie silence, broken by an occasional cry of jackals or roars of wild beasts broadcasting territorial possession.

Muhammad paced back and forth along the battlements, checking and double checking the line of defense. Every now and then he heard the enemy's drunken taunts coming from unsuspected areas: turning their indiscretions to his advantage. He used their vociferations like an indicator of their positions. He shifted archers and pike men around until stretching his small force to counter any rush. Finally, seeing his men so thinly spread out, anxiety began to creep over him. He stopped and stared out across the expanse into the pagans camp: there were still about three-hundred fires burning.

Before dawn's thread of light slivered the darkness, Muslims nourished themselves to last through the day in keeping with Ramadhan. Back in position, they kept glancing over their shoulders toward the eastern sky, listening and expecting to hear the sound of rain. They heard nothing save the sound of their own men drawing swords, archers selecting arrows from quivers, and the nervous tapping of spears.

Muhammad stepped from his tent, looked up at the sky, then addressed his forces. "Oh, ye who believe, Allah hath responded to our prayers. We shall be victorious over the kafirun in the battle ahead, and he who is slain in Allah's Cause will be honored with the Eternal Home of heaven! Therefore, be ye not afraid, for The Ever-Living is with thee and there is none like unto Him."

The tidings electrified them and lending credence to the Prophet's speech, a subdued and distant thunder rumbled out behind Muhammad, followed by a warm, gentle rain. Spirits rose as their excitement grew. They became restless, eager, wanting to commence the battle even before the customary preliminary challenges were issued. Someone bellowed, "Allahu Akbar," which was immediately roared out along the line of defense. Next, when the sun's rays crested over the mountain tops it fissured through the clouds and bathed the battlefield in golden light which made the rain sparkle as it dropped. The Muslims were ever more anxious to engage the fight. Again, "Allahu Akbar," thundered out repeatedly, until the chant instilled fear to course through their enemy's veins.

Abu Jahl sprang to his feet and rushed from his tent upon hearing the rising crescendo of voices. Across the field he saw an indistinct band of weapon waving and shouting Muslims. From where he stood it was impossible to count their numbers. What he could see was a line of bow-men nearly stretching the valley's width. Feeling a little unnerved by their fervor, he looked to his own army thinking the numbers would strengthen him. But what he saw disappointed him: their faces were filled with fear. Angrily he shoved aside several men and stepped onto the field of battle where he began to shout at the top of his lungs.

Muhammad, knowing the significance of Jahl's actions, raised his arms for silence, abruptly cutting off their intonation. Jahl issued challenge for three Muslims to come forward and meet a like number of Qurayshies in a duel. Before any had the opportunity to volunteer, Ali, Hamzah and Abdullah ibn Rawahah, bounded forward to meet the challenge. But for reasons unknown Muhammad stopped Abdullah and asked him to remain in the ranks. Ubaydah, then, jumped to replace him. Muhammad said to them as they started to cross the field: "Put thy trust in Allah, the Subduer. That is better for ye than any known way. Allahu Akbar!"

"Allahu Akbar," roared back the Believers.

Ut'bah and his two sons, Shaybah and Walid, waited in the center of the field. Sure of victory, they insolently stood poised for battle. They watched the three Muslims approach until they stopped fifteen feet away. Then, with earsplitting cries of "Allahu Akbar," Ali, Hamzah and Ubaydah, attacked with the violence of wounded tigers.

There was a flurry of sword thrusts. Clanging steel reverberated across the empty field as the two sides viewed the ferocious entanglement with bated breath.

Hamzah skillfully fended off Ut'bah's lunges and with fluid-like movements slew his opponent, severing his head while Ut'bah stared with open mouth disbelief.

Ali, learning the art of deadly combat as he fought, crippled Walid with a deflected swing of his sword which cut deeply into his enemy's shoulder. Seizing the moment, Ali drove his weapon straight into Walid's chest, killing him instantly.

Ubaydah, wounded in the first minute of combat, fought in desperation until Shaybah finally knocked his weapon from his grasp. Neither cringing at the pain of a nearly cleaved leg, nor showing any sign of fear, he stood bravely as Shaybah coiled back to deliver the death stroke.

Unexpectedly, Hamzah intercepted the blow with his own weapon. No match for Hamzah, Shaybah was dead in less than a minute.

There was a moment of silence, pregnant with pagan irresolution as they watched the victors retrieve their dead's weapons and aid Ut'bah back to the Muslim defenses amid deafening shouts of "Allahu Akbar." It was a startling defeat, leaving the pagans stunned at having witnessed the unexpected. The infidels who were without incentive, sense of duty or love for The Eternal, Self-Sufficient Master, felt no inspiration.

The Prophet glanced about cautiously as if spies might have suddenly been planted among their midst. Actually, he was analyzing the positives and negatives of the enemy's strength. Then in a symbolic gesture of blinding the infidels, he scooped up a handful of sand and cast it toward the enemy. His motion galvanized the Muslims into action and the cry "Allahu Akbar" erupted with volcanic fury as they charged the Disbelievers.

The ground started to tremble like spasms of an earthquake as the pagans counterattacked. At bow shot range, the vanguard of charging Muslims dropped to one knee, allowing archers to let loose a blur of feathered death.

Muhammad's uncalculated generalship took the enemy by surprise and over a hundred men and animals screamed out in pain, falling dead or wounded. A moment later, the opposition answered with a volley of their own arrows. Another cacophony of sound rent the air as agonizing screams, whinnies and snorts, filled the battlefield.

For some minutes, clouds of shafted death flew back and forth between both sides with the pagans receiving the worst end. They fell from their mounts shrieking in anguish, grasping frantically at the wooden missiles lodged in their bodies. Others jumped away as their wounded beasts floundered and reared or dropped to the ground, trampling the fleeing to gore and splinters of bone. Then, after a last volley of arrows the Muslims charged en masse.

Since the enemy had never seen or heard of Ali fighting before, they paid him little mind as the Muslims charged, regarding his earlier victory as mere luck. Ali, however, proved the overpowering forerunner in the battle. Nimble footed, he flung himself upon the enemy, heedless of danger. None could match him, nor stand in his way. He finished off his challenger with celerity uncommon in a novice swordsman, dismembered the third, dealt a mortal blow to the forth. He was swift, his blade hit sharply: true to it's mark, and before the battle was over he killed more than thirty infidels.

Hamzah and Dujanah also performed exceptionally well as did all the Muslims. Bilal was able to requite his one time master, ibn Khalaf. In totality, the Islamic forces were remarkable in their fighting techniques, easily finding their opponents point of weakness.

Muhammad, calling to mind tactics of warfare from his early years directed them, encouraged them, and they in turn responded with unconstrained vengeance.

After an hour of fierce close quarter fighting there was near hysteria amid the Mekkan army. Many started throwing down their weapons and scattering all points south to escape the flashing swords of retribution. The wounded hauled themselves behind carcasses of horses and camels, or laid where they fell holding their wounds with bewildered looks on their faces as they watched the blood spurt from severed arms, hands and punctured torsos. One of Islam's arch enemies, Abu Jahl, had fallen from his stallion mortally wounded in the first volley of raining death. Crushed to red mush, he lay groaning in pain. His face had been trampled beyond recognition, his bull hide armor was pierced in several places from well thrown spears, and a score of arrows protruded from his neck, arms and legs. He died a slow death.

Eleven of the fourteen tribal leaders who conspired to murder the Prophet two years back, now remained silent and motionless. Enemy casualties totaled seventy-three dead, hundreds injured, and seventy prisoners. But what was most miraculous, only fourteen Muslims were slain and thirty-two wounded.

What the Muslims lacked in numbers they more than compensated with unfailing courage and belief in God. They saw their enemy as representatives of Satan's dark forces who were trying to extinguish God's Light. To them, they weren't slaying human beings but the devil's minions.

In the end, Ali, Hamzah and Abu Dujanah, emerged as heroes of the battle. They stood out with their tremendous versatility and unbounded courage. Each was a shinning example to say the least. Ali, the most outstanding of all, quickly became known as the bravest of the brave, and was shortly nicknamed "Asadullah-ul-Ghalib," by the Prophet.

It was impossible, without the aid of God, for such a small and ill-equipped force as the Muslim band to defeat the large and well-equipped army of the enemy. But their faith, zeal and discipline, won them Divine assistance. Enemy prisoners were later overheard saying the Muslim force appeared to be larger than it actually was.(9) Perhaps Muhammad's gesture of tossing sand, blinded the enemy?

Once the dead were buried, booty, arms, and animals collected, the Prophet sent Abdullah ibn Rawawhah and Zayd ibn Harithah ahead, back to Madinah to break the news of their victory.

In Madinah, the city was alive with wild speculation as it's population discussed the battle. The Hypocrites, taking advantage of Muslim concerns started spreading rumors that the Prophet had been killed and the force decimated. To many, it was inconceivable that God's Prophet and His servants could have suffered defeat. Yet, it was such talk that sparked doubts which kept the pharisaic element brewing. Thus, with no real way of knowing the truth, the Believers were beleaguered with mixed emotions and unconsciously gathered at the learning hall. They talked well into the evening about "What if?"

Their Jewish brethren who sincerely converted knew better and started relating accounts of Allah's Mercy from narratives in the Old Testament, and soon had the community back in good spirits. Then, as one of God's subtler signs, the two Muslim warriors arrived. Immediately they were besieged with questions. Jubilantly they put into words their victory over the pagans.

"Allahu Akbar" and "Al-Hamdu lillah" roared out from where the warriors stood like waves rippling out from a stone dropped in a pool of water.

Early next morning, the Islamic force was flushed with a sense of great accomplishment as they entered Madinah. Ali, Hamzah, and a few others, led the bound prisoners to an area where they could be watched until their fate was decided. The city's inhabitants, upon hearing the sudden sound of voices, stamping horses, spiting camels, and clanging weapons, turned out of their homes in droves, hungry for information about the battle. Excitement ran through the crowds as individuals reported their version, turning the mood festive. However, as details of the victory spread a certain segment of the populace's hearts hardened with hatred.

Numerous chiefs and leaders of the Jewish tribes, along with the Hypocrites, having their hopes dashed in returning to power turned to one another in commiseration, expressing sentiments like: "Wouldst I rather be dead than follow the Arabs" and "God's Way doth not allow liberties such as our religion." As quiet as it was kept, their real fear was that once Islam firmly established itself they'd be exposed for perpetuating a false doctrine.

Ka'b ibn al-Ashraf, one of the Hypocrites secretly intriguing with the Confederacy, became so enraged by the Muslim conquest, summoned together his accomplices to discuss their next plan of action. Following a long and tense meeting it was decided he'd ride to Mekkah and assure their counterparts of their continued effort to destroy Islam.

Finally, after a number of hours repeating the battle particulars Muhammad begged leave and retreated into the mosque for meditation. Plagued with questions regarding the spoils of war and prisoners, he contemplated till the Call to Prayer sounded without reaching any definite solutions. Following prayer he returned to the hub of excitement seeking advice of elder Muslims. Again, he was set upon to relate portions of the battle. Grinning in shared appreciation, he explained he was on his way to consult with elders and respectfully the questions stopped. Finding them gathered in the marketplace, he asked their opinions about the prisoners. He listened carefully, weighing their suggestions, and when he left it was settled to use their advice along with Islamic Law.

When the Prophet made it back home, he stepped through the doorway into a room suffused with the warm glow of sunset. Sawdah, Ali and Fa'timah, froze at his sudden entry, staring at him with innocent guilt. Anas, the only one to react, cried out Muhammad's name and ran to him, throwing his small arms around his waist in an embrace of affection

Muhammad saw their expressions and sharpened his gaze, suspecting his family of being up to something. Sawdah was smiling easily. Ali's broad tanned face looked as if it were filled with happiness. Fa'timah's face beamed, rising with a flush of color. The prisoners momentarily slipped to the back of his mind as he tried to fathom the joy permeating their faces.

"Hath victory over the kafirun filled ye with happiness? Or is there more than meeteth the eye," Muhammad asked with increasing curiosity.

"Father," Ali and Fa'timah said simultaneously. Ali stood and looked at Fa'timah tenderly. He said: "Fa'timah, doth thou wish me to speak the news?"

"Nay. Ali, with thy permission wish I to convey the reasons for our excitement."

"As you wish," returned Ali.

Smiling, Fa'timah radiated as she began to tell her father. "Dear father," she colored slightly, "Allah hath not only blessed us with victory over the infidels but hath blessed me with child."

"All praise and gratitude is due to Allah," said Muhammad while he crossed the room to embrace his daughter. "Daughter, wilt thou excuse Ali for a short time whilst I speak with him?"

Fa'timah acquiesced shyly and rose to exit the room. Sawdah followed suit. Young Anas, hoping he'd be allowed to remain tried to make himself as tall as possible as he walked over to stand next to Muhammad. Ali chuckled. Muhammad grinned and tousled the boy's hair before hugging him in affection, permitting him to stay.

"Ali," started Muhammad, "in the matter of the captured prisoners, have I sought the advice of elders to determine several decisions regarding their welfare. Firstly, thou wilt unbind all the prisoners and place them in the homes of our brethren to be held until ransom is remitted for their freedom. Next, give strict instruction that they are to be treated with respect and dignity. Those whose clans cannot afford to pay the tithe but possess skills of reading and scribing, they will each be required to teach ten of our youths their skills before they are set free. And those who neither possess the skills nor have kindred to ransom them, set them free. As to the booty, share it equally amongst the warriors with extra portions to the widows or families of those slain."

Some days later the excitement of victory died down and the routine of life returned to normal. For the Prophet and sixteen families, however, death had struck: fourteen men during battle with two more succumbing from their wounds; and, Muhammad's daughter Ruqayyah who suddenly took sick and passed on.

At the same time Umar started fearing for his daughter's well-being. Hafsah who recently lost her husband at Badr, had no prospective suitors vying for her attentions and started to withdraw from the community. He approached Uthman who just suffered Ruqayyah's death, with Hafsah's hand in marriage. He declined, but did remarry to the Prophet's daughter Umm Kulthum later that year. Umar next went to Abu Bakr who also declined. Vexed, he sought out the Prophet to voice his concerns.

Muhammad, already gripped in the clutches of grief, understood Umar's worries. And knowing Hafsah's age and plainness would be a hindrance in finding a husband, felt compassion. He said: "Umar, trouble thyself not. After things settle down, insha'a Allah, I will assume the responsibility and take her as my wife."

That evening while the Prophet consoled himself with prayer, his last conscious thought before the Sublime's emissary enfolded his mind was: Glory be to Allah, The Most High, Full of Grace and Mercy. Then, the Angel Gabriel's voice echoed through the chambers of his mind.

CHAPTER TWENTY-NINE

The pagan soldiers straggled into Mekkah with heads hung in shame. The wounded, bandaged with makeshift blood encrusted wrappings, gloomily followed in their wake. Stripped of the arrogance with which they departed, the Disbelievers entered in small groups or individually, seemingly ashamed of each other's actions. Ayyub, Mikraz, Utwa, Budayl, Russal, Wahshi, and a host of others surviving Badr, either slipped away from the throng of questioning Mekkans to inform their masters or to lick their wounds. Sufyan, twice humiliated, became angered with the unceasing questions and went straight away to his house where he sequestered himself.

Within hours of their arrival details of their rout started to circulate. By the time the majority of soldiers arrived, the plaint: "How could that small insignificant band of Muslims overcome our army?" "By the gods, Muhammad used sorcery!" "What a catastrophe!" And the like sentiments were expressed throughout the city. It appeared as if every other clan had lost a relative or someone dear to them, such was the grief.

Ka'b, meantime, had to convince himself of his plan's success as he leisurely trekked across the desert. In high spirits he rode the last few miles to Mekkah envisioning himself emerging a great man. When he arrived he was unprepared for what greeted him. Everywhere, it looked to him like the city had given itself over to despair: grieving women walked the streets wailing for loved ones; malcontents criticized the Confederacy's ineptitude; and drunken men condemned the Qurayshie leaders to any who stopped to listen. Shaking his head in disgust, Ka'b kicked his steed's sides viciously and sped for Abu Lahab's house. Once more he was caught off guard: for Islam's chief nemesis lay dying in bed. Expiring from self-induced grief, after the One God's servants rendered him powerless, thought Ka'b.

Russal, who had been lingering near his master's side, upon Lahab's request departed to summon what remained of the Confederates.

Ka'b took the opportunity to explain his plan, hoping for approval. He reiterated when the others arrived. Gaining their support, he bid leave and made his exit. He gazed out over the city trying to decide where to start his campaign, when Russal slipped out the house and stood behind him.

"Oh, great one, may I speak with thee before you depart," Russal asked in a condescending tone.

Ka'b suddenly turned to face Russal. "Waste not my time with foolishness and say what thou hath on thy mind!"

"If thou knowest not where to begin, may I suggest speaking with Hind, Abu Sufyan's wife. Since her husband's return, she has been stirring up the people: calling for revenge. It is said amongst the knowledgeable that she wisheth to avenge the deaths of her father, brother and uncle, slain at Badr. Furthermore, she will not share her bed with Sufyan until seeketh he retaliation. Thou wilt no doubt find her in the marketplace rousing the people."

Ka'b was about to rebuff Russal for stating the obvious when he thought better, deciding to use him instead. Feeling contempt for the pock faced evil one, he stared scornfully and said: "Very well, let us make for the square."

Ka'b scanned the crowd mutely for several minutes looking for Hind. Sighting her amidst a throng of men and women, he instructed Russal to enter their midst and direct them to the Ka'bah. He crossed the square watching Russal, surprised at how well he maneuvered and manipulated. He thought: couldst I surely use such an oily character. Then before he could continue his train of thought, Hind asked him his business. He spoke with her for some minutes, confiding his plan, then asked her to accompany him while he addressed the crowd.

Near the Ka'bah, he climbed atop a stack of furs to better facilitate his appeal. He started singing in a loud voice which pealed out over their heads. "Oh, Wadd! O' Nasr! O' Lat! O' Yaghuth! O' Uzza! O' Ya'uq! O' Suwa! O' Manat! O' masters of the city! I beseech thee to hearken unto my petition and give succor to thy worshippers. Aid us to overcome the loss of kindred. Strengthen us so we may seek revenge against Muhammad who wisheth to change the ways of our service unto thee..."

As planned, Ka'b's insidious obtestation along with Hind's agitation, awakened the baser instincts of those within hearing range. They in turn took up the cry which eventually roused the city from it's commiseration. And over the course of time the call for vengeance gained in numbers while Ka'b, Sufyan, and other infidels formulated new plans against the Muslims.

Back in Madinah, the city of the Prophet, the peace from threat lasted but a few short weeks before Jewish plan manifested itself openly. Embittered over the Muslim victory and fearing the increasing advancement of Islamic dominance, the Jews of Khaybar and Wadi-ul-Qura, counseled with the local tribe, Banu Qaynuqa. In the end it was decided that the area's natives would begin a cold war of propaganda. They started spreading slogans and stories of Muslims viciously abusing their prisoners. In itself the aspersions weren't much, but when they set about perverting God's Word and dishonoring His Apostle, Muslim emotions effervesced. Tensions quickly mounted, out-breaking in strife throughout the city.

The Prophet, in warning, visited the Jewish marketplace and delivered a fiery speech. "Oh, Banu Qaynuqa, thou knowest what fate befell the Quraysh. It is an instruction for thee. If ye take not heed, fear I the same will befall upon thy heads. In thy midst are many learned men and religious scholars. Question and verify from them as to who I am and that they may tell ye clearly that I am Allah's Prophet, recorded in thy own Scripture."(1)

Ali, Hamzah, Dujanah, Miqdad, and several other trusted companions, surrounded Muhammad in a circle of protection upon his last word.

A Jewish agent from Khaybar, not content to let matters lie, obstinately retorted in vulgar tone: "Doth thou think us weak and unaware of thy strategy? Verily, thou didst face an army without knowledge of battle! The sons of Qaynuqa are strong and valorous and if thou tempteth fortune, thou wilt indeed feel their strength upon the battlefield!"(2)

Muhammad and his trusted Companions took their leave. The Islamic hand was tied. The Prophet would not violate the principles of Qur'anic Law. He would wait knowing the cold war would escalate into acts of aggression. As it invariably happens, Evil could not recognize it's respite. In an incident involving an Arab woman's honor and her champion's death at the hands of a Jewish mob, stirred the Muslim moral sense. Al-Mustafa knew he could no longer wait to take action against the instigators. He put aside his personal grief and summoned his closest Companions. In the hall which was guarded against eavesdroppers, he met with the trusted and raised the issue of Banu Qaynuqa's pretended alliance and treachery. The Companions, having their suspicions substantiated by the man never known for invention, clamored for their death. At first, Muhammad was inclined to agree but vetoed the recommendation as too harsh a measure. The council, then, for the next hour debated different ways to deal with Qaynuqa until a course of action was decided upon.

Before dawn the following day, two-hundred fifty armed Muslims moved out toward the city's outskirts where the offending tribe lay in slumber. Surrounding the small hamlet, Ali and Uthman entered the chief's dwelling and brought him before Muhammad while the remaining warriors rounded up the men. At daybreak, the men of Banu Qaynuqa were in front of the Prophet, encircled by stern looking Muslims who were ready to take heads at the first indication of resistance.

"Oh' ye of Banu Qaynuqa," intoned Muhammad gravely. "Thy oaths of allegiance have been mere screens for evil minded schemes to disparage the Message of Allah. Thou mayest plot to lure men away from Islam, or slight the Believers, but never wilt thy deception overcome the Truth. Thus, for thy treachery thou art henceforth banished from the region."

A collective sigh of relief escaped from the censured men's throats after Muhammad pronounced judgment. Fearing a Muslim change of heart they hurried to their homes and gathered their womenfolk, belongings, and departed the area in haste, leaving behind some arms, livestock and possessions.

Following Qaynuqa's exile a general unrest among the idolatrous, and the Jewish tribes in the territory began to make itself felt. In addition, the disturbing news from Mekkah brought on the need to firmly institute the Islamic position.

The Prophet convened council of the area's chiefs and advised that Qur'anic precepts would be enforced with vigor. He told them to inform their allies that any who violated the treaties to which they had agreed would be adjudged accordingly. The warning drove the Hypocrites underground and incited others outside the city to step up their dangerous designs.

As Islam stretched forth it's message beyond Arabia's frontiers; Jews, Christians, and Pagans alike within the Peninsula started renouncing their ways of falsehood and embraced the Way of Truth. Then reports of Mekkah's Disbelievers forming treaties with the desert tribes along the trade route began to reach the City of the Prophet.

In the central region of Banu Salim; at Kadar, information was received that the ungodly were collecting arms to attack Madinah. In response Muhammad led a force to quash their planned aggression. The enemies, however, had caught wind of the impending incursion and scattered. Upon the Prophet's return he commanded his forces to revisit Kadar. The resulting skirmish left three Kadarians dead and the Islamic army victorious.

In the region of Ariz, at a place known as Saweeq, Abu Sufyan marched with two-hundred men. His army murdered a Muslim and set fire to a palm grove. The Prophet responded, but by the time his force arrived Sufyan's army had fled back to Mekkah.

In the interior, Banu Ghatfan amassed an army intending to retake Madinah. Muhammad raised the battle cry and rose up four-hundred fifty soldiers. The enemy panicked and absconded into the mountains.

A year had passed since Badr. Abbas, who had not declared his faith openly, believed his nephew Muhammad to be a man changing life for the better and kept him informed as to the Confederacy's actions. It was through his uncle that the Prophet learned Ka'b met with Qurayshie leaders, incited the people for war, and were building up another army to march against Madinah. Some weeks later, Ka'b ibn Ashraf met his destiny through the hands of his foster brother.

The dispatch, with it's account detailing the number of soldiers, arms and mounts, raised unexpected apprehensions in Muhammad. He anticipated a certain amount of nervous tensions but the feelings of mishap were altogether new and left him baffled. And with less than three weeks before the enemy reaching the city, he dwelled but little time trying to decipher it's significance. Instead, he sent for his Companions and appraised them of the information contained in his uncle's communique.

Military defense, according to signed treaties with the Jewish and neighboring tribes, befell the duty of all able bodied men. And under Muhammad's organization, he consolidated the Muslims into a force of seven-hundred fighting men: utilizing weapons; armor; horses; and camels, taken at Badr and from Banu Qaynuqa.

Ali, as next in command, contacted Sa'd ibn Ma'adh, chief of the Jewish tribe Aws, to speak with his people about fulfilling their obligations. Abd ibn Ubayy, Abdullah ibn Sallul, and Kulthum of Quba'a, sent three-hundred men with Ubayy and ibn Sallul in charge of the Jewish forces.

At the end of two weeks, the Islamic army and their allies were ready for battle. Muhammad, by way of alliances along the trade route learned the pagan army was within a week's march from Madinah. He was of the opinion to fortify the city and make the fight inside where his force would have the upper hand, but before committing his men he called a council of elders to hear the their opinions.

Inside an hour the hall was packed. Back and forth the suggestions went. Most of the elderly agreed with the Prophet. However, before the matter was settled upon, numerous voices were raised in objection: the younger men wanted to meet the infidels in face to face battle. Muhammad listened to the voice of the overwhelming majority. He raised his arms for quiet and declared the rights of the people to decide their own fates were inviolable under God's Law. They would confront the enemy out in the open.

Following early morning prayer the next day, the soldiers of God began to move out. Muhammad cast his eyes about, seeing the enthusiasm and determination written on their faces. Then looking to the Jewish force, a shadow streaked through his thoughts. Dismissing the abstraction as an effect of the anxiety coursing through him, he raised his arms for quiet.

"Oh, ye who believe, ever keep The Restrainer in remembrance. He alone is thy Light and Strength. So fight ye the good fight, and dispute not over booty: that is for Allah to bestow. Men of faith act and obey.(3) No man of heart or spirit or constancy can ever be cowed down by the odds or evil forces against him. We fight not for spoils or for captives, but for the glory of Allah, Truth and Faith..."(4)

Thunderous cries of "Allahu Akbar" sounded when the Prophet paused. In that moment Muhammad felt an emotion only a general could appreciate when he knows his men are prepared to fight to the death. Raising his arms once again to quell their fervid roars, he continued.

"Our destination is Mount Uhud. Ali will carry my standard and will bear the banner of Truth . At the Mount will we, insha'a Allah, set station and make ready our defenses." He tugged Duldul's reins and headed towards the mountains.

Once more the cries of "Allahu Akbar" sounded as men mounted their beasts and those afoot formed ranks to follow. The coming battle would be a time of great trial: testing Muslim mettle; strength; and wisdom of the Prophet. Though much courage was shown at Badr, the Mekkanese were determined to avenge their humiliation and smash the Islamic nation. With a year to prepare the Confederates had amassed an army of over three-thousand fighting men under Abu Sufyan's command. So sure of victory, even the womenfolk came following behind to collect the spoils of war.

A mile out, Muhammad doubled back along the ranks to offer suggestions to ibn Sallul. But as he tried ibn Sallul interrupted, fabricating some story of imminent danger back in Madinah and withdrew, taking the three-hundred man Jewish force and leaving the Muslims with their original seven-hundred men.

Muhammad rode midway up a small hill upon attaining Uhud's base which marked the mountain's northern edge. He stood silently in the stirrups for better part of an hour scanning the terrain. Calm and motionless, he stared into the barren landscape. Overhead, he watched clouds roll by in slow motion. Except for an erne's occasional shriek, or clatter of stones blown off the heights, it was eerily quiet. Then, closing his eyes in reproach he forced himself to put aside the majesty of God's creation and concentrate on the task of analyzing different strategies. Moments later, he started envisioning a variety of battle scenes, and brought to mind all the tactics of war he knew or even heard of. He recalled the way men guided their beasts, unless directed they mindlessly adhered to the land's contours. Next, taking into account the dry river bed to the south, the wind's velocity, the land's natural fortifications, and the mountain pass at their backs, he decided his strategy.

Finally, he looked toward his men and said: "Jabir, take fifty archers and station thyselves up in the pass behind us and under no circumstances are ye to leave thy positions until relieved. Ali, appoint Sahl ibn Hanif to take one-hundred archers and line the eastern flank along Uhud's base for two bow shot's length." Turning to study the terrain again, he then placed the remainder of his men in position.

Next day, just before the sun climbed to it's peak, Muhammad watched from the hillside a dark wall of men approach and stop in the distance, pikeheads ablaze in the sunlight. Several horsemen, then, broke away and came galloping toward his defenses. Stopping out of bow shot range to scan the Islamic forces, they watched with hands raised to block out the sun. After a few minutes reconnaissance they were satisfied that they knew all the Muslim positions and rode back to inform their superiors. They failed to see, however, the archers concealed above the pass and the others along Uhud's base.

Following a short consultation with his captains, Sufyan splintered the army, assigning each captain different areas to assault. Ikramah would lead the left flank along the chain of mountains. Khalid to bring up the center if needed. And Sufyan would lead the right side. The command was given and they began to close the distance.

In a huge cloud of dust the pagan war machine arrived amid a cacophony of sound. Standard bearers whooped and yelled, shouting maledictions in kind of peremptory sentence. Drummers drummed out wild staccatos of mood altering cadences. Abu Sufyan's wife Hind, led the women in shrilling out invocations to the gods while others carried idols to encourage their men to fight bravely. All in all, they were in a frenzy, ready to rush blindly in their lust for revenge.

On the other side, the Muslims presented a picture of nervous calm. Having different ideas and goals they called upon the One God for help: praying for nothing but victory or martyrdom. With heart pounding readiness they quietly watched the maddened horde approach.

Stopping some three-hundred eighty feet away, the two sides faced one another as in the Battle of Badr. Abu Amir rushed ahead into no-man's land with fifty archers and fired the first volley. The Muslims retaliated likewise, driving them back to their own ranks. Talhah ibn Abi Talhah, one of the Qurayshie standard bearers, strutted to mid-field, drove the standard into the ground, and with puerile gestures accenting his challenge defied any to the passage of arms.

Ali, the first to leap forward, unsheathed his double-edged sword and crossed the field. Warily he watched his opponent with narrowed eyes, examining Talhah's visage. No doubt, thought Ali, hath he the control of a warrior. Aside from Talhah's scarred face, both men could have passed for relatives. Like the flag bearer, Ali had the same dark piercing look of predaciousness and heavy boned stature. Ali knew he was about to engage in a fierce and brutal fight to the death.

"So, at the last we meet Ali," said Talhah with Goliath-like self-importance. "Have I heard much of thy exploits, but then thou didst fight men of no skill. Prepare thyself to die Muslim dog!" With mercurial motion Talhah brought up his sword and slashed at Ali.

Nearly caught off guard Ali jumped back, twisted in mid air and raised his own weapon to turn the blow aside. Cautiously the two men danced around full circle, mindful of the other's agility. Ali began to say something when Talhah suddenly lunged with deadly intentions. The ring of steel again rent the air as Ali blocked the thrust. Talhah followed up with a flurry of hammer-like strikes. Ali intercepted every swing with deft maneuvering. Enraged, Talhah cursed, rushed and swung wildly. Ali ducked and spun around, allowing Talhah's momentum to carry him past. He grabbed his hilt with both hands and before Talhah realized, delivered a slash of his own that severed Talhah's leg. Talhah screamed and fell to the ground where he begged for mercy. Ali struck him no more.

Mus'ab, Talhah's brother, stepped forward and retrieved the fallen standard. He was about to say something when Asim ibn Thabit shot an arrow and killed him. Uthman, another brother, recovered the standard and was also killed by Asim's well placed arrow.

Talhah's slave Sawab, treading on the heels of his masters met with Ali. Sawab charged. Ali easily side stepped and parted with a mortal strike, which opened a large gapping wound in Sawab's throat. As the whistling blade sliced into his neck he dropped his weapon and reflexively wrapped both hands around his throat, trying to staunch the bleeding. He gurgled horribly, his eyes nearly bulged out their sockets as he ogled the blood squirting through his fingers. Seconds later he dropped to the ground dead. Ali stepped away, raised his sword, roared "Allahu Akbar" and severed the Qurayshie standard. Several more challenges were issued which the Muslims accepted and came away victorious. Ali alone killed eight more standard bearers before the infidels charged en masse.

Sufyan, at the vanguard of a thousand man flank, witnessed the defeat of some of their best warriors with growing apprehension. Summoning his captains, a short consultation followed. Taking Khalid's advice, he ordered him to take a hundred horsemen to circle Uhud and come down the pass in attack from the rear. He, then, from atop his spotted Arabian screamed out the command for mass attack.

The front ranks kicked their mounts, goading them toward the Muslim line. A third of the horses, frightened by the suddenness, reared and tried to buck their riders. The men used their reins and lashed the beasts into submission and joined the charge. In an angry maelstrom of humanity, the tide of infidels sped for the Muslims from a dozen different trails. At mid point where the dead challengers lay, the animals calmed and began to gallop full speed. Archers dropped their reins and notched arrows, spearmen leveled their weapons, axe men raised their instruments of death, and the swordsmen waved their blades with deadly menace.

Muhammad squinted at the wall of attacking pagans, watching intently as they prepared to initiate the battle. Looking to his own archers, he raised his arm, signaling his men to notch their arrows. He waited until the enemy could be hit with a degree of accuracy before dropping his arm.

The pagan bowmen at some unseen sign began shooting their arrows from two-hundred seventy feet out. Firing from moving animals was difficult at best. The Muslims, employing the terrain's natural convexities, easily evaded the incoming shafts. The Disbelievers nevertheless continued to rain arrows at the Muslim line.

Finally, at sixty-five yards the mounted enemy came into range and Muhammad dropped his arm in signal. A gray shadow streaked over the sand as Muslim bowmen unleashed volley after volley of flying death. Pagans fell from their mounts screaming in pain. Wounded animals shrieked in terror, then tumbled end over end as they crashed to the ground.

Muhammad heard the horrible sounds of dying men and screeching beasts. He could smell the sickly sweet odor of fresh blood. It was not a sound or emanation he cared for, nor did it distress him. He was fighting in God's Cause and would not allow himself to be troubled by the sounds of war.

Screaming and cursing, the pagans hit the Muslim line. A sharp, earsplitting peal of clanging steel echoed off the flanking mountains. Eagles and buzzards took to the air screeching and cawing. Muhammad watched but an instant; the men hewing and battering; the flashing scimitars; battle axes; krises; broadswords; spears; and rising dust, then pushed into the seething horde of combatants with a roar of "Allahu Akbar." The Muslims immediately responded with a resounding "Allahu Akbar," that even drowned out the constant tumult of beating drums, chanting women, and screaming animals.

The medley of shrieks, groans and cries, was close and fierce. The clash of weapons swift and deadly. Blood chilling war cries and more shocked yells of pain rang out as Muslims from the mountain's base loosed another flurry of missile death. Men fell wounded, dying and dead. Injured horses and camels stumbled and fell, crushing dozens of men who were either hobbling or crawling away. Within an hour, the terrain was partially lost in a sea of dust, thick as smoke with an occasional flash of steel. The sound was horrendous: piercing screams; squalling camels; whinnying horses; metal clanging against metal; and the crazed requiems of chanting women filled the air. The pagan onslaught started to flounder, becoming a confused, frightened attack as anarchy set in. Thus, with the enemy turning to flee in abject fear, the fight turned in favor of the Muslims.

The womenfolk, suddenly quiet, watched in stunned silence their men turn tail and run for their lives. Hind, the first to find her voice started screaming at the men which set off a chorus of shrieking: urging their men back into battle. It was all to no avail for the growing shouts of "Allahu Akbar" had put terror in the enemy's hearts.

The Muslims pursued the infidels relentlessly until their pursuit landed them in the enemy's camp. Most of the Muslims stopped the chase and gathered supplies, discarded weapons, abandoned mounts, and just about anything of value. The others searched out tents, slaying the ungodly wherever they were discovered. The women wailed as they could only watch helplessly their men put to the sword.

High above the field of battle, the archers protecting the pass watched their brothers-in-arms slowly beat the Disbelievers back. When the gaps opened up allowing the Muslims to flank the pagans on three sides, it appeared as if the enemy stampeded in every direction.

Ta'imah ibn Ubayraq, never one to miss an opportunity for gain exposed his hypocrisy, when just before deserting his post greedily called out to the others: "By Allah, He hath granted us victory! The field is clear, let us not delay and join our brothers in gathering plunder!"

Jabir and Umar ibn Hazm simultaneously looked at each other in surprise. Jabir, fearing an all out rush down the mountain for the spoils of war, barked out with menace: "Nay! Stay ye where ye are! The Apostle of Allah hath commanded us to remain at our posts no matter the situation!"

"He hath ordered thee to do that without knowing the matter would come to what we see now," replied the hypocrite.

Jabir's admonition did no good, for the lure of loot had the majority of archers running down the mount to get their share.

Meanwhile, Khalid sensed an opportunity. He and his force of horse warriors were minutes away from entering the pass. Signaling his men for silence, he stopped fifty yards short of the opening and ordered Amr and Russal to dismount and spy out the battle's progress. With exaggerated stealth they approached and rounded the bend. Unaware of the remaining archers concealed in the heights, they proceeded until taking in the scene below. Amr sucked in his breath in stunned disbelief. Russal cursed his gods vilely.

What they saw were Muslims searching their camp: leading prisoners; horses; camels; and carrying away weapons, tents and supplies. As they stared, a falling stone drew Russal's attention away from the scene below. Instantly, he flattened himself, pulling Amr with him behind a protrusion of rock. Together then they peered out from behind the outcropping and counted eleven men. Returning as they came, they reported back to Khalid.

Shaken by the news, Khalid's shoulders sagged as he took a few moments to analyze and digest the information. Then, abruptly his head snapped up, his back straightened.

"Men, we must make a great diversion to draw our enemy's attention. So, bind ye a piece of garment or anything to drag behind thy mounts. This will cause the Muslims to think an enormous force is attacking." At Khalid's command, the pagans came around the mountain amid an immense cloud of dust, shouting: "Death to the Muslims! Death to the Muslims!"

Alerted by the charge and shouting infidels, the archers waited until the enemy came into sight. A moment later, they fired volley after volley into the churning mass of horses and men, killing and wounding a score of men and causing the animals to stumble over fallen bodies which added to the confusion.

Khalid bellowed the order to mount assaults up the mountain. Each time, however, they were greeted with a shower of arrows. The sheer number of Disbelievers soon overwhelmed the Believers' valiant effort and one by one they fell.

Of the eleven Believers, four lay dead, three dying and the others wounded. Tamyeez al-Sahabah, speared with a javelin to his thigh had managed before collapsing, to yank free the iron tipped shaft from his limb and return the spear. Thrown with the force of desperation, it pierced the back of Russal's skull, partially exiting through his left eye and pinning him to the ground in a grotesque portrayal of death.

In the valley below, Muhammad's thoughts were suddenly interrupted by the deafening sound of pounding hooves rolling off the mountain like thunder. And compounded with billowing clouds of dust surging out the pass, created the illusion of hundreds of attacking riders.

Mass confusion broke out among the Muslim ranks, causing a sudden turn of events. Aside from the Holy Apostle and Ali, who were able to retain their wits, everyone in a five yard radius surrounding their location thought of their own safety and fled for their lives.(5) Recognizing the immediate danger, the first two men of God braced themselves for the coming onslaught of rancorous idolaters bent on annihilation. Muhammad and Asadullah-ul-Ghalib with an abruptness that took God's enemies by surprise, counterattacked with a bold violence rarely seen or recorded in the annals of warfare. With a united voice, "Allahu Akbar," thundered out as they warred against the irreligious; gaining precious time for the Muslims to collect themselves and rejoin the battle. Amid renewed roars of "Allahu Akbar" some of the soldiers of God started converging around the Prophet in protection.

In the chaos, Khalid's horsemen swarmed down Uhud. The pagan prisoners, taking advantage of the disorder, shook free from their captors, rallied, and turned back on the Muslims. Several hundred men of the enemy, lagging far behind Sufyan's fleeing army, also turned to attack again. From the front, left and right, an explosion of guttural yells sounded as the infidels retrieved fallen weapons and pursued the panicked Muslims. At the rear, despite the terrain's unevenness and jolting impacts from leaping horses, the horse warriors maintained balanced with uncommon skill as they neared the mound holding God's Holy Apostle.

In those first few disorganized minutes a vicious and deadly fight ensued with no quarter given. Abu Jahl's son, Ikramah, and what remained of his flank were the first to about face and support Khalid's rear charge. At fifty yards from the hill holding Muhammad and his Companions, Khalid's men dismounted and started hacking and slashing their way through escaping Muslims.

Meanwhile, on the small hillock Muhammad was now surrounded by Ali and seven others. They fought hard, using the lethal power of their weapons to cleave the infidels to pieces, littering the mound with heads, limbs and bodies. Muhammad's leadership was superb. He alone slew and wounded more than a score of Disbelievers. Ali, Dujanah, Sahl and the others, strengthened with the Spirit of Faith battled off wave after wave of attackers. Mus'ab, after killing and incapacitating a good number of men was struck from behind and killed. His slayer, mistaking him for the Prophet, bellowed out triumphantly: "I have slain Muhammad! I have slain Muhammad!"

For an instant the fighting paused, then one of the Believer's refuted the Prophet's death: trying to halt the fleeing men and give heart to others, who had thrown down their weapons in defeat. Albeit, eventually thirteen Muslims returned to join Ali at Muhammad's side and made up the human wall defending the Apostle of God.

The Disbelievers, realizing their err, turned and zeroed their attention upon Muhammad's standard. Over two-hundred malignant souls intent on bloody murder charged. Unprecedented bloodshed, mayhem and violence erupted: men screamed wildly; steel clanged and crunched bone; blood and gore splattered everywhere. So massive was the assault, tumbling bodies and parts accumulated at the mound's base and dyed the earth maroon in a forty yard circle.

During the last seconds of combat for Muhammad's hill, he fell from his numerous wounds. In reaction, his trusted Companions furiously pitched themselves into the fracas. Ali, through the periphery of his sight, observed the Prophet's state and swiftly covered the ground to his side. He knelt and administered aid while miraculously fending off the myrmidons of disbelief.

"Ali, what hath the people done?" Al-Mustafa asked.

"They have broken their pledge and turned their backs in flight!" Ali could say no more as he had to engage several infidels coming up the mound. Returning, the Prophet again questioned him.

"Why didst thou not flee with the people?"

"Oh' Apostle of Allah, how could I flee after submitting to Allah?"

"Oh' Ali, doth thou not hear the praise for thee in the heavens? As Allah liveth in Whose presence my soul standeth, the Angel Ridwan was calling out: 'There is no sword which rendereth service except Zul-Fiqar and there is no champion except Ali."(6)

Off to the Prophet's far side, Hamzah measured swords with no object in mind other than killing the enemy. He heard nothing as he dispensed havoc and fear: slaying and maiming the ungodly. Wahshi, a slave of one of Hamzah's many victims, watched him from concealment as he decimated those crossing his path. Tensely, he waited until Hamzah's back was all he could see, then struck him down dead with a well thrown javelin.

On the valley's far side, near Uhud's base, a battery of Muslims were engaged with a band of idolaters when the cry: "I have slain Muhammad," sounded. Already on the verge of dispatching the remaining Disbelievers; they, in that bleak moment were engulfed with discouragement. With heavy hearts they threw down their weapons and quit the fight, allowing the infidels to escape with their lives.

Anas ibn Nadhr, having just slain one of the fleeing Mekkans, turned and saw a group of Muhajirun and Ansari sitting gloomily on the ground. He quickly glanced around, making sure no pagans lurked about, then ran over to them. Looking at Umar ibn al-Khattab, Talhah, and several other prominent Muslims he addressed them with a tone of protest.

"Why art thou sitting here?"

Someone replied as ibn Nadhr ran his eyes over the area. "The Prophet hath been slain and there is no use fighting."

"What! Ibn Nadhr retorted sharply. "If the Prophet hath been slain, what will ye do with thy lives now? Get up! Meet martyrdom in the same path in which he hath been killed!"(7) Seeing that his words had no effect on them, he put his back to them and rushed to unite with Believers rejoining the battle. Redoubling his efforts, he fought courageously, killing and crippling opponents braving his sword. After receiving more than seventy wounds he fell to his death.

Muhammad, exhausted and bleeding from his injuries as were the majority of Believers around him, began thinking of regrouping his scattered forces as his men drove back the enemy. He gave the order to charge a nearby mound where it's elevation could be used as a focal point to collect the Muslims.

In a roar of "Allahu Akbar" that reverberated throughout the basin, they charged as one toward the designated hill. The tactic worked beautifully: frightening the pagans into further retreat; and marshaled the Muslims from every direction. Grouped together, supporting each other, the Muslims presented an indomitable force of fighting warriors as they drove through the opposition. Without exception, they cut down any who stood between them and their objective. As the battle raged on, the Muslims started spreading in an ever lengthening line of slashing, killing machines, dealing out death as they effectively warded off the enemy's assaults.

Sufyan, from a distance, watched the Muslims wipe out nearly a third of his army. Contorting his face into a scowl, he glared at his subordinates and said: "Tell the drummers to sound a withdrawal!" It was beyond his powers of imagination to understand how the Muslims could withstand and repulse their repeated attacks. He thought, while his men retreated that for every Muslim having fallen, better than a dozen of his own soldiers lay dead or wounded. Nevertheless, he intended to reorganize his army for another assault. The fleeing pagans, however, after having crossed a battlefield littered with the bodies of their own men, were now too afraid to fight even though they had to some extent succeeded in routing the Muslims.

When the enemy turned on their heels, Muhammad ordered his forces to pull back and attend to the wounded. It was then, to their horror they discovered the atrocities committed by the pagan women.

Sometime during the battle the women came onto the field. Hind, who initiated the outrage, disemboweled Hamzah and flung his organs about while chewing on his still warm liver. Then to encourage others in like manner, she raised Hamzah's liver above her head and with blood dripping from her red smeared face, screeched out her hatred for God's Prophet, the Muslims, and Islam. She next joined the women in hacking ears and noses off the bodies while others sliced the Muslims corpses to shreds. It was a gruesome scene which understandably incited the Believers into seeking revenge. But the growing number of casualties unsettled Muhammad and he instead ordered the burial of their dead.

At nightfall, Muhammad posted guards as a precaution against surprise attack then had the men form ranks so he could lead them in prayer. Normally standing to begin the prayer, he instead sat facing the Ka'bah's direction. The change wasn't due to bodily pain, or the pain in his heart: for Muslim loses were one in nine with hundreds wounded and a good many crippled for life. Every Muslim was pained over the looses and many took offense at those who withdrew from battle under false pretenses. But as the Prophet neither criticized nor condemned, they could do no less.

The following day after morning devotions, Muhammad announced that they would pursue the Disbelievers. The Muslims, as if energized by the Prophet's words, rose like a dynamic force: ready to fight again. They rallied around Muhammad, listening to his instructions, then circled round the field of death and began the six mile march towards Sufyan's camp.

The pagan guards, half asleep at their posts snapped alert in alarm: for the sound of horses; camels; and marching men, carried clearly over the crisp morning air. They watched for several seconds with mounting terror the ranks upon ranks of Muslim warriors coming at them. Leaving their weapons, they hastily scrambled from their positions and took to their heels in wild eyed panic to inform Sufyan.

Wakened by yelling guards charging into his tent, Sufyan angrily demanded silence and asked the reason for the intrusion. The guards were besides themselves with fear and all at once blurted out there were hordes of Muslims on the march. Sufyan's face drained of color, along with his remaining reserves. With twenty-eight of his captains killed and hundreds of dead and wounded, the situation was bad. Intuitively he knew the moment favored the Muslims. So, in frightened rage he cursed the Islamic forces and solemnly declared a formal and ritualistic desire that Quraysh would again measure swords. Next, he went over to the tent's flap and saw the huge cloud of dust darkening the horizon. He gulped involuntarily, gave one of the guards a message to give Muhammad, and issued the command to decamp for Mekkah.

The Holy Apostle saw from Duldul's back a lone rider in the distance galloping toward his army. Suspecting some devious plot, he halted the march. Ali, Dujanah and Zubair, rode up to the Prophet's side, wondering over the stop until Muhammad nodded in the direction of the oncoming rider. Together they watched, warily glancing every few seconds towards their flanks. Unconsciously they moved their mounts into a protective wedge in front of Muhammad.

The emissary, terrified by the reputations of the men surrounding the Prophet, stopped his mount fifty yards away. Cupping his hands around his mouth, he shouted across the stretch of sand: "Oh, Muhammad, hearken thou. The lord Abu Sufyan hath invested me to speak in his behalf. He challenges thee to another battle at the fair of Badr next year. Doth thou accept the challenge?"

"The challenge is accepted," bellowed back the Splendor of Prophets.

272

Thus, instead of another engagement, the battle was left undecided.

With a number of Muslims having been slain, the Prophet nearly killed, an amount of wounded, the soldiers of Islam returned to Madinah in a state of somberness. And when details of the battle became generally known, a great feeling of resentment arose. One group of Muslims wanted to put the archers who disobeyed Muhammad's instructions and the Jewish hypocrites to the sword. Others wanted to banish them from the area. One thing remained clear, they were a danger to the community. So before passions could incite mob action, Muhammad ordered an end to further suggestions until he contemplated the matter. The day, however, was not all downcast: Muhammad's daughter Fa'timah had given birth to a man child, Al-Hasan.

The Jewish tribe Nadheer, meanwhile, refusing to heed Banu Qaynuqa's example, seized the moment of indecision and cautiously began sowing seeds of sedition amongst the tribes in treaty with the Islamic city-state. Insidiously, they broadcasted insurgence until the Prophet revealed Qur'an's latest Revelation dealing with community social problems, including the lure of evil and treachery.

Selecting a day the mosque was apt to be filled, Muhammad led prayer as usual, then followed with the recitation of God's Message.

"In the name of Allah, The Beneficent, The Merciful."

"Oh' men! Take shelter in your Lord Who hath created you from a single self and created from it, it's pair, and spread from these two, men manifold and women, and fear Allah in Whose name ye importune one another, and (be mindful) of kinship; verily Allah is vigilant over you."

"And give unto orphans their property, and substitute not (your) worthless things for (their) good ones, and devour not ye their property, along with your own; for verily it is a great crime. And if ye fear that ye can not act justly among the orphans, then marry those who seem good to you, two, or three or four, and if ye fear that ye shall not deal justly (with so many) then (marry) one only, or (the slave woman) whom your right hands have acquired; that is nigh keeping you from transgressing."

"Give away women their dowry freely (without any restraint); but if, they of themselves remit unto you anything thereof, then (ye may) consume it with pleasure (and it shall be) wholesome (to you). And give not away to the weak in mind, your property which Allah hath made for you (a means of) your sustenance but maintain them therewith, and clothe them, and speak to them with kind words (for their good)."

"Worship ye Allah (alone) and associate not aught with Him, and do good to parents, and to kinfolk, and to orphans, and to the needy, and neighbor close to you and neighbor who is a stranger , and to a companion by your side and to the wayfarer, and to that which your right hands possess; verily Allah loveth not the proud, the boastful."

"Those who are misers and bid people miseredliness, and hide away what Allah of His bounty hath given them; We have prepared for the disbelievers a torment ignominious. And those who spend their property (in alms) to show to the people and believe not in Allah and in the Last Day (of Judgment); and he whose companion be Satan (what) an evil companion then is he! And what (harm) would it have done them if they had believed in Allah and the Last Day of (Judgment) and spent (benevolently) of what Allah hath provided them with; verily Allah is (fully) aware of them."

"Verily, Allah doth not injustice (even) to the weight of an atom, and if there be any good deeds He multiplieth it and giveth of His own accord a great reward. How will it be (then) when We shall bring forth from every people a witness and when We shall bring thee a witness over those (witnesses)? On that day will those who disbelieve and disobey the Prophet shall wish that the earth were leveled with them, but they shall not hide from Allah (even) a word."

"Hast thou not seen those to whom is given a part of the scripture? They but error and wish that ye too go astray from the (Right) way. But Allah best knoweth your enemies; and suffices Allah as your Protector and suffices Allah as a Helper."

"Of the Jews are those who (purposely) change the words from their places (to alter the meaning) and say 'We have heard, and we have not obeyed,' and hear, but as one that heareth not and RA'INA look at us, distorting (the word) with their tongues and taunting about the religion; but (instead) if they had said 'We have heard and we have obeyed,' and if they had said 'ISMA' (hearken) and 'UNZURNA' (look at us) it were better for them, and more upright, but Allah hath cursed them for their disbelief, so they believe not, but only a few."

"Oh, ye, whom the Scripture hath been given! Believe in what We have sent down confirming what is (already) with you, ere We change their faces and turn them towards their backs, or as We cursed the people of Sabbath; and (know ye, that) the Command of Allah is ever executed."

"Verily Allah forgiveth not (anything) be associated with Him, but He forgiveth what is besides that whomsoever He pleaseth; and whoever associateth (aught) with Allah, hath indeed devised a great sin. Hath thou not seen those who consider themselves pure? Nay, it is Allah Who purifieth whomsoever He pleaseth, and they shall not be wronged (even) the husk of a date-stone. Behold how they forge a lie against Allah! And that (itself) is sufficient as a manifest sin."

"Oh' ye who believe! Obey Allah and those vested with authority from among you; and if ye quarrel about anything refer it to Allah and the Apostle if ye believe in Allah and in the Last Day (of Judgment); this is the best and fairest way of ending (the dispute)."

"Hast thou not observed those who think they believe in what hath been sent down unto thee and what hath been sent down before thee? They intend to resort to the judgment of TAGHOOT (the Satan) though commanded were they to abjure (reject) him; and Satan intendeth to mislead them far astray. And when it is said unto them, 'Come (let us refer) to what Allah hath sent down (the Holy Qur'an) and to the Apostle (Muhammad)' thou seest the hypocrites turn away from thee with utter aversion."

"Hast thou not seen those unto whom was said, 'Withhold your hand (from war) and establish prayer and pay the poor-rate,' but when fighting was prescribed for them, lo, a party of them fear men as the fear of Allah, or even (with) a greater fear and say "Oh, our Lord, why hast Thou ordained upon us fighting, wherefore didst Thou not grant us respite to a near end;' say (O' Our Apostle Muhammad!): 'The provision of this world is scant and the Hereafter is better for him who guardeth (himself against evil), and ye shall not be wronged (even to the extent of) the husk of a date-stone."

"Wherever ye be, death will overtake you, even if ye be in towers (strong and) lofty; if good befalleth them they say, 'This is from thee;' say (O' Our Apostle Muhammad!) 'All is from Allah;' but what hath happened to these people that well-nigh they understand not anything spoken (to them)."

"Do they not think (carefully) in Qur'an? And if it had been from any other than Allah, they would surely have found in it much discrepancy. Allah! There is no god but He! He will certainly gather you all together on the Day of Resurrection; there is no doubt in it; who can be more True in Word than Allah?"

"Verily, We have revealed unto thee (O' Our Apostle Muhammad!) as We did reveal unto Noah and the Apostles after him; We did reveal unto Abraham, and Isma'il and Isaac and Jacob and the tribes, and Jesus and Job and Jonah, and Aaron, and Solomon, and gave We to David the Psalms. And apostles We have w(already) mentioned unto thee before and Apostles We mentioned not unto thee; and Allah spoke unto Moses, directly discoursing. (We sent) apostles as givers of glad tidings and warners, that there may not remain any argument for people against Allah, after (the coming of) these apostles, and Allah is Mighty, Wise."

"Allah (Himself) beareth Witness, that what He hath sent down unto thee (O' Our Apostle Muhammad) sent He that down, with His knowledge; and the Angels (too) bear witness; and sufficient is Allah for a Witness. Verily those who disbelieve and obstruct (people) from Allah's way, indeed have they strayed off, far away (from the Right Path). Verily, those who disbelieve and act unjustly, it is not for Allah to pardon them, nor is it that He will guide them to a way, except the way to Hell, to abide therein for ever! And this, for Allah is easy."

"Oh' mankind! Verily, the Apostle (Muhammad) hath come unto you with truth from your Lord; believe (then in him), it is good for you; and if ye disbelieve, then, Allah's is whatever is in the Heavens and the Earth; and Allah is All-Knowing, All-Wise. O' People of the Book! Overstep not in your religion, and say not upon Allah except the Truth; verily, verily, the Messiah Jesus, son of Mary, is only an apostle of Allah and His Word which He conveyed unto Mary, and a Spirit (Proceeding) from Him; believe therefore in Allah and His apostles, and say not (that there are) Three (gods); desist! It is good for you; verily, verily, Allah! (There is) Only One God! Far be it from His (Absolute) Purity that there be for Him a son; His is whatever is in the Heavens and whatever is in the Earth; Allah is sufficient as a Protector."(8)

Sufyan halted his army a distance from Mekkah, wanting to convince them of their victory. For more than three hours he blustered about their mightiness, the blow dealt to Islam, and lavished praise on those killed or wounded. Finally, when the army entered the city, the fraudulent fruit of his labor worked it's deception. The Mekkanese were overjoyed: they wanted revenge and they got it, seemingly. For those who knew better it was a hollow victory, ringing false to any looking beyond the rhetoric: no prisoners were in evidence; nor spoils of war; they could not enter Madinah; neither did they dare engage the Muslims the following day when marched upon.

In the City of the Prophet, al-Mustafa took three more wives: two, whose husbands had been martyred at Uhud, were married out of compassion and clemency; the other to cement ties with a neighboring tribe.

Soon afterwards, Muhammad held secret council with his trusted Companions, probing into Banu Nadheer's treachery and intrigues. Information had come to light of their instigating the area's tribes in committing acts of aggression. The Prophet ordered siege to their stronghold and led his battle weary men against Banu Nadheer. Setting his base of operations in a dry river bed, orders were issued to begin the investment. Guards were posted and Muslims settled in for the duration. At nightfall one of the Jews stole past the sentries and shot an arrow into the Prophet's tent. Near panic erupted as Muhajirun and Ansari surrounded God's Chosen one in shielding. Headquarters were moved further back, and in the confusion, the Lion of God vanished from the scene.

"Oh' Apostle of Allah, where is Ali," questioned the alarmed warriors.

He answered: "Worry not thyselves. Assuredly he is involved in some task which will bring benefit unto the message."

Before long Ali returned with the head of the individual responsible for attempting to assassinate Muhammad. He unceremoniously threw it to the ground before al-Mustafa.

"Ali, how didst thou accomplish this?"

Ali delayed before replying, allowing the pumping adrenal glands to subside. "Oh' Prophet, upon the arrow striking thy tent and knowing the craven manner of Allah's enemies, I set out to oversee the vigil. This infidel and nine others were advancing with drawn weapons. I charged and killed him for the reason that he carried the only bow. His companions escaped whilst I fought; however, they are yet near. If thou wilt send me with some men, insha'a Allah wilt we overtake them."

Muhammad turned and called out: "Dujanah, Sahl, follow Ali after selecteth he seven others, and seek out the enemies of Truth."

Ali's party discovered the squad of assassins before they could gain safe haven. The contest was quick and deadly and God's soldiers came away without injury. Their opponents were killed, decapitated and their heads thrown down the cooperative's well.

The following morning Banu Nadheer surrendered.

Other Jewish tribes around the area paid no mind of the lessons to be learned. Consequently, by virtue of Qurayshie propaganda, they ushered in schemes to murder the Believers.

A recent convert from Persia, Salman al-Farisi, wise in the ways of intrigue saw through the whispers and suspected an invasion. Fearing for the safety of his newly found Brotherhood, he took his apprehensions and knowledge of such affairs to the Prophet.

Muhammad was alarmed by the battle proven Persian's suspicions. He thought furiously while looking Salman over. Then in a voice tempered with restraint, asked: "Hast thou revealed thy suspicions to anyone?"

"Nay, my Prophet," returned Salman, wondering over the question.

"Wouldst thou come to the assembly hall after evening prayer and relate thy account to the council?"

"Thy word is but what I follow and heed, O' Prophet."

That evening the hall filled to capacity. Speculation about their sudden summons kept the hall alive with chatter as elders and

Companions tried to discern the reason. Then, with filial respect the din vanished when the al-Amin entered with Salman on one side and Ali on the other.

"As-salaamu alaikum," greeted Muhammad.

"Wa alaikum as-salaam," returned the assembly as one.

Muhammad positioned himself atop a small dais and said: "Come I unto thee with a matter of grave concern to seek thy counsel. Thus, I petition thee to give audience unto Salman al-Farisi, whom thou knowest as Salman the Persian. He is a man confirmed in war who fought under the Persian king Parwiz while their armies conquered Aleppo, Antioch, Damascus, and other chief Syrian cities. They crushed the idolatrous Christians in Jerusalem,(9) and was he in the battle at Issus, and in Constantinople. Hence, he is knowledgeable about matters of war and bringeth he wisdom to the passing words against us. Hearken ye unto his counsel well, then wilt we decide upon a course of action."

After Salman rendered his past experience in gathering information, he detailed his analysis of the rumors which confirmed their suspicions. However, as wise and alert to the complicated machinations of contention, he could not provide a time of attack.

There was an angry silence across the room while people looked to one another as their thoughts fell into place. Without so much as a word between members of the council, all were in accord that some of the surrounding tribes had broken treaty with acts of duplicity and instigation. Agitated murmurings erupted in varying degrees of reaction: some favored banishment while others called for their death. The sit down ended in a unanimous voice for offensive action. So, it was decided that measures by which to set an example would be taken.

"Ali, Dujanah, Salman, Bilal, Jabir, Zubair, wouldst thou remain behind," said Muhammad as the council broke up and started to leave. Understanding time was of the essence to stave off any surprise attacks, he waited for the hall to clear before instructing the men what to do. Thus, for the next several months the Muslims led one preemptive strike after another.

CHAPTER THIRTY

Some years had now passed since the Prophet left Mekkah for Madinah. The years witnessed tremendous activity as people by the numbers came into the folds of Islam. Actively they studied the Qur'an and learned the Way of life, even while the confederacy again wove another network of alliances and conspiracies.

One day, a group of polytheists entered Madinah declaring their tribe's desire to learn God's Message. They were claiming with such sincerity that once the Truth had been given to them their entire tribe would convert. Word quickly reached the Prophet that another tribe wanted to enter Islam's embrace. So, when the men humbly approached Muhammad requesting teachers, he was delighted and assigned six versed Muslims to accompany the men back to their tribe

The day they departed it seemed as if the whole Muslim community came out to wish the six preceptors well, turning the event into an impromptu festival. People enjoyed themselves, talked and watched the children in amusement. It was a joyous occasion: gathering men into Islam's breast always brought out the best in Muslims. Delayed for more than an hour, the Believers along with the men from the petitioning tribe finally rode off amid shouts of "Allahu Akbar" and "Laa ilaaha illal-laah."

All through the journey, the men kept the Muslims occupied with discussion. But when they entered the small Valley of al-Raji, Marsad suddenly sensed a double-cross. He called to the other Believers and they immediately drew near to one another for protection. Their hosts laughed chillingly as they sped away in the opposite direction. Unsheathing weapons, the Muslims formed a rough circle and started searching the countryside for ambush. Moments later, from behind boulders and rises in the earth, an armed band of over fifty Lihyan youths attacked, screaming and cursing as they charged. Marsad and the others backed their mounts rear to rear, flank to flank, roared in unison: "Allahu Akbar," and fought with a fury which momentarily surprised the youths. But with the numbers so heavily favored against them, it was only a matter of minutes before they were overtaken. Three lay dead, Zayd ibn Dasinah, Khubayb Adiy and Taarah were taken prisoners.

Bound and gagged, the surviving Muslims suffered humiliation upon humiliation while preparations were made for the journey to Mekkah where they would be turned over to the Qurayshies. The second night out, Taarah freed himself from his bonds and started to untie Zayd and Khubayb's bonds. They pleaded with him to flee, as they were severely injured and would only hinder his chance to escape. Torn between compassion for his Brothers in faith and the instinct for survival, he wept. Then, with a Herculean cry of "Allahu Akbar" he struck the nearest guard senseless, snatched his weapon and flung himself against his captors.

Hampered by his own aches and pains, it wasn't long before the Disbelievers overpowered him. In an act of vengefulness, one of the youths reared his horse to allow the beast's forelegs to come down and crush Taarah's legs: pulverizing them into dangling mush.

Groaning, as the throbbing pain racked his body and nearly unconscious, the pagan youths bound his arms behind him, fracturing his arms in the process. Next, they shoe-laced his shattered legs with wet strips of hide and dragged him to an igneous area of broken rock. Doused with water, he regained his senses while the burning sun dried and shrank his leather bindings. The strips cut into his encrusted flesh and renewed the bleeding, adding to the pain of his already ravaged body. Insects, drawn by the sickly sweet coppery smell of blood, began crawling toward Taarah's withering body. Using their mandibles and pincers, they started tearing away bits of torn flesh. Incapable of flinging away the voracious little creatures, his pain increased to intolerable heights. He realized with sudden clarity that he had not long for this world. So, disregarding the torment his shell endured, he focused his mind on God. In a voice pierced with agony he bellowed: "Allahu Akbar" and began reciting the seven most oft-repeated verses of the Qur'an.* His act of devotion and respect to the One God, so incited the tribe, they started stoning him until Allah's Mercy released him from the physical plane of existence.

The chief, fearing the Muslim's effect of dying for what he believed in so courageously, ordered his men to take the prisoners forthwith to Mekkah lest they convert any in his tribe. Zayd and Khubayb were enchained to prevent further attempts at escape, thrown unceremoniously into a cart and taken that evening. Burdened only by it's human cargo, the train made fast time and encountered Safwan Umayyah's caravan as it returned from Syria.

Safwan, whose father was slain at Badr, recognized Zayd and Khubayb. Smiling malevolently, he purchased the two captives for the sole purpose of avenging his father's death. He replaced the chains with prickly grained fetters and manacles with lengths of chain extending down to their leg shackles. He couldn't wait to inflict the torture he dreamed of doing to any Muslim and stopped in Tan'im. There in the presence of a large assemblage of Mekkanese he had his prisoners yoked to iron pillars.

---

* The Al-Fatiha, opening chapter of the Holy Qur'an

For hours the infidels circled round about them: cursing, spitting, and bombarding them with refuse. Neither Zayd nor Khubayb cowed or surrendered their dignity under the abuse. Instead, they spent the time glorifying God. Finally incensed by their unshakable faith, the Pharaoh of Mekkah, Abu Sufyan stepped to Zayd.

He said: "If I put thee on oath to tell me with the name of Allah whether thou wishest Muhammad to be slain in thy stead that thou mayest be set free, wouldst thou be inclined to do so?"

Zayd replied, pity for Sufyan inflecting his tone: "Wish I not that even a thorn prick his foot." Sufyan glowered menacingly and ordered both Muslims whipped until their bodies sagged in unconsciousness. Still not satisfied, Zayd was drenched with sewage and hung to die.

Later that day, Khubayb, before facing the hangman sought leave to offer ritual prayer. Performed with perfect solemnity, he addressed the chiefs of Quraysh. "Had it not been the fact that ye would have thought I feared death I would have offered more salat and lengthened my kneeing and prostration." Tilting his face to the heavens, he said: "Oh, Allah! Fulfilled we the duty mandated by Thy Prophet. O' Allah! Thou seest there is no well-wisher who could communicate my salaam unto Thy Holy Prophet. O' Lord! May Thou convey my salaam unto him. O' Lor-" Khubayb was suddenly killed with a sword by Abu Uqbah.

In the territory of Nejd, a sizable area of Arabia resisting the Way, agents of Quraysh commissioned Abu Bara'a in their conspiracy. Renowned for his talent at persuasion and skills of deception, they instructed him to go to Madinah.

Once there he took several days investigating the Muslim state of mind, because they were still discussing the treachery at al-Raji. Learning all he could, he implemented his plan and started inquiring about Islam. With an innocence belying his evil intentions he made a show of seeking the truth to all who he came in contact with. So convincing was his desire to acquire Islamic knowledge, that inside of three weeks he had Believers lauding his enthusiasm to the Prophet.

Muhammad, yet uneasy over the warrantless deaths of his six missionaries, kept bringing to mind their murder whenever Abu Bara'a's zeal was mentioned. Finally, in a move calculated to counter any treachery, he appointed Amr ibn Umayyah to discover what he could about the man. Two weeks passed; Amr, satisfied with the man's straightforwardness, introduced him to the Prophet.

God's Holy Apostle received him with great welcome, immediately noticing his accent and style of dress. After an hour's audience he was taken with the man's eagerness and relaxed his concerns. But when the man mentioned the tribes in his area needed twenty teachers of Islam, an alarm bell sounded in mute warning.

"Where are these men needed," asked Muhammad, masking his growing suspicions with interest.

"Bi'r Ma'una," answered Abu Bara'a.

In tense silence Muhammad regarded him as he considered the area, his tone and attire. He hesitated to delegate any Muslim for the task. Bara'a, seeing the Prophet's concern, brought to bear his silvery tongue. Still harboring misgivings, Muhammad started sifting through the man's words while he spoke, searching for anything that would expose his motives. Abu Bara'a sensed Muhammad's scrutiny and smoothly changed tactics, promising the learned Muslims safety would be protected with his life, and even going as far as to invoke God as his witness. To Muhammad, there was no better witness over man's affair than God. He agreed to dispatch a group of Muslims into the area.

Two days later, Prophet Muhammad thought a large number of Muslims would better serve to safeguard each other and sent forty missionaries to Bi'r Ma'una. Again, the Islamic community turned out to cheerfully bid farewell, even as their optimism was undermined by the six recent deaths.

The Nejdian, having made friends while in Madinah, knew most of the learned Muslims making up the caravan. He kept them in high spirits, especially after leading them around several settlements full of Jewish and pagan malcontents. So, when the group reached Bi'r Ma'una, the Muslims did not expect any foul play and were caught in ambush by over three-hundred men of Banu's Amir and Sulaym. From seemingly nowhere volley after volley of arrows sailed through the air, finding their marks with deadly accuracy. The Muslims could not escape the fatal shower of death and fell dead or wounded. Wounded camels spit and snorted as they staggered about without direction while the injured writhed in pain. An instant later two-hundred horsemen thundered into view and mercilessly fell upon the surviving Muslims, killing thirty-nine out of forty.

Left for dead, Ka'b ibn Zayd regained consciousness a few hours after the attack. He had lain where he fell, hearing nothing but the loud buzzing of insects. He tried opening his eyes but couldn't, the blood from his wounds had dried into a thick crust over his face. For a few moments he panicked, thinking himself blind when in his reflexive struggle to open his eyes the crust of blood cracked and a golden streak of daylight pierced the darkness. Peeling away the encrustation, he propped himself up and stared at the carnage around him. It was horrible, a blow to his senses. All his companions were slain, a number of them mutilated and recognizable only by their clothes. From the tracks he surmised the polytheists had dragged away a number of the dead. Stripped of weapons and anything of value, he scanned the vicinity for any kind of implement with which to bury his fallen brethren. But seeing nothing he could use, he began to weep, beseeching The Forgiver to forgive him for not being able to bury His servants. He said several prayers for the dead, consigning them to God's care, then started the trek back to Madinah.

News of the slaughter devastated the Muslim community, thrusting them into deeper mourning. More than thirty families had the heads of their household slain, orphaning in a sense the women as well as the children.

Prophet Muhammad, during Jumu'ah service looked out over the assembly, seeing faces full of grief. He thought: why do the Christian and Jewish tribes continually aggress upon us and force us to defend ourselves; we are a peace loving people who desire only to spread Allah's Word... O' Allah! Let Thy Message be a guide for the betterment of humanity. Pained by the memories, he wiped at his eyes as they threatened to spill.

A young child began to cry, bringing Muhammad back to his sermon.

"In the name of Allah, The Beneficent, The Merciful. The Hypocrites and kafirun think they can deceive Allah with their deceptions. They plot, plan, mock the Way, and slight Muslims at every turn. If ye wonder why the good suffereth and evildoers thrive, keep ye in mind the Final Goal, where true adjustments will be made. The gainers here will be the losers there,(1) in the Hereafter."

"Nations and men of yore assumed arrogance and perished because they were unjust, but that destruction was only a foretaste of the Doom to come in the next life.(2) Waste not nor misuse thy life. Time through the ages beareth witness that remaineth nothing but Faith and Good deeds.(3) What endureth if ye deny all Faith and private responsibility?(4) The man of faith holdeth fast unto his faith, because he knoweth it to be true.(5) All resistance is vain and perdition is the end of all evil.(6) Thus, guard ye well Allah's Truth and close not the door. His Wisdom will foil the treachery of those who rebel against Faith and He will turn their plots against them. There is no god but He, Allah! The One and Only, The Irresistible! Hearken unto what the Lord hath Promised."

"Nay! The record of the wicked hast been preserved in the SAJJIN, and what will make thee know what SAJJIN is? It is a Book Written; woe on that day unto the beliers: those who belie the Day of Judgment. And belieth it not (any one) save every transgressor, a sinner. When, are recited unto him Our signs, saith he: '(These are only) the stories of yore!' Nay! Rather, has rusted their hearts, what they used to do. Nay! Verily that day they shall be shut out away from the mercy of their Lord. Verily, they shall be committed to the flaming Fire, then shall it be said (unto them): 'This is that which ye belied!'"

"Nay! The record of the righteous shall be in the ILLIYUN. And what will make thee know what the ILLIYUN is? (It is) a Book Written. See it those who are the near ones unto Allah. Verily the righteous ones shall be in bounteous bliss, on exalted couches will they view (the delightful sights)."(7)

"Verily, the chastisement of thy Lord shall indeed come to pass, there is none to repel it. On the Day when the heaven shall reel a (Terrible) reeling, and the mountains shall fly an (awful) flight. Woe then that Day unto those who belie the Truth, those who, in vain sport do play. The Day on which they shall be driven unto the Hell-Fire with a violent drive. (And it shall be said unto them): 'This is the Fire which ye used to belie!'"(8)

Finishing, Muhammad took a moment to study his audience. After observing the faces staring back at him, he sensed rather than felt the service accomplished the curative effect he'd been hoping for. Praise be to God, he thought before asking the congregation's assistance in providing shelter for the orphaned families. The response was overwhelming, even the poorest offered their homes, making him select who were most capable of furnishing lodgings. With matters settled he restarted the instructional classes in Islam, and under his guidance the Muslims numbers increased dramatically.

Months passed without further incident. Islam started to crack the walls of resistance as it ingressed into the interior and spread beyond Arabia's borders. Muhammad entered his sixteenth year of Prophethood and took two elderly wives to further relations with surrounding tribes. The Confederacy, through it's network of allies and hypocrites continued their hostilities with occasional strikes against budding Islamic communities. Abd ibn Ubayy, through cunning and deception managed to maintain his hypocritical endeavors secret, and enlisted Banu Mustaliq's support against the Muslims.

It wasn't long with the amount of intrigue taking place in and around Madinah before Islam's enemies contrived another scheme aimed to slay the Prophet. One afternoon, while Muhammad expounded God's Message, a Jewish emissary from Banu Nuzayr arrived, asking for an audience with the Prophet. Following what constituted a visual search for weapons, permission was granted. He was then surrounded by the trusted Companions and escorted into the assembly hall where he requested, in his tribe's behalf, Muhammad's presence to renew their treaty of mutual defense.

Prior to committing himself, Muhammad flashed on past treacheries. He said: "Tell thy elders wilt I come to their quarter before nightfall." True to his word, he visited the burgh ringed by Muslim warriors who were all of imposing stature, battle proven, heavily armed, and renowned for their fierceness.

Asked to wait next to a wall while the elders were summoned, Muhammad felt exposed: like a target which triggered his senses in alarm. Instinctively, his eyes narrowed to slits as he panned his vision over the vicinity scanning for signs of peril. Turning back toward a small group of men, he zeroed in and noticed they repeatedly glanced in his direction. Convinced their actions were at the least suspicious, he decided it best to depart. No sooner had he and his companions moved away, a huge boulder crashed into the earth where they'd been standing. The warriors spun around with lightening-like reflexes, drawing their weapons as they did so. Seeing nothing but a five or six-hundred pound boulder and rising dust, Muhammad ordered a quick retreat back to the city.

The Muslim community, after hearing about the incident fell to discussing it amongst themselves. In the end they were convinced chance had nothing whatsoever to do with the mishap. The general consensus being that the tribe responsible was, of late conducting itself in a manner like the ousted tribes had. Consequently, they converged on the Prophet's home, where in angry protest they raised their voices against the offending tribe: for the attempt brought home the point that all were still in danger. Something had to be done, patience also had it's limits.

The act of aggression, however crafty, was the last link in a chain of events which prompted the Prophet into delivering an ultimatum. Abhorring violence and it's ugly ramifications, Muhammad, following much consultation between the elders, decided against attack and granted Banu Nuzayr ten days time to evacuate Madinah's region.

In a predawn raid, Ali and his party of warriors converged on the chief's house. Easily slipping through unsuspecting defenses, the Muslims penetrated the chief's abode and took him by surprise. Ali stepped forward, nodded to Muhammad ibn Maslamah who issued the Prophet's ultimatum.

"The exalted leader of God's Way hath sent ye a message through me. Ye of Banu Nuzayr should quit this area within ten days at the latest, and if ye refuse to depart from this region, war will be declared."

"F-for wh-what reason doth thou dare to exile Banu Nuzayr," sputtered out the chieftain in frightened rage.

"The elders of the city have determined that Banu Nuzayr hath practiced treachery and infidelity unto the treaty with the city," ibn Maslamah returned sternly.

The chief glanced around his room furtively as if seeking a means to escape their withering stares. Thinking of the secret agreements with the Mekkans to come to their rescue, the allied Hypocrites within Madinah, and the strength of his stronghold, he said defiantly: "We will not depart!"

"It is thy choice," returned Ali and spun to depart, followed by his men.

Immediately informed of Banu Nuzayr's refusal. Muhammad thought a moment then paired off Ali's men and gave them new instructions. All through the evening and most of the night, Ali and his men knocked on doors, gathering men until they had a full complement of warriors. Just before true dawn sliced the horizon, three-hundred men had amassed outside the assembly hall to hear the Prophet speak and measure swords if need be.

Muhammad ended his all night prayers, drawn by the sound of men and clanging armaments. He stepped out of the mosque. The odor of bull hide shielding assailed his senses. He scanned the area searching for the best vantage point to say what he had to say. Long seconds passed, the men settled down. Muhammad decided upon the ledge running the hall's length which afforded the elevation he needed to be seen and heard by all.

Banu Nuzayr had been expecting eventual hostilities for the last ten days and were prepared to engage in warfare. Promised by ibn Ubayy that in their hour of need two-thousand armed soldiers would come to their aid, they defied the city's directive.

In light of the challenge to the Prophet's authority, Muhammad nevertheless kept to his pledge and waited the allotted time to elapse before enacting contingency plans.

Early morning of the eleventh day, Muslim warriors again grouped around the assembly hall. Muhammad stepped upon the same elevation. "Oh, ye soldiers of Allah," God's Apostle solemnly commenced.

"In the name of Allah, The Beneficent, The Merciful.

"Halloweth Allah whatsoever is in the heavens and whatsoever is in the earth; and He is The Ever-Prevalent, The All-Wise."

"Oh' ye who believe! Why say ye what ye (yourselves) do (it) not? Most hateful is it unto Allah that ye say what ye (yourselves) do (it) not. Verily Allah loveth those who fight in His way in ranks as if they were an unbreakable metal wall."

"And when said Moses unto his people: "Oh, ye my people! Why do ye pain me? While indeed ye know that verily I am the apostle of Allah unto you;' but when (yet) went they astray, Allah (too) allowed their hearts (to stray); and Allah guideth not the people who transgress."

"And when said Jesus, son of Mary: "Oh, ye children of Israel! Verily I am an apostle of Allah* unto you, confirming what is before you of the Torah and bearing (unto you) the glad tidings of an Apostle who shall come after me, his name being Ahmad (i.e., Muhammad);' and when came he (Muhammad) unto them said they: 'This is a manifest sorcery!'"

"And who is more unjust than he who forgeth a lie against Allah while he is invited unto Islam? And Allah guideth not the unjust people. Intend they to put out the Light of Allah with their mouths, but Allah will perfect His Light; though averse may be the disbelievers. He it is Who hath sent His Apostle (Muhammad) with the Guidance (Qur'an) and the Religion of Truth, that He may make it triumph over all the (other) religions, though averse may be the polytheists."(9)

"Thus, temper thy anger when ye have the enemy at sword's point and deal kindly and justly with all: it may be that those whom ye hate now, will love you later. And keep in remembrance Allah's promise: trust in Him and strive thy utmost in His Cause. Allahu Akbar!"

"Allahu Akbar," roared back the warriors and set off toward the fortified township a few miles away.

By sunrise the Muslims besieged the burgh. They encircled the nest of insurrection in preparation to attack, keeping a safe distance from the bowmen perched atop the walls. Half the men started erecting tents while the other half began hacking down surrounding trees: using them to dam up the water supply. At regular intervals around the small municipality, Muslim bowmen drove arrows into the sand for easy access and rapid firing, spearmen adjusted shields and loosened their biceps, mounted soldiers unsheathed swords and swung spiked maces through the air.

The siege commenced.

The Jews, after eleven days with no help coming from their secret alliances, combined with their water shortage, sent a tribal representative bearing their banner downwards which signified surrender to all. But there was no discussion. Instead, they had to vacate the area immediately. They were stripped of weapons and forced into exile under escort.

Miles away from Madinah the Muslim guard withdrew their escort and left the Jews to decide their own fates. Most departed from their brethren for Syria, wanting to flee from the Truth. The others went onto Khaybar and Fadak: fortress cities ninety miles north of Madinah.

---

* See Luke 13:33

Months later, Muhammad led fifteen-hundred of Islam's fiercest warriors towards Badr's plains to meet Abu Sufyan's challenge. After a week's time it became obvious the Disbelievers weren't coming. Thus, seizing the opportunity to propagate the Word, Muhammad and the Muslim force stopped at Badr's fair. They returned to Madinah not only unharmed but strengthened with the addition of new converts, enriched with new friendships, new alliances, and once again Muhammad was a grandfather: Fa'timah had given birth to another man child, al-Husayn.

Emperor Heraclius, following a succession of victories along the Black Sea's southern shore, drove the tenacious Persians into the region of Kars and Trebizond where they were finally repulsed from the area. Thereafter, the Avars, fearing the string of Roman successes, betrayed their treaty with the Byzantine government and united with the Persians.

Heraclius, with Constantinople again under siege, made treaties with the Turks. And with their help all but quelled the hostility against the city. Now, by force of arms he marched his army through Armenia, toward Mesopotamia where he planned to strike at the very heart of the Persian Empire.(10)

CHAPTER THIRTY-ONE

Pagan Quraysh and its allies, after many years persecuting the Muslims, could not do away with or beat back the Islamic spirit. Moreover, as reports started arriving with alarming regularity of different tribes and clans reverting the old way of life, the Qurayshis began to experience a subtle pressure against their own unjust aristocracy. The Confederates were now in desperation against Islam's growing influence and power, and sent out additional agents to seek those resisting the change.

Armed with highly exaggerated propaganda about Muslim strengths and weaknesses, they scoured the country. Banu Ghatfan, a large tribe of Bedouin Arabs from the interior, the Ghanam of Quba'a, the Sulaym of Hunayn, the Khuzaymah, the Tayy, and a half dozen others all lured by promises of riches, affiliated themselves with the Quraysh. Also joining this evil minded league of oppressors were the expelled Jewish tribes of Qaynuqa, Nadheer and Nuzayr.

Midway during the Prophet's fifth year in Madinah, most of the troublesome tribes in and around the city had been ejected from the region. The Muslim community had grown so large it now dominated the city and it's environs. Holy Scripture continued their manifestation and Islamic knowledge increased. Emphasis, in this time of relative peace was in spreading the Truth.

Nearing year's end another threat reared it's ugly head. Agents of Quraysh, through secret communications convinced Banu Qurayzah, one of the remaining Jewish tribes in Madinah, to start a war of propaganda against Islam hoping to undermine it's growing respect and dynamic power. The Hypocrites, feeling they had the upper hand and fueled by promises of financial gain, began orchestrating the Confederacy's allies into attacking small Muslim outposts and killing its men which produced an undefined disquiet throughout the territory.

Almost immediately the Islamic forces retaliated and struck before any more Muslim lives could be lost. All but exposed for their treachery, the Hypocrites and Disbelievers were suddenly silent, ominously so.

Most in the Islamic community attributed the cessation of threats and hostilities as nothing less than fear of reprisals and were content to let matters be. But al-Mustafa saw beyond the forced smiles and insincere salutations of those who a short time ago were turning their backs to him. Muhammad was wise to his enemy's wiliness and thought the non negotiated armistice as some kind of lull before the storm. Yet, he allowed the benefit of doubt to shade his decision against taking retaliatory action against the suspected tribes. He, instead, summoned the trusted Companions and revealed his suspicions.

Hours of discussion ensued, reaching its conclusion when Muhammad, seeing no end to the rhetoric, asked Ali, Salman the Persian, Abu Dujanah and Dihyah Kalbi, to ride for three days towards each point of the compass to find out what they could about their enemies.

Six days later all four men returned with varying reports. Ali, Dihyah and Dujanah, gave accounts of the pagans beguiling nature. Salman, on the other hand, spoke of something he couldn't quite define and added that agents of Quraysh were enlisting men.

Over three-hundred miles southward, Qurayshie and Mekkan leaders had been joined by scores of influential Jews wanting to fight the Islamic arrogation of authority. Pooling their resources, they accomplished a feat never before equaled in Arabia's history, and surpassed only by the Prophet in years to come: uniting men so massively for a common cause.

Abbas, a Qurayshie leader in his own right, had never been summoned to attend the city's councils, or shared confidences with it's political body because of his relationship with Muhammad. Nonetheless, he kept alert and abreast of the Confederacy's transactions for his nephew.

One day he became curious after noticing an influx of soldierly looking men and ventured out into their midst to listen. At first, he thought their talk was the usual resentful remarks about Islam. But as the days passed, the crowds of new faces grew into hordes of hard drinking men who boasted of their proficiency in war. Even Amr ibn Abdwid, Arabia's most feared warrior, pitched his tent outside the city in what was fast becoming a temporary township. Then, shipments of dried foods, supplies, weapons, horses and camels, started arriving with every incoming caravan. Now alarmed at the massing of men and provisions, Abbas dispatched a messenger to Muhammad, detailing everything he saw and heard.

All in all, the infidels had amassed over ten-thousand men, an unprecedented number ever put together for war in Arabia. There were thousands of cavalrymen equipped with full body armor, thousands of cameleers, and thousands of foot soldiers, also outfitted in mail.

* * * * *

Back in Madinah, young Anas was up in the uppermost part of the mosque cleaning. From the corner of his vision he detected some movement in the distance. Pausing, he watched until the diminutive form took shape. Then, as if prodded with a spear jumped back, knocking over his pail of water, and ran down the stairs shouting at the top of his lungs. Hearing him one would have thought an army approached. He was as close as one could get to the truth.

Ali, alone with his two children in his house next to the Prophet's, chilled when he heard Muhammad's attendant excited yelling. Snatching the boys up, he placed them under his arms and ran to Fa'timah. He said but few words, surrendered al-Hasan and al-Husayn, then raced to find the Prophet. He found Muhammad just as Anas ended his report. Seeing no signs of danger or looks of apprehension, he sighed in relief and returned to his family smiling over Anas' excitability.

Muhammad on the other hand, felt a sense of foreboding upon hearing the youngster's first outcry. He hoped his anxieties had exaggerated themselves while calming Anas down. But before probing his feelings, the rider rapped his knuckles against the door. Dreading to hear what he felt, he answered the door. Anas, sensitive to al-Mustafa's moods, followed closely behind in case he was needed.

"As-salaamu alaikum," greeted Muhammad, smiling warmly as he recognized his uncle's friend.

"Wa alaikum as-salaam," replied the Mekkan.

"Hast thou news from Abbas?"

Muhammad was stunned by the information. Never before had an army of such magnitude been gathered to crush an opponent. He closed his eyes, momentarily losing track of his visitor and surroundings as an infusion of ideas assailed the depths of his mind.

Anas and the news bearer stared, waiting for some instruction. Long minutes passed, concern growing in both their eyes. Muhammad suddenly snapped his eyes open and without intending, spoke sharply to Anas.

"Summon Ali!" He turned to face his uncle's emissary. "Doth thou wish to return to Mekkah?"

"Nay! My place is with thee, O' Prophet."

Before noon prayers, Muhammad met with elders and trusted Companions to discuss the latest turn of events. He listened to numerous suggestions, many of which he dismissed as impractical while others made food for thought. Back and forth they voiced their opinions; until, in the meeting's dying stages Salman interjected a proposal that galvanized the represented government into a renewed frenzy of speculation. Muhammad agreed immediately and the council adjourned in unanimous agreement to follow through with the Persian's recommendation of excavating a trench stretching between two elevations surrounding the city.

Realizing there was no time to waste as enemy forces were expected to reach Madinah inside of six days. Muhammad exercised his options and requested assistance from Banu Qurayzah. They refused to engage in a battle not of their own making, and only provided tools to aid with the digging of the ditch. Technically, they filled the obligations of their treaty with the Islamic city-state, but fell short of the moral ramifications.

Thus, using every available implement the city had to offer, the digging began that same afternoon and continued night and day. Tirelessly the Muslims toiled, redoubling their efforts as a matter of course when "Allahu Akbar" sounded. Homes considered in danger areas were abandon and others were fortified into offensive platforms. Then, just before the pagan army arrived the trench was completed, averaging fifteen feet in width and twelve feet in depth.

* * * * *

Abu Sufyan for the second time was chosen to lead the army of infidels against the Believers. He was so confident, he halted his army two days out from Madinah and had the standard bearers place their idols upon an elevation. He, then, made a show of praising the images: hoping to foster within his soldiers a sense of dedication. Remounting, he went up a nearby dune and reviewed his army which stretched back for miles. Yea, he thought, surely wilt Muhammad surrender upon sight of my forces.

At the same time fifty miles away, the Prophet stared out his tent's flap which had been erected well back of the yawning trench where he could overlook his army. Oblivious to preparations of war, he sat cross-legged devising different strategies for directing less than three thousand Muslims. After making several decisions, he summoned Ali and disclosed his assessments. He watched Ali leave to carry out his orders, then prostrated to pray for strength and guidance. In the midst of his prayer, The Beneficent, Merciful God, did give answer through His Archangel Gabriel.

In sunset's last stages, Muhammad exited his tent to a cloud covered heaven, the color of vermilion. He maintained an indecipherable look on his face while surveying the area searching for Bilal. Locating him atop the battleground's highest point, the Prophet gave his signal.

Bilal raised his hands to cup his ears and melodiously chanted the Adhan: "Alla-a-a-hu Akbar, Alla-a-a-hu Akbar," pausing long enough to face the other direction, he continued. "Alla-a-a-hu Akbar, Alla-a-a-hu Akbar." Facing forward, he trolled out: "Ash-sh-sh hadu an laa ilaa-ha il-lal-la-a-ah, Ash-sh-sh hadu an laa ilaa-ha il-lal-la-a-ah, Ash-sh-sh hadu an-n-n-na Mu-u-u-ham-m-m-m-ma-a-dan Rasu-u-ul-lu-ul la-a-a-ah, Ash-sh-sh hadu an-n-n-na Mu-u-u-ham-m-m-m-ma-a-dan Rasu-u-ul-lu-ul la-a-a-ah." (A) Turning to face the right, "Hi-yya alas Sa-a-la-at, Hi-y-ya alas Sa-a-la-at," facing left, "Hi-y-ya alal Fa-la-a-ah, Hi-y-ya alal Fa-la-a-ah." Facing forward again, "Hi-y-ya ala Khai-ai-ril-amal, Hi-y-ya ala Khai-ai-ril-amal. Alla-a-a-hu Akbar, Alla-a-a-hu Akbar. Laa ilaa-ha il-lal-la-a-ah, Laa ilaa-ha il-lal-la-a-ah."

Except for the Muslims assigned to strategic points of defense, all others answered the Call to Prayer and arranged themselves in close ranks behind God's Mercy of the World. At prayer's end, al-Mustafa faced his warriors and spoke.

"To Allah belongeth all Wisdom and Guidance and wilt He bestow it according to His Wise and Universal Plan. So let not the world's foolishness divert ye from the service of Allah.(1) The issue of all things dependeth on Allah alone: we must put our trust in Him as The Guardian of all things, both great and small,(2) for the keys of Life and Death are in His hands,(3) and justly wilt Allah enforce His Law. Learn ye from the doom upon the people of ancient times. If the kafirun could but see how the End will shape itself, how the Good will be sorted out from Evil. If they learn not now; alas, it will be too late when Time's wings are furled.(4) Allah's Plan canst not ever be frustrated, nor changed, and pagan Quraysh along with their followers canst not escape the inevitable doom for their sins. Hearken ye well unto His Word."

"In the name of Allah, The Beneficent, The Merciful."

"Praiseth whatsoever is in the heavens and whatsoever is in the earth the Glory of Allah; and He is The Ever-Prevalent, The All-Wise. He it is Who caused those who disbelieved among the people of the Book to go out from their homes unto the first banishment; ye deemed not that they would go out; while they thought that their fortresses would protect them against Allah, but came upon them Allah from whence they looked not for Him, and caused (such) terror into their hearts that they demolished their homes with their own hands and the hands of the Believers; therefore get warned O' ye who have eyes! And were it not that Allah had decreed against them the exile, certainly would He have chastised them in this world; and for them in the Hereafter shall be the chastisement of the Fire. That is for that they opposed Allah and His Apostle and whosoever opposeth Allah, then verily Allah is severe in retribution.""Oh' ye who believe! Fear ye (the wrath of) Allah! Let every soul (carefully) look well to what it hath sent on for the morrow (the Day of Reckoning); and fear ye (the wrath of) Allah; verily Allah is All-Aware of whatever ye do."(5)

Concluding, Muhammad remained silent, motionless, his attention fixed somewhere behind his troops. Following a deep breath, he asked the archers to step forward. He divided them into thirty groups of ten, instructing them to take extra sheaves of arrows and spears to positions behind the mounds of displaced earth and up to the fortified defenses. Next, he gave orders for the rest of the men to line themselves along the trench. When all was in readiness, a strange type of quiet settled over the area, full of nervousness and expectation.

The waiting began.

Early next morning, shortly before the sun made it's appearance, the sound of an approaching army could be heard. Even the earth trembled underfoot as thousands upon thousands of soldiers, horses, camels, livestock and women, tread through the basin. The women, who were following the men, trolled out chants for encouragement and victory. Bearers, in the fore, carried idols for the pagans to take heart.

As the sun crested over the mountains, the Muslims were able to see the huge cloud of dust which appeared to cast the plain behind their enemy in shadow. And when the whole formidable army of the Confederacy came into the valley, Hypocrites among the Islamic ranks began their best to undermine confidences. With innuendo they started circulating defeatist attitudes: telling all that overcoming the enemy was nothing but delusive hope. Next, they pretended to withdraw for the defense of their homes, even though their homes were not exposed. Muhammad noted their traitorous actions and would bring them to account at a later time, if Allah willed, he thought.

Sufyan, overseeing the battle to come a half mile back, thought to forgo preliminaries and confidently ordered the attack. Thousands of pagans surged forward. They went galloping on their mounts, others ran, all screaming in their lust for blood. The rush was so tremendous it raised enormous clouds of dust, obscuring the vision of those bringing up the rear. The noise was intense and deafening. All of a sudden the clamor of frenzy changed to one of confusion as the Muslims let fly their deadly weapons.

Realizing there was some kind of trouble, Sufyan cautiously rode forward. He looked left, right, seeing a ditch running the length of his attacking army. A knot of resentment formed in his breast. He felt Muhammad had again outmaneuvered him. Wouldst I give gold dinar to know how many Muslims lurk beyond the mounds of earth, he thought, then realized he'd never know unless he crushed them. He turned to the Jewish leaders, openly scowling at them. He started to say something spiteful but the crafty leaders converged on him before the words left his mouth. They convinced him of the value of besiegement, promising that seven hundred men of Banu Qurayzah would be drawing swords against the Muslims from within their midst at any time. Sufyan considered the last bit of information while bile crept up his throat as the bitterness of failure made itself felt. But stubbornly he refused to surrender to his instincts and ordered his army to lay siege.

Once the dust settled, it was then that the Muslims truly saw the size of their enemy's army. Many felt overwhelmed: a feeling of deep anxiety; the odds insurmountable. They worried over the consequences of falling short in warding off the infidels. The Prophet, however, somehow sensitive to their thoughts, traversed the lines of defense where with words of encouragement, soothed their hearts and minds. Then, charging Ali with the command, retreated to his tent.

Having to lay a lengthy investment in an area three thousand feet above sea level during Madinah's coldest month(6) was not to the Disbelievers liking. They had come for a two or three day encounter, prepared to crush Islam and steal, loot and destroy, everything the Muslims had. Now faced with the trench and an unknown number of Muslims concealed behind the mounds of earth, it was impossible.

Already disheartened by their ill-success, the pagans within a week's time rued the day when their bonds of common hatred for Islam drove them together. Then the frowns of fortune befell them. Weather went from bad to worse. Dark gray clouds started swirling and piercing cold winds began to blast through the region which cut through their garments. Shelters were ripped from their stakes, fires were extinguished, rain pounded their faces. Furthermore, besides the physical forces of nature to contend with, there was their own mutual distrust of each other which resulted in bickering and fighting. While on the trench's other side the Muslims were no less feeling adverse to the icy winds but maintained perfect discipline.(7)

The Jewish leaders and Sufyan could not help but observe the sharp decline of belligerency among their troops. Moreover, fearing their endeavor would come to nothing but humiliation, they countered the growing disillusionment with promises of gold dinar to any man crossing the ditch. For a time the pledge enlivened the army, until the reality of crossing and confronting the Muslims bore through their castle building.

From hour to hour, day to day, the Jews solicited men to take up their invitation to fight. All the while hoping their brethren of Banu Qurayzah would usher in the uprising from within the city. They waited in vain, not realizing their sister tribe were masters of cowardice.

Inside Madinah, the schismatic elements were not content with their own disloyalty but tried to infect others as well. They were ready to betray the city(8) only if the Confederacy breached the defenses and provided an overwhelming force of power.

Nu'aim, of Banu Qurayzah, who in secret had been learning the truth and on the verge of accepting Islam before his tribe's discord became apparent, feared a sneak attack against the Muslims. Hence, forsaking his treacherous brethren, he fled their presence and alerted

Prophet Muhammad of their designs if the Disbelievers gained entry to Madinah.

Alarmed by the information, Muhammad quickly thought of the consequences in engaging several hundred men from within the city while trying to defend against thousands from the outside. It was a dilemma, impossible to resolve at first thought. Leaving Nu'aim to join the ranks along the trench, he placed Ali back in command and retired to his tent to ponder the new variables.

A short time later, he emerged and briskly climbed up a small mound of dug up earth to inspect the enemy's position. After a moment, he was satisfied that no sudden attack was coming. He summoned Ali and apprised him of Qurayzah's intentions, then disclosed his plan to neutralize any revolt.

Ali assembled a detachment of two dozen warriors, specially chosen for their aggressiveness. Together they slipped unseen into the city, toward the Jewish sector. And in order to achieve the desired effect of Muhammad's plan they let it be known they were seeking those who conspired against Islam.

The men of Qurayzah, heeding the information, filled with dread: wondering over their fates now that their actions had been discovered. They terminated all treasonous acts and not only imprisoned themselves within their sector, hoping to escape the Muslims, but began strategic measures against attack. Ali and his force, with the streets now emptied of traitors, returned to their defenses.

Next day, it was an hour after dawn when weather conditions changed: sunshine finally broke through from behind darkened rain clouds. Arabs from the interior, who were regarded as the more mercenary, had been waiting for such a break. Around noon, once the puddles drained away and the terrain somewhat hardened, nearly a thousand of them charged the ditch at it's narrowest point.

As Muhammad and the others maintained their vigil, a subdued thunder seemed to roll out toward them. A dark band of pike waving and yelling pagans appeared cresting over a rise five hundred yards out. Muslims squinted at the line, watching it intently as if they could count their number through obstinate study. Silently, each petitioned God's Protection and commenced their preparations. Archers notched arrows, spearmen poised to launch their weapons, catapults were loaded with heavy stones, and sling men whirled rock filled slings through the air.

Fifty yards from the trench, Muhammad raised his sword and the Muslims fired, launched and slung, their weapons. So dense was the volley of projectiles it cast a shadow like the sun momentarily retreating behind a small cloud. The material, finding their marks struck with damaging consequences. For all at once the vanguard of mounts and riders crashed to the ground, spilling pagans everywhere. Men fell dead or wounded atop the rotting corpses already littering the field. Following the volley, pagan lines became a muddle as more than a few panicked Bedouins turned to flee, running headlong into mounts and men.

After the attack which lasted less than eight minutes, scores of infidels either dead or wounded were added to the field of death. As both sides caught their breath and attended their injured, a challenge suddenly rent the air.

During the churning melee, Amr ibn Abdwid along with a few others managed to cross the ditch at it's narrowest point. Amr, a huge black bearded hunk of humanity known for his fierceness, strength, murderous instincts, and as a killer of a thousand challengers, bellowed across the expanse between him and the Muslims.

"Where are the claimants of Paradise? Is there not amongst ye anyone who will dare my sword in single combat? Doth not the followers of God's Way profess that those who are slain in Jihad will go to Paradise and those from amongst us will go to Hell? Is there not one of you prepared to send me to Hell or go to paradise at my hands?"

The pagan army fell silent. Excitedly they watched Amr thrust his standard into the ground for all to see. After all, they thought, who could beat Amr? None in all Arabia had ever bested him. Yea, he was ruthless, fearless and his reputation as a fighter unquestionable.

In the meantime, Muhammad had upon hearing the challenge asked who wanted to accept the affair of honor. The Muslims, somewhat unnerved by the huge lumbering killer remained silent, except one. Ali, the Brother of God's Apostle, quickly tread a path to the fore. "I am here for him, O' Prophet of Allah!"

Muhammad wanted to see someone else take the dare. He disliked the idea of Islam's Guide after him taking such risks. He was about to ask the Muslims again when Amr yelled.

"Are ye cowards that ye have to conceal thyselves from me? Indeed, ye act like women!"

Muhammad repeated his request for one to step up. Once more it was none but the Lion of God who sued for the challenge.

Amr, full of confidence, roared: "I am weary of shouting and challenging. Behold, wilt I alone approach and fight any Muslim."

As Amr crossed the distance through the rubble, Muhammad invited: "Is there none to relieve us from Amr's mischief?"

For the third time it was only Ali to speak out and volunteer. "Oh, my Prophet, accept I his wish to cross swords!"

One of the Muslims, finding his tongue, called out: "Oh, Prophet, thou askest us to face Amr, going against him is going against death. We have seen him fighting single-handedly a huge number of men using only a young camel as his shield."

The matter could not be delayed further: Amr had to be faced. Muhammad gestured to his Successor. Ali dashed to the Prophet's side, where the Holy one placed his turban upon Islam's hope and gave him Zul-Fiqar, the sword of champions. He exclaimed as Ali ventured forth: "The whole of Faith proceedeth against the whole of infidelity!" Without further ado Ali climbed a small flattened mound and ripped away his tunic from his upper body in order to be free of any constraint. He was the model of physical perfection: tanned a rich creamy umber.

He rippled his muscles, loosening them for the deadly fight to come. There was absolute silence, save the buzzing insects over the field of dead pagans. Both sides waited breathlessly. Amr rammed his sword into the earth and began guffawing derisively with his hands on his hips. A twisted look covered his face. He said sarcastically: "Oh, Muhammad! Is there none in all thy ranks to fight me, save this boy? Why doth thou deliver unto me a mere boy to fight a man's battle?"

Ali was feeling like David against Goliath. He looked up and locked eyes. He said in a chilling voice, thick with menace: "If thou likest not to meet me, like I to meet thee on behalf of Allah and His Apostle. Meet thou, this boy of the Apostle of Allah! Wilt I be more than sufficient for thee!"

Amr returned resentfully, "Oh, nephew, had I once been the guest of thy father Abu Talib and eaten at his table. Like I not to slay the son of the one who had been my host and was known to me as a friend."

Ali retorted: "Canst there be no true friendship between a faithful one and an infidel."

Amr's resentment flashed into rage as he thought how Ali referred to him as an infidel and his father a Believer. With measured belligerence, he said: "Be that as it may, like I not to fight with a boy like thee!" Ali instinctively knew his next remarks would bring them to arms and readied himself. "Oh, Amr, since thou hast come against Allah and His Apostle, and even thou likest not to fight with me, have I come to fight with thee defending the Cause of the One God, His Apostle and His religion!"

"Attack thou then!" Amr fired in return.

"We of the Holy Prophet's Ahlul Bayt never initiate any offense on our behalf, we only meet it. Attack thou first, for it is thou who hast challenged, and then thou wilt be dealt with."

Amr could not believe his ears. Blood rushed to his face. Enraged, he jerked free his sword. Ali bellowed out a blood curdling yell of "Allahu Akbar," and both men charged, swishing their weapons until clanging steel pealed the air. They jumped back out of each other's sword's reach, feeling the steel's vibration shoot up their arms and into their shoulders. Wearily they circled the mound's top, each seeking to strike a crippling blow. Amr feinted a thrust to Ali chest, then with a nimbleness belying his size, raised his sword and swished it towards Ali's neck. Ali ducked and delivered a slashing swing which cut deep into his adversary's thigh as he spun away. The gaping wound seemed to infuriate Amr, for he started slicing the air wildly, hoping to strike any part of Ali's body. Ali parried every swing and meted out a number of punishing blows in return. They fought relentlessly, blocking each other's thrusts. Finally, Amr was stunned insensibly by the flat of Ali's sword upside his head which drained his strength away. Ali, then swung mightily and sliced into his foe's shoulder. It was a blow that sent shock waves of pain, slamming Amr into the ground, robbing the breath from his lungs. He thought, at first, that his legs had been severed, then his vision clouded as his oxygen starved brain refused to function. He lay in a stupor, his only connection to the world was the gritty earth against his face.

Ali drove Zul-Fiqar into the earth. Unsheathing a wicked looking serpentine dagger, he waited for Amr to regain his senses. Amr started to rise after a few moments but Ali's arm shot forward and snatched Amr by the hair, forcing his head back to expose the throat. Ali pressed the blade's point into Amr's windpipe and said: "Say thou there is no god but Allah and Muhammad is His Apostle and thou wilt live to see another day."

Taken down several pegs, Amr fumed with murderous hatred. Bereft of reason, he speechlessly eyed Ali as the capillaries in his eyes burst. All he could do was blather incoherently in his rage. Never before had he been beaten. He could not take the humiliation any more, seeing the youthful Ali on top of him digging the blade's point into his neck. In an act of defiance he spit into Ali's face.

Ali jerked aside the infidel and allowed him to rise, giving him another chance to fight. Amr, driven by pure adrenaline, charged and savagely slashed at Ali. Ali countered back furiously, inflicting a score of slashes. And in a matter of minutes, Amr impacted the earth for a second time, bleeding profusely from deep gashes in his body. Ali retrieved his opponent's sword, looked upon him pitilessly, roared "Allahu Akbar" and sliced off Amr's head.

Returning to Muhammad's side, he threw the head to the ground and said: "Here, O' Apostle of Allah! Here is the head of Allah's enemy and thine enemy."

Muhammad embraced God's Lion and declared: "The one stroke of Ali on this day of the Ditch is superior to the prayers of both the worlds."(9)

The Muslims, who had been watching the encounter with bated breath followed Ali's lead with a thunderous roar of "Allahu Akbar." Graced with victory, spirits soared and they wanted to cross the ditch and engage the infidels. The Prophet, wanting to end the bloodshed maintained discipline and cautioned them against bloodlust, then said: "The embodiment of Faith hath crushed the personification of Evil!"

On the other side, pagans looked at one another in disbelief. They had just witnessed their hero fall, slain with his weapon no less. And to add insult to injury, Ali who was half Amr's size, dispatched him so easily. Thus, in consequence, they all but lost their feeling to continue the battle, or even express any enthusiasm for it. Then, by Divine Command, the dark dreary clouds roiled, the heavens thundered, lightning blitzed the mountains, the weather grew colder, winds gusted, and the rain poured which sent fear into pagan hearts.

A few hours later night fell and the blustering storm increased in intensity. Thunder and lightning played havoc as animals broke free of their restraints and started running in different directions, knocking over men and what few tents happened to be standing. Then, one of the Mekkans screamed: "Muhammad's men are in the camp! Save thyselves! Save thyselves!" That's all it took, for the infidels started running helter skelter for their lives, leaving their possessions behind.

Next day, the morning broke clear and sunny. A cheering shattered the calm as Muslims realized the Disbelievers had fled during the night. Muhammad raised his arms for quiet and quickly got their attention. "Oh, ye who believe! All praise and gratitude is due to Allah. Thou hast again proven Allah's Word. Never shall Evil conquer Good. The battle is yet unfinished, for Evil still remaineth in out midst. This day shall we cleanse the city of it's Hypocrites. Whilst we defended Madinah from Allah's enemies, others rose up at our backs. They intrigued with those from Mekkah, and had they breached our defenses, Banu Qurayzah was ready to rise up against us..."

With that said, several warriors mounted up and left for different points around the city to collect those still guarding it's perimeters. Subsequently, Muhammad ordered his men to surround the Jewish sector and sent Ali with a squad of soldiers to bring the tribe's leader forward. The chief demurred, relying on their strengthened position to withstand any aggression against them. So, as with Banu Nadheer, essentials were cut off and the siege began. After the third week, they were out of meat, cooking fuel and water. The tribe's leader, seeing no alternative other than surrender, asked for Sa'd ibn Mu'adh, chief of Banu Aws, to arbitrate the differences. Prophet Muhammad agreed and Banu Qurayzah capitulated without incident.

Sa'd, one of the many Jewish men who turned to Islam, had been wounded during the battle and was slowly dying from infection.

Nevertheless, when notified of his election to pass judgment upon his one time sister tribe, he asked for time to give the matter thought. Finally reaching his decision, his nurse Rufaydah dressed him with fresh bandages and departed to relay his readiness.

Meanwhile, Muhammad, encircled by warriors, approached the Jewish leader's house and ordered him to bring his tribe into the square. Muslims, old and young joined the warriors in surrounding and escorting the tribe. Frightened, the people of Banu Qurayzah assembled in a confused bunch, refusing to meet the eyes of angry Muslims.

Sa'd, in a voice weakening from coming death put into words his judgment. "Oh, ye men of Banu Qurayzah, thou hast chosen me to determine thy fates. And it was agreed by both sides to adhere to my decision without question." He looked to the Prophet and Qurayzah's leader and watched them both nod in agreement. He continued, turning back to the men under indictment: "Thou wast counted amongst the citizens of Madinah and were bound by solemn treaties to aid in it's defense.(10) But, instead of honoring thy covenant ye intrigued with the Confederacy to destroy Allah's religion and slay His Apostle. Hath thy treachery for some time been suspected and now proven by thy actions. Thus, that none may lay claim to Islamic intolerance, I, Sa'd ibn Mu'adh, of Jewish ancestry will judge thee according to Old Testament law. Thou deserveth total annihilation, however, that ye mayest know Muslims are a people of compassion I adjudge thee the most lenient of punishments for thy treason." He paused a moment to catch his breath before pronouncing sentence. Those versed in God's Scriptures fell to their knees begging for mercy. The women started wailing for their men. And many Muslims who were knowledgeable in religious lore, silently wept for the loss of life to come. Turning to face Prophet Muhammad, he said: "Thou shall smite every male thereof with the edge of the sword: but the women, and the little ones and the cattle, and all that is in the city, (their sector), even all the spoil thereof, shall ye take unto thyself; and ye shall eat the spoils of thy enemies, which the Lord thy God hath given thee."(11)

It was a grisly scene: the men with no meed of valor, cried, pleaded, and had to be forced onto the block. The executions lasted for hours. The women were taken as captives of war and all their properties and possessions were divided among the Muhajirun.(12) The Hypocrite, Abdullah ibn Sallul, having witnessed Banu Qurayzah's fate fled the city unnoticed.

In the days following, a tremendous sense of relief permeated the city, especially in the Muslim community. Madinah was now clear of all enemies.

At this stage, Prophet Muhammad wanted to provide for suffering widows who were too old to provide for themselves and married those requiring protection. Some of them. Like Sawdah helped Muhammad with the women who had to be instructed in keeping the family together: where women and men had similar social rights. Muhammad's daughter Zaynab, who was specially devoted to the needy was called the "Mother of the Poor." The other Zaynab, also worked for the poor: using the leather working skills taught by her mother Jahsh, and provided the proceeds of her craft to those in need. All the Prophet's wives who were able to work assisted as Mother's to the Faithful.(13)

Months later: areas stretching to the Yemen coast; throughout the territories of the crumbling Persian and Roman Empires; across the Red Sea; in Mekkah, still talked of the Trench Battle.

Sallam ibn Abi Haqiq, a dangerous instigator of the Jews, was put to death.

Qurayshie agents again visited king Negus in an attempt to halt the advance of Islam, all to no avail.

Muhammad led an armed expedition against Banu Lihyan for murdering Islam's missionaries. Days following his return to Madinah, an infidel plundered a herd of camels, killing its shepherd and kidnapping a Muslim woman. Islamic forces moved to the defense in a battle known as Zi Qarad.

Abu Sufyan's daughter Umm Habiba, whose husband embraced Islam then regressed to Christianity so he could indulge in drink and games of chance, had died in Yemen. She, as an elderly Muslim lady and daughter of Islam's arch enemy, turned unto the Mercy of Believers for help. Muhammad; because of her struggles to survive, took her in hand and provided shelter: trying to further relations with Banu Ummayad.

CHAPTER THIRTY-TWO

In the sixth year of Hijra, Islam entered a new era. Cities, townships, settlements, and areas beyond Arabia's borders were being swept into the Islamic fold. Yet, all was not well: several regions under Jewish control remained hostile and actively plotted against God's Truth.

Muhammad kept close watch on the enemies of Truth. Every day intelligence reports were received and verified. The latest described Banu Mustaliq's intentions to besiege Madinah. Thus, in an action to check the conspiracies and neutralize the increasing fervor for aggression, the Prophet marched against the provoking tribe and routed them out of the territory.

* * **

Stimulated by recent dreams of Pilgrimage to God's House, Muhammad had an overwhelming desire to journey to Mekkah. The city and Ka'bah, however, were under Qurayshie dominion. So with regard to their enmity and safety to the growing number of cells within Mekkah, he sought ways to circumvent the likely outbreak of hostilities if he led the Muslims into the city Abraham once purified. He could find no answers. Frustrated, he sojourned into the nearby mountains in quest of harmony which he needed to derive solutions. After two days fasting and prayer, his guidance came.

The next afternoon, following Jumu'ah Prayer, Muhammad began the khutbah with his usual enthusiasm and intensity. "Oh, ye people of the True Faith. Thou knowest that for no other reason than devotion to the One God, were we driven from our homes. We came to this city in peace and the Ansari welcomed us with open arms, but the mischief loving Disbelievers pursued our trail. Then Allah in His Mercy permitted us to take up arms, and by His Grace alone didst we defeat the enemy."

"Our Lord has enjoined Pilgrimage to His House in Mekkah. His House is not for the Qurayshies, nor for one people, but ALL people from every clime be it fast or far. Have we a right to be in Mekkah to worship."

He paused a moment to evaluate the congregation's reaction. It was as he expected, for the instant he stopped speaking the assembly erupted with exclamations of "Allahu Akbar." Feeling a sense of gratitude, he smiled broadly and raised his arms to still their exuberance.

"In the name of Allah, The Beneficent, The Merciful."

"And (remember O" Our Apostle Muhammad!) when We fixed for Abraham the place for the House, (saying): 'Associate thou not with

Me aught, and cleanse My House for those who make the circuits and stand in prayer, and bow and prostrate themselves (unto Me). And proclaim thou unto the people the Pilgrimage (Hajj)! They will come unto thee on foot and on lean camel, coming from every remote (high)way. That they may witness the advantages unto them, and mention the name of Allah during the appointed days over what He hath provided them of the cattle quadrupeds (as sustenance), then eat of them and feed the needy (and) the poor.' Then let them get cleansed and smarten themselves and fulfill their vows, and let them circuit the Ancient House (the Ka'bah). That (shall be so); and whoever respecteth the sacred ordinances of Allah, it is best for him with his Lord; and the cattle are made lawful unto you, save that which is (already) specified unto you, shun ye therefore, the pollution of the idols; and shun vain words. Being upright for Allah, not associating (anything) with Him; whosoever associateth with Allah, is like that which hath fallen from heaven and (a vulture) bird snatcheth it away or the wind wafted it to a distant abyss. That (shall be so); and whoever respecteth the signs of Allah verily it is (the reflection) of the piety of the hearts. For you therein are benefits till a fixed time, and the place of their sacrifice is the Ancient House, (the Ka'bah)."

"Unto every people We have prescribed a rite (of devotion) that they may mention the name of Allah on what He hath provided them of the cattle quadrupeds, (as their sustenance), so your God is One God, so unto Him submit ye (all) yourselves; and thou (O' Our Apostle Muhammad!) give glad tidings unto the humble ones, who, when Allah is mentioned, get thrilled their hearts (with awe for His Glory); and the steadfast on what befalleth them, and the establishers of prayer and of what We have provided them with they spend (benevolently)."

"And the camels (of sacrifice) We have made them for you among the signs of Allah, for you in them is good; so mention the name of Allah on them (when they are drawn) in rows (to be sacrificed); and when fall they down (sacrificed), on their sides, eat of them and feed the contented (poor ones) and the beggar; thus have We subjugated them unto you that happily ye may give thanks. Never doth reach Allah their flesh nor their blood, but reacheth Allah the piety on your part; thus hath He subjugated them unto you that ye might pronounce the greatness of Allah for what He hath guided you aright; and thou (O' Our Apostle Muhammad!) give glad tidings unto the doers of good. Verily, Allah loveth not any of the unfaithful, ungrateful (ones)."

"Oh' ye people! A parable is set forth (unto you) so listen ye unto it! Verily, those whom ye call upon besides Allah can never create (even) a fly, even though they all gather together for it; and should the fly carry away any thing from them, they can not take it back from it;

(how) weak the invoker and the invoked! They estimate not Allah His rightful estimation; verily, Allah is All-Strong, and All-Mighty. Allah chooseth from among the angels messengers and from among the men; verily, Allah is All-Hearing, All-Seeing. Knoweth He what is before them and what is behind them, and unto Allah are returned all affairs."

"Oh' ye who believe! Bow ye down and prostrate ye and worship ye your Lord, and do ye good, happily ye may succeed. And fight (endeavor) ye in (the Way of) Allah as it behoveth you to fight (endeavor) for Him; He hath chosen you and hath laid not upon you any hardship in religion; the faith of your Father Abraham; He (God Himself) named you Muslims before and in this , that the Apostle (Muhammad) may be a witness over you and ye be witness over the people; so establish ye prayer and pay ye the poor-rate and hold ye fast by Allah; He is your Master, how Excellent The Master and how Excellent The Helper!"(1)

Muhammad concluded and was about to ask the assemblage if anyone had any questions, when a young man sprang to his feet

"Oh' Prophet of Allah, at the last thou recited about witnesses, are we to be them over the people?"

"Nay, there are only Thirteen men who are addressed in this verse. Myself, my Brother Ali and his eleven sons.(2) Therefore, outstrip them not, for then shall perish ye and fall not short of them, for then you shall perish. Do not teach them for they are more knowledgeable than you.(3) I am the Warner and Ali is the guide. And the rightly guided will be guided by thee, O' Ali, after me.(4) Therefore, whomsoever desireth to live my life and die my death and enter the heavens unto the Lord of Leal (Paradise), which Allah hath promised, he should follow the guide of Ali and his offspring after him. Verily, they shall never take ye out of the door of guidance and never bring ye into the door of misguidance."(5)

With no more inquiries, the excitement grew two-fold. A wonderful feeling spread as Believers realized their guidance was assured after the Prophet. Next, they started expressing their eagerness to renew old acquaintances, visit old haunts. Daily, passions continued to rise as preparations progressed for Hajj. Sacrificial camels, sheep and goats, were selected and separated from the herds: becoming symbolic by which they could demonstrate their willingness to share with the needy.

The young Muhajirun, who frequently were the recipients of stories about Muslim valor and battles, were now coming of age. And with the Hajj's commencement a few days away, the young men's memories of their early years in Mekkah surfaced. Memories of mothers, fathers and kinsmen, being hated, abused and tortured. They were anxious to prove themselves warriors, and discussed retaliation. But when rumors of reprisals against the Mekkanese started circulating, Muhammad summoned all young men of the community

For more than two hours, Muhammad listened as each young man spoke of his experiences, silently reliving the brutalities. Finally, the last story was related and he could no longer contain his emotions: tears spilled from his eyes. Somberly, he glanced from face to face, feeling their pain along with his

"It is so," said Muhammad, "but we owe duties to Allah. We must respect the laws and customs of His House and it's Sanctity. We must not retaliate, or return evil for evil. Hatred from the wicked doth not warrant hostility on our part, is it not commanded of us to aid one another in righteousness and piety? Not in perpetuating feuds of bad blood and enmity.(6) Thus, we go in peace seeking only the rites of Pilgrimage."

It was the month of February, the middle of winter and fairly cold. Hundreds of Muslims in response to Prophet Muhammad's call for Pilgrimage, trekked into Madinah to join in the pious undertaking: swelling their numbers to nearly fifteen-hundred.

On the day of departure, Muhammad requested that all weapons of war be left behind which caused most of the desert tribes to hang back and make excuses for not going: their faith being but lukewarm,(7) and so shaky, they thought the worst would happen.(8) But had there been the promise of pillaging and booty, assuredly they would have made the journey. For the desert Bedouin were found of fighting, plundering, and understood such motives for war. The higher motives of spiritual enrichment seemed to be beyond them.(9) Nevertheless, the Prophet, amid deafening roars praising God, led the multitude toward the city's outskirt's where he addressed them.

"Oh' ye people, from a certain point on the road wilt we don the unstitched cloth of pilgrim garb and begin the dedication to worship and prayer and denial of all vanities. Upon arrival in Mekkah, shall we then round the Ka'bah seven times, then stop at the Station of Abraham to offer prayer unto Allah. Then unto the hills of Safa and Marwah. After a time, wilt I give a khutbah to the whole assembly on Hajj's meaning. The day following we as one body journey to the Valley of Mina and camp the night. Next day, we will proceed to the hill and plain of Arafat. Finally, we return to Mina's valley for the Day of Sacrifice."(10)

He ended his instruction and searched their faces, expecting some questions. There were none so he faced about and began the journey toward the point where the Pilgrimage would begi

News of a great number of Muslims traveling down the Madinah-Mekkan road quickly reached Mekkah's hierarchy. Caught completely off guard, they took alarm and started conscripting fighting men by the scores. Days later, the small army was placed under Khalid's command and started for the advancing Muslims.

At the same time the pagan force departed Mekkah word sped down the trade line causing al-Mustafa to change routes. Hence, in taking another road the Muslims were not only able to avoid the fast approaching Mekkans but avoided the possibility of bloodshed on this most holiest of occasions.

Khalid's two-hundred man force arrived at an area where the desert's expanse and its road to Madinah could be seen as far as the eye could see. The Muslims were nowhere in sight. Khalid felt outwitted and stared silently into the distance. All kinds of dire thoughts flashed through his mind, creating graphic scenes of Muslims attacking Mekkah. Abruptly turning in his saddle, he shouted in a voice full of alarm: "We must make haste for Mekkah, the city is unprotected!"

Meanwhile, the Muslims had reached the plain of Hudaybiyah and set up camp in the area of Dhi al-Halifah: a day's march from Mekkah. Muhammad ordered the men to stow their personal weapons and don the pilgrim garb. And while the camp waited to learn what would happen next, Prophet Muhammad retired to his tent and started contemplating ways of avoiding the violence he felt sure to come if they progressed further. It was anyone's guess whether they'd be allowed to continue in peace or not.

An hour after Muhammad retreated into his tent, the Confederates learned the Muslims were less than a day's ride away. Feeling vulnerable and open to attack with their army still somewhere out in the desert, they themselves, took to the streets seeking fighting men to protect them. Finding but few, they returned to Sufyan's house where they met in council and quickly reconsidered their stance against Islam. Finally, fearing an imminent assault they charged Suhayl, Urwa ibn Mas'ud and Budayl, to lead a delegation to Hudaybiyah and discover Muhammad's intentions.

In the Muslim camp, the men tensed and drew near their personal weapons when alerted of incoming riders. Ali, Dujanah and several other trusted Companions, immediately formed a wedge of protection around Muhammad as he crossed the grounds to greet the horsemen.

"As-salaamu alaikum," hailed the Prince of Peace.

"Why art thou and the Muslims near Mekkah," questioned Budayl without acknowledging the salutation.

Looking from one to the other, Muhammad said: "Rest thy minds, for we come in peace to perform the Pilgrimage which Allah hath ordained. Behold, there are no weapons of war in our midst." Following a cursory inspection and short consultation, the three man commission unanimously agreed that the Muslims had indeed come with peaceful intentions. Suhayl told Muhammad that he would report their findings to the city's fathers.

The Mekkan leaders, despite assurances of Muhammad's peaceful motives, still felt intimidated with his presence in the area. So to delay matters until their army's arrival, they dispatched another delegation with Urwa in charge. Bringing to bear all his skills of diplomacy, Urwa attempted to intimidate the Apostle of God with subtle references to Qurayshie strengths.

Muhammad interrupted and reiterated Muslim intentions. Then putting the 'D' in diplomacy, the Splendor of Prophets arrested further innuendo of power with an act of ablution.

The commission not only came away with the previous conclusions of Muhammad's purpose, but were more than a little apprehensive. Upon reaching the assembled Qurayshie chiefs, Urwa expressed his fears.

"Have I witnessed great kings and powers like the Emperor of Persia, Kaiser of the Roman Empire and the king of Abyssinia. None amongst those powerful nations commandeth the respect and loyalty accorded unto Muhammad. Have I witnessed with my own eyes that his Shi'a wouldst not allow even one drop of water to spill onto the ground whilst he performed ablution. Even if a hair falleth, they pick it up immediately. O' chiefs, ponder over this situation most carefully."(11)

Afterwards, when darkness hid one's actions, Urwa returned to the Muslim encampment. For hours he spoke with Muhammad, probing in depth Islam's ideals. At the end, he converted and returned to Ta'if, sure his position would keep him out of harm's way. But, the inhabitants upon learning of his conversion surrounded his home, and killed him with a shower of arrows when he stepped out to investigate the commotion.

Prophet Muhammad the next day, in a move to counter their obvious attempts at procrastination, sent his son-in-law Uthman to negotiate their entrance into Mekkah, thinking his family's power and influence would help their cause. Uthman was a long time in Mekkah, gone much longer than expected. And around the camp Believers started voicing their opinions of foul play. Muhammad suspected Uthman may have been killed to show the city its leaders remained in control. Then seeing their anxiety ridden faces, he addressed the camp.

"Oh' ye Muslims! If anything untoward hath befallen Uthman, pledge I unto thee I will fight, insha'a Allah, till the death in avenging him against the kafirun!"

There was nothing but silence while the Spirit of Truth's words took effect. Then, as Muslim morals and somatic strength manifested itself, they suddenly erupted with roars of "Masha'a Allah." Charged with resolve, they came individually and in groups to lay their hands atop the Holy Prophet's hands, swearing fealty to God's Cause. In times to come the demonstration of fealty became known as Bay'ah al-Ridwan. Muhammad next ordered the men to prepare for departure and started for his tent when a new cry arose from the camp's fringes.

"Uthman has returned! Uthman has returned!"

Moments later Uthman rode up and stopped in a cloud of dust. Dismounting, Muhammad promptly embraced him then the others started shaking his hands in affection. Not realizing the significance of his long absence, he glanced around trying to understand the overwhelming show of fellowship. He faced the Prophet, feeling an indefinable strangeness.

"Oh' Muhammad," he began, "the enemies of Truth are a very difficult bunch to negotiate with..." His debriefing lasted well over an hour as he recounted every detail of the parley with Mekkah's leaders. Finally ending his report with information that a representative of Quraysh would bring their decision on the morrow.

The Confederates, with all their self-importance smugly felt in command of the situation now that their small army had returned. Yet, they still feared engaging the Muslims, remembering their unflinching resolve of past battles. Thus, dreading their prestige would suffer irreparable damage if Muslims entered the city by force, they broke from custom which allowed Pilgrims the rites of Pilgrimage. Calculating against criticism, they again sent Suhayl. This time he was to contract a treaty which they thought saved face.

Shortly after sunrise, Suhayl and his escort of armed soldiers arrived with an air of pomposity and theatrical pretensions. Muhammad immediately convened council thinking the Disbelievers might prove difficult. Turning to Ali, he asked him to act as scribe knowing his eloquence would serve Islam's interests. Negotiations lasted all morning and into late afternoon. Finally, an agreement was reached and the symposium concluded in a peaceful treaty with several stipulations:

1.) Peace between Muslims and Quraysh would henceforth extend to cover
a period of ten years so security may be established throughout Arabia.
2.) Any Qurayshie leaving Mekkah without permission from his or her guardian and converts to Islam must be returned to Quraysh. And any

Muslim wishing to come back to Quraysh there is no obligation to surrender that person back.

3.) Any person of age, clan or tribe, has the liberty to join either of the signing parties or form alliances with them.

4.) Muhammad and the Pilgrims could not enter Mekkah until the following year on condition that they carry no weapons of war and stay no longer than three days.(12)

5.) Any Muslim in Mekkah is free to perform their religious rites with complete safety.(13)

6.) Property belonging to the signatories would be respected.(14) 7.) Life and property of the Muslims entering Mekkah from Madinah would be respected.(15)

Upon the delegation's departure, some of the Muslims raised their voices in protest, thinking the conditions too harsh. Muhammad, however, was looking toward the future and considered the treaty a great victory: for it ended Mekkan hostilities which defrayed an immediate sense of security; opened the door to teach True worship; and, paved Islam's way to spread unhindered.

Umar ibn al-Khattab, raising his voice above the others, angrily asked: "Oh, Muhammad, art thou not truly Allah's Prophet?"

Shocked by Umar's outburst, the dissenting Muslims fell silent.

Prophet Muhammad masked his feelings, zeroed in on Umar and stared him directly in the eye. He coldly answered in a voice underscoring his displeasure, "Thou knowest that I am."

"B-but, are we not in the right and our enemies wrong," Umar returned under the Prophet's withering look.

"Yea," said Muhammad simply.

"Why then do we humble ourselves and render shame upon Islam?"

Surprised by Umar's annoyance, Muhammad nevertheless remained calm and collected. He said: "Oh, Umar, I am the Messenger of Allah and never will I disobey Him, for He is my support."

Again Umar persisted in annoying the Apostle: "Didst thou not tell us that we would come to the House of Allah?"

"Yea! But didst thou hear me say this year?"

"Nay."

"Then, thou art coming to it and going around it!"

With Umar having been silenced, Muhammad looked around, waiting for questions. None came. He said: "Go and slaughter the beasts chosen for sacrifice, shave thy heads, and shear but a lock from the women."

Ali and several other Believers immediately departed to fulfill the Prophet's command.

Muhammad at first thought the others hadn't heard him, so he repeated his orders. Again, no response. He reiterated for the third time. When no one moved to obey, he turned and followed the Believers. Speaking to no one, he joined the Believers at the animal pen, selected one of the sacrificial animals, slaughtered it and portioned the meat out, then had his head shaved. When the disagreeing Muslims saw the Prophet's actions, they slowly began to follow suit.

Once the animals were put to the spit, Muhammad explained all that had transpired during the negotiations. Then while the camp shared the offerings, relatives and friends of the Muhajirun started arriving. The mood turned festive as people rejoiced. Discussions on Islam abounded everywhere. Umar, who remained rankled, approached Abu Bakr.

"Oh' Abu Bakr, need I to speak with thee, for thou art wise and can aid me with my misgivings about this treaty. Is Muhammad truly Allah's Prophet?"

Taken aback by the heretical question, Bakr regarded Umar in the fading illumination of glowing coals. "Umar, thou shouldest know that Muhammad is the Messenger and Prophet of Allah. And as such never wilt he violate the sanctity of His Word, so hold ye fast unto him."(16)

At sunset, Muhammad, who had spent hours going from group to group nurturing the spirit of Hajj, pleaded weariness and retired for the evening. Alone, he performed the sunset prayer after the red disappeared from the sky, then fell to contemplating the day's events and dissenting voices. Of late, he noticed their questioning his direction, even going as far as to challenge his motives. He could not understand their carping at things they knew not.

On the way back to Madinah, Angel Gabriel came with the revelation of manifest victory.

"In the name of Allah, The Beneficent, The Merciful."

"Verily, We have caused victory for thee a manifest victory, (so) that Allah may grant protection for thy (Muhammad's) sake (against) that which hath gone before of thy (followers) shortcomings and that which hath to come later, and thus He perfected His bounty unto thee, and guideth thee (firm-footed) on the way straight (unto the Lord), and that Allah might help thee with prevailing triumph."

"(Such hath been) the course of Allah that hath passed into effect before, and never shalt thou find in the course of Allah a change. And He it is Who withheld their hands from you and your hands from them in the valley of Mekkah, after He hath given you victory over them; and Allah is seeing whatever ye do."

"They are the ones who disbelieved and obstructed you from reaching the Sacred Mosque and the offering (which was) prevented to reach its destined place (of sacrifice); and were it not for the believing men and the believing women, not having known them, ye might have trodden down, would have afflicted you a crime on their behalf without knowledge; that He may admit to His mercy whomsoever He pleaseth; had they been separated, certainly We would have chastised those of them who have disbelieved (with) a painful chastisement."(17)

Next morning, one of Muhammad's uncle's arrived with Maymuna bint Harith, a widowed Muslim woman who needed a husband to support her. But being of advanced years, and a daughter of the enemy, none would accept her hand in marriage. The Prophet, however, opened his heart and consented. Thereby, not only providing for the needy, but furthering Islamic relations with the influential Mekkans.

Within days after the treaty's ratification, a young man named Jandal joined the Muslim camp, lacking his father's consent. Well received, no one inquired as to his age. He quickly declared his belief and plunged himself into learning God's Religion. Two days afterward, his father Suhayl arrived and put to test the treaty's strength. Without so much as a word to anyone, he searched the encampment amid curious eyes until locating his teenaged son. Jandal was bound in iron fetters and literally dragged away. It was horrible, tearing at the hearts of Believers as the boy pleaded for help; but Muslim hands were tied.

Muhammad, fearing the camp's Muslims losing control, rushed to Jandal's side and explained the situation which the boy more or less understood, for he ceased his struggles and with tears streaming down his face stood and returned to Mekkah with dignity.

As the rising Light of Islam filtered through man's cloud of ignorance, people began seeking a new direction in life. At the Prophet's behest, Mughirah composed a number of formal letters inviting Emperors, Kings, Shahs, Emirs and Sheikhs, to Islam.

Heraclius, in the course of time, had neared Mosul on the Tigris, part of the Persian Empire. Battling for months, the Persians capitulated and sued for peace. Returning to Constantinople to celebrate his victory, he vowed that after his trip to Emessa, he'd march to Jerusalem to further commemorate his triumph and return to its place the Christian cross which had been carried away by the Persians.(18)

CHAPTER THIRTY-THREE

North of Madinah atop a volcanic tract of mountains nestled between the two main Jewish cities of Khaybar and Fadak, the expelled tribes continued to subvert truth and slander the Comforter. Combining their resources, they started bribing, pressuring, and in some instances hired mercenaries to attack small Muslim communities.

Muhammad, alarmed over the sudden outbreaks of violence, thought the aggression too coincidental, too organized, and dispatched men into the area to discover those responsible. Two nights later, he summoned his trusted Companions to council.

Following a short prayer, he said: "Oh, ye who believe! Have ye noted the rising hostility toward our Brothers northeast of here? Through information some of you have obtained, it is clear that our enemies at Khaybar are responsible. Therefore, let us suppose that the Persians or Romans fleeing their war torn lands made treaties with the Jews. Thus, supplied with arms and men, would not our enemies descent to make war?"

"Yea," "Indeed," "Surely," sounded from more than a few voices throughout the assembly hall.

Muhammad raised his arms for order. He decided the threat to any Muslim life, be they rich or poor, Arab or non-Arab, was not in Islam's best interest to leave unanswered. "We must aid our brethren and take to battle! The kafirun must know they cannot oppress our Brothers without retaliation. Did not Allah command the Believers to fight oppression?" Hence, a state of war was declared and Muslims from all walks of life converged on Madinah in answer to the declaration.

Meanwhile, some of the Jews having anticipated a showdown against God's forces, had in fact for sometime been enlisting absconding soldiers from the collapsing empires and stockpiling weapons. They felt invincible in their fortress cities with its many outcroppings of rock that provided numerous advantages in defense. Unknown to them, God had judged them in the like manner of their brethren of ancient times for their repeated distortions of His Law.

Seven days following the hue and cry for battle, sixteen hundred Muslim warriors and a number of women needed for nursing, marched out of Madinah. Dedicated, united in purpose, there existed no greater cause than service to God. At Isr, they tread a path toward the Valley al-Raji where Muhammad warned Banu Ghatfan, Jewish allies, to keep their distance from Khaybar's region or face annihilation. Then, setting a fast clip, they reached the cluster of mountainous fortifications. Despite the grueling pace the Muslims were surprisingly robust, showing no indications of fatigue from the five day march. Ali, however, had suddenly fallen ill with a violent malady, which affected his sight and balance. Unable to catch their enemies unaware, Muhammad selected a site and ordered the camp's construction. After insuring Ali's care, he stepped from his tent to examine the heights of Khaybar. Surprised at how well fortified their stronghold was, he thought the Jews would give no quarter as this battle would establish their status in Arabia. Facing skyward, he raised his arms in supplication: "Oh, Allah, Lord of the seven heavens and what they shade. Lord of the seven earths and what they maintain. I seek from Thou the goodness of this dwelling place and the goodness of its inhabitants and seek refuge in Thee from its evil and from whatever is in it.(1) The siege began.

As days passed into weeks, the Muslims could not breach Khaybar's defenses. Night after night Believers returned to gather in front of Muhammad's tent. With no end in sight the Prophet stepped from his command center and stood in front of his men. Silently he reviewed his troops as he contemplated his next move. Suddenly he called out.

"Abu Bakr, on the morrow thou wilt take charge and lead the attack!" Honored at being chosen above the rest to lead the offensive, he accepted the privilege with zeal.

Next morning, cold and pristine, dawn sliced the horizon to reveal countless bow men roosting atop the ramparts. Muhammad crossed the rocky terrain to stand three hundred yards from Khaybar's stony base. He scanned the hewed rock walls, searching for weaknesses to exploit. But as he studied the mountain and its ramparts, the Jews raised their bows and fired off a volley of shafted death, more in a display of might than to kill, for he was well out of range. Ending his inspection, he gave Bakr last minute instructions. Bakr bellowed at the top of his lungs:

"Insha'a Allah!" The warriors instantly followed with "Allahu Akbar!"

Muhammad's heart started pounding as the vociferation's reverberated thunderously off the volcanic rock.

The archers manning the ramparts notched arrows upon hearing the Islamic battle cry and waited for the Muslims to come within range. Moments later a black cloud of feathered death and catapulted balls of flaming pitch sailed down through the air. Over forty Muslims fell wailing in anguish while a score of others screamed in terror as the blazing pitch stuck to their skin and garments. Unprepared for the orbs of spreading fire, they ran wildly for the safety of the rocks and ensconced themselves.

Pinned at the mount's bottom, the Muslims could only reciprocate arrows haphazardly, and then ineffectively: for their arrows seemed to hang in the air like floating debris carried along up-drafting wind currents. The battle, for now was at a standstill, saving the occasional Muslim who at risk of death or bodily injury exposed himself to let loose an arrow with a degree of accuracy.

Muhammad watched the offensive until it became too disturbing to see dead and wounded Muslims lying helplessly in the field. Feeling discouraged, he left his observation point and headed for his tent to rethink tactics. When he pulled back the tent's flap, he saw one of the nurses applying cool compresses to Ali's forehead. "Yaa Allah," he cried in a whisper.

Deep in thought over the day's outcome, he wandered through the deserted camp searching for answers. Aimlessly he roamed, twinging at the sight of a dead Believer's personal possessions. He wondered if his army would have proven successful under a different leadership, for in previous engagements either he or Ali had led the men, or if he should quit the area. "Nay!" He exclaimed aloud. He knew if he didn't crush the Jews they would never stop arguing against the Religion of Truth.

Finally night fell and the torches were lit. Muhammad breathed a sigh of relief when his men started returning. The day's casualties tallied seven dead and a score injured. Their loses, thought the Prophet, reflected all too well the difficulty of their campaign. As the women attended the wounded, the others started assembling to hear God's Apostle.

Ali at that moment broke his fever and awakened to hear a multitude of voices outside the stopgap infirmary. Disoriented, his eyes nearly swollen shut, he gazed through oozing slits trying to get his bearings. As he rose from his pallet to find Muhammad, he knocked over a cistern full of water and toppled to the ground.

The nurse, standing just outside watching the Prophet speak to his men, heard the crashing receptacle and rushed in to find Ali struggling to rise. "Ali! Thou shouldst be resting!"

"How can I rest when we are at war with the enemies of truth," replied Ali vapidly.

"Aye, but thou canst do no good if ill."

"Nevertheless, must I help and insha'a Allah, wilt I regain my strength in a few minutes." It was not meant to be, Ali's knees buckled. He started swaying and had to be helped back to his pallet.

In the interim, Muhammad had raised his arms to quiet the soldiers. Gesturing Umar to his side, he said: "Oh, ye warriors of Allah, Umar wilt command on the morrow. The enemy was victorious this day. And inasmuch as they show no sign of venturing out from behind their walls to engage in open combat, insha'a Allah, wilt we find a way to counter their strategy. So rest ye now, for the morrow wilt prove another difficult day."

After daybreak, Umar assembled the troops. Atop the ramparts, hundreds of Jews had gathered to watch. Muhammad also watched, interested in their reactions. As if on cue, the Disbelievers all at once began to shout invectives and waving closed fists in defiance to emphasize their slights. The Muslim army roared its rallying cry and started marching towards the mountainous cluster of seven fortifications.

Minutes later, volleys of arrows flew back and forth. Again, the area filled with gut wrenching cries of anguish. Jews, by the dozens somersaulted off the battlements and fell to their deaths. Muslims fell wounded, dead or dying. The engagement was long and severe, and once more the Muslims could not overcome the war of position.

Muhammad saw the repeat of his army's inability to conquer the mountain, he again cried: "Yaa Allah," and turned to wander the camp until nightfall.

The men gathered in front of the Prophet's tent, accusing Umar of cowardice while he charged them like-wise.(2) All accusations ceased the instant Muhammad's tent flap slapped against canvas. It was eerily quiet as they waited for him to speak. Prophet Muhammad stared out over the crowd for several minutes before articulating his thoughts.

"On the morrow wilt I give the mantle of leadership to a man who loveth Allah and His Apostle and who is loved by Allah and His Apostle. One who will not withdraw until Allah hath granted conquest. He is a man who hath never showed his back unto the enemy and doth not flee the battlefield."(3)

Early the following morning Muslims massed in front of Muhammad's tent, excitement and expectation filled the air. They waited, spoke in whispers, and wondered who would be named by the Holy Apostle of God and given the honor.

Muhammad emerged from his tent and had to raise his arms to quell their enkindled passions. "Oh, ye men of Faith, the best of peoples. It is thy good that wilt endure and the evil that wilt be crushed. Allah, The Best of Planners, Who created all mighty forces wilt shower His Wrath upon the Disbelievers in His Own good time. Every man, whether concealeth or revealeth he his thoughts, all are under Allah's watch and ward. His Grace encompasses everyone, and again and again protecteth him, if only he will take the protection from evil."(4)

"Allah, Most Merciful, is not intent on punishment. It is only when man hath made his own sight blind and changed his nature away from the virtuous cast in which He fashioned it, that His Wrath will descend on him and the favorable position in which He placed him will wax and wane.(5) His Design is not for us to know. Thus, hearken now unto His Word that ye mayest be strengthened."

"In the name of Allah, The Beneficent, The Merciful."

"Oh' ye who believe! Remember ye the bounty of Allah unto you when came upon you hosts, then sent We upon them a strong wind and hosts that ye saw them not; and seeth Allah what (all) ye do. When came they upon you from above you and from below you, and were turned dull the eyes, and reached to the throats the hearts, and ye did imagine about Allah diverse thoughts. There were tried the believers and they were shaken a tremendous shaking."

"And when saw the believers the allies, said they: 'This is what Allah promised unto us and His Apostle, and Allah and His Apostle had spoken the truth;' and it increased not in them but faith and submission. Of the believers are the men who are true to what they covenanted with Allah; of them is he who hath fulfilled his vow and of them is he who awaiteth (its fulfillment); and they have changed not in the least, that Allah may recompense the truthful ones for their truth, and chastise the hypocrites if He willeth or turn unto them (merciful); verily Allah is Oft-Forgiving, The Most Merciful."(6)

Ending, Muhammad inhaled deeply and scanned the sea of expectant faces. He suddenly heralded before making the announcement all waited to hear: "Declare I that there is no god but Allah, the One God, One without equal," His declaration provoked the already excited army into roars of "Allahu Akbar" and "Subhan Allah." Raising his arms, he asked: "Where is Ali?"

Two warriors immediately departed to bring Ali, the Lion of God. Whispers erupted: "Hath he bad eyes." "Why doth the Apostle call for Ali?" "He can but barely see and needeth help to walk!"

Muhammad retorted: "The standard of Islam is not for anyone to carry whom they can accuse of cowardice to me. It is for Ali ibn Abi Talib." Moments later the warriors returned, supporting Ali between them. The Prophet gazed upon his Vicegerent with parental affection and soundlessly prayed. He wet his fingers with saliva and touched Ali's eyes. To the amazement of all, the redness faded and the swelling depreciated noticeably. He was ready for battle.

The crowd exploded with unparalleled exultation. Muhammad had to wave his arms for some minutes to quell their excitement. Turning to his Brother, Deputy and Successor, he said: "Oh, Ali, take thou the standard and set forth with it. The Archangel Gabriel is with thee. Victory is in front and terror is spread into their hearts. Be thou aware that they have found in their Book that the name of the one who will destroy them is Iliya,(Elia). When thou meeteth them, say: 'I am Ali,' insha'a Allah wilt they forsake the battle. But first call the people to God's Religion and inform them of their obligations under an Islamic

Government. Should they refuse then thou mayest resort to battle. If Allah guideth even one person through thee it is better than spending red-haired camels in the Way of Allah.(7) Ali is the leader of the pious and the slayer of the kafirun. Victorious is that who helpeth him, and defeated is that who disappointeth him."(8)

As the men dispersed for their places, Ali mounted a coal black Arabian stallion and raised Zul-Fiqar in the air. He looked to Khaybar's heights, glanced back at the formation of men, then bellowed: "Allahu Akbar." Hundreds upon hundreds of voices instantly echoed with roars of their own. Ali's stallion reared, blasted steamy vapor through it's nostrils in skittishness, and bounded towards the mountain of rock in an all out charge.

The Jewish archers, unnerved by the intensity of earsplitting fulmination's reverberating through their parapets, fell into inaction long enough for the Muslims to gain a foothold upon Khaybar's escarpment. The archers seemed to raise their bows in concert and fire their arrows. The fusillade sliced through the air and caught God's soldiers off guard. Muslims fell dead and wounded. Seconds passed before arrows were returned. Men started falling off the fortress walls, wailing until thudding the sharp volcanic rock. The tempo suddenly picked up, volleys of death started streaking between the walls' base and its top. Slowly but steadily Muslims made their way towards the massive iron gates leading into the stronghold.

After five hours of fierce battle and before the entrance was reached, a monk called out: "Who is this man that turneth not his heels in the face of death?"

"I am Ali ibn Abi Talib!"

Upon hearing the name Ali, the monk paled and set about warning that Ali would not withdraw without capturing Khaybar. Harith, a Jewish champion, could not bear having one of his own extolling Ali. He issued challenge.

The huge gates creaked open. Ali came forward and met with Harith in single combat. The fight was over in seconds, Harith lay dead. His brother Marhab stepped from the gates.

"I am Marhab. All of Khaybar knoweth of me as unequaled in valor amongst the Jews. Fight me!"

Ali drew near, measuring the enemy and his three-pronged lance. As they closed the gap between them, Marhab twirled his sword in distraction and lunged with his spear. Ali skillfully warded off his strike and delivered Zul-Fiqar into his opponents head, killing him instantly. "Allahu Akbar," boomed out Ali.

Six more champions challenged the Lion of God, all were felled. The Muslims charged roaring "Allahu Akbar" and set ablaze the wooden beams supporting the iron gates.

Three hundred yards away, Muhammad could smell the biting smoke and coppery odor of spilt blood drifting down off the slopes. As he watched, a portion of volcanic rock around the framed iron gates crashed to the ground. An instant later the Jews were discarding their bows and drawing their swords as they abandoned their posts.

Ali, meanwhile, had his shield splintered to pieces by the numerous impact of arrows and sword strikes. He had thrown what remained aside, daring the bowmen's aim as he made for the burning frame encasing the iron doors. In a superhuman feat of strength Ali twisted and yanked free a slab of iron from its hinges. His stallion abruptly neighed, reared up to pump its forelegs wildly. Ali phenomenally hefted the section of iron over his head and entered the fortress shouting "Allahu Akbar."

A multiplicity of throats roared back the rallying cry and combined with the rising clamor of clanging weapons, screams of wounded and dying men, sent shivers of terrifying fear among the Jews.

Closing in on the enemy, Ali charged ahead, cutting down any who dared his sword. His men following, hacked and slashed their way behind him: driving the enemy back. Once passing into the court, a shower of arrows and spears unexpectedly came raining down from the ramparts and parapets. The Muslims, despite the consequences, showed no fear and eventually forced their opponents deeper into the fortress. At nightfall the warring stopped. Muslims, dead and wounded were taken back down the mountain; while the Jews, fearing the possibility of ambush left their dead and injured where they lay.

A few days later, as the stench of rotting bodies permeated the area, the first of the citadels was taken and secured. Next morning, Muslim spirits were high. Eagerly they waited for Ali's command to cross swords. Again, before engaging the enemy, the dreaded roar of "Allahu Akbar" sounded, causing renewed tremors of fear amongst their adversaries. And as the rallying cry echoed throughout the fortress, the Muslims charged across the courts amid a rain of missiled death. By sunset, after having secured another section, hostilities halted for the night.

The following day, near noon, the battle reached it's severest point as the fighting became particularly vicious. Muslims, selling their lives dearly, returned arrow for arrow, spear for spear, and sword thrust for sword thrust, killing and wounding six for every one of their own slain or injured. The Jews, desperately defending the last rampart separating their main stronghold, al-Kamus, from the Muslims, fought with intense energy.

Ali realized the significance for their sudden vehemence and called a tactical retreat to reorganize his forces. He had the bowmen refill their sheathes, assigned new positions, and instructed them when to loose their arrows. While waiting for them to station themselves among the captured steeples and ramparts, he ordered the swordsmen to form ranks behind the spearmen, also instructing them when to attack. He then calculated his chances for success, studying the last remaining battlement: its ramparts and flight of steps. Next, he roared out "Allahu Akbar" and launched himself toward the stairway.

Atop the walls, Jewish archers shifted positions, focusing their attention upon Ali running across the courtyard. When he reached the staircase's bottom, they loosed their arrows. Ali signaled, and before they could re-notch their arrows the Muslim bowmen and spearmen stepped from behind their shielding and released a barrage of deadly projectiles. Ali charged up the steps. Three quarters of the way up he had to measure swords with enemy soldiers. Quickly dispatching his opponents, he gained the upper most parts while his men swarmed in behind him.

The Jews, caught between defending the staircase and Muslim bowmen firing volley after volley, turned away and quit their posts to battle against the host of Believers spilling into their stronghold.

In a matter of hours they were beaten back into a walled enclosure where they surrendered. Then, beneath the eyes of Muslim bowmen, they were stripped of all weapons and imprisoned where they took themselves. Ali instructed his men and departed the mountain top to locate the Apostle.(9)

Muhammad recognized Ali's black stallion as it pranced in front of the command center. He exited with open arms to receive him. "Al-Hamdu lillah," the Prophet declared and embraced Asadullah-ul-Ghalib as soon as he dismounted. "Oh, Ali, in you there is a parable of Jesus, the son of Mary, alaihimus salaam, who was detested by the Jews to the extent that astonished his mother, and was loved by the Christians till imparting upon him the position that he was unfit for.(10) Hadst I not feared the Muslims regarding thee as the Christians regards Jesus, alaihis salaam, wouldst I have said things about thee which would have made Muslims revere thee and deem the earth falling from thy sandals as something worth venerating. Suffice it to say that thou art from me and I from thee. Thou wilt inherit me and I wilt inherit thee. Thou art unto me what Aaron was unto Moses, alaihimus salaam. Thou wilt continue to fight for my cause and thou wilt be nearest unto me on the Day of Judgment, next to the (heavenly) Fountain of Kauthir. Enmity against thee is enmity against me. War against thee is war against me. Thy friendship is my friendship and to be at peace with thee is to be at peace with me. Thy flesh is my flesh and thy blood is my blood. Whosoever obeyeth thee obeyeth me, for truth is on thy tongue and in thy breast. Thou hath as much faith in Allah as I have. Thou art the Gateway unto me as Allah hath ordered. Give I unto thee these things so that thy shi'a wilt be rewarded in Heaven and thy enemies be doomed for Hell-Fire."(11)

Ali could do nothing but weep in humility as the Holy Prophet rendered testimony of God's blessings for his service to the Divine Cause. He hugged Muhammad and requested permission for leave to oversee the Jewish surrender.

Later that same day Muhammad rode Duldul through the smoldering aperture. At once, he was taken aback by the pall of death, the stench of gore, and destruction. Enemy bodies blanketed the courtyard and hung over ramparts and parapets. A mordant haze from burnt up combustibles covered the area, adding to the surrealism. Solemnly, he gazed heavenward and thanked God for sparing his men the dreadful task of taking more lives than necessary. Finding Ali, he had him release the captives so they could collect their dead and provide proper burials. Afterwards, the Jewish leaders were brought before him and he dictated terms that would insure Muslim safety.

In days following the wounded recuperated from their injuries while the able bodied helped the Jews with construction. The Muslim women, having done everything within their power in treating the injured Believers, laid aside their personal losses and started comforting the grieving womenfolk of their enemies.

Zaynab bint Harith, a Jewish widow, distraught and embittered over her father, husband, and uncle's death, concocted a scheme designed to kill the Prophet. Pretending an interest in learning about Islam, she constantly asked questions, knowing it would attract Muhammad's attention. Then, in furtherance of her planned atrocity she started going out of her way to please the Believers, always saying a kind word or bringing an ewer of cool water for them to quench their thirst while they labored. She secretly watched from behind drawn curtains Muslims point out her house whenever Muhammad came through the area. After nearly two weeks she was satisfied her insidious plot had achieved its goal. She stopped Muhammad one morning and invited him along with several others to supper. Upon his acceptance for the next evening, she purchased and slaughtered a plump lamb along with the makings for a sumptuous meal. Marinating the meat in poison over night, she concealed it's toxicity with tangy spices and roasted it until her guests arrived.

At the appointed hour a knock sounded at her door. She graciously welcomed and seated her company, smiling at the men's mouth watering expressions. The aroma of roasted meat promised a delicious meal. After a few amenities, she poured them fresh juice and withdrew into the cooking area. Moments later she returned with a steaming trencher of food. Everyone reflexively swallowed and licked their lips in anticipation.

Muhammad asked the men to bow their heads while he invoked the Lord's name to bless the food. Afterwards, the men hungrily dug in while the Prophet stepped after the woman to thank her. When he turned to join his Brothers, a fleeting signal of danger flashed through his mind. He crossed into the room, the men were eating heartily and lauding the woman's cooking skills. The sense of danger passed. Resuming his place, the Prophet abstractedly examined their faces and began to eat. At the first taste he spit the food onto the floor.

"This meat tastes strange!" Muhammad unequivocally declared.

The Muslims at once stopped eating, expectorating mouthfuls of food, and looked at one another in disbelief. At the same instant, Bashir who had eaten more than the rest groaned and clutched his stomach as if his innards were afire. Seconds later he started vomiting then collapsed and died.

During the commotion the woman made her escape.

Within minutes news of the poisoning spread throughout the mountaintop, causing an angry outcry. Scores of Muslims cried for revenge, wanting to slay the surviving Jewish males. But Muhammad, already in the depths of misery over the loss of human lives, calmed the crowd.

Shortly thereafter, Zaynab was apprehended attempting to steal past the guards protecting Khaybar's entrance from any Jewish allies. Returned to answer for her crimes, she faced the Prophet and began sobbing. She dropped her head, fell to her knees, and admitted her wrong doing. Muhammad thought, that all at once she appeared helpless. And from the look of her, her evident penitence, he forgave the woman to the shock of all.

During the following year, while Muslims held true to Hudaybiyah's treaty terms, Banu Bakr joined forces with Quraysh against Islam. A host of tribes and clans either converted, or came into league with the emerging Islamic power. The Najranian Muslims, understanding the falsity of worshipping Jesus, sent an embassy to Madinah to entreat Prophet Muhammad to commission delegations into surrounding Christian countries to teach The Word of God. Thus, deputations were dispatched to Syria, Egypt, Abyssinia, the Byzantine capitol at Constantinople, the Sasanian dynasty at Ctesiphon, the Persian capitol at Mada'in which practiced no religion but followed the ways of their forefathers, and to Yamamah, an area east of the Hijaz where numerous Christian tribes were located.(12)

More often than not, instead of converting to Islam wherever they learned of the Truth, people would undertake long arduous journeys to Madinah to have al-Mustafa himself hear their declaration of faith. On one such occasion, Baseer, a young man under guardianship arrived. For two days he wandered around the city. He listened to every discussion on Islam he came across, learning all he could. Mid-afternoon of his second day he heeded the Call to Prayer. He tried to be as unobtrusive as possible, taking a position near the rear where he could observe Muhammad lead the Prayer.

Upon it's completion, Muhammad turned to face God's congregation and noticed a fresh face staring back at him with a look of expectancy. Smiling to take the sting out of any embarrassment his remark may cause, he said: "There is a new face amongst us this day. Al-Hamdu lillah!"

As the Apostle spoke every head in the mosque turned to see who he was directing his comments to.

"Where doth thou alight from young man," asked Muhammad.

Baseer colored slightly at having drawn so much attention and answered in a voice just shy of maturity. "M-Mekkah. I wish to declare my belief, O' Prophet."

Subsequently, it was learned that Baseer was still under guardianship. Al-Amin, in keeping with the covenant of Hudaybiyah, sent the young man back to Mekkah. Baseer departed Madinah in a state of depression. On his way back he decided not to return to Mekkah and its Disbelievers. Instead, he set out for the foothills just off the main route between Mekkah and Syria. Blaming Banu Quraysh for his troubles, he set up camp and resolved to give the pagans as much distress as possible.

Once establishing his base, he camouflaged it to blend in with the terrain. Next day, he spent collecting needle sharp bramble and thistle, anything the desert provided with a sturdy point. Another day was used in binding the collection of spinous material into star-like clusters: designed to disable caravan animals. Following a day of rest, he mapped out his strategy and set out with a pouch filled with over a thousand of the spiky little weapons. He planted them under the road's surface along a half mile stretch of the trade route.

Within a week the first caravan traveling to Syria for trade made it's way toward the concealed anti-animal devices. Baseer, watching intently from a nearby dune, waited until the last animal passed over the hill where his caltrop-like instruments would soon demonstrate their effects before jumping to his feet. In a shout that rocketed across the sands, he roared: "Laa ilaaha illal-laah," turned and disappeared into the desert's wilderness.

The caravaners, startled by the bellow, underwent flashes of fear thinking they were going to be attacked. But seeing no Muslim army they started to jeer and curse the vanished figure, saying things as : "The poor devil is lost and cannot find his God," and "the Truth must drive one to madness." The ridicule continued until the first beast screeched in pain.

Suddenly apprehensive, the merchants remembering the lone Muslim glanced around nervously, expecting an attack. In the meantime, the other animals started stamping their legs attempting to dislodge the spiny thorns imbedded in their hooves and foot-pads which caused the caltrops to penetrate further. As a result, the beasts erupted in a cacophony of screeching, bawling and braying. Spooked, the uninjured animals bucked off their riders and fled into the desert. Those able to maintain their saddles became unnerved and refused to continue the journey.

Upon their return to Mekkah, the news rapidly spread that a lone Muslim managed to turn back their entire caravan. Other young Muslims who were under guardianship thought this their way out of Mekkah without breaking the treaty. They banded together and fled the city to join their Brother in his campaign against Banu Quraysh. Posing a threat to future caravans, they became a new threat and unexpected headache for the Disbelievers.

Over the weeks and causing all sorts of misfortune, the young Muslims played havoc with Mekkah's commercial trade. It became so troublesome and menacing to their financial well being that an outcry was raised. Merchants and traders pleaded with city leaders to allow any Muslim the right to migrate to Madinah.

Qurayshie leaders, after an expedition of soldiers failed to capture any of the youngsters, started fearing a boycott of their businesses if they didn't handle the situation soon. Thus left with no options, they dispatched Walid ibn Mughayrah to the City of the Prophet with a sealed scroll. Traveling alone, he reached Madianah in under three weeks. Then with the intervention of several intermediaries, the known hater of Islam was finally passed through the organized structure of Islamic security and allowed an audience with the Prophet.

Entering the assembly hall, ibn Mughayrah found himself confronting Ali, Dujanah, and other trusted Companions. They were all standing around Muhammad protectively, issuing warning with their eyes as they watched him. Feeling insecure and frightened by their reputations, he put on a mask of defiance and swaggered toward Muhammad, scroll in hand. Before his second step he was sharply commanded to halt.

Ali collected the rolled parchment, eyeing the infidel with suppressed feelings and handed it back to Muhammad who in turn presented it to another.

In the few moments it took to break open the seals and unroll the scroll, a strain of tension gripped the air. Ali and the others never once removed their sight from Walid while Bakr quickly perused the document. A trace of a smile creased his mouth and the corners of his eyes crinkled. He read aloud in a satisfied voice that shattered the infidel's impudence.

"Oh,' Muhammad, we of Banu Quraysh, in order to further better relations, implore thee to stop the band of Muslim youths from vexing our caravans along the trade route. Take ye them into Madinah and any who wish to depart Mekkah."

"Al-Hamdu lillah," voiced Muhammad in acknowledgment of the Sublime Master. "Tell thy masters they will be collected."

In Abyssinia, the group of Muslims who fled Mekkah to avoid persecution had for more than ten years carefully watched events in Arabia. Homesick and encouraged by the changing attitudes towards their Faith, Ja'far decided the time had come to return to their homeland. At about the same time Bakr led the first assault on Khaybar, Ja'far started organizing the Muslims for travel. The farewell was several days long and heartbreaking owing their large numbers. After some time of traveling they reached the City of the Prophet.

The reunion, the successful campaigns, God's Revelation purifying and blessing Muhammad's Ahlul Bayt(13) and the threat to Islam or Muslim lives all but eradicated, prompted life in Madinah to explode with activity. Streams of people arrived daily from all parts of the Known world, wanting to learn the Religion of Truth.

Muhammad al-Amin al-Mustafa, in his earnest desire to continue the Message had more than once proclaimed: "I am the City of Enlightenment (knowledge) and Ali is it's Gateway"(14) and "My Ahlul Bayt is like that of Noah's Ark, he who embarketh upon it will have saved himself, and he who turneth away from it, is drowned and lost. So do not outstrip them, for then you shall perish, and do not fall short of them, for then you shall perish. Do not teach them for they are more knowledgeable than you.(15) Therefore, adhere and follow them in the same way ye adhere and follow the Book of Allah."(16)

He shrouded the protection of Islam on all who sought the Right Path and poured forth his love and wisdom. Without stint, he fulfilled their spiritual needs with God's inexhaustible Treasures.(17) With a pure heart he taught the worship of One God: to draw nigh unto Him; and to serve all creation with charity and love.(18) Wisely he guided, gently he counseled(19) and made known the Truth in marvelous ways.

As peace began to stabilize throughout the Arabian Peninsula, great events and changes were taking place as underdeveloped countries with their primitive but sincere performance of duty were learning how to decipher truth from falsehood. With the exception of a few nations, the empires and sovereignties gave little attention to events unfolding in Arabia.

Steeped in arrogance, their consciences deadened, they not only victimized their souls but deprived them of it's spiritual needs. The Roman Pontificate, who some thirty years earlier, presumptuously introduced a new Christianity which had in effect, planted the seed of ruination within the mighty Empire.(20) Its great system of laws, organization, and universal citizenship were sinking into the mire of ecclesiastical formalism, dogmatism, and self-importance.(21) Thus, in the course of time, the Christian respect for the individual's right became little more than tolerance, which caused an enormous amount of disillusionment. And the Empire, with it's internal stresses, along with the Persian Empire, were being pressed by the Turks and Avars, adding to their collapse. In the heart of Persia, the Sasanian dynasty also started to crumble under a wave of lawlessness.

In China, the renowned Buddhist, Yuang Chwang, had embarked upon his journey in search of religious truths as the first indications of trouble with the Tibetans and Khitans arose.

In Egypt, the Coptic Church had their hopes for gaining authority shattered and became the "Stipendiary slave-official"(22) of the state.

In India, the countless castes were canceling out the unity of Buddha's teachings. And with the span of each nation's gloriousness entering its last stages, Islam's spiritual significance made itself felt.(23)

CHAPTER THIRTY-FOUR

Far to the north, in Mesopotamia, the Persian Monarch Khusraw Parwiz had just received Abdullah ibn Hudhayfah, Prophet Muhammad's courier, with an air of effrontery. Years earlier, after hearing numerous reports of a Prophet in Arabia, he dispatched spies to determine the information's veracity filtering in from the Peninsula. Full of self-praise and greatness, he despised any near or far who vied for peoples attention. His agents, soon had the potentate appraised of Muhammad's teachings, of his exemplary life, the way people flocked to him, his increasing power, and his growing spiritual influence over Arab lands. Thus, when Parwiz read the contents of the Prophet's letter, he rebuked the bearer. In a spiel of invectives insulting the Voice of Unity, Islam, and man's Brotherhood, he ripped to shreds Muhammad's manifesto and slung its pieces into the emissary's face. He burst into paroxysms of fury and had Abdullah manhandled out from his presence. An hour later, he sent orders to Bazan, his governor in Yemen, instructing him to arrest Muhammad for his audacity in daring to address him, the grandson of Anawshirwan, the Just King, on equal terms.

At about the same time in Jerusalem, Dihyah Kalbi, Muhammad's representative, had made it past palace bureaucrats to Emperor Heraclius' inner domain. Standing before a set of gilded doors leading to the Emperor's presence, he met another bureaucrat who demanded he state his business. Raising the sealed scroll for emphasis, he said: "I bring tidings to Emperor Heraclius from the Servant and Messenger of God."

The official studied Dihyah's dusty and ragged appearance disdainfully, sneering in disapproval. Turning, he whispered to one of the palace sentries guarding the doors.

Following his instructions, the sentry opened the doors and disappeared down the hall. The functionary watched the retreating guard a moment before whirling to face Dihyah. Full of self-importance, he contemptuously put forth his hand, thumping his foot as he waited for the scroll. But not knowing court etiquette, the Muslim emissary simply stared at the bureaucrat. Finally, after a moment of barely masked animosity, the administrator said: "Pass thy weapons, for no doubt thou hath them hidden beneath thy robe."

Dihyah frowned, reluctant to relinquish his only means of defense but the official would not withdraw his hand. "It is a matter of propriety," he explained in a voice full of haughtiness, then added: "for no one but palace sentries may bear arms in the Emperor's presence."

Moving aside a pleat in his robe, he unloosed his dagger and scimitar and handed them over. The bureaucrat goggled in surprise as he took and passed the weapons back to the remaining sentry guarding the doors. He never suspected a sword of such lethal dimensions to be hidden among Dihyah's robe. Just then the other sentry returned and escorted both courier and official into a large antechamber where Emperor Heraclius sat upon a golden throne surrounded by upper echelon administrators.

The guard stepped to the first step leading up to the throne, bowed and stepped back to stand behind the emissary. Dihyah took the moment to glance around. He saw the walls lined with guards and felt his stomach fill with maddened hummingbirds. Apprehensive of saying the wrong thing, he decided to address the king exactly as Muhammad had instructed.

"Oh, Emperor Heraclius, I bri-" said Dihyah, then stopped abruptly because every one of the bureaucrats gasped, shocked that the Arab would dare speak without being spoken to.

Heraclius, with a flick of his hand simply waved aside the breach of protocol and silenced their objections. To the astonishment of all he smiled benevolently and said: "Tell me Bedouin, what tidings hath thou?"

"Oh,' Emperor, I bring thee a message from the Prophet and Messenger of Allah," he replied and started forward to present the scroll. Within his first step he was stopped by several guards rushing to block his advance with spears pointed at his chest. He swallowed hard. Heraclius sat bemused. The chief chamberlain stepped forward, collected the scroll and gave it to his king.

After perusing the rolled parchment, Rome's sovereign did not realize the seriousness of Muhammad's intentions, or understand the way Islam would reshape the world. Nonetheless, he was impressed with the message's articulation and invitation. But owing to his Empire's existing grandeur, subjects' pride, and his own vanity, he refrained from openly accepting the renewed Message. Instead, in something short of secrecy he initiated a local search for Arabs sufficiently acquainted with the Prophet to tell him more about Muhammad.

Oddly enough, Abu Sufyan had been among a group of Arab merchants discussing business when the emperor's men started making inquiries about the Prophet of God. At first, he was going to ignore the queries, but since Hudaybiyah's treaty he realized the wave of Islam and its Truths would sweep the world. Never, he thought while palace officials questioned the Arabs, did Muslim numbers decrease even in the worst of times, they just kept growing. So, shrugging his shoulders in resignation, he spoke up: "Thou needest not to look further. I, Abu Sufyan ibn Harb, am a distant cousin of Muhammad and know him well."

The bureaucrats, with a small retinue of guards, escorted Sufyan back to the palace. At the gilded doors, another detachment of guards he assumed to be palace defenders by their finery, took over and marched him directly into the throne room.

Abu Sufyan could not help but gawk at the ostentatious atmosphere of the emperor's inner sanctum as he imagined his own personage amid the splendor. Beams of sunlight spilled in through intersecting vaulted ceilings, revealing richly painted murals of Heraclius' victories. And as he lowered his gaze he noticed another detachment of guards against the walls. He knew they were the king's personal bodyguard by their royal colors. Suddenly one of the dozen or so chamberlains surrounding Heraclius cleared his throat and snapped him out of his reverie.

The administrator, by gesture, indicated Sufyan to remain where he stood then stepped three paces towards the throne. He said: "Oh, Emperor Heraclius. Mighty ruler of the land, thy humble servant brings forth Abu Sufyan ibn Harb who layeth claim to personal knowledge of Muhammad ibn Abdullah, the Prophet of Islam."

Heraclius nodded impatiently and drummed his fingers on the throne's armrest while the bureaucrat went through the motions of formality. Sufyan stepped to where the official stood. Heraclius wasted no time with courtesy and came right to the point.

"Art thou acquainted with this Prophet Muhammad?"

"I know him well, O' Emperor. Many a time hath our paths crossed, and he is a distant cousin."

The king was pleased at his good fortune in finding a kinsman of the Prophet. He edged forward on his throne and fired his next question. "Is he of noble lineage?"

"Of the noblest, O' Emperor.

"Hath there been a king amongst his kindred?"

"Nay, Oh,' Emperor."

"Are these followers of God's Way rich or poor?"

"At first, Oh,' Emperor, they were poor and lowly. But even as we speak, people of substance are entering the fold of submitting unto God."

"Doth thou know of him to speak falsehoods?"

"Nay," Sufyan hated to admit.

"Doth he ever break his covenants?"

"Nay."

Heraclius suspected a reluctance in Sufyan and took several moments to study the Arab. Sufyan grew nervous, wondering if he'd offended the king with the brevity of his answers.

Finally, in a voice manifesting his rising excitement, Heraclius asked: "Hath thou ever engaged him in battle?"

"Aye," Sufyan replied, unable to keep his responses from one word syllables.

"What were the results?"

"Never did we prevail against him," he managed to say with more than one word.

"What doth he proclaim?"

Sufyan felt entrapped by the emperor's shrewdness and sighed. He said: "To worship the One God and assign Him no partners. To fulfill one's duty to Him with devotion and praise. To be chaste, straightforward, truthful, and keep thy union with kindred." Inwardly he was surprised at his answers, for it sounded like he himself advocated The Message.

"Hath any of his followers ever turned apostate?"

"Nay."

Satisfied with Sufyan's answers, Heraclius slid back in his throne and closed his eyes as he called up his knowledge of Scripture. A few moments later, he opened his eyes and looked around the room, letting his vision wander from face to face. He was certain, beyond any doubt. He said, voice filled with sudden humbleness: "If what thou saith is true, verily Muhammad is the one prophesied by Jesus. For only PARACLETOS,(1) who is a Comforter and Mercy unto all creatures could tame the wild lands of Kedar."(2) As an afterthought, he added: "Should I ever lay sight upon Prophet Muhammad, would I lave his feet with my own hands!

* * * * *

When Prophet Muhammad heard Abdullah's account of Persia's monarch shredding the invitation to Islam, he simply said: "Thus shall his kingdom be rent."

In Egypt, Prophet Jesus' simple teachings had evolved from the Oneness of God to irrational descriptions which culminated in the doctrine of the Trinity. And as the Church split into idolatrous sects, conditions started deteriorating. Thus when the invitation to Islam arrived, which could redress the discontent, the church sought to appease its population and welcomed the renewed Message.(3)

Bazan, Governor of Yemen, after receiving the emissary from Persia began to question the monarch's edict to arrest and execute Prophet Muhammad. He, instead, started investigating the Way of life the country was hailing. Once enlightened, he became convinced Islam was not some new religion but was in fact the Truth taught by prophets of old. He ignored Khusraw Parwiz's orders, converted, and joined the growing Islamic community in Yemen. Journeying to Madinah, Bazan informed the Prophet of his monarch's injunction, his

330

subsequent investigation, and conversion to Islam. Muhammad was delighted and kept him on as Governor to Yemen. Thus, another province came under the banner of Islam.

* * **

Nearly a year had passed since the treaty of Hudaybiyah. And as more and more people came into God's Way of life, discussions started focusing on the Umrah and Hajj as the sacred months neared. The Muhajirun, anticipating their return to Mekkah and believing they'd be able to stay in Mekkah to complete the Pilgrimage, became feverish with activity. Everywhere one went, in and around Madinah, the topic of conversation revolved around the Prophet's place of birth, or the Mountain of Light.

Weeks prior to their departure, Muhammad ordered a hundred man party of warriors to scout their route and make certain the Mekkans were living up to their end of the treaty. Two weeks later the patrol returned to report that it was safe to proceed.

On the eve of departure over two thousand Muslims amassed for the Pilgrimage. The trusted Companions, following Muhammad's instructions, selected and separated sixty camels for sacrifice, and gathered the fattest stocks for sustenance. At daybreak, after a short speech and prayer, the Prophet began the march to Mekkah.

It took over three weeks marching the mass of humanity across the Hijaz to reach the point where Prophet Muhammad had everyone change into Pilgrim garb. From there, the Most Holiest of cities was less than a day's march away, the mood turned solemn. Next day, after morning prayer, the Muslims moved out with hearts pounding in anxiousness. By mid afternoon, they were at the bottom of Cave Hira where the Word of God came down, and camped the day out.

The pagan Mekkans, alerted to the approaching Muslims were now faced with the consequence of their own doing. Imagining insult, the leaders couldn't endure what their hands had wrought. It was too much for them, for their hearts still continued to burn with hatred. Over the years they had lost so many people to God's Religion that an intense fear gripped them. They thought if the populace, especially the young, watched the act of true worship they'd forsake their idols and convert to God's Way as so many others had. So, hoping to avoid the inevitable they convinced all but the Believers to vacate Mekkah while the Muslims performed the rites prescribed by God.

Before noon the next day, Prophet Muhammad led the Muslims across the last three miles to God's Sacred House. The Disbelievers, at a distance atop the surrounding mountains, pretended to ignore the Believers. But the two thousand plus throats calling out, "Labbaika,

Allahumma labbaik," reverberated through the mountains, making them impossible to ignore.

The Disbelievers stood in awe, unable to turn away from the scene of true Brotherhood. Silently they watched with creeping admiration, feeling the raw power of belief radiating out in waves. Some of the tribal and clan leaders, wondering why their idols weren't using their powers to drive away the Muslims, started reevaluating their convictions. And as the train of their thoughts continued to develop,more than a few of the leaders began to wonder: was it worth the loss of lives to battle the Muslims, or to prevent Muhammad from delivering the Message.

After the sun started it's decline, Bilal called the Adhan. Muslims went from milling about to forming close knit ranks until they encircled the Ka'bah. And as the Prophet commenced prayer, the Mekkanese were again electrified by the scene of harmonious Brotherhood as Believers bowed and prostrated in true obsequiousness to the One God.

Again, the idols, crosses and images, did nothing. More than any could know, save God, pagan hearts were indelibly imprinted with the act of worship. For none could deny the magnetism of True submission as the Muslims prayed, seemingly to sing God's Glory.

Three days later. Two men from the pagan camp arrived to tell Muhammad the Mekkan leaders had lived up to their end of the treaty and would like him to take the Believers and leave the area. But when they entered the square they found him in the midst of telling the Muslims their time was up. At first, there were a few grumbles but the Prophet explained that with patience and perseverance they would soon complete the Hajj. One of the men immediately returned to rejoin his camp while the other waited for Muhammad to finish his delivery, then asked to be accepted into the Brotherhood of man.

Khalid, who years before contemplated joining the ranks of Believers had for the past three days observed the Muslims closely. Now, as he watched them march away he started to feel an emptiness, like his soul yearned to be with the People of Truth. He wanted to feel the spiritual uplifting so plain on Muslims faces, to serve the One God. He wanted change.

Sometime later, he approached the Mekkan leaders and boldly announced his intentions. "It is clear unto me and should be clear unto all men of sound mind that Muhammad is neither a poet nor sorcerer. He is the Prophet of Allah and what saith he is the Message of the Righteous Guider. And saith I unto thee in truth, it is the duty of a people seeking wisdom to learn and live God's Way."

The leaders were too stunned to respond. Then, one by one they opened fire with arguments against him becoming a Muslim. But seeing his resolve they almost all at once changed their course of action to one of persuasion. Failing, they started offering gold dinar and promising him the position of general over the army. Nothing worked, he remained impervious to their inducements and seemed to be gaining strength in his determination.

Suddenly, someone from the gathering crowd yelled: "I am with thee, O' Khalid! For none can permanently suppress the Light of Truth from the people."

Amr ibn As broke from the crowd and stood besides Khalid. That's all it took to shatter the walls of ignorance, for several others then followed ibn As. All wanted to share in the Brotherhood of man, to have the honor of serving God in Truth. Thus, with nothing more to be said, the group of men left for Madinah, forsaking their homes and possessions.

The Mekkan leaders were left trembling with anger and began blaming each other for Hudaybiyah's treaty. It dawned on them that as soon as word spread of their strongest supporters converting to Islam, hundreds of others might also convert and flee the city. Left without the nerve to openly make a stand against the Prophet they again started intriguing with their allies.

Meantime, Khalid and his group rode into Madinah amidst the wary eyes of countless Muslims. "Where can I find the Prophet Muhammad," Khalid asked the first man he recognized. Given directions, he led his party to the mosque.

"As-salaamu alaikum," said Khalid for the group.

"Wa alaikum as-salaam wa Rahmatul-laah," Muhammad returned. "How can I help thee and thy men Khalid?"

"Oh,' Prophet of Allah, if thou wilt forgive our past transgressions we would like to declare our belief in Allah, the One God, and our loyalty unto thee."

Muhammad was not surprised, for he knew if one looked with a sincere heart the Truth would knock the brains out of falsehood. He looked from Khalid's face to the other faces. He saw no treachery, only the countenance of genuine desire. He said: "I am only a man as ye are and ye have no need to petition my forgiveness. Implore Allah, The Acceptor of Repentance, for forgiveness. He is Most Merciful. Say ye..."

During the year that followed, numerous Muslim missionaries were sent out to the furthest parts of Arabia and into the middle east to propagate the Message. In Mu'tah, of the new Roman province, an ill-disposed Governor defied Emperor Heraclius' edict regarding Islam and had Muhammad's emissary arrested. He tortured him in public, hoping he'd renounce the Way. But he would not recant his belief and was put to death.

Prophet Muhammad, within a week of hearing about his emissary's death, marshaled together an army of over three thousand fighting men and set them off toward Mu'tah. He was intent on demonstrating to all enemies of Islam how prompt the Muslims would respond to protect their interests and retaliate against willful murder. It was time once again to crush the contumacious Disbelievers.

At the time of Muhammad's call to arms, the spies fled Madinah to inform the Roman army near Mu'tah who were preparing to mobilize against the Persians. Apprised of an exaggerated number of Muslim soldiers, the generals flew into a panic. They dreaded the idea of engaging the massive Persian army on one side and the fiercest Muslim warriors on the other. So, working against time, they dispatched messengers requesting additional forces and were able to augment their army to well over two hundred thousand men before the Islamic force arrived.

All along the way, Muslim faces steadily darkened with resolve. Each knew the enemy's lust for power and perilous ideas, which concealed something more obscenely dangerous. Eventually their thoughts ran their course and they invariably took solace in God's immutable Law of Truth: the Good will overcome the Evil, no matter the guise it wears. They marched somberly, musing on the conditions imposed by the Prophet if peaceful solutions failed. They were not to harm women, children, or the elderly, destroy vegetation, or lay waste to property.

Never before in mankind's history had an army set out with such noble instructions. The distinction, however, made no difference, for they considered not their place in history but occupied their time with prayer and meditation. Finally, after several weeks treading through the blistering desert, advance scouts returned to disclose that an enormous Roman army lay beyond the next series of mountains.

Ja'far ibn Abu Talib halted the army, ordered the camp's construction, then sent scouts out to reconnoiter their enemy. They were taken aback, unconsciously gawking at the sheer size of the Roman encampment which appeared to extend back to the horizon. A short consultation ensued and it was estimated that their numbers were in excess of two hundred thousand soldiers. Suddenly feeling the continuity and bond of Brotherhood, they turned toward the Qiblah in silent prayer. Ending, they returned to camp.

Ja'far, Zayd ibn Harith and Abdullah Rawahid, entered the largest tent which served as command center. They took places around a large platter of food, each feeling a quiet desperation as the whole enormity of the situation struck their senses. Deeply agitated by the sea of trouble less than a thousand yards away, two thoughts were uppermost in their minds: how would the Prophet handle the problem and what would Ali do? Ja'far, the commander-in-chief, sought ways to diplomatically resolve the differences while the other two leaders spent their time superimposing offensive strategies over the terrain. So absorbed were they in their concentration they did not realize several warriors entered the tent until someone 'a-hemmed'.

One of the commanders selected two negotiators and said: "Foremost, trust ye in Allah, for He is The Best Disposer of affairs. Ye have full authority to sue for peace without compromising Islam's standards. Hence, when breaketh the new day approach the Romans from the opposite side of our position."

After the mediators departed, word was given to have the warriors assembled. One of the leaders, speaking for the others, raised his arms for quiet. He said: "Oh, ye men of Faith, there is no god but Allah! If negotiations for a peaceful settlement fail we will confront an enemy with far greater numbers than any of ye have imagined, perhaps in numbers exceeding two hundred thousands." He paused a moment to allow the information to sink in before continuing. He thought he'd see shock, incredulousness and fear, but saw elation instead: the warriors felt honored at having the opportunity for martyrdom. "For now, let us await the outcome of our arbitrators," he added to end the gathering.

Late morning two days later, just as the sun crested over the mountains and touched the command post, the two negotiators came riding into camp. Escorted into the tent, the eldest began speaking. "Oh, Ja'far, saith the Romans they will not bargain with the likes of us."

"So be it. Please wait outside, we will be there shortly," said Ja'far. With their hopes dashed, they steeled themselves against the trial to come then stepped out to address the men as they massed in front.

"In the name of Allah, The Just, The Most Compassionate," began Ja'far in a voice that rang out over their heads. "Amongst men, who has higher chances in the realm of heaven than the servants of Allah?"

"None," came the reply from the army of Believers.

"All praise and glory is due to Allah," Ja'far roared back as the fervor of battle started to warm his blood. "The jealously of Cain against Abel, which led to the slaying of innocent Abel is the type of jealously existing between Disbelievers and Muslims."(4)

"Those in obstinate rebellion against Allah are merely deceived and deceive one another, their wickedness is but wickedness against their own souls.(5) They treat His Signs lightly or as jest(6) and would fain put out His Light, but the Truth will shine for aye.(7) The Just God worketh His world in mercy for His servants, and in just punishment for those who do wrong."(8)

335

"Fighting in defense of Truth and Right is not to be undertaken lightheartedly, nor to be evaded as a duty. Life and death are in the Hands of Allah. Thou knowest large armies can be routed by those who battle for Allah, as shown by the courage of David, alaihis salaam, whose prowess single-handedly disposed the Philistines."(9)

"Oh,' ye who believe, hold together thyselves in unity and discipline, for ye know thy mission is righteousness for mankind.(10) Allah's loving care doth encompass us round and delivereth us from dangers, He is the Only Protector.(11) To the pure in faith, He will give the mind and resources to conquer.(12) Our duty is to stand firm, unswerving in steadfast courage, thinking nothing of self-sacrifice for our reward is His good pleasure."

"Stand ye not in despair nor in fear of the enemy, but stand with firm hope in The All-Seeing, The All-Hearing.(13) The Battle of Uhud showed how dangerous it was to disobey orders or lose courage, where He helpeth can no harm befall.(14) Hence, fight the good fight and never want for confidence, for this life is short and the Hereafter eternal.(15) And, regard unmoved the taunts of thy enemy who mock ye in battle, nor allow their falsehoods to raise questions in thy minds.(16) Hearken ye unto the Word of Allah."

"Allah! There is no god but He, The Ever-Living, The Self-Subsistent (The Sustainer of all things). He hath sent down unto thee the Book with Truth confirming what was before it; and He sent down the Torah and the Evangel aforetime, a guidance for a people and sent down the Distinction (Qur'an); verily for those who disbelieve in the signs of Allah, for them is a sever punishment; Allah is Mighty, Lord of Retribution. Verily, Allah, nothing hidden is there from Him, in the Earth and in the Heavens. He it is Who fashioneth you in the wombs (of your mothers) as He liketh; there is no god but He, The All-Mighty, The All-Wise."

"Oh,' ye who believe, fear ye Allah as ye should; and (see that) ye die not but as Muslims. And hold ye fast by the cord of Allah all together, and be not divided (among yourselves) and remember the bounty of Allah bestowed upon you, when ye were enemies (of each other) He united your hearts together with (mutual) love, and thus by His favor ye have become brethren and (while) ye were on the brink of the pit of the Hell-Fire then He delivered you there from; thus doth Allah clearly explain His signs for you, so that ye may be guided."

"Oh, ' ye who believe! If ye obey the disbelievers they will make you to turn on your heels so ye will turn back losers. Nay! Allah is your Guardian and He is the Best of the Helpers."

"Say: "Oh, Allah! Master of the Kingdom, Thou givest the kingdom unto whomsoever Thou likest and takest away the kingdom from whomsoever Thou likest! Thou exaultest whomsoever Thou likest and abasest whomsoever Thou likest; in Thine hands is all good; verily Thou art over all things Mighty. Thou causest the night to pass into the day, and Thou causest the day to pass into the night, Thou bringest forth the living out of the dead, and Thou bringest forth the dead out of the living, and Thou givest sustenance to whomsoever Thou likest, without measure.'"(17)

After delivering the Surah's portion he wanted, Ja'far continued with last minute instructions on the loftiness of their purpose. "Let us fight the evilness, but acquit not evil in its own coin, however great the temptation: for no chance will there be to retrieve our conduct once Allah's angels call the kafirun to account.(18) To Allah we belong and to Him is our return."

The Muslims en masse jumped to their feet, their passions swelling beyond human comprehension. Then all at once they turned towards the enemy's camp, began brandishing swords, spears, bows, and charged while shouting at the top of their lungs: "Allahu Akbar," "Na'uuzu Bil-laah," and "Ta wakkal-tu Alal-laah."

Beyond the mountain's bend, Roman sentinels were joking and ridiculing Islam and it's followers as they watched the direction from which the negotiators had ridden in two days earlier, never suspecting the Muslim camp behind them. Their camp, certain of victory, maintained a high level of activity thinking none could stand against their numbers. Suddenly guards and soldiers alike smothered their cavalier attitudes. Speechlessly, they looked at each other with growing alarm as the ground started trembling. An instant later, in an ever rising crescendo they heard the rolling rumble of pounding hooves and the deafening sound of three thousand roaring voices.

At first, widespread panic ran unchecked through the Roman rear lines of defense, which now became the primary lines and caused a stampede for the rearmost area. In their haste to flee the hordes of Muslims rounding the mountain behind them, they were knocking aside their own men which added to the confusion. Thus allowing the Muslims to inflict a great deal of death and casualties. The warriors of Truth and Right were like mechanical men, unrelenting in their dispensation of retribution. They fought with a will that knew no retreat. Striking with vehemence, their ferocity fountain-headed the enemy's imagination to amplify the valorous charge out of proportion and fancy themselves under attack by like number of Muslims.

Nearing day's end, the Roman generals were able to reorganize their terror stricken soldiers and counterattack. The Muslims started losing their momentum and began losing ground: falling dead and wounded.

Ja'far was fighting on the battle's far side when he realized their press forward started slowing down to a snail's pace. He knew it was time to call a tactical retreat before the enemy overwhelmed them. But being heavily engaged, he neither had the time nor opportunity and soon fell under the sword.

Across the field, Khalid, an accomplished tactician himself, also recognized the battle's tide turning and wondered why any of the leaders hadn't sounded the withdrawal. After dispatching his opponent, he stepped back four or five paces to look for Ja'far and the other leaders. Seeing them down, he took it upon himself to sound the retreat.

As both sides fell back they gathered their wounded and dead. An eerie calm fell over battlefield. The air smelled of the rank odor of disemboweled bodies and spilt blood. And adding injury to the senses were the suffering cries of wounded men and animals, making the cessation of hostilities nightmarish rather than peaceful.

That night amid burning torches, Khalid appointed captains and held council. Bent on developing new stratagems, it was well after midnight before a number of tactical agreements were reached. Khalid, about midway through, had departed the circle of men in a state of excitement and issued instructions. Two dozen men with puzzlement on their faces started scouring the land for dead shrubs. He, then, directed another group to bind the bushes into small bundles. And, finally charged a third group with placing the bundles every fifty feet across the countryside.

At dawn, following prayers and another soul stirring speech, the assigned horse warriors moved into action. With a bundle tied to drag behind their mounts, they galloped to and fro from each cluster of tied brush and put it to fire. Then rode up to form the vanguard where they began cantering back and forth, creating a huge cloud of dust which mixed with the smoldering shrubs.

In the Roman camp, soldiers came alert with trepidation as the rising stridency of voices and drumming hooves reverberated through the valley. And when they saw the human wall of Muslims stretching for over two thousand yards in width amid thickening clouds of dust, they started inventing Muslim reinforcements. Next, they refused their orders to attack. Instead, they kept to their side praying to their gods to protect them against attack. Even the generals thought better of initiating the offensive after yesterday's charge.

Consequently, the Muslims stopped short of bow shot range while a hundred horsemen paced their mounts far behind the lines. Both sides waited tensely for the onslaught of death and mayhem. Hours later, the combatants remained at a standoff and eventually began to withdraw.

Though withdrawal of Muslim forces was the wisest thing to do under the circumstances, the people in Madinah were inappropriately displeased. They never believed in retreats and understood only two things in such situations: martyrdom or victory. Upset, they began to shame the warriors and Khalid for leading the withdrawal. It was an unexpected reaction.

Muhammad, nevertheless, adamantly defended Khalid's actions. He knew with the passage of time people would eventually realize the judiciousness of their retreat.

* * * * *

It was only a matter of time before varying accounts of events at Mu'tah reached Mekkah and its querulous tribes. Qurayshie leaders, particularly pleased with the report of Islam's forces being driven from the area, thought the Islamic power structure was rendered impotent. And under that premise they opted to break the treaty of Hudaybiyah. Clandestinely they worked through their network of allies and in a relatively short time raised the levels of contention against the Muslims around Mekkah's precincts. With the city's Disbelievers backing their supporters, they bribed and coerced chiefs Nawfal and Malik ibn Awf al-Nasari, of Banus Bakr and Hawazin respectively, into attacking Banu Khuza'ah, a small tribe which recently converted to Islam.

The two chiefs joined forces and began planning their assault. Days afterwards, in a predawn raid, Khuza'ah's first victims were a number of adolescent shepherd boys who were taking the settlement's animals out to graze. The raiders, then fell upon the dwellings, completely catching the Believers unaware. Viciously, they slaughtered combat aged men and any who even looked threatening. And finally ended burning and looting the settlement.

Within days of the savage attack, an outcry for help arose out of Khuza'ah's ashes and reached Madinah. The ignoble Disbelievers remembering just how well established the Islamic Empire had become started having second thoughts about their involvement. Fearing the return in kind they tried to distance themselves from the butchery and persuaded Abu Sufyan to sue for another treaty, or at the very least renew the old one.

Sufyan, who had assumed leadership of Quraysh and the Disbelievers, traveled to Madinah like a man attempting to stay his own execution. Driven into a corner of his own making, he desperately wanted to convince Prophet Muhammad into reinstating Hudaybiyah's conditions as they were, or allow him the opportunity to ransom the loss.

Upon his arrival, however, he immediately encountered a wall of difficulty. His pleas for an audience with Muhammad were ignored. People turned their backs to him, realizing his motives, his brutal disregard for the rights of others, his inherent dislike of Islam and suppressed hatred for Muslims. Discouraged and a bit put off by their stonewalling him, he resentfully made his way sensing the situation's gravity. Yet, he refused to succumb to his instincts.

Pessimistically, he sought out familiar faces who at one time had been friends. Without direction he strolled the streets feeling the cold stares of those around him. Children fled from his path, seemingly detecting his cold violence and ruthlessness. Rounding a corner, he nearly bumped into Abu Bakr. He raised his head and slowly met Bakr's eyes. His peppered brows drew together propitiously as he greeted his one time friend. Bakr returned his salutation with less than common courtesy and his spirits sank a little lower. Nonetheless, he asked him to intercede on his behalf with the Prophet.

Bakr did not reply, just regarded him in silence, scrutinizing him with a look of irony. He understood all about him, his conceits and evil mindedness. His manner became stern, uncompromising and imperative.

"This I cannot do, Sufyan," he finally said.

Curse thee, thought Sufyan, inwardly shrinking from Bakr's icy stare. Red in the face, his ego damaged, he was on the verge of panic when he saw Umar.

"Umar! Umar!" Sufyan hailed. "Wilt thou take me to see the Prophet?"

Umar responded as Bakr had.

Sufyan then saw his daughter Habiba who was married to the Prophet. Smiling to conceal his dejection, he greeted her. Her return was also less than desired.

"What art thou doing in Madinah? Hast thou come to proclaim Allah's Oneness," Habiba asked hopefully.

"Nay, I came to speak with Muhammad but none will take me to him. I must warn him if he retaliates against Mekkah, the Muslims will be slaughtered," he answered falsely.

Habiba stared at her father, taken aback by his statement. Her voice trembled with resentment when she next spoke. "I cannot take thee to see my husband. Perhaps thou shouldest take thy warning back into the streets," she added before turning around to do something else.

Walking near a group of men he recognized and called Ali. After a lengthy conversation, Ali suggested he take his news to the community. Thinking his chances to better address the Muslims as a whole, he followed Ali's advice and waited in the assembly hall while word went out that he wanted to speak to the ummah.

As the learning hall started to fill, he recognized many faces and gained confidence in his ability to persuade them to stay their hands. Then when the doors closed, he decided to switch tactics and use every trick of the tongue.

Even though he was considered chief of the largest tribe in Arabia and had a considerable amount of influence, not a single Muslim displayed emotion, or the slightest interest in his proposals. He could see how little esteem in which he was held through their stares. Feeling inveighed against, his face reddened in humiliation. His heart pounded in uneasiness. Finally unable to bear their regard any longer, he left the hall and departed Madinah in a state of heightened apprehension.

* * * * *

Inasmuch as the infidels of Mekkah had chosen to break Hudaybiyah's treaty, Prophet Muhammad no longer felt an obligation to remain bound by any agreement made with the Mekkans. Consequently, Ali and trusted Companions were called for council and advice sought. Following hours of discussion, war was declared. Word was then secretly dispatched to Muslims across the Peninsula, informing them to prepare for a major offensive and where to assemble. None however were told who they were going to battle.

As the days passed, Prophet Muhammad spent his time in contemplation while the Islamic communities throughout Arabia prepared for war. Muslims up to the midway point between Mekkah and Madinah, and from all points north converged on Madinah by the thousands. Muslims south of the half way mark began gathering an hour away from Marr al-Zuhran, where they'd eventually link up with their Brothers from Madinah.

It was a massive undertaking, comparable to the war craft of the declining Persian and Roman Empires. One day, weeks before the scheduled date set to march on Mekkah, Muhammad told Ali that Angel Gabriel disclosed information regarding a woman on her way to the Mekkans with a letter describing their mobilization and plans to take Mekkah.

Ali was suddenly alarmed as he stared at Muhammad. In view of what the Prophet told him he feared the loss of the element of surprise, and felt failure as second in command. He shook his head in disgust, clenched his hands into fists and turned away. After a moment or two, he faced his mentor, his voice hard as he asked if he could personally run down the informer.

Muhammad regarded Ali calmly and with affection. Ali felt a surge of nostalgia rush through him as Muhammad's expression cast the familiar gentleness of his childhood.

"Ali, none other wouldst I trust but thee, for thou art to me as my own brother," said the Mercy of all creatures.

Minutes later Ali rushed out, collected Zubair and Miqdad, and departed in hot pursuit. After three days of hard riding they finally overtook a lone woman on camelback.

Ali immediately recognized the woman, but felt neither compassion nor the need for courtesy. Speaking in a hard cynical voice, he sternly asked: "Doth thou carry any letter to the kafirun in Mekkah?"

The woman averted her gaze, shaking, denied the accusation. She even went as far as swearing to it without invoking God's name, claiming she was only going to visit relatives. Nearly bursting into tears, she goaded her beast ahead.

Zubair and Miqdad turned in unison to face Ali. Miqdad said as Ali stared after her with distrustful eyes: "The poor woman is innocent, perchance stopped we the wrong woman."

Ali knew better: the Prophet had never erred nor spoken falsely; besides, he noticed the woman would not call upon Allah as her witness when she made her oath. Gesturing his companions to follow, he rode up to the woman and ordered her to stop. Without so much as a word he unsheathed his sword and raised it high above his head, poised to deliver a death stroke if need be. "Woman," exclaimed Ali menacingly, "if thou doth not give me the letter, by Allah, Most Wise, wilt I cut thee to pieces!"

The woman's blood drained from her face. She started trembling uncontrollably with fear. Blubberingly she said: "W-wait my lord, smite me not! Have I what thou seekest. I beseech thee, O' noble one, have mercy upon me for I-"

"Silence!" Ali said harshly. "Doth thou not realize the peril thou couldst have placed the Muslims in? Ask not I for mercy, but seek thou the Lord thy God for mercy." With the danger of exposure now neutralized, Ali's granite-like exterior cracked away. He asked the woman to reveal nothing of their preparations for war to which she not only acquiesced, but invoked Allah as her witness. She was allowed to continue on and the letter was taken back to Madinah.

Prophet Muhammad, upon receipt of the letter thanked Ali, Miqdad and Zubair, and retreated into the mosque. Two days he fasted, contemplated and prayed, neither speaking nor moving from his position. On the third day, the day of Jumu'ah, he rose from his niche and performed the service. Afterwards, he stepped onto a small base and stared into the crowd. The congregation, after several long minutes in silence started whispering in concern until he cleared his throat. Holding the letter up for them to see, he said: "People, what I hold before ye is a letter to the kafirun of Mekkah. And, I regret to say it was written by someone in this very assembly divulging information about our secret plans for war. Hence,-" He could say nothing further because the congregation erupted with angry cries. He stood silently, his gaze fixed on the perpetrator while they vented their anger. Then raising both arms for silence, he waited for the man responsible to come forward of his own accord.

Hatib ibn Amr, who after a minute of enduring the Prophet's relentless stare, started shaking in fear. He cast his sight to the floor guiltily and rose to step forward. He felt a great sense of shame as the densely packed mosque fell quiet and ogled him unbelievingly. Standing next to the platform, he slowly looked up and faced the Prophet remorsefully then turned toward the assemblage.

He said penitently: "Didst I scribe the letter but not with intentions of causing harm. Thought I only to save my small family still in Mekkah, for I feared losing the confrontation with the Mekkans and my family would be put to death for my belief in God's Way. I realize now it was wrong and foolish to go against a people whom I regard as kin, so slay me for my infidelity if ye must. But I beseech thee to protect my babies and woman."

In every respect his arguments were something all could understand and the Muhajirun could relate to. Compassion and reason now governed the assembly's emotions, for no harm had actually been done. Embarrassed by their earlier condemnation, they looked to Muhammad for adjudication.

Al-Mustafa had upon hearing Hatib express his reasons, lapsed into an era decades beforehand. He was seeing beyond his present dimension: espying horrid scenes of torture and sufferance. Devoid of focus, he stared out into the congregation until they started getting restless which snapped him out of his reverie. He blinked several times as if to clear away the last vestiges of his nightmarish vision and raised his arms to calm the crowd before he spoke.

"Seeing as how his cause was prompted neither for selfishness nor gain, and that secrecy hath been preserved, no harm shall befall Hatib."

On the day of the march on Mekkah there were over seven thousand fighting men gathered at Madinah's entrance, ready to give their lives in defense of Islam. Muhammad sat atop Duldul and watched the furor of his army. They are the soldiers of Allah, he thought, and they came to reclaim Mekkah and crush the Disbelievers, al-Hamdu lillah! Then, as the women employed to care for the wounded brought up the rear, he waved his arms to silence the multitude.

"In the name of Allah, The Beneficent, The Merciful," pealed out the Comforter's words distinctly over their heads. "Say I unto ye what relation should one hold with men whose hearts are filled with rancor, who hate both Allah and His servants? Seek protection from The Faithful, The Giver of Security, and not from His sworn enemies.(19) for only The Guardian can put in order all things."

Muhammad then tugged Duldul's reins in the direction of Mekkah and the expedition began. Following their intrepid leader, the Muslims started roaring out "Allahu Akbar" which thundered off the nearby mountains. It had been the dream of many to return to Mekkah, cleansing it of it's idols as Prophet Abraham had done more than millenniums earlier. Indeed, reflected Muhammad, their hearts were full of faith and they would not be held back from delivering the Truth and bringing justice and decency into the holy city.

In Mekkah, at about the same time Prophet Muhammad launched the march, his uncle Abbas and some others were searching out individuals who had expressed a desire in becoming followers of God's Way. They were disgusted with Mekkan autonomy and jurisprudence, and sought redress that could only come with Islam. But upon discovering a mysterious lack of Believers they regrouped to discuss its significance. Eventually deciding their absence signaled a warning of some kind, they departed for Madinah with a sense of urgency.

Ten days out, they awoke to a monstrous cloud of dust spreading across the horizon. Abbas, having never before seen a cloud of such magnitude darkening the sky, immediately realized the potential danger of attempting to trudge their way through the coming onslaught. So as eldest he issued orders that they waste no time in taking steps to shield themselves against the storm's violence.

Within minutes they were huddled along side their mounts for protection and wrapped in robes, awaiting the leading winds to assault their position. But the expected gale never arrived. Instead, the ground gave to vibration and a rolling cadence too indistinct to make out which began increasing in intensity. Confused by the inconsistent elements, Abbas and the others, one by one, unwrapped themselves to cautiously peer over their animals. To their surprise they saw in the distance coming down a small rise Prophet Muhammad's white Arabian followed by a wave of humanity. Abbas was the first to find his voice and exclaimed: "It is no storm, it is the Prophet and his army that has caused the horizon to darken!"

Mounting up, Abbas led the small party toward Muhammad whose horse stood out like a beacon of invitation. They rode in silence, each lost in thought, wondering whom the Muslims were going to battle with. Before any could reach any conclusion, they were greeted by the Prophet and his trusted Companions. Afterwards, the riders declared their belief and joined the march on Mekkah.

Abbas rode in the vanguard, near his nephew's side, immersed in speculation. Unable to refrain from conjuring up visions of Mekkans cowering in fear amidst death and destruction. He worried over those whom he knew wanted to convert but were frightened of retaliation. What will become of them, he mused, will they be put to death in the heat of battle, mistaken for the enemy? In the end, recalling his vow to The Eternal, Self-Subsisting God, that come what may he would fight God's enemies till the death if need be against those he once called friends.

After three weeks traversing the Hijaz, the Muslim military force arrived at Marr al-Zuhran where an additional three thousand plus fighting men joined the ranks. With less than an hour's trek to Mekkah, Muhammad gave final instructions to Ali who in turn passed them onto his captains. And the war machine moved into the city's surrounding precincts.

Despite the moon's luminescence, Muhammad had the soldiers build small fires every forty paces which made the countryside glow. Opting for a peaceful solution before having to take the city by force, he summoned Ali for instruction. Ali in turn appointed Sa'd ibn Abbadah Ansari to captain an advance party into the city for mediation. But as Sa'd made preparations Abbas overheard him making remarks inconsistent with a peaceful entry. Abbas, fearing a massacre, reported the comments to Muhammad. The Prophet, then asked Ali to take command of the party and carry the Standard himself. Ali requested Abbas to accompany the group, thinking his vale of years and wisdom would help against the Mekkanese. Abbas agreed without hesitation and asked Muhammad if he could use Duldul, thinking the highly recognizable animal would better serve their mission. With dawn but a short while away, they entered Mekkah.

Meantime, all across Mekkah's hilly section, late night revelers were growing alarmed by the thousands of small fires lighting up the countryside. Feeling uneasy about its implications, many of the hedonistic Mekkanese rushed home in a state of panic. Three men, without the other's knowledge hastily departed for Sufyan's hilltop dwelling to inform him of the matter. It was impossible not to glimpse the fires as each man passed openings between the structures around them. By the time they reached their destination fear ruled their thoughts.

Ali's party rounded the last corner before Sufyan's house and nearly trampled the three men about to enter the courtyard. They reined to a halt, startling the men as the mounts peppered them with dirt.

As it happened, the infidels were discussing the forces outside the city and conspicuous lack of Muslims within Mekkah when Ali's party came charging up like a bolt of retribution. Taken by surprise, they turned with a jump and instantly recognized Ali and Duldul. Frightened, they started darting their eyes around the area in panic, expecting an attack. After a moment, Hakim felt safe enough to timidly ask: "What bringeth thee here?"

Ali ignored him and said with unqualified conviction: "By Allah! Verily, it is He Who guideth the minds of men. For now ye can spread the monition amongst thy people." Without another word he spun on his heels and led the way toward their enemy's carved doors. Lifting the lion headed knocker to announce their arrival, the door suddenly opened.

Sufyan gasped as he recognized Ali and the pearl white mare near his courtyard gate. He was about to speak but fell silent with renewed apprehensions.

Ali came directly to the point. "I have come unto thee as emissary of the Holy Apostle Muhammad. Hath he invested me with authority to parley and sue for peace if thou wish it. Sufyan, the city is ringed about and the hour of confrontation is at hand. For when the sun rises we will enter Mekkah by force if necessary, or in peace. What saith thou as leader of Mekkah? Doth thou yield or feel the want of battle?"

No one spoke as the Disbelievers worst fears were substantiated. Then not daring to voice their opinions the three men looked to the chief of Quraysh who wielded the authority. Sufyan, having the most to lose simply stared at Ali, his mouth agape as feelings of gloom overwhelmed him. Perceiving his reign over Mekkah at an end his mouth became cottony. His legs grew rubbery and his heart started thumping in humiliation.

Abbas, seeing Sufyan's pathetic condition, felt pity. So before the tyrant's obstinacy reappeared, and hoping to avert a senseless war, he suggested that Sufyan return with them to council with Muhammad. With no other viable option save certain death, the leader of Quraysh gave in and placed himself under Abbas' protection.

During their ride through the encampment, Sufyan couldn't help but look around enviously at the multitude under Muhammad's command. He coveted status and loved the prestige that came with it. He even imagined himself as Caliph of the Islamic Empire, inventing scenes of tens of thousands paying him homage. Wistfully, he said: "Oh, Abbas, the son of thy brother hath indeed become a great leader of men."

At that moment, Umar's jaw dropped open in surprise as he recognized Islam's greatest enemy. In disbelief he watched the riders pass by. Recovering his wits, he became incensed and began racing on foot to see where they were going. After guessing their destination, he veered away from their path and ran through the maze of fires, thinking one thing: kill Abu Sufyan, the leader of the opposition! Gasping for breath, he reached the Prophet's tent and scanned the immediate area looking for Sufyan. He saw no sign of him. Without thinking he charged into Muhammad's quarter's yelling: "Oh, Muhammad, let me smite Allah's enemy!"

Sufyan's face paled.

Consequently, following a short question and answer session, Islam's number one antagonist became Muslim. None knew with certitude, except Allah, if Sufyan converted out of fear to save his life. But it didn't matter because he would now be a troubleshooter instead of a troublemaker.

Back in Mekkah, inner city infidels were growing alarmed over the pall of smoke blanketing the city. They started turning out of their dwellings by the hundreds. They gathered in the streets, giving utterances to their suspicions. A Christian idolater in the crowd seeing the futility of speculation suggested their attention should be turned toward finding the source. After canvassing the inner city and finding no visible flames in evidence nor any sign of danger, the throng wove their way to the city's edges where they saw the Muslim army.

All speculation abruptly stopped. An intense feeling of fear began to creep over their hearts. Men, women and children, stared in awe while others turned and fled for their lives. It was a frightening scene, soldiers and their fires were covering the countryside, extending beyond the periphery of their vision. The dogs didn't even bark, sensing the phantoms of death staring back through the eyes of Muslim warriors. Then, without warning, Abu Sufyan and Abbas broke from behind the ranks and came charging across the terrain. Surprised, the Mekkans stood transfixed, each thinking their own thoughts as they approached.

"Oh,' ye people," Sufyan heralded. "The Muslim army hath encircled the city and prepareth to enter within the hour, by force if necessary. Hence, make not mischief or warlike actions, for it is foolish to oppose Muhammad, the Prophet and Messenger of Allah, the One God.

"Hold thy tongues and hearken unto him," someone bellowed sharply to still their cries. Then added: "many were the years I rebelled against submitting myself to God's Way for selfish and greedy reasons, all of which came to naught. This past hour spent I pondering over the Message in sincere examination. Al-Hamdu lillah, didst my eyes open."

"Through Muhammad al-Amin al-Mustafa ibn Abdullah, came Allah's Scripture in our tongue, not as a Message to inflict distress but to shed light upon ignorance. Thought I as ye think now that Jesus was the Son of Allah, but Almighty Allah, The One God, The Opener of hearts, showeth the fallacy of man's fabrications. If you but stop and use thy vision, thou wilt see that saying Jesus is the Begotten Son of Allah is a notion most monstrous and blasphemous to the majesty of The Creator. For begetting is an act assigned only to animals of which man is a higher form. How then, can one ascribe such carnality to the Supreme Being? Jesus' birth was indeed miraculous but only because Allah said "Be," and he was. That however, doth not mean man is to worship him. There is but One God! Not the invented fancies of a Trinity! Even Jesus himself saith to ascribe not such things.(20) Thus, go ye forth and spread the word that the One God's Apostle arriveth shortly."

Near the appointed time, fires were extinguished and the Holy Prophet of God issued final instructions before mounting Duldul. "Oh,Ali, insha'a Allah can we take the Holy City without war and bloodshed. However, Ikramah ibn Abu Jahl, Habbar ibn Aswad, Abdullah ibn Sa'd Abi Sarah, Migyas Subabah Laythi, Huwairath ibn Nuqayd, Abdullah Hilal and four women, should be put to death upon capture for their crimes of willful murder and other related offenses. Notify all thy captains, for they will endeavor to instigate war."(21)

The soldiers of God, under strict orders not to engage the Disbelievers unless attacked, stood and started forming ranks until the lines of humanity completed circle. Ali, Khalid and Bakr, leading the other quarters, waited for the wall of men to move before launching their sections. From the north, east, south, west, and all points in between, they advanced on Mekkah, converging on the square and Ka'bah.

The streets were empty as they made their way. The only sound issued from thousands of Muslims chanting "Allahu Akbar." Muhammad thought of God's promised victory, how it was being fulfilled without war. Silently, he rendered thanks and praised The All-Mighty. He rode through the city seeing the frightened faces peering from behind doors, windows, any opening which afforded a view. Unbidden, the years began to unreel in his mind like an unrolling scroll: the ugly years of mockery; abuse; torture and worse.

At the same time in another quarter, a man harboring a grudge against Khalid incited several others into attacking as he led a phalanx of horse warriors through Mekkah's passage ways. Khalid and the soldiers made short work of the troublemakers and continued on. The incident marred an otherwise peaceful entry.

Before the Messenger and Apostle of God realized it, he reached the square filled with Believers. A hush fell over the area, bringing him back to the present. Bodies moved aside, clearing a path to the Ka'bah's steps. Dismounting, he walked down the aisle, climbed the steps and waited for Ali.

By now the ever watchful Mekkanese had nervously exited their homes and crowded in behind the thousands. On edge, they waited to hear their fate.

As Ali took his place next to the Prophet of Islam, Muhammad struck the side of God's ancient House with the palm of his right hand and declared: "By the One Who is The Master of my soul, this person (Ali) and his Shi'a will be the successful ones on the Day of Judgment!(22) He turned, pointed to the Black Stone of Remembrance and bellowed: "Allahu Akbar."

The Believers roared back: "Allahu Akbar."

Before pivoting to enter the Ka'bah, Muhammad gestured for Ali to join him and together they set foot into God's House. There were over three hundred sixty idols fashioned in all manner of shapes and images. One by one they started toppling the tribal gods, images and crosses. Afterward, Muhammad asked Ali to climb upon his shoulders to reach the roof of the Ka'bah, where the massive stone idol Hubal stood in domination. As Ali climbed the square fell silent: wondering how one man could upset the huge rock. Ali put his back against the gigantic stone, invoked the name of God and pushed. To the gasps of all, Hubal crashed to the ground.(23) Straight away the Prophet intoned: "Truth hath prevailed and Falsehood hath withdrawn. Verily falsehood is destined to perish."

In no time the rubble was cleared and the Ka'bah washed. Now purified of it's blasphemous perversions, all was in readiness for worship to the One God.

Muhammad emerged from the interior and delivered a short speech emphasizing the abolishment of revenge, shedding blood unlawfully, and belief in superstitions. He declared the equality of all peoples and ended with the only people who excelled were the righteous and pious. Then following a brief period of silence, he blazoned out in a voice that sliced through the stillness

"Oh,' ye people of Quraysh! What doth thou think I shouldst do with thee?"

There were pleas for clemency, others gulped in fear, while the majority abstained from voicing any opinion, knowing whatever befell them they deserved it for the atrocities committed against the Muslims over the past twenty years.

Muhammad held his tongue, allowing several minutes to pass which only increased the tension. Consequently, the unlettered Prophet feeling love for his fellow man, took a stand that would forever show the excellence of his character and spirit of Islam. He announced: "Henceforth, there is no blame on thee. Go then thy own ways, thou art free of indictments."

Everyone started renewing old acquaintances and making new ones. Eventually, as the morning wore on, they started drifting back to their homes discussing Arabia's new era. It was a time of great optimism, for many began to realize Islam not only did away with one's injustices and unreasonableness against his brother, but provided spiritual completion.

At half past noon, Bilal ascended the Ka'bah's steps and in his celebrated voice, trolled out the Adhan which inexplicably resonated throughout the Holy City. More than a few were impressed and had wanted to join Khalid's party awhile back but feared repercussions against their families. Now, however, they were free to do as they liked without fear and followed the tide of Believers rushing for the square. They lined the inner walls silently, feeling the power of faith wash over them. In an air of solemnity they watched the Muslims encircle the Ka'bah, aligning themselves shoulder to shoulder to await Prophet Muhammad's lead.

Following prayers, the moment dictated that the Spirit of Truth impart the spiritual implications of regaining God's Holy City.

"Oh,' Children of Hashim and Mut'talib! Have I been sent unto ye by Allah as His Messenger and the ties of love and kindness between ye and myself are unbreakable. Think ye not that only relationship with me will ensure thy salvation on the Day of Judgment. All shouldst understand that my shi'a from amongst ye and others is he who is pious and virtuous, and my connection with those who come before Allah with a heavy burden of sins is cut off. Shall I not be able to intercede for ye on the Day of Judgment. That Day all will be responsible for their own actions."(24)

"Oh,' people! Hath Allah abolished from amongst ye, under creed of His Way, the bases of pride of the Age of Ignorance and self-glorification on account of lineage. All are the descendants of Prophet Adam, alaihis salaam, and was he created with clay. The best person amongst ye is one who refrains from sin and disobedience."

"Oh, people! Being an Arab is not the criterion of thy character or a part of thy being, but only a mode of expression. Ancestral pride is not of any use to a person, who dost not carry out his duties properly, and dost not make amends for deficiency in actions."(25)

After Muhammad's recital the Disbelievers were in an emotional turmoil. He had shown them a great sense of forbearance the like of which they had never seen. Only hours ago they believed they held the upper hand. Then the Muslim army marched in, descending like starving locusts. And Sufyan's conversion, his urging to desist all enmity, their objects of worship smashed into heaps of trash. Indeed, it was an unsettling day. Yet, The Most Beneficent God enkindled the Truth to blazon forth within their hearts and new feelings for Islam blossomed.

In groups, one after another, they came yearning for the Way of life which neither worshipped miracle workers, idols, images, nor symbols. Even Hind, the hateful woman who during the Battle of Uhud mutilated Hamzah's body, sheepishly came forward to embrace the Faith that served One God.

CHAPTER THIRTY-FIVE

In the days following Mekkah's conquest, Prophet Muhammad spent the time teaching Islam's Truth. Daily, he imparted portions of Qur'an, which were recorded, checked and double checked for accuracy. After two weeks, a friend of Islam arrived from Ta'if bearing news which jolted the city.

Two powerful tribes, the Hawazin and Thaqif, did not take kindly the news of Islam's acceptance in Mekkah. Thus, for no other reason than to demonstrate the power of their gods, the chiefs organized their tribes into a force of four thousand fighting men and concerted plans for annihilating the Muslims. They marched toward Mekkah, making boast of their military capabilities and issued warning that they would crush the Muslims. Stopping some fifteen miles away from the Holy City, they concealed three quarters of their army amid the mountainous entrance to Hunayn's Valley while the remaining soldiers set up camp out in the open, a thousand yards behind the entrance.

In Mekkah, Muhammad had over ten thousand warriors at hand with another two thousand untried Muslims hankering to join the army preparing to march. For the first time the numbers were in their favor and they felt no army on earth could defeat them. However, therein lie the danger, for the rank and file had more enthusiasm than wisdom, more a spirit of elation than of faith and confidence in the righteousness of their cause.(1)

A day after the contentious tribes took their positions, Islamic forces reached the valley's entrance just before dawn broke through the darkness. Unsuspecting, sure of themselves, they never imagined their enemies lying in ambush as they passed the flanking mountains. Midway through the enemy unleashed a devastating crossfire of arrows and spears, which wounded and killed a number of Muslims.

Still too dark to see clearly, the besieged warriors swiftly fell into disorder. The wounded cried out in pain, injured horses rent the air with earsplitting screeches of terror and threw their riders. The horses, blindly stampeding away, trampled the wounded. Adding to the confusion were the un-saddled men running every which way, shouting in alarm as the shafts of death relentlessly rained down. In the midst of their panic, the enemy swarmed down off the mountains and furiously exacted a heavy toll.

In the moment of seemingly disaster, dawn sliced the horizon revealing scenes of horrifying carnage. Infidels were chasing down fleeing Muslims while others mercilessly cut to pieces the wounded. Then, the horde's momentum turned toward the Prophet. Muhammad, however, was surrounded by nine sons of Banu Hashim and one

Companion, all others turned in flight.(2) Ali, Abbas, his son al-Fazl, and the others, tightened their ranks around the Chosen one and battled with a violence that sent quivers of terror into their attackers hearts. The defense of God's Holy Apostle was first priority no matter the cost.

"Abbas," called Muhammad upon seeing his army flee in panic, "call thou unto the people and remind them of the covenant."

Abu Sufyan, still resenting his deposal, could not hide his inner feelings and contemptuously cried out: "Behold! These are the people who conquered Quraysh, verily they will not stop fleeing till they reach the sea."

Abbas, having heard Sufyan, immediately countered with a bellow that pealed out above the tumult and turmoil: "Oh, ye Muslims! Remember the pledge of allegiance at the tree. Forsake not the Prophet! Forsake not the Prophet!"

Next came the roar of Muhammad: "I am the Prophet of Allah! There is no falsehood in me! Hold ye fast unto Allah and turn not thy backs to the enemy!" His bellow worked like a miracle and stopped the retreat. For in the twinkling of an eye, it came without shadow of doubt that come what may God watched over them. Thus inspired, the Muslims reversed directions and seemed to yell all at once: "Allahu Akbar." And in defiance of the danger became instruments of death as they slashed their way to protect the Mercy of all creatures.

The enemy, which had been giving no quarter moments before were startled by the sudden turnabout. Muslims who were running for their lives abruptly checked their flight, turned, and began fighting without thought to life or limb. And immediately following up on their heels came the rear guard, charging in waves and roaring: "Allahu Akbar." The counterattack ripped into the offensive, driving the enemy back through the pass into the valley where the remainder of their army waited.

As Muslims erupted out from the gap between the mountains, the enemy was overwhelmed. Instead of battling or surrendering, the infidels threw down their weapons and fled toward Nakhlah, abandoning their womenfolk and provisions. Pursued, they changed directions for Awtas and finally headed for Ta'if.

Muhammad suddenly found his army in control of the valley. He issued instructions to secure the area and the prisoners taken to al-Jir'rana, then set out for the foothills where he could contemplate the day's events. Alone, he sat atop an outcropping of rock, absently watching Ali put things in order. All the while his mind pealed back the years of his Prophethood. He thought back upon his visit to Ta'if, it's irreligiousness, it's mockery of Truth, and of Urwa ibn Mas'udh's death. In accordance with his current of thoughts, he decided to rid Arabia of it's last pocket of resistance. That being the case, he and Ali posted fifteen hundred men throughout the valley, conferred with elders, then led his army toward Ta'if.

Daybreak the following day, the rolling terrain leveled out and revealed a fortress-like city in the distance. From what Muhammad could see, Ta'if had been expecting attack: the countryside was empty of livestock and the verdure scythed short. Even now, the infidels were manning the city's walls.

Nodding at the barren patches of land, Muhammad asked: "What doth thou think, Ali?"

Ali squinted, scanning the sheared areas of earth and walls as if he could magnify the setting through intense observation. It was a look characteristic of his close study, expressing his singleness of purpose that was the core of his essence. Ali finally completed his examination. "Wouldst I say the city is prepared for attack," he announced.

Muhammad nodded his head in agreement. "Yea, they are in battle array. Thus will we encircle and lay siege to the city." He turned to face Ali, "If we attack the enemy it would take many lives."

As things go, nothing entered or left Ta'if and it's environs. With the beleaguerment in full force, al-Mustafa requested Ali's presence and instructed him to destroy the symbols of idolatry and polytheism wherever found.

Nightly, Ali organized small parties and led them in assaulting Ta'if's precincts. Just before dawn one night, he encountered a troop of horsemen testing Muslim vigilance.

Shihab, surprised by Ali's sudden appearance, called out: "Is there not one amongst you who will draw the sword against me in single combat?"

Ali turned to face his men. "Which of ye will fight this affair of honor?" When no one took the challenge, he dismounted and drew his weapon.

"Oh,' Ali, thou art to much for the kafir!" Someone said to Ali's back as he faced Shihab.

"Indeed," replied Ali without taking his eyes off his opponent, "but if I am slain thou art in command of the men." He moved forward praising God and said: "It is the duty of every commander to wet his blade with blood! Strike thou first infidel!"

Shihab charged, swinging his sword for Ali's head. Ali ducked, spun and came up delivering a sweeping slash that nearly decapitated his assailant as he passed by.

The enemy surrendered without further fight.

After smashing the idols and symbols, Ali returned to inform the Apostle. Muhammad upon sight of Ali, exclaimed: "Allahu Akbar," and led him into his private quarters. A time later, several Muslims complained over their exclusion from the Prophet's conference.

Umar ibn al-Khattab, questioned Muhammad the instant he exited his tent. "Why doth thou take Ali aside and counsel with him and not with us?"

"Umar," said the Prophet, "it is not I whom hath made Ali my confident. Allah hath made him His confident. It is for that reason he was engaged for so long."(3)

Finally, after a number of injuries, two weeks investment without any significant results, Nafi ibn Ghaylan ibn Ma'tib and a force of men emerged from the fortress of Ta'if. Ali met him in battle and killed him, scattering his men to the winds.

Muhammad saw no end in sight. He relented and gave the command to withdraw. The consensus being an outright charge would produce no gain and many deaths, and that the Truth would eventually overcome their obstinate rebellion.

Stopping once more in Mekkah before returning to the City of the Prophet, Muhammad addressed the multitude.

"In the name of Allah, The Beneficent, The Merciful."

"Oh, ye people of the True Faith! Of late, the Jews and Christians lay claim that we Muslims are a hate mongering people because we object to their hindering man from the Right Path with their teaching of false doctrine. Even the holy Prophet Jesus, alaihis salaam, said: 'Well hath Esai'as prophesied: This people honoreth me with THEIR lips, but their heart is far from me. Howbeit, in vain do they worship me, teaching FOR doctrines the commandments of men.'"(4)

"Shun ye idolatry and polytheism in whatever manner it may manifest itself. Ascribing partners unto Allah is abomination and a sin most grievous. Saith Jesus, alaihis salaam, Allah, the Author of all is greater.(5) Thus, Allah hath not partners in His Godhead, for no part of the same substance can be greater than itself. For as many as are led by the Spirit of Allah, they are the sons of Allah.(6) Look ye sincerely into thy Books and ye can yet see glimpses of Allah's Truth. Be not deaf, dumb and blind when ye read thy Books, look to the context and if Allah willeth you will see that blind faith is clear error."

"In the Muslim House, believe we that Prophet Jesus, alaihis salaam, was one of the mightiest prophets of Allah, that he was born miraculously, that with Allah's leave gave life to the dead like Prophet Ezekiel,(7) alaihis salaam.

"Allah! There is no god but He! Hath He no son or partners! Heed ye His Word."

"And indeed sent We Noah unto his people, and he said: "Oh, my people! Worship ye Allah (alone) ye have no god other than Him; will ye not then guard (yourselves against evil)?' But said the chiefs of those who disbelieved, from among his people: 'This is a man like unto yourselves who intendeth to exalt himself above you; but had Allah willed (to send any apostle) He would certainly have sent angels. We have heard not of this among our fathers of old; verily he is not but a man maniac, so bear ye with him for some time.'"

"He (Noah) said: "Oh, my Lord! Help me against what they belie.' So revealed We unto him that: 'Make thou (Oh,' Our Apostle Noah!) the Ark before Our eyes and (as per) Our revelation (direction) and when cometh (unto thee) Our command, gusheth forth water from the oven, take into it two of every species a pair and thy people except those among them about whom had already been issued the word; and address Me not in respect of those who are unjust; for verily they shall be drowned. And when thou art settled (in the Ark), thou and those with thee, then say thou: 'All praise be unto Allah Who delivered us from the unjust people!' And say thou: "Oh, my Lord! Disembark me with a blessed landing, for Thou art The Best of all who cause to land!' Verily, in this are signs and We do only try (the people)."

"(And the apostles were commanded by God): "Oh, My apostles! Eat ye of the good things and do good; verily I know what ye do. And verily this your group is one group, therefore fear ye (only Me). But they have rent the unity among themselves into sects; each party rejoiceth in that which is with them. So leave them in their overwhelming ignorance till a certain time. What! Think they that We aid them with of wealth and children, We are hastening unto them the good things? Nay! They (only) perceive not."

"Say thou: "Oh, my Lord! If Thou wilt make me see what (chastisement) they are promised, Oh,' my Lord, then place me not amidst the unjust people!' Verily, We are well able to make thee see (the chastisement) what We have promised them."

"Repel evil by what is best; We know best what they attribute (against thee). And say thou: "Oh, my Lord! I seek refuge unto Thee from the (evil) promptings of the satans! I seek refuge unto Thee, O' my Lord, from their access to me.' Until, when cometh death unto one of them, saith he: 'My Lord! Send me back again (into the world), that I may do (the) good which I have left undone.' By no means! It is but a word he saith; and after them shall be a barrier until the day they shall be raised (again)."

"And when the Trumpet is blown, there shall be no ties of kindred between them on that day, nor shall they ask of one another. Then (those) whose scales (of good deeds) are heavy, they shall be the successful ones; and those whose scales (of good deeds) are light, they are those who shall lose their souls, abiding in Hell. The fire shall scorch their faces and they therein shall be grinning (of the affliction)."

"(Then will God ask them): 'Were not My signs rehearsed unto you? Then ye used to belie them.'"

"They shall say: "Oh, our Lord! Overcame us our ill-luck and we were people gone astray. O' our Lord! Take us out of it; if we return (to evil) then verily we shall be unjust.'"

"(God will) say: 'Be ye driven down into it, and speak ye not unto Me!'"

"Verily, there was a party of My servants who said: "Oh, our Lord! We believe, so forgive us and have mercy on us, and Thou art The Best of The Merciful ones!'"

"What! Think ye then that We created you in vain and that unto Us ye shall not be returned?"(8)

Back in the City of the Prophet, the inhabitants began to settle down. The Islamic intelligence network reported thousands of infidels were massing in the Valley of Ram. Muhammad issued orders, the coded call sounded and warriors headed for the mosque. He distractedly watched God's battle weary soldiers file in, thinking of the engagement to come. "Yaa Allah," he expressed before stepping onto the pulpit.

Praising and glorifying God, the Apostle divulged his information and plans. "Oh, my people! The mischief mongers have gathered at Ram and are formulating designs to attack Madinah at night. The enemies of Allah and of all Believers are hoping to catch us unaware." Before Muhammad could add anything further, a group of Muslims stood and volunteered for the mission.

The spokesman declared: "Oh, Apostle of Allah, give us the chance and insha'a Allah wilt we crush the enemies of Truth and His Way! Appoint whomsoever to command us and wilt we fight unto martyrdom or victory. To Allah we belong and unto Him we return. Allahu Akbar!"

"Allahu Akbar," thundered back the assemblage.

Abu Bakr was named to lead the force. Hours later the soldiers of Islam moved out. Arriving well after sunrise, Bakr's advance was observed and suffered enemy countermeasures. One of the chief's from Banu Saleem contemptuously rode forward and demanded an explanation for the military expedition.

Bakr said: "Have I been appointed by the Prophet of Allah to present the Message unto Banu Saleem and to fight against ye to prevent further mischief if ye decline to accept God's Way."

The chief signaled and the infidels attacked, killing a great number of Muslims before Abu Bakr fled with his troops.

Muhammad next gave the Standard of Islam to Umar ibn al-Khattab, then to another after the same results. The commanders had suffered a disastrous defeat, suffering heavy losses and were put to flight. The Prophet delayed appointing another commander for several days, while he prayed against the Disbelievers. He wanted all to have the opportunity to lead, but he refused to sacrifice lives. In the end he selected Ali for the command, declaring: "Have I sent him as one who will attack, not one who will flee!"

Ali led his force in a different direction as not to alert the enemy by their passage over the rocky terrain. Traveling by night and concealing themselves by day, he prevented any information of their whereabouts from reaching the enemy. Reaching the valley before dawn, Ali ordered his men into strategic positions and initiated the attack with a roar of "Allahu Akbar."

The infidels woke to pounding hooves and sparks of fire as God's army charged across the stony desert. Ali's leadership provided an easy victory. Most of the enemy were killed, those surviving the sudden attack were put in chains and taken before the Prophet.(9)

As God's Master Plan steadily unfolded, the propagation of Islam spread faster than before. The City of the Prophet filled with delegations from every part of Arabia, lest the city of Ta'if, wanting to learn the Message. Jews and Christians from as far away as Jerusalem, Bethlehem, Nazareth, Ma'an, Syria, Abyssinia, and places where they were known to gather, conceded that not only did their Book confirm the advent of a Prophet from the wild lands of Kedar, but Prophet Jesus, son of Mary, foretold of him by name six hundred years earlier. They along with the Bedouins flooded into Madinah.

With the annexation of several Roman provinces under the Islamic banner, tragedy struck. Umm Kulthum, the Prophet's third eldest daughter took ill and died. Then rumors of a Roman invasion, bent on revenge, started circulating in and around Madinah. At first Muhammad attributed the common talk to disgruntled Christians who adamantly clung to their irrational theories of three gods in one. But when the hearsay persisted with increasing details, he took no chances and issued the call to arms.

Not all of the eligible men, however, answered the summons. Weak willed, daunted by the dangers and difficulties ahead, they made all sorts of excuses against service. Nevertheless, more than thirty thousand Muslims responded: ten thousand on horseback; and the remaining warriors either on camels or on foot. Also, among their number mingled Madinah's leading Hypocrite, Abdullah ibn Ubayy who still managed to keep his anonymity.

Days prior to the march for Syria's border where the Roman soldiers were gathered, the Prophet requested Ali to stay behind and take charge of Madinah in his absence. Ali began feeling uncomfortable and went to ask Muhammad to reconsider his decision since he always participated in military endeavors. He found him in conversation with the trusted Companions and waited until they finished before addressing the Prophet.

"Oh, Prophet, have I fallen in disfavor with thee? Some of the people are saying thou hast left me behind because of finding me burdensome."

"Nay, indeed not!" Muhammad returned while stepping back till the others were in front of him. "Heed not the common talk, for jealously maketh men liars. They are the hypocrites and infidels who wouldst beget sedition. I left thee behind because thou art the only one who can properly look after the City in my absence. Thou art the guardian of my Ahlul Bayt, my kinfolk and the Muhajirun, and there is none save myself and thee fit for this position. Thou art my Khalifa and thou art unto me what Aaron was to Moses, alaihimus salaam, excepting that thou canst not be a prophet like him; I being the Last of the Prophets."(10)

"The Muslims will victimize thee, though thou followeth my path.(11) Thou wilt be obligated to fight against the renouncers, transgressors and deviators. Furthermore, thou wilt fight against matters of Qur'an's interpretation as thou hadst to fight on the side of it's disclosure.(12)

"Verily, he who insulteth thee, insulteth me, and he who insulteth me insulteth Allah. And he who insulteth Allah, Allah will cast into Hell-Fire.(13) Ali, my beloved Brother, loving thee is belief and hating thee is hypocrisy.(14) As I am the source of peace and protection for mankind on earth, my Ahlul Bayt are also the same for them.(15) Hence, it is only thee suited for this task to manage the City's affairs."

Finally, the mobilization got underway. The Muslims, in spite of the summer's blistering heat, went forth with energy and enthusiasm. Two miles out, ibn Ubayy rode up to Muhammad and explained he could not continue because he'd fall victim to the bewitching charms of Syrian women, thereby placing others in jeopardy.

Prophet Muhammad regarded him with cool detachment. His only sign of study were his thin brows which had arched and the vein between them had swelled. Saying nothing, he nodded as if in understanding, realizing ibn Ubayy had been feigning his belief all along. Canst I not, he thought, compel anyone to believe, but I can see to it that he influences not another into unbelief upon my return.

Weeks later and three hundred fifty miles northeast of Madinah, the Islamic force reached Tabuk, a large city near Arabia's frontier. Recalling the city's particulars from his travels, Muhammad directed his army to an ancient fort, owing to it's supply of spring water. After situating his troops, he sent parties of scouts into the Byzantine territory to discover the Roman's readiness to invade. Hours later, each party reported back with information suggesting the Romans would be mobilizing within the next two to three days.

At the same time, Roman spies from the nearby towns of Ayla, Adhruh and Jibra, were reporting the Muslims arrival, their location, and numbers which they greatly exaggerated. Many of the generals, remembering the Muslim valor and fierceness during Mu'tah's skirmish, dreaded another engagement and planned accordingly. Three days later they advanced their armies to within a quarter mile of the fort and made camp.

Meanwhile, sentries posted atop the ramparts saw the advance and sounded the alarm. Horse warriors and cameleers jumped to their feet, mounted up and moved out, their line of defense stretching a half mile on both sides of the stronghold. Inside, foot soldiers poured through the crumbled gates and took positions behind the mounted warriors, save five thousand who formed ranks, ready to charge out at Muhammad's direction.

The moment was tense, pregnant with nervous expectation. Minutes passed as if time had retarded. After two hours of waiting for them to attack, Muhammad issued orders for the men to stand down and to remain alert.

The following day, again, there was no offensive nor any signs of preparations for attack. That evening while Muhammad held council with his captains, it dawned on him that had the Romans wanted battle they would have charged tooth and nail, not set up camp as if to keep the Muslims from invading.

For twenty days without so much as exchanging a word, the Muslim army held their position until the Romans withdrew. Muhammad then decided to secure the frontier and dispatched messengers to all the surrounding towns, inviting its chiefs and inhabitants to hear the Word of God.

At the time, few if any had actually heard firsthand Prophet Muhammad speak, though all had known of him and his propagation of Islam. So when the request came, thousands of people journeyed to Tabuk to hear the Truth.

Muhammad was pleased by the interest God's Word generated and stepped onto an elevation constructed for the occasion. He raised his arms to quiet the multitude. Dressed in clean white garments, he stood taller than a short man with the alert grace of one at ease. His whole appearance presented a dignified picture of authority. "In the name of Allah, The Beneficent, The Merciful," declared Muhammad in a bellowing voice to carry out over their heads. "Verily, the most veracious disclosure is the Book of Allah. The most trustworthy handhold is the word of piety. The best of religions is the religion of Abraham, alaihis salaam. The best precedents is the precedent of

Allah's Messengers. The noblest speech is the invocation of Allah. The finest narrative is the Qur'an. The best of affairs is that which has been firmly resolved. The worst in religion are those things which are created without sanction. The best of ways is the one trodden by the prophets. The noblest death is the death of a martyr. The most miserable blindness is waywardness after guidance. The best of actions is that which is beneficent. The best guidance is that which is put into practice. The worst blindness is the blindness of the heart."

"The upper hand is better than the lower hand which giveth in charity. The little that sufficeth is better than what is abundant and alluring. The worst apology is that which is tendered when death stareth one in the face. The worst remorse is that which is felt on the Day of Resurrection.

"Some men come to Jumu'ah salat, but with hesitance and delay. And some of them do not remember Allah but with reluctance. The tongue which is addicted to false expression is a bubbling spring of transgressions.

"The most valuable possession is the contentment of heart. The best provision is that of piety. The highest wisdom is fear of Allah, The Mighty and Most Great. The best thing to be cherished in the heart is faith and conviction; doubt is infidelity.

"Impatient wailing and fulsome laudation of the dead is an act of ignorance. Betrayal leadeth one to the Fire of Hell. Drinking the fermented juices amounts to burning. Obscene poetry is the work of the devil. Wine is the mother of all evil. The worst thing eaten is that which belongeth to the orphan. Blessed is he who receiveth admonition from others.

"Each of ye must resort into a place of four cubits of ground and thy affairs will be decided ultimately in the next life. The worst dream is a false dream, for whatever is in store is near.

"To abuse a Believer is transgression; raising arms against him is infidelity. To backbite is a disobedience unto Allah. Violation of his property is like that of his blood.

"He who sweareth by Allah falsely, in fact falsifieth Him. He who pardons others is himself granted pardon. He who forgiveth others, is forgiven by Allah for his sins. He who holdeth his anger, Allah rewardeth him. He who faceth misfortune with perseverance, Allah will compensate him. He who acteth only for fame and reputation, Allah will disgrace him. He who showeth patience and forbearance, Allah giveth him a double reward. He who disobeyeth Allah, He will chastise him..."(16)

After successfully defending against any possible Roman invasion and forging alliances that secured the frontier, Muhammad led his army back to Madinah where much had been happening. Zaynab, the Prophet's daughter took ill and died. Abdullah ibn Ubayy had also died, but not before laying the groundwork to assassinate Muhammad upon his return. Ali, however, discovered the plot and brought it to an end with several expulsions. Thus, with virtually every pocket of contention wiped out, a new age of autonomy spread across the Peninsula and the deputations began.

By this time most of the Qur'an had been revealed. Prophet Muhammad repeatedly explained the importance of following his Ahlul Bayt, emphasizing Ali's closeness, his vast knowledge and contributions to Islam.

A delegation of twenty elders from Ta'if arrived to announce their city's readiness to accept Islam. The group's spokesman, after stationing his party at the square's rear, stepped through the throng amid a growing spread of excited whispers which attracted Muhammad's attention. Al-Hamdu lillah, was Muhammad's first thought as he recognized the man coming through the parting crowd.

"Oh, Prophet," said the spokesman humbly, "can thou forgive our obstinacy?"

Muhammad silently stood as he flashed back across their ill-treatment. He felt no ill-will toward the people that tried to kill him. "There is nothing for me to forgive," he returned kindly.

Visibly relaxing, the elder turned and waved his companions over, then turned back to face the Comforter. "Have I lived these past twenty years in various cities throughout Arabia and felt the stir of new beginnings since thou revealed Allah's Message. But during my years in Ta'if, I often heard discussions about thee and the reestablishment of God's Way. Was I not interested at the time and regarded the conversations tiring, but courtesy demanded that I listen. And now, since the siege much of the talk in our councils centereth around religion. Hence, we know the future is in the Truth thou bringeth, not in other ways of worship."

"The Message thou bringeth is one of true peace and prosperity, and encourageth every idea which promises the betterment of a people. Thus, wouldst we welcome thou to teach us the truth."

Following hours of negotiation, an agreement was reached that all idols and polytheistic fetishes would be destroyed, and from then on forbidden. Mughirah would be sent to educate and Abu Sufyan, who previously advocated idolatry, would accompany him to insure the destruction of idolatrous representations.

A few weeks later, on the Day of Assembly, the Holy Apostle led the service as usual and revealed another of God's Revelation. He started the khutbah, saying: "Oh, ye who believe! The best of peoples. The Mu'mineen do their duty and make not excuses, unlike the Hypocrites who are a burden unto thee. No help doth thou accept of them, as they are false and insincere. They will be found out and receive due punishment."(17)

"Thy hardest striving and fighting are needed to combat evil and hypocrisy; for sin can reach a stage when the doors of forgiveness are closed. Eschew all evil as unclean, and welcome all chances of service and sacrifice as bringing thyselves closer to the Presence and Mercy of Allah."(18)

"To be true in speech and deed is to hold selfish desires at bay. In this is the fullest satisfaction and reward. One's striving shouldst include study and teaching for our brothers benefit. Allah's Message increaseth one's faith, and leadeth one to love and trust Him.(19) Thus, that thou mayest know His Word, rehearse I unto ye His Holy Message."

"In the name of Allah, The Beneficent, The Merciful.

"Verily, alms are only for the poor and the needy and the workers (in the administration of the poor-rate) and those whose heart's alliance is sought and (the ransoming of) the captives, and those in debt, and in the way of Allah and the wayfarer; a duty ordained by Allah; and Allah is All-Knowing, All-Wise.

"Among them are those who hurt the Apostle (Muhammad) and say they (that), 'He is (all) ear' (i.e., one who believes in everything he hears); say, (He, Muhammad) is the Ear of good for you; he believeth in Allah and hath faith in the believers and a mercy unto those of you who believe, and those who hurt the Apostle of Allah, for them is a grievous chastisement. Swear they by Allah unto you that they might please you; and (whereas) Allah and His Apostle (Muhammad) hath a greater right that they should please Him, if they are believers. Know they not that whoso opposeth Allah and His Apostle (Muhammad), verily for him is the fire of Hell to abide therein? That is the grievous abasement.

"What! Came not unto them the news of those before them; of the people of Noah and Ad and Thamud, the people of Abraham and the inhabitants of Midian and the cities overthrown; came unto them their apostles with clear proofs (of their truthfulness). Thus it was not Allah to do injustice unto them, but they unto themselves were unjust.

"And the believer men and the believer women, they are guardians to one another; they enjoin good and forbid evil and they establish (the regular) prayer and pay the poor-rate and obey Allah and His Apostle(Muhammad), these, Allah will bestow on them His mercy; verily Allah is All-Mighty, All-Wise. Allah hath promised to the believer men and the believer women gardens 'neath which flow rivers, to abide therein, and the excellent mansions in the gardens of Adn (of perpetual bliss). But the goodwill of Allah is the greatest; that is the grand achievement.

"And (as for) the foremost, (degree of attainment to the Divine Will and Order), the first of the Muhajirun and Ansari, and those who followed them in goodness, Allah is well pleased with them and they are well pleased with Him, and He hath prepared for them gardens 'neath which flow rivers, to abide therein for ever; that is the great achievement.

"Nor is it Allah to lead a people (leaving them to their own reactions to God's guidance) astray after He hath guided them (aright), He even maketh it clear unto them what they should abstain from; verily Allah knoweth all things. Verily Allah, His is the kingdom of the heavens and the earth; He bringeth to life and He causeth to die; and there is not for you besides Allah any guardian or helper."(20)

* * * * *

Months later, as the time for Pilgrimage neared, the Spirit of Truth received Revelation forbidding idolaters and polytheists from participating in the sacred rites of Hajj. Muhammad praised and glorified God for the remedy to end the transgressions against mankind and destroy the causes of society's immoral practices. He summoned Abu Bakr and instructed him to deliver the Message of Renunciation upon Mekkah's citizens.

At Bakr's hasty departure with a force of men, the Muslims gathered and converged upon the Prophet in a state of alarm. Muhammad quickly reassured them and explained. "Oh, ye who believe! Allah, High and Exalted is He, hath given unto all the freedom of faith as long as it doth not harm the moral sense. Freedom of faith is respectable only when it fulfilleth godly direction, otherwise it is a bane unto the God-fearing."

"Hajj is one of the greatest religious rites and acts of worship. No longer will polytheism and idolatry be allowed in Allah's Holy House, nor will they have the right to perform Hajj.

"All the tribes which have faithfully carried out their obligations under the signed treaties will be respected until their term ends. Those who have not signed treaties will have four months to cease their blasphemous habits or prepare for war. The Hajj is for the worship of the One True God. Allahu Akbar!"

"Allahu Akbar," roared back the gathering as al-Mustafa retreated back into his home.

Days afterward, Archangel Gabriel descended. The bands of Divine Disclosure encircled and tightened upon the Prophet's breast, God's Emissary said: "Oh, Holy Apostle, sendeth Allah His greetings. And saith He the delivery of the Verses of Renunciation shouldst be conveyed by none but thou or one who is of thee."(21)

Muhammad immediately called Ali and apprised him of God's command. Ali was dispatched with the Prophet's fastest camel and instructed to reclaim the proclamation and pronounce it himself. Ali, Jabir ibn Abdullah and several trusted Companions, in short time overtook Bakr and his men.

"As-salaamu alaikum," greeted Bakr, then asked before Ali could reciprocate the salutation. "Art thou to escort us into Mekkah?"

"The Apostle of Allah hath ordered me to retrieve the Verses thou wast to recite unto the people. And he hath given thee the choice to accompany me or return to Madinah."

"Indeed," Bakr retorted, "wilt I return to him!" He reluctantly turned over the Verses and returned to seek out the Prophet. Finding him amidst a group of believers, he questioned Muhammad's motives.

"Thou deemed me fit to fulfill this mission, but after some days of traveling thou hast relieved me. Is thy decision based on any command of Allah!?"

The Apostle answered: "Angel Gabriel came to me and said Allah Commanded that I shouldst not let anyone deliver the Verses of Renunciation except myself or someone who is of me. Ali is of me and I of him. His purity and excellence is indistinguishable from myself. He is my Brother, my Vicegerent, my Successor, and the Executor of my will. Ali is the only one outstanding in merit. His high rank and noble position amongst the Mu'mineen is well known and giveth evidence to the abrogation of treaties with the infidels."

Ali arrived in Mekkah on the last day of Hajj ceremonies. He mounted an elevation and expressed with a booming voice that left no uncertain terms. "(This is a declaration of) immunity from Allah and His Apostle towards those of the idolaters with whom ye have (mutually) covenanted. So go ye about in the earth for four months, and know ye that ye are not weakening Allah, and that Allah bringeth shame unto the infidels. And an Announcement from Allah and His Apostle unto the people on the day of the great pilgrimage, that Allah is immune (from any obligation to) the idolaters, and (so is) His Apostle; therefore if ye repent, better will it be for you, and if ye turn back, then know ye that ye are not weakening Allah; and announce thou unto those who disbelieve, a painful chastisement; except those (with whom) ye have entered into a pact, from the idolaters who thereafter failed not you in aught and have backed not any one against you, then fulfill their pact unto the end of their term; verily Allah loveth those who guard themselves (against evil)."

"So when the sacred months are past then slay the idolaters wherever ye find them, and seize them and besiege them and lie in wait for them in every ambush, then if they repent and establish prayer, and give the poor-rate, then leave their way free to them; verily

Allah is The Oft-Forgiving, The Most Merciful. And if any one from the idolaters seeketh protection from thee, grant thou protection to him till he hears the Word of Allah, then convey him to his place of safety; this because they are a people who know not.

"How can there be a covenant for the idolaters with Allah and with His Apostle except (for) those with whom ye made a covenant at the Sacred Mosque? So long as they stand faithful to you, then be ye too faithful to them; verily Allah loveth those who guard themselves (against evil). How (can there be any alliance!) while they overcome you they regard not in you any tie nor of any covenant; they allure you with (the sweet words of) their mouths while their hearts are averse (from you), and most of them are transgressors. They have bartered the signs of Allah for a small price, so they turn others away from His way; verily evil is what they do. They pay not regard in the case of a believer, to any tie nor to any covenant; and these are they who transgress the limits.

"But if repent they and establish regular prayer and give away the regular charity, then they are your brethren in faith; and We explain the signs for the people who know. And if they violate their oaths after their covenant and revile your religion, then fight the leaders of infidelity, verily there is no oath for them, so that they may desist. What! Will ye not fight the people who violated their oaths and aimed at the expulsion of the Apostle, and they attacked you first; what, do ye fear them? Whereas Allah is the most deserving that ye should fear Him, if ye are believers..."(22)

* * * * *

Far to the south, in Najran, the Christians were in council discussing the Prophet's invitation back into the Religion of Abraham. Shurahbil, an elder held in high honor for his store of knowledge and wisdom, humbly addressed the members.

"Oh, noble ones, thou knowest me to be an honest man who rarely speaks out. But have I spent tens of years in pursuance of Allah's Truth and if ye will permit me the floor would I like to speak."

Every head nodded.

"My knowledge of religious matters is but little. However, as a man of truth I am duty bound to point out that our clerical leaders have constantly reminded us that the Apostleship would one day pass from the descendants of Isaac unto the descendants of Isma'il. Praise be to Allah for the day is upon us! Muhammad is the descendent of Isma'il and he is like unto Moses.

"I admit I believed the Promised Prophet was Jesus whom Allah spoke of in our Book,(23) but with study and sincere reflection one can see that only Muhammad is like unto Moses. Didst not Moses and Muhammad bring Law, whereas Jesus only came to fulfill the Law.(24) The Almighty God giveth warning about not following the Promised Prophet.(25)

"The Jews didst not believe Jesus for the reason that they awaited Elias. When Jesus said unto them that Elias hadst already come(26) they questioned him again, asking if he was 'THAT PROPHET'.(27) Therefore, it is clearly evident that we must send a delegation unto Madinah to investigate further. Let us not be obstinate or we may suffer these continued disasters, which I have heard attributed to Mother Nature. That is ridiculous, for it is none but Allah Who controlleth the forces of nature!"

The council was stunned, never had they heard Shurahbil vocalize his insights so passionately. Another elder, taking advantage of the silence, jumped to his feet the instant his friend seated himself.

"Truly hath Shurahbil spoken most eloquently. Yet, wouldst I like to add one thing by a disciple who actually walked with Jesus. Saint Barnabas records the Prophet of Israel saying: 'After me shall come the Splendor (Muhammad) of all the prophets and holy ones, and shall shed light upon the darkness of all that the prophets have said because he is the Messenger of Allah.'"(28)

Following the elder's comments, the chamber was cleared and committee members discussed Islam's merits. No more than ten minutes had passed before the advisory council reached its decision: a delegation would be dispatched.

Nearly a month later, the dusty commission arrived in Madinah under the auspices of Bishop Abu Harith and Abdul Masih. Once securing lodgings, the representatives bathed and dressed in all their finery: silken garments, golden baubles and crafted crosses.

The legation set out for the mosque, drawing amused stares as they paraded through the streets. Muhammad turned as sounds of sixty men entering the mosque attracted his attention. His eyes imperceptibly widened with displeasure as he took in their pageantry. Bishop Harith, the first to speak, introduced himself and explained their business, while the Prophet abstractedly regarded them, thinking: this is Allah's House of worship! Not a place to display tawdriness!

Without a word in return, he pivoted around and put his back to them in dismissal.

Abdul Masih realized Muhammad had been displeased, but could not fathom the reason. Tugging the Bishop's sleeve, the delegation withdrew back into the streets. One of the elders, recognizing former acquaintances, whispered to Bishop Harith and approached Uthman ibn Affan and Abdur Rahman ibn Awf.

Addressing them both, the Bishop said: "Thy Prophet scribed unto us a letter and invited us, but when we visited him would he not acknowledge us nor even speak to us. What doth thou advise? Shouldst we return to Najran or await another time?"

Uthman and Abdur Rahman faced each other with blank expressions, unable to comprehend the situation. Finding his tongue, Uthman said: "I know not the reason for thy rebuff. However, I can lead ye to one who hath never failed to provide a solution to any problem."

Ali took one look at them and advised before they could explain: "If ye wilt remove thy glittering baubles and conspicuous attire for simple garments, the Holy Apostle wilt receive thee with honor and respect."

Exchanging their finery for dress befitting men of God, they presented themselves before the Prophet. Muhammad responded to their salutations and ended the amenities saying: "By Allah Who hath appointed me His Apostle, when ye first entered the mosque earlier shaitan was in thy midst. So rest and refresh thyselves this day and on the morrow wilt I , insha' Allah, answer all thy questions."

The following day after courtesies, Muhammad said: "I invite thee to the religion of true belief and worship unto Allah and submission unto His Will."

"If thou meaneth belief in only the Lord of the world, indeed believe we in Him and obey His Laws," returned Bishop Harith.

The Spirit of Truth raised his brows dubiously then replied, "How doth thou profess belief when thy actions say otherwise? Is it not an abomination unto Allah, the Lord our God, for thy crosses, the work of the hands of the craftsman? (29) Is it not forbidden to eat the meat of swine? And how can thou slander the Lord of the Worlds by attributing Him a son? Far above is He from begetting sons."

"Didst not Jesus raise the dead and cure the sick? All these things show he is Allah," the Bishop persisted.

"I put to thee, didst not Prophet Ezekiel, alaihis salaam, also raise the dead?(30) Doth that make him Allah? Nay, Jesus, alaihis salaam, was the Word of Allah communicated through the chaste and pure Holy Lady Mary, alaihas salaam. He is the created not The Creator and he is the servant of Allah(31) whom He chose for the people of Israel."(32)

"Aye!" One of the representatives exclaimed. "Doth thou not see he is the Son of Allah, because Mary birthed him without a human father and it is therefore necessary that Allah is His father."

No stranger to man's obstinacy, Muhammad sighed in exasperation. He said: "According to thy standards, if one who is born without the intervention of a male is a Son of Allah, then one who is born without mother or father is doubly deserving to be a Son. Is not Adam, alaihis salaam, then also a Son?" He stopped to let his question take effect, then quick as thought, God's Revelation descended upon him. He said: "Verily, the similitude of Jesus with Allah is as the similitude of Adam. He created him out of dust then said He unto him 'Be', and he became. The Truth is from thy Lord, therefore be not thou of those of the doubters."(33)

"Thy words impress us not," another of the representatives ejected.

Muhammad retorted: "If Truth impresses ye not, Allah The High and Mighty, hath disclosed unto me the prayer of Mubahala. By this, will Truth manifest itself and Falsehood be known. Saith Allah, the Lord of the Worlds: ' And unto him who disputeth with thee therein after the knowledge hath come unto thee say: (O' Our Apostle Muhammad!) (unto them) Come ye, let us summon our sons and (ye summon) your sons, and (we summon) our women and (ye) your women, and (we summon) our selves and (ye) your selves and then let us invoke and lay the curse of Allah on the liars!'"(34)

Bishop Harith requested leave to consult with his companions. In the end, both the Prophet of God and Christians agreed to settle the issue through Mubahala following Muhammad's period of meditation and fasting. He and Abdul Masih watched Muhammad depart in silence, each wondering whether they would see the sunset in days to come. Suddenly frightened, Bishop Harith called council and advised the representatives: "When Muhammad returneth look to see if he hath entered the field amongst warriors and officials of his government, then we shall take up the Mubahala for believeth he not in the Way He teacheth and true submission unto Allah. However, if he cometh with his loved ones without pomp and power of numbers, be thou warned for he is kthe Promised Prophet and engage him not in Mubahala."

A couple of days later, Muhammad requested his trusted Companion, Salman the Persian, to prepare the area where he and those intended for the Mubahala would take place. Treading on the heels of Salman's departure, Muslims with their sons and daughters gathered in the mosque: hoping for the selection that would establish their spiritual purity and openly prove beyond all doubt they were the best ones of God's creation to be used in the contest of Truth.

A number of Muslims claiming to be Muhammad's close Companions and their families, along with the Prophet's wives kept the mosque alive with whispers. Muhammad raised his arms for quiet, praised and glorified God, then chose two children from the hundreds of children of his followers. From the females, he selected one lady. And to personify his Self, he chose one male.

At the appointed time Muhammad stepped onto the field with al-Husayn on his arm and al-Hasan walking next to his side holding a finger of his other hand. Fa'timah and Ali trailed behind. Heading for the site cleared by Salman, the Prophet removed his mantle and flung it over the branches of interconnecting trees and stationed himself along with the Holy ones under its shade. Facing the godly souls, he said: "When I utter the invocation of Allah's Wrath upon the liars, pray ye for its acceptance by saying ameen." Muhammad then raised his hands to the heavens in a supplicate manner saying: "Oh, Allah, these are my Ahlul Bayt..."

Meanwhile, at the appearance of Muhammad and those with him, Bishop Harith exclaimed with awe: "By Allah! Have I never seen such faces radiating light, which can be no other than Divine. I fear if they lift their hands in prayer for mountains to move, the mountains will move immediately. Verily, this Muhammad has the true belief and Call, for none but the truthful would bring such people with the glow of Heaven onto the field where Divine Wrath is to be invoked. Who are they?"

He was told: "The child on Muhammad's arm and the other child next to him are his grandsons, al-Husayn and al-Hasan. The ones following are his daughter Fa'timah and son-in-law Ali."

The Bishop turned to his people: "Oh, believers in Jesus, say I that shouldst ye fail to come to terms with Muhammad and if these pure souls curse you, you will be wiped from existence. If it were not for the emperor's authority over us, wouldst I submit. But now, let us make peace with the Holy Apostle of Allah."

Every one of the Christians, having observed the phenomenon of celestial light surrounding the Holy Ahlul Bayt, fell into consultation the moment Bishop Harith terminated his counsel. The discussion was a foregone conclusion as one and all had determined to sue for peace.

"Oh, Holy Apostle of the One God," the Bishop called out. "Wilt we not enter the Mubahala with thee. In its stead, let us seek peace."

Muhammad again extended the invitation to accept the true submission to God. He closed with: "Say, "Oh, people of the Book, come ye to a Word Common between us and you, that we worship none but Allah and shall not associate anything with Him, and take not any others for lords other than Allah.' And if they turn back, then say ye: 'Bear ye witness that we are Muslims (those surrendered to God).'"

"Oh, ye People of the Book! Why dispute ye about Abraham when the Law and the Evangel were not sent down till after him? (What?) Do ye not then understand (so much)? Lo! Ye are those who disputed about which ye had no knowledge, but why dispute ye about which ye have no knowledge? And Allah knoweth and ye know not!'"

"Abraham was neither (a) Jew nor (a) Christian, but upright in faith, (was he) a Muslim and he was not of the polytheists. Verily, of men the nearest to Abraham are surely those who followed him and this (Our) Prophet (Muhammad) and those who believe; and verily, Allah is the Guardian of the Faithful."

"A group among the people of the Book would fain mislead you, while they mislead not but themselves, but they sense it not. O' People of the Book why do ye disbelieve the signs of Allah while ye yourselves witness (them)? O' People of the Book: why confound ye the truth with falsehood, and why hide ye the truth while ye know (it)?"(35)

Cried out an elder, when the Prophet paused: "Holy Messenger of Allah! Have we not the conviction of thy faith nor the will to engage thee in battle. Let us therefore come to terms."

At the last a treaty was signed: the Christians offered to pay an annual tribute which gave them full freedom of faith in their religious practices; and, full protection for themselves, religious places, property and personal integrity.(36)

CHAPTER THIRTY-SIX

The declaration of limited immunity read by Ali during last year's Hajj had it's desired effect upon the idolaters and polytheists. Yet, there remained a few tribes of the Peninsula's coastal regions unwilling to forsake their evil practices. A plot to assassinate the Prophet by Banu Amir crumbled with the sudden death of its conspirators and conversion of it's deputation.

Another Revelation from God indicating the Guardianship of Believers after the Holy Prophet was revealed and clarified. One day while Ali prayed in the mosque, a pauper entered and begged for alms. None attended him and when he turned for the door, he observed Ali's small finger waving. The man was hesitant about disturbing Ali while he bowed in prayer, but his hunger drove him forward until he removed the ring from Ali's finger.

At the same time in Muhammad's private apartment Angel Gabriel revealed: "Verily, verily your Guardian is (none else but) Allah and His Apostle (Muhammad) and those who believe, those who establish prayer and pay the poor-rate, while they be (even) bowing down (in prayer)."(1)

A time afterwards, Muhammad ordered those who had constructed their homes with doors connecting to the mosque sealed, save his and Ali's. At the injunction, some of the companions complained and wrangled against it. The Prophet took offense and verbalized his thoughts and God's Command.

"Verily, didst Allah charge His Apostle Moses, alaihis salaam, to construct a House of Worship and allowed him, Aaron, alaihis salaam, and his two sons to dwell therein. Was I likewise charged, wherein myself, Ali and his two sons, al-Husayn and al-Hasan, are allowed to live. Do I only what I am ordered to do. Never undertake I to act upon my wishes. Know ye with certitude have I not ordered of my own accord to close thy doors or to let Ali's door open. It is Allah, High and Exalted is He, Who granted Ali an abode in His House of Worship.(2) Allahu Akbar!"

* * * * *

Mu'adh ibn Jabal, having been dispatched to Yemen to propagate Islam, returned to inform the Spirit of Truth of his failure to reach the Yemenites. Muhammad then sent Khalid ibn Walid with troops for protection to carry out the mission. Months had passed before reports were relayed to the Apostle of Khalid's inability to extend the Islamic influence. With no other viable alternatives, Muhammad summoned the Guide of Believers after him.

"Oh, Ali, the Hajj is nearly upon us and now that the way is free of infidels, wished I thy Companionship. However, my desires are second to matters of God's Way. Therefore, am I assigning the region of Yemen unto thee for invitation to the Right path. Be thou warned, the Yemenis are a proud people and known for their knowledge of scripture. Inform them of God's Divine Laws, the things which are lawful and unlawful and how to pray. Then, so please Allah, on thy return collect the jizyah from the people of Najran."

Ali replied, "Oh, Prophet, am I but a young man without the skill needed to convince scholars."

Muhammad smiled warmly as he placed his hand over Ali's heart. He prayed: "Oh, Allah, protect the tongue of Thy servant from error. Worry thyself not, for truth needeth not support. Do not argue with the deaf, dumb and blind, just use logic and comport thyself with benevolence. Swear I by Allah, if Allah guideth one by thy doing it is far nobler and better than all the wonders on which shineth the sun!"(3)

* * * * *

Shortly after Ali's departure, the Comforter began dispatching messages throughout Arabia informing Muslims that Hajj was at hand. Accordingly, a new kind of excitement filled the air. There were no obstacles, nothing to stop them from performing the complete Pilgrimage to God's Sacred House.

The following two months brought Believers pouring into Madinah from every part of the Peninsula and areas extending beyond it's borders. The desert Bedouin, mountain folk, rich and poor, they came by the tens of thousands to learn how to discharge their duty and be with the Holy Prophet. Tents were pitched, dotting the countryside for miles around the city. In all, over one hundred twenty thousand Muslims were in Madinah's vicinity waiting for The Chosen One to commence the march to where they'd don the pilgrim garb and begin the sacred rites of Hajj.

On the day of departure, Muhammad exited the mosque after finishing the noon prayer. Before taking Duldul's reins from Anas, he gazed upon the thousands lining his way to the City's entrance. Mounting, tears started falling from his eyes. He praised God, for only the True God could amass so many different people in one place without the trouble associated with such numbers. He began to smile as he mounted. Goading Duldul into a slow pace, he absorbed the ambiance of spiritual purpose. He glanced back over his shoulder, the people had closed in like a vortex swallowing water. He looked at the mosque, it stood strong and square, luminous by the sun. Its windows were darkened and seemingly testified that everyone was making the Hajj.

At the city's gates, the Muslims had decamped and gathered, waiting for this moment. Muhammad, again, ran his eyes over the multitude and urged Duldul through the sea of humanity until reaching the city's wall. He stood atop his mount to step onto the wall. The Believers watched in silence.

Muhammad became thoughtful while observing the Muslim pack themselves in as close as possible to hear his words firsthand. Suddenly, he bellowed: "Labbaika Allahumma, Labbaik," which caused the faithful to thunder back likewise. Raising his arms for quiet, he continued: "The future of Islam is unlimited. Already, the spread of Allah's Message has liberated man from the stultifying ignorance of idolatry and has given insight in which to educate thyself, and gain the good life in the Hereafter."

His voice, for all it's resonance, became intense: "I am the City of Enlightenment and Ali is it's gateway. He who wants to attain this locality, should come through it's gateway.(4) Ali is from me and I from him, and nobody can discharge my duty except myself or Ali,(5) thus I leave unto you my Ahlul Bayt. The similitude of Ahlul Bayt is like that of Noah's Ark, he who taketh it will be saved, and he who forsaketh it will be drowned.(6) Verily, whosoever wisheth to live and die like me, and to abide in the Garden of Bliss after death should acknowledge Ali as his patron and follow Ahlul Bayt's ways after me, for they are created out of the same knowledge and understanding as myself. Woe unto those who will deny my Ahlul Bayt their distinctions and disregard their relationship and affinity with me. May Allah never let them benefit from my intercession.(7) So, keep ye in justice, honesty and decent living. Remember thy allegiance to one another and be true to the Law of Allah, for He and He alone hath sent down the Qur'an. All praise and gratitude is due to Allah, the Lord and Sustainer of the Worlds!" Finishing, he took saddle and began the pious undertaking.

In the meantime, Ali had upon reaching Yemen's frontier informed Khalid the Prophet ordered his return. He then selected a Mu'edhdhin with a booming voice to make the Call to Prayer. At the first sliver of light in the horizon, the Adhan filled the crisp morning air that compelled Muslims into forming ranks and Yemenis out to investigate. Ali's execution of the Prayer was surpassed only by the Prophet. Ending, he approached the area's inhabitants of Banu Hamdam and articulated Muhammad's invitation. He fielded questions with spellbinding clarity, and by day's end the whole of Banu Hamdam embraced Islam.(8)

Up till the time needed to carry out the Holy Apostle's orders, Ali held daily discussions with Jews and Christians. His enlightening lectures on the Oneness of God and Islamic values impressed all. And once the Christian authority accepted Islam, it was only a matter of time before the others followed suit.

After weeks of crossing the Hijaz, the concourse from Madinah finally arrived at the fixed point where pilgrim garb was donned. Muhammad raised his arms to halt the procession. Suddenly double taking the distance in front of him, he lowered his hand to shield the sun's glare from his eyes. "Al-Hamdu lillah," he exclaimed jubilantly as he recognized Ali's idiosyncrasies. The Prophet jumped off Duldul and awaited his Successor. Embracing Ali warmly, they talked several minutes before Muhammad issued instructions and rode off towards the mountains.

Ali watched the Prophet ride away in a state of distraction, his mind working on ways of how best to implement his orders. Some minutes later, he had the trusted Companions pass word among the multitude to dress in their unsewn cloth and instituted prohibitions against all high spiritedness as it was time for devotion to prayer and worship. Then allowing time for them to change, he rode down the train's line dividing it into bow shot lengths, informing each section that they were to enter Mekkah at half hour intervals. Returning to the point, he found Muhammad ready to began the Hajj.

Once ingressing the Holy City's limits, Muhammad's section encountered hundreds of Believers waiting to join the ranks. He directed them to fall in behind, then took them through the streets and into the square where he led them in seven circuits around God's House. Afterwards, he offered prayer at the Station of Abraham, then guided them onto the hills of Safa and Marwah. Hours later, the last of the Pilgrims reached the hills where Prophet Muhammad sat alone atop Safa. When he stood he neither had to raise his arms nor ask for quiet.

He said, his voice powerful: "There is no god but Allah. Hath He no partners nor sons. He is All-Powerful and Supreme over all things. Hath He fulfilled His promise, He helped His servants, and He alone vanquished all the forces of disbelief." Ending his declaration, he gave an exposition on the meaning of Hajj, then retired for prayer and meditation.

A few days later, Muhammad led the whole body of Muslims to the Valley of Mina where the Pilgrims studied Qur'an, prayed and worshipped Allah. In the morning, they proceeded to Mount Arafat, eleven miles north of Mekkah where the Prophet again addressed the multitude.

"In the name of Allah, The Beneficent, The Merciful. All praise be unto Allah, The Cherisher and Sustainer of the Worlds. We glorify Him, seeking His help and forgiveness. We take refuge with Allah from the evils of ourselves and from the evil consequences of our deeds. There is none to lead him astray whom Allah guideth aright, and there is none to guide him aright whom Allah lets stray. I bear witness that there is no god but Allah, He is alone, having no partner with Him, and I bear witness that I am His Messenger. I admonish thee, O' ye bondsmen of Allah, to fear Him and I urge thee to His obedience, and I open this speech with that which is good.

"Ye people! Hearken unto my words: I will deliver a message unto thee, for I know not whether after this year, I shall be amongst thee. O' people! Verily thy blood, property and honor, are sacred and inviolable until ye appear before thy Lord, as this day and month is sacred unto all. Verily, ye will meet thy Lord and ye will be held accountable for thy deeds. Have I not conveyed the Message? O' Allah, be Thou my witness."

"He who has any trust with him should restore it unto the person who placed it with him in its entirety."

"Oh, people! Heed my words and understand them. A Muslim is brethren to another Muslim and together ye form one Brotherhood. Nothing of his Brother is lawful for a Muslim except what he himself alloweth willingly. So thou shouldst not oppress one another. O' Allah, have I not conveyed the Message?

"Behold! All practices of paganism are now beneath my feet. The blood revenges of the days of Ignorance are remitted. The first claim on blood I cancel is that of Rabi'ah ibn Harith who was slain by Banu Huday!

"Usury is forbidden, but ye are entitled to recover thy principal. Wrong not and thou wilt not be wronged. Allah hath decreed that there should be no usury and I make the beginning by remitting the amount of interest which Abbas ibn Abdul al-Mut'talib has to receive. Verily it is remitted entirely.

"Oh, people! Fear Allah concerning women. Verily hast thou taken them on the security of Allah and have made their person's lawful unto thee by words of Allah! Verily hast thou certain rights over women, and thy women have certain right over thee. It is incumbent upon them to honor their conjugal rights, and not to commit acts of impropriety which if they do ye have the authority to chastise them, yet not severely! If thy wives refrain from impropriety and are loyal to thee, clothe and feed them suitably. Behold, place injunctions upon them, but kindly."

"Oh, people! Hearken and obey, though an Abyssinian slave is thy emir if he performs the laws of the Book of Allah amongst thee.

"Oh, people! Verily hath Allah decreed unto every man the share of his inheritance. Belongeth the child to the marriage bed and the violator of wedlock shall be stoned. He who attributes his ancestry to other than his father or claimeth clientship to other than that of his masters, the curse of Allah, that of angels, and of the people be upon him. Allah will not accept from him neither repentance nor righteousness.

"Verily, have I left amongst thee the Book of Allah and my Ahlul Bayt which if ye hold fast, ye shall never go astray. And if thou were asked about me, what would ye say?

One by one, by groups, then by the thousands Muslims started calling out:

"Do we bear witness that thou hast conveyed the Message and fulfilled thy obligations."

The following day, Eid day, Muhammad led the Believers back to the Valley of Mina where the sacrificial animals were brought forward for sacrifice. Afterwards, the Prophet shaved his head to signify Hajj's completion and addressed the assemblage.

"In the name of Allah, The Beneficent, The Merciful. Unto Allah do we owe gratitude, for He it is Who giveth life and taketh it away."

"Oh, people! Verily the changing of prohibited months increases faithlessness. Thereby are the Disbelievers led to wrong. For they make it lawful one year and prohibit it in another year. To be in compliance with the months which Allah proclaimed unlawful, they consider violable that which Allah declared to be inviolable and they consider inviolable what He decreed to be violable."

"Verily, time has passed from the day when Allah created the heavens and earth. He made twelve months to a year of which four are Sacred: Dhul-Qa'dah; Dhul-Hijjah; Muharram; and, Rajab.

"Oh, people! Dost thou know what day it is, what province it is, or what month it is?

At first everyone looked around, then started answering: "It is the Day of Sacrifice; the region is the Sacred territory; and, the month is the Sacred Month."

Muhammad continued: "I tell ye that thy lives, property and honor, must be sacred to one another as this Sacred day, in this Sacred Month, in this Holy City."

"And thy bonds people! See that ye feed them with such food that ye eat thyselves, and clothe them with garments ye wear thyselves. And if they commit a fault which ye are not wont to forgive, then leave them alone for they are Allah's servants and are not to be punished."

"Behold! Hearken unto me. Worship thy Lord, offer thy obligatory prayers, observe the fast in the month of Ramadhan, make pilgrimage to the Sacred House, remit the Zakat and Khums, and comply with whatever I tell ye, only then will ye get to heaven!"

"So, let him who is present appraise those not here. Verily, many people to whom the message is conveyed may be more mindful of it than those present."

The next day, Muhammad decided to stay for another three days, devoting the time to instruction, prayer and praise. Before sunset, he delivered another speech, picking up the thread of his previous oration.

"Oh, people! Verily thy Lord is One as thy father is one. All of ye belong to the lineage of Adam, alaihis salaam, and he was made from clay. There is no superiority for an Arab over a non-Arab or a non-Arab over an Arab, nor for white over the black or black over white, except in piety and righteousness. Verily the best amongst thee is he who is the most pious.

"Behold, the closest of thee should relate the message to the furthest. Have I now conveyed the Message?"(9)

* * * * * *

As the Prophet, Ahlul Bayt and Companions, departed the Holy City's precincts for Madinah, the great numbers of Muslims followed. Muhammad rode Duldul in silent contemplation as his Holy Mission drew to a close.

Have I left anything unclear, Muhammad explored. *Nay! Have I designated my Ahlul Bayt as the Ark of Noah and made the love of them incumbent upon the Believers.* Without warning the voice of God's Archangel overwhelmed his thoughts with one of the last Revelations that would complete God's mercy upon mankind.

Oh, our Apostle Muhammad! Deliver thou what hath been sent down unto thee from thy Lord; and if thou dost it not, then(it will be as if) thou hast not delivered His message (at all); and surely will Allah protect thee from (the mischief) of men; verily, Allah guideth not an infidel people.(10)

Muhammad stopped near a dry pond at Ghadir Khum, three miles north of Juh'fa. He spoke with Ali and his trusted Companions, then stepped between two acacia trees to await the outcome of his instructions. He watched with tears of happiness filling his eyes as Muslims surrounded him: Ali, his grandsons, his daughter Fa'timah helping the women, his trusted Companions directing the elderly forward where they could clearly hear God's Commands, while others erected a pulpit out of saddles.

A short time later everyone was in place, quietly awaiting the Mu'edhdhin. At Muhammad's signal, Bilal called the Adhan. After leading prayer, the Apostle motioned Ali to accompany him on the pulpit, where he addressed the tens of thousands.

"All praise and gratitude are due unto Allah. To mankind did Allah give a special place in His creation. He honored him with understanding, purified his affections and gave spiritual insight, so that man should understand nature, himself and know Him through His wondrous signs.(11)

"There is no god but Allah! He is the One and Only God. Hath He no sons, nor father or mother, nor partners and there is none like unto Him. He is The Beginning and The End.

"Behold! Allah hath informed me the Angel of Death will soon come for me. What then say ye?"

The multitude replied: "Bear we witness that thou hast done thy duty."

"Do ye then bear witness to the Oneness of Allah and the Apostleship, who speaketh now unto ye by His command and do ye bear witness that the Day of Judgment and the life Hereafter are certainties?"

"Aye," "Indeed," "Verily," were answered.

"Hearken unto me carefully: leave I amongst thee my legacy of two weighty things; the Book of Allah and my Ahlul Bayt. Allah hath informed me that never shall these two be separated from one another until they reach me in Heaven at the Fountain of Kauthar.(12) Verily, should you be attached to these two; never, never shall ye get astray after me.(13) Do not seek precedence over the Qur'an and over my Ahlul Bayt, nor lag behind them. But follow them and tread their steps and will they guide ye unto the Right Path."

"Am I not master unto the Believers more than their own selves?"

The sea of Muslims roared out their agreement.

Muhammad turned to face Ali and raised his arms until the white of his underarms could be seen. He said: "Of whomsoever I am the master this Ali is his master."(14) The Prophet repeated the declaration three times to prevent any misunderstanding. Then raising his hands heavenwards, he prayed: "Oh, Allah! Be Thou a friend to him who is a friend of Ali and be an enemy to him who is an enemy to Ali. Support him who supports Ali. Forsake him who forsaketh Ali."(15)

Abruptly the Holy Apostle fell silent, motionless, his eyes fixed. His chest heaved with labored breath as the invisible yoke of Divine manifestation constricted around his upper body. Perspiration started dripping from his forehead. He was undergoing the Revelation of God's Last Will and Testament.

Prophet Muhammad returned his attention to the Believers. He swallowed several times as if to replenish the lost fluids, then revealed the crowning Message. "Saith the Lord thy God: 'This day have I perfected for you, your religion, and have completed My favor on you, and chosen for you ISLAM (to be) the Religion.'(16) Allahu Akbar," he bellowed before directing Ali to his tent, where the Believers could give their allegiance.

As the men lined up to congratulate God's first Guide to the Islamic nation, Harith ibn Nu'man exposed his hypocrisy before leaving. "Oh, Apostle, thou wanted us to abandon idol worship, we did. Thou wanted us to perform salat, fast, Hajj, give zakat and khums, to do jihad, we did all that thou asked. And now thou hast put Ali above us. Doth thou doest this of thine own accord or in accordance with the command of Allah?"

Muhammad retorted: "Whatever I have done is nothing, but the execution of the revealed will of Allah!"

"By Allah," Harith prayed, "if what thou saith is true, then let the penalty come from heaven!" As soon as the words left his mouth, a small meteorite slammed into his body, killing him instantly.(17)

Meanwhile, Umar ibn al-Khattab approached to render homage to his new superior. "Greetings be unto thee, O' son of Abu Talib! Thou hast now become my master and master of all the faithful men and women."(18)

"Umar!" Muhammad inveighed. "Henceforth, address not Ali as son of Abu Talib, but as Amir ul-Mu'mineen!(19) He is the master of the Muslims and Imam of the pious, and leader of the immaculate pure ones."(20)

"Oh, ye who hath ears to listen, when thou sendeth salutations of peace and blessings upon me, cut me not away from those of me, (my Holy Ahlul Bayt)."(21)

* * * * *

Once back in Madinah, one could sense a feeling of complacency as the city's inhabitants discussed Islam's triumph across the land and Muhammad's affirmation of the Imamate; declaring: The stars are safety for inhabitants of the earth against (getting lost) drowning, and my Ahlul Bayt are safety for my ummah against disagreement, whenever being opposed by any Arab tribe, disagreement will prevail amongst them, after which they will turn to be a party of Iblees (Satan).(22) At the same time, there were those who made wry faces at the institution of the God's Vicegerency. Some going as far as to circulate rumors imputing the character of God's Holy Apostle: relating he was bewitched and remained so for days not knowing what to do, to the extent that he was imagining having sexual intercourse with different women, and not doing so(23); performing ritual prayer in a state of impurity(24); of him exposing his lower extremities to people entering his house(25); and, being unable to correctly reach decisions without the help of others.(26)

The true Believers, however, paid no mind to the slanderers as God Himself chose Muhammad above all mankind to deliver His Final Book, exalted him above others,(27) made him the most honored,(28) removed the capacity for error,(29) endowed him with sublime morality,(30) and made him the pattern of conduct(31) for all time. They knew without doubt The All-Wise God, The Discerner of hearts, would never entrust man's guidance to those subject to err, lie, mislead, misinterpret or deceive; for it made no sense to follow the example of a wrongdoer or sinner. Ali, on the other hand, was hard-hit by the fabrications. He approached the Prophet with his sentiments.

Muhammad listened with a warm and knowing smile. He waited for his Successor to express his concerns, then said: "They recognize the bounties of Allah, and yet they deny them, and most of them are infidels.(32) Either out of envy for Allah's favors upon thee or begrudging you for killing their relatives in battle and crushing their heroes, driving them to kneel, subduing them and destroying their pride through thy sword and bravery till they surrendered and embraced the Truth.(33) O' Ali, I know that there are vindictive feelings harbored inside the bosoms of people which they will divulge for thee after me. If swear they allegiance unto thee, accept it, otherwise thou shouldest forbear till ye meet me while being wronged.(34) The Muslim ummah will victimize thee though thou wilt keep to my course. The one who loveth thee, loveth me, and the one who disliketh thee, disliketh me, and certainly this (beard) wilt be wet with the blood from this (wound on thy head).(35) Ali, thou wilt in truth demonstrate unto my ummah all that which they differed regarding it after me,(36) and thou wilt fight against matter of it's misinterpretation (of Qur'an) as thou hadst fought on the side of it's disclosure.(37) After me wilt there be leaders that can never follow my guide, and never adopt my sunnah, among whom wilt rise up men having hearts of devils inside a body of a human being.(38) My ummah will be divided after me, into seventy three sects of which only one will be on the right and will be saved, the rest will go to Hell-Fire.(39) (And) on the Doomsday my Companions will be brought unto the left, whereat I wilt inquire: whereto (art they brought)? The reply shall come: unto the Hell-Fire, and wilt I say: O' my Lord, these art my Companions. It will be said unto me: thou art unaware of what they have done after thee. Thereat I wilt say: remote be whoever changed after me, and I canst not see anyone delivered from amongst them save a few as the forsaken cattle.(40) (Thus worry ye not, for thee and thy issues art Rightly Guided, and this) Religion remains established till the Doomsday or Twelve Successors rule over ye, all being from Quraysh."(41)

A month later, two men from Yamamah arrived from Musaylimah: claiming a share in prophethood and demanding half the lands under Islam's standard. Shortly thereafter another impostor rose in Yemen.

Muhammad advised Ali, who in turn relayed the information. He dictated a letter to Musaylimah: In the name of Allah, The Beneficent, The Merciful. This is a letter from Muhammad ibn Abdullah, the Apostle of Allah to Musaylimah the Liar. Peace be unto the adherents of guidance. Belongeth the earth unto Allah, High and Exalted is He, and giveth He it unto those pious servants of His whom He pleaseth. And the pious servants will have a good end."(42)

Even though Muhammad knew the Governors of Yamamah and Yemen would deal with the impostors, his main concerns were over the Romans as the Truth of Islam forced the false doctrines of Christianity out of Arabia and surrounding areas. In the second month after Hajj, he further inflamed the malcontents passions by appointing eighteen year old Usamah ibn Zayd ibn Harith as Commander of an expedition to the region of Balqa in Syria, near Mu'tah.

During the following days, while Islamic forces assembled the insurgents contemptuously objected. So vehement became their disobedience to the Prophet's orders, the army remained encamped at al-Jurf, three miles away.

Meanwhile, the Holy Apostle fell ill: suffering severe headaches and mercurial rises in temperature. He lay bedridden, all the while his headaches growing more persistent and increasing in severity. Upon learning of the army's immobilization, he had no choice other than to rise from his sickbed. He entered the mosque and mounted the pulpit. Dizzy from high temperature, he wavered for nearly a minute before glorifying God. Afterward, he upbraided the men.

"Indeed, O' people! Am I heavy hearted the army has not departed. Many have objected my placing Usamah at the command. Thy dissent and disobedience is nothing new. Ye took exception to Usamah's father Zayd when he had the command. By Allah, he was fit for leadership and so is his son Usamah. Is he of the good ones, therefore obey him!"(43)

Muhammad returned to his bed. That night he called for Ali and took him by the hand to the cemetery of al-Baqi. Ali followed without question, but the people trailing after them inquired.

He said: "I have been commanded by Allah to seek forgiveness for the souls buried in al-Baqi." As he entered the graveyard, he verbalized his orders: "Oh, people of the graves. May the condition in which ye are be one of comfort as opposed to the disturbances which have come upon the people like the parts of a dark night when the first of them will come after the last." He then faced Ali, "Oh, Ali, the Angel

Gabriel used to present the Qur'an unto me once every year, but this year he presented it twice. I can only regard this that the time of my departure is at hand... I was given the choice of prolonged life   or of going to heaven. I have chosen to meet my Lord and enter Paradise."

No longer able to endure the cold night air, Muhammad terminated his requiem: the cold had aggravated his migraine as septicity engulfed him. He reached out for Ali and requested help back to his quarters. Several days later, he realized he was not long for this world and summoned Ali and Fazl, his uncle Abbas' son.

"Ali, Fazl, wilt thou help me to the mosque?" Even as death approached, the Prophet remained humble and courteous. Feverish, his head draped with cool towels, the two nearly carried Muhammad up to the pulpit.

"Oh, people, the shades of death draw closer unto me with each day. Therefore, those with whom I have something on trust, come so that I may return it. Those with whom I owe a debt, inform me. By Allah! Who sent me as His Apostle with His Last Will and Testament, let no one lay claim to nor wish salvation without good works."

Descending the rostrum, he led a short prayer before being assisted to his spouse's apartment. Next day, A'isha made an appearance and asked Umm Salema to move the Holy Apostle to her dwelling, where she could attend him. Muhammad's illness continued, worsening with each passing day. He suffered high fevers, spells of lethargy, weight loss and persistent migraines.

Bilal, who had not wanted to disturb the Prophet, hesitantly knocked on the apartment's door. Admitted, he petitioned an audience with Muhammad. "Oh, Prophet of Allah," he choked out as tears of sadness spilled, "forgive my intrusion, but may I call the Adhan for the morning prayer?"

Muhammad smiled weakly and acceded to Bilal's wishes. He added: "Ask

Ali to lead the prayer."

A'isha quickly interjected: "Muhammad, order Abu Bakr for this honor!"

Another of the wives in attendance, intervened: "Or order my father Umar.

Muhammad's brows arched with displeasure, recognizing their attempts to exalt their fathers. He said: "Hast thou removed the shroud of Allah's Apostle whilst he yet lives? Verily, art ye like the mistresses of Joseph, alaihis salaam." Dismissing them, he rose as fast as his weakness allowed, only to collapse. "Call Ali and Fazl!" He exclaimed while pulling himself back onto his bed.

Ali and Fazl had to literally carry the Prophet into the mosque. Immediately noticing Abu Bakr leading the prayer, Muhammad ordered his release and motioned Bakr to step aside and took up his place. Vocalizing "Allahu Akbar," he repudiated Bakr's leadership by restarting the prayer. Afterwards, his weakened state in conjunction with the energy spent in leading the Service completely drained him and he crumbled to the floor, startling all present. He tried to rise, but fainted from the exertion. Awakening, he found himself back in his own residence and ordered Abu Bakr, Umar and several other Muslims present in the mosque to present themselves.

At the group's arrival, Muhammad gave voice to his anger: "Did I order ye to march with Usamah?! Why hast thou disobeyed me?"

Bakr, the first to reply, said: "I had gone, but then thought it best to return."

Umar quickly added: "I did not go because I wished to know about thee."

Muhammad did not respond, but observed them with quiet regard. Then, without addressing their acts of disobedience, he instructed them: "Dispatch the army of Usamah!" He fell unconscious.

The wives and women lamented, the men wept. The Prophet regained consciousness a moment later to say: "Bring quill and ink pot so that ye may scribe and follow it and thou wilt never go astray."(44)

As someone rose to carry out the Prophet's order, Umar hastily dictated: "Nay! Muhammad is delirious and overwhelmed with his sickness. We have the Qur'an which is sufficient being the Book of Allah."(45)

Unfortunately, Ali was not present to enforce the Prophet's orders. However, some of the men gasped with fear and argued against Umar's decision: for God had clearly revealed the Apostle spoke not of his own inclination.(46) The ensuing dispute rapidly degenerated into a shouting match, which roused the Holy Apostle.

An elderly man cried for silence and said: "Oh, Prophet, have we been ordered not to obey thee or retrieve the materials thou asked for."

Annoyed, Muhammad declared: "May Allah remove him who made thee say, 'No'". Then stared at the two groups of men before telling them to leave his home. Following a short period of rest, he asked one of the women to summon Ali and his uncle Abbas.

"Ali, uncle," welcomed the Prophet, "sit near me. Uncle, wilt thou accept my testamentary bequest, fulfill my promises and carry out the religion of Allah?"

"My Prophet of Allah, thy uncle is an old man with obligations unto a large family. Thou viest with the wind in liberality and generosity and made covenants which this old man could never fulfill."

Turning to face Ali, the Holy Apostle said: "My Brother, wilt thou accept my testamentary bequest, fulfill my promises, carry out Allah's religion and look after the affairs of my family after me?"

"Aye, Oh, Apostle of Allah." Ali replied.

"Come closer my Brother," Muhammad requested. He called for all his personal possessions and gave them to Ali. At the last, he removed his finger ring and asked Ali to put it on his finger.

Tearfully, Amir ul-Mu'mineen humbly thanked al-Amin al-Mustafa. Following several minutes of anguished silence, Ali cleared his throat and requested admittance for Bashir's mother. The audience was granted.

"As-salaamu alaikum O' Prophet, and may the peace and blessings of Allah be upon thee and thy progeny," she said upon seeing Muhammad.

Muhammad smiled weakly and replied: "Wa alaikum as-salaam wa Rahmatul-laah. How can I help thee?"

"Oh, Prophet, I came to inquire about thy health."

"Oh, mother of Bashir, the poisoned meat which killed thy son at Khaybar, which I only tasted has been effecting me since. And now it
is having its play cutting off the vein in my neck."(47)

* * * * *

Next morning, the Angel of Death stretched forth his hand and Muhammad's coloring paled alarmingly. His family, Ali, the trusted Companions and wives, were in attendance. All tried to comfort him, but his condition steadily deteriorated. After an hour of their vigilance, he called his grandsons to his side. Repeating one of the many maxims regarding the Leaders of the Youths of Paradise: "The one who loveth al-Hasan and al-Husayn will have loved me, and he who detests them, detests me."(48) Then turning to his wives, he zeroed in on the youngest and prophesied: "I wonder who of you will be the instigator of the Jamal (camel) affair, at whom the dogs of How'ab will bark, and she will be the one who has deviated from the Straight Path. As to you, Humayra (A'isha), I have warned you in that regard."(49) Weakened by the exertion, Muhammad fell into an uneasy rest. Ali took the time to attend the Prophet's pledges.

Muhammad woke to the ministrations of his wives. Drained of energy, barely able to speak he glanced around the room before saying: "Call my Brother and Companion."

A'isha immediately departed to call her father, Abu Bakr. Hafsa followed suit minutes later to call Umar. Both were summarily dismissed by the Prophet turning his face away from them.

Umm Salema, having witnessed Bakr's and Umar's dismissal, said: "The Holy Apostle of Allah, meaneth not anyone but Ali."

Ali returned at once. He bent over to hear the Prophet clearly.

Rising, he cleared the room and resumed his place. The family gathered in the main room of the house. A time later, Ali exited and informed Fa'timah her father wished to speak with her.

"Daughter," said Muhammad feebly, "come closer so I may tell thee something. Was I given the choice between the treasures of this world with assurance of their enjoyment or of Paradise. Chose I to be with my Lord and heaven."

Fa'timah burst into tears and buried her face in her father's beard. Muhammad lovingly embraced her and whispered something that curbed her sobs. Sniffling, she wiped her eyes, started smiling and actually became cheerful. He smiled back wearily and drifted off into sleep.

Meanwhile, Ali was asked what Muhammad had told him. He answered: "He taught me of a thousand doors of knowledge and each door opened for me another thousand doors.(50) And made he a bequest of me of what I will undertake, insha'a Allah."

Fa'timah emerged from her father's room. Ali returned. A'isha asked the question burning in everyone's mind.

Fa'timah, what hath Muhammad told thee to cause such a transformation?"

"First, father said he was not going to recover his health, which caused me to weep. Then he said I would be the first of his family to join him and that made my grief go away."(51)

Minutes before the Trustworthy, the Chosen one, the Comforter, the Prince of Peace, the Mercy of all creatures, the Spirit of Truth, the Splendor and Seal of the Prophets expired, a strange stillness pervaded the room. His fever dropped and eyes cleared. "Ali, cradle my head in thy lap, for Allah's Order hath come. As my soul leaveth, rub my last breath over thy face and point me in the direction of Allah's ancient House. Keep my commands and be the first to pray over me. Do not leave me until thou hast put me in the earth. Seek Allah's help, High and Exalted is He!" Muhammad shifted his vision to the ceiling, seemingly to the world beyond.

He said to the Unseen: "Oh, Allah, aid me in my moment of death. Aye, I have made my choice... It is the Hereafter with my Lord in heaven. Verily... I have... and I swear...by... Him Who hath sent thee."(52)

EPILOGUE

Allah, Dios, God, or any of His Illustrious Names by which He is called, says: "THERE IS NONE BESIDES ME."

In light of the Bible's numerous contradictions: Egyptian and Chaldaean terms, LUKE's declaration(1:1-2), and later miscellaneous interpolations, Bible scripture can no longer be assigned as the Pure Word of God. It now becomes incumbent upon the sincere seeker to decipher Truth from invention and distortion; the Almighty IS NOT the Author of confusion (1 CORINTHIAN 14:33), and draw the whole truth from His Final Testament: the Holy Qur'an according to those whom God Himself blessed and purified. A Book subjected to intense scrutiny and scientific examination by scholars, theologians and scientists, of every denomination. They have affirmed the Holy Qur'an as a Scripture beyond human creation. For over fourteen centuries, the Noble Qur'an's text remains unchanged from it's original and is deeply revered by Believers throughout the world. It's conformity to humankind's natural thought process, it's majesty of style, clearly expresses the subjective states of human beings in the most precise manner possible. Readers of the Holy Qur'an are immediately struck by the absence of innovation and Islam's simplicity. Thus, the Bible's testimonials and the Qur'an's refuted Truths unequivocally avow that worshipping Jesus, peace be on him, as Allah or as the Son of Allah is Disbelief in God's Word.

"Unto thee it wast showed, that thou mightest know that the Lord He is God; THERE IS none else besides Him DEUTERONOMY 4:35

"Cursed be the man that maketh ANY given or molten image, an abomination unto the Lord, the work of the hands of the craftsman, and puts IT in A secret place. And all the people shall answer and say amen." DEUTERONOMY 27:15

HOLY JESUS FURTHER ELABORATES ALLAH'S ONENESS:

"The first of all commandments is, O' Israel; the Lord our God is One Lord." MARK 12:25

"Why callest thou me good? THERE IS none good but one, THAT IS God." MARK 10:18

"I can of mine own self do nothing: as I hear, I judge: and my judgment is just; because I seek NOT MINE OWN WILL, but the Will of God which hath sent me." JOHN 5:30

"MY doctrine is not mine, but His that sent me." JOHN 7:1

"If I bear witness of myself, my witness is not true." JOHN 5:31

"Then saith Jesus unto him, get thee hence, Satan: for it is written

Thou shalt worship the Lord thy God, and Him only shalt thou serve." MATTHEW 4:10

GLOSSARY

ADHAN: (AZAN) Call to Prayer

AHAD: God is One

AHLUL BAYT: Fourteen Divinely Purified Individuals, the Prophet Muhammad, his daughter Fa'timah, Ali ibn Abi Talib, Hasan ibn Ali, Husayn ibn Ali, and nine others of the Prophet's bloodline through Ali and Fa'timah.(A.S.)

ALAIHAS SALAAM: Peace be on her

ALAIHIMUS SALAAM: Peace be on them

ALAIHIS SALAAM: Peace be on him

AL-AMIN: The Trustworthy, one of Prophet Muhammad's epithets

AL-HAMDU LILLAH: Praise be to God

ALLAH: Proper Name of God that neither signifies gender nor pluralization

ALLAHU AKBAR: God is Greatest of All

AL-MUSTAFA: The Chosen one, one of Prophet Muhammad's epithets

AMEEN: Amen (so be it)

AMIRUL MU'MINEEN: Commander of the Faithful, an exclusive title bestowed by God's Prophet Muhammad upon the First of the Twelve Holy Imams, Ali ibn Abi Talib

ARSH: The Throne of Mighty Power

ASADULLAH UL-GHALIB: The ever victorious Lion of God, an exclusive title bestowed upon Ali ibn Abi Talib by the Prophet Muhammad

AS-SALAAMU ALAIKUM: Peace be unto you

AS-SALAAMU ALAIKUM WA RAHMATUL-LAAH: Peace be unto you and the mercy of God

BANU: Tribe

BAY'AH AL-RIDWAN: Fealty of God's Good Pleasure

BINT: Daughter of

EID: Commemoration

FA TA BARA KUL-LAAH: With the Blessings of God

FI AMAAN ALLAH TA'ALA: In God's, The Most High, Protection

HAJJ: Pilgrimage to God's Oldest House of worship in Mecca, (the Ka'bah)

HIJRA: Prophet Muhammad's flight from Mecca and start of the Islamic calendar

HOLY IMAM: Divinely Appointed Guide, Leader of the Believers

IBLEES: Satan

IBN: son of

IMAMATE: The Twelve Divinely Designated Imams of the Holy Ahlul Bayt with Leadership and Universal Authority in all Religious and Secular Affairs

INSHA'A ALLAH: If God Wills

IQRAA: Read, Recite, Proclaim

ISLAM: Peace, surrender to God's Will

JALABIYYAH: Long pull over shirt

JAZAA KALAAH: May God reward you

JIHAD: Earnest and ceaseless striving (to righteousness), fighting for God's Cause

JINN:Ethreal beign created from fire

JIZYAH: Protection Tax

JUMU'AH: (Friday) Day of Assembly

KAFIR (UN): Disbelievers

KALIMAT: Words, i.e., there is no god but Allah and Muhammad is His Servant and Messenger

KAUTHAR: Abundance

KHALIFA: Successor

KHUMS: The 1/5th rate of the Annual Net Profit remitted by believers to the Holy Imam or his delegate

KHUTBAH: Advice, guidance on living, sermon given at Jumu'ah Prayer

KUFIYAH: Head scarf

LAA ILAAHA IL-LAL-LAAH: There is no god but Allah

LABBAIKA ALLAHUMMA LABBAIK: I am here at Thy service, I am here O' Lord! I am here

MASHA'A ALLAH: What God has willed

MUBAHALAH: An agreement between two parties to earnestly invoke God's Wrath on the lying side

MU'EDHDHIN:(Mu'ezzin) the Caller to Prayer

MU'MINEEN: Believers

MUSLIM: One who submits to God's Will

NA'UUZU BIL-LAAH: We take refuge in God

QIBLAH: Direction facing God's First House of worship, the Ka'bah

RAMADHAN: (Ramazan) Islamic Holy Month of Fasting

SALAAM: Peace

SALAT: Prayer

SHAITAN: Evil force, Devil

SHARIAH:Islamic Jurisprudence

SHI'A: Friend, Follower, Partisan

SUBHAN ALLAH: Glory be to God

SUNNAH: Tradition of the Prophet

SURAH: Chapter of the Holy Qur'an

TA WAK-KAL-TU ALAL-LAAH: I place my trust in God

TAYAMMUM: Ablution for Prayer using clean dry earth
TORAH: Scripture given to Moses
UMMAH: Islamic society
UMRAH: Lessor Pilgrimage to Mecca, at any time of the year
WA ALAIKUM AS-SALAAM: And unto you be peace
WA ALAIKUM AS-SALAAM WA RAHMATUL-LAAH: And unto you be peace and the Mercy of God
WA AL-HAMDU LIL-LAAH RABB AL ALAMEEN: And All Praise and Gratitude is due to God, the Lord of the worlds
YAA ALLAH: O' God, (distress)
ZAKAT: Regular charity

BIBLIOGRAPHY

INTRODUCTION

(1.) Amana Corporation's new revised edition of Holy Qur'an, note 2762. (Hereafter A.C.n.)

CHAPTER ONE
(1.) Commentary on the life of Prophet Muhammad, by al-Qummi.

CHAPTER TWO
(1.) Deuteronomy 27:15. (2.) Numbers 23:19. (3.) Deuteronomy 4:39, 6:4; Isaiah 42:8, 44:6, 8; Matthew 4:10; Mark 12:29; Luke 4:8; John 20:17; Ephesians 4:4-6; 1 Timothy 2:5; James 2:19; Jude 25.

CHAPTER THREE
(1.) A.C.n.6276. (2.) A.C.n.6277. (3.) A.C.n.6279. (4.) A.C.n.6276.

CHAPTER FOUR
(1.) A.C.n.8. (2.) "Tarikh," by al-Tabari, Vol.1, pp.33-34; "Seerah," by ibn Hisham, Vol.1, pp.180-183. (3.) Amana Corporation's new revised edition of the Holy Qur'an, Commentary no.18-19, p.5. (Hereafter A.C.Com.no.)

CHAPTER FIVE
(1.) A.C.Com.no.24, p.7. (2.) A.C.Com.no.25, pp.7-8.

CHAPTER SIX
(1.) Ibn Sa'd, Vol.1, p.129. (2.) Ibid.

CHAPTER EIGHT
(1. to 3.) A.C.Com.no.27, p.8. (4.) References: "Decline and Fall of the Roman Empire," by E.Gibbon; "Arab Conquest of Egypt," by A.J.Butler. (5.) References: "History of Egypt," by Sir W.M. Flinders Petrie; "Introduction to Egyptian Religion," by A.W.Shorter; "Hypatia," by C.Kingsley; "History of Dogma," by Adolf von Harnack; "Rise and Fall of Christianity," by R.W.MacKay.

CHAPTER NINE
(1.) Holy Qur'an according to the Version (Interpretation) of the Blessed and Purified, the Holy Ahlul Bayt, note 3095, page 1880. (Hereafter A.B.V.n.).   (2.) A.B.V.Surah 96:1-5. (3.) A.B.V.n.3095,

p.1880. (4.) A.C.Com.no. 33, p.10. (5.) See CHAPTER EIGHT no. 4.
& 5.

CHAPTER TEN
(1.) A.C.Com.no.26, p.8. (2.) A.B.V.Surah 74:1-6.

CHAPTER ELEVEN
(1.) A.B.V.Surah 93. (2.) A.B.V.Surah 68:1-16, 34-52. (3.)
A.C.Com.no.202, p. 1174.

CHAPTER TWELVE
(1.) A.C.Com.no.35, p.11. (2.) A.B.V.Surah 81. (3.) A.B.V.Surah 87.
(4.) A.C. Com.no. 31, p.9. (5.) Ibid. (6.) A.B.V.Surah 74:7-56. (7.)
A.B.V.n. 1672, pp.1134-1138. (8.) A.B.V.Surah 26:214. (9.) "Kitab al-
Irshad," by Shaykh al-Mufid, p.30. (10.) See #7. (11.) "Tarikh," by al-
Tabari,Vol.3, pp.1171-1173. (12.) "Tarikh," by al-Tabari,Vol.3, p.1162.
(13.) Matthew 15:8-9.   (14.) A.B.V., pp.6-7. (15.) Deuteronomy
24:16. (16.) A.C.n.3389.

CHAPTER THIRTEEN
(1.) A.C.n.1940. (2.) A.C.n.5626. (3.) A.C.Com.no.248, pp.1510-1511.
(4.) A.B.V. Surah 68:34-41. (5.) John 16:12-13. (6.) A.C.Com.no.57,
p.143. (7.) A.B.V. Surah 96:6-19.

CHAPTER FOURTEEN
(1.) A.C.Com.no.44, p.16. (2.) A.C.Com.no.34, p.19. (3.) "Tarikh," by
al-Tabari,Vol.3, p.1170. (4.) A.C.n.5746. (5.) "Seerah," by Halabi,
Vol.1, p.311. (6.) A.C.n.2019. (7.) A.B.V.Surah 111. (8.) A.B.V.n.3183,
p.1920.

CHAPTER FIFTEEN
(1.) A.B.V.Surah 78. (2.) A.C.n.1205. (3.) "Hilyat al-Awlia," Abu Nu'aym
quotes the Holy Prophet Muhammad. Also, see A.B.V.n.2838, p.1796.
(4.) A.B.V.Surah 102. (5.) A.B.V.Surah 104. (6.) A.B.V.Surah 105.
(7.) A.B.V. Surah 106. (8.) A.B.V.Surah 107. (9.) A.B.V.Surah 109.
(10.) A.B.V.n.3143, p.1899. (11.) A.B.V.n.3159, p.1906.

CHAPTER SIXTEEN
(1.) A.C.n.854. (2.) A.C.Com.no.88, p.394-395. (3.) A.B.V.Surah 30:11-
19,
28-40,58-60. (4. & 5.) A.C.n.2057. (6.) A.C.n.3140. (7.) A.C.n.3141.
(8.) A.C.n.3173. (9.) A.C.n.3174. (10.) A.C.n.2335. (11.) A.C.n.3664.
(12.) Ibid. (13.) A.C.Com.no.181, p.1012. (14.) A.C.Com.no.182,
p.1019.   (15.) A.C.n.92. (16.) A.C.n.95. (17.) A.B.V.Surah 27:91-

92. (18.) Matthew 7:6. (19.) "Seerah," by ibn Hisham, Vol.1, pp.295-296. (20.) A.C.n.1155.   (21.) See #19. (22.) A.C. introduction to Surah 45. (23.) A.B.V.Surah 41:1-13. (24.) See #19. (25.) See #20.

CHAPTER SEVENTEEN
(1.) A.C.n.1169. (2.) A.C.n.1170. (3.) A.C.n.876. (4.) A.C.Com.no.115, p.593.
(5.) A.C.n.881. (6.) A.C.n.3969. (7.) A.C.n.3828.   (8.) A.C.Com.no.114, p.585. (9.) A.C.Com.no.117, p.602.   (10.) A.C.Com.no.119, p.619. (11.) A.C.Com.no.120, p.624.   (12.) A.C.Com.no.124, p.643. (13.) A.C.Com.no.127, p.664. (14.) Matthew 15:24. (15.) A.C.n.84. (16.) A.C.n.102. (17.) A.C.n.95. (18.) Ibn Hisham, op.
cit., Vol.1, p.336. (19.) Exodus 20:3-5. (20.) Luke 4:41; 9:20-21. (21.) Luke 3:38; Exodus 4:22; Psalms 2:7, respectively. (22.) Numbers 23:19.   (23.) Romans 8:14. (24.) Mark 12:29. (25.) A.B.V.Surah 19:1-36. (26.) A.C.
Com.no.138, p.743. (27.) Matthew 27:33, 35. (28.) Acts 5:30. (29.) Revelations 11:8. (30.) 1 Corinthians 14:33. (31.) Luke 1:1-2; 2 Timothy 2:8. (32.) A.C.Com.no.141, p.758. (33.) Matthew 12:18; A.B.V.Surah 43:59. (34.) A.B.V.Surah 20:1-8, 55, 130-135. (35.) A.C.Com.no.77, p.301.   (36.) A.C.n.853. (37.) A.B.V. p.10. (38.) A.B.V.Surah 36:1-50.   (39.) A.B.V.n.1967, pp.1320-1321. (40.) A.B.V. introduction, p.130a.   (41.) A.B.V.Surah 10:35. (42.)A.B.V.Surah 67:22. (43.) A.B.V.Surah 29:2.   (44.) Matthew 21:11. (45.)A.B.V.n.1969-1970, p.1322.

CHAPTER EIGHTEEN
(1.) A.C.n.134. (2.) A.C.n.1287. (3 .) A.C.n.4244. (4.) A.C.n.167. (5.)A.B.V.
Surah 27:1-6, 59-66, 83-93. (6.)A.C.Com.no.40, p.12.

CHAPTER NINETEEN
(1.) Genesis 17:20. (2.) Deuteronomy 18:15. Gospel of John. Gospel of Saint Barnabas, which for several centuries remained a Canonical Gospel
until the Nicene Council in 325 C.E., ordered all original Gospels written in Hebrew destroyed; followed by an Edict of death for the possession of Hebrew Gospels. In 478 C.E., Barnabas' remains were unearthed and there atop his ribcage lay the original Gospel written by his own hand. It is no wonder the Church placed this particular Gospel on its list of forbidden books, as it was written by one who actually walked with and recorded Jesus' Gospel. This surviving Gospel directly contradicts Church dogma and prophecies the advent of

Prophet Muhammad by name. This prophesy came to fruition some 600 years later.

"…Barnabas about whom ye received instructions: if he cometh unto thou, receive him" Colossians 4:10. (3.) Luke 1:1-2. (4.) 1 Thessalonians 4:15-17. (5.) 2 Timothy 2:8. (6.) Matthew 6:9-12. (7.) Isaiah 1:2-5. (8.) Isaiah 3:8.   (9.) Isaiah 42:9-11. (10.) Isaiah 42:14-17. (11.) Isaiah 43:28.

(12. & 13.) A.C.n.2668. (14.) A.C.n.2669. (15.) Mark 14:35. (16.) Matthew 12:18. (17.) Matthew 14:5; 21:11; Luke 24:19; John 4:19; 6:14; 7:40.   (18.) Luke 13:33. (19.) Deuteronomy 31:25-29; Jeremiah 8:8; Matthew 15:1-6; 23:1-33. (20.) A.C.Com.no.148, p.800. (21.) A.C.Com.no.150, p.815.   (22.) A.C.n. 3385. (23.) A.B.V.Surah 29:41-69. (24.) A.C.n.3190.   (25.) A.C.Com.no. 129, p.680. (26.) A.C.Com.no.130, p.685.   (27.) A.C.Com.no.131, p.691. (28.)A.C.Com. no. 134, p.714. (29.) A.C.Com.no.133, p.706. (30.)A.C.Com.no.129, p.680. (31.)See #24.   (32.) See #23.

CHAPTER TWENTY

(1.) A.B.V.Surah 67:1-14, 29. (2.) A.B.V.n.2632, p.1716. (3.) Matthew 6:9-10.

(4.) Isaiah 42:8. (5.)A.B.V.n.2628a, pp.1712-1714. (6.) A.C.n. 1978. (7.) A.C.n.1950. (8.) A.C.n.1565. (9.) Genesis 11:31. (10.) See #6.

(11.) First Book of Ezra. It must be presupposed for obvious reasons that the Original Law of Moses was not only Hallowed, but also a valued treasure. Thus the likelihood of the priest Hilki'ah actually discovering the Original Law (intact) in the Temple, 2 Kings 22:8, is highly suspect and very farfetched in light of recorded history: after several kings ransacked, looted, and ravaged the Temple of it's wealth and sacred objects over several centuries. See 1 Kings 14:25-26; 1 Kings 15:18; 2 Kings 12:18; 2 Kings 16:8; 2 Chronicles 12:1-9; 16:2; 25:23-24; 28:24. An opportunity presented itself to adulterate recollected parts of authentic Law with law suited to Jewish liking and disseminate it as the original scriptural Law. Consequently, this distorted "law" became the foundation of Judaism and by extension, Christianity. (12.) A.C.n.2013.   (13.) A.C.n.84. (14.) A.C.n.103. (15.) Authorities: "Bible," by Encyclopedia Britannica; "Divine Library of the Old Testament," by A.F.Kirkpatrick.   (16.) A.C.n.6290. (17.) A.C.n.6291.

CHAPTER TWENTY-ONE

(1.) A.B.V.Surah 42:1-9,13-15, 21-23, 25-26, 42-43, 47. (2.) A.B.V.n.2991, p.

1443. (3.) John 16:13. (4.) A.C.n.2921. (5.) A.C.n.4692. (6.) Ibid. (7.) A.C.n.
4699. (8.) A.B.V.Surah 44:1-14, 43-59.

CHAPTER TWENTY-TWO
(1.) "The name of Abu Talib," by Obaiddullah Amratsari. (2.) "Seerah," by
Halabi, Vol.1, p.390. (3.) "Madarijun Nubawwat," by Shaki Abdul Haqq Mahaddis Dehalvi. (4.) A.C.Com.no.11, pp.3-4. (5.) A.C.Com.no.36, p.11.   (6.) A.C.Com.no.219, p.1302. (7.) Ibid. (8.) A.B.V.Surah 40:1-20, 38-44,   51-52, 55-60. (9.) A.B.V.Surah 42:39.

CHAPTER TWENTY-THREE
(1.to   4.)   A.C.n.4581.   (5.)   A.C.Com.no.255,   p.1564.   (6.) A.C.Com.no.256, p.1570. (7.) A.C.Com.no.259, p.1591. (8.) See #6. (9.)See #7.   (10.) A.C.Com.no.231, p.1386. (11.) Hafiz ibn Qayyim, op.cit., Vol.2, p.124.   (12.) A.C.n.599. (13.) A.C.n.494. (14.) A.C.n.753.   (15.) A.C.Com.no.252, p.1543. (16.) A.C.Com.no.253, p.1550. (17.) Ibid.   (18.) A.B.V.Surah 72:20-28.

CHAPTER TWENTY-FOUR
(1.) A.C.n.2169. (2.) Exodus 19:20. (3.) Exodus 20:3-5. (4.) A.C.n.2170.   (5.) 2 Chronicles 3:1. (6.) 2 Ezra 5:12. (7.) 2 Kings 24:10-11; Jeremiah 39:1; Daniel 1:1. (8.) 2 Kings 24:14-16; Jeremiah 39:9. (9.) 2 Ezra 1:1. (10.) Books of Ezra and Nehemial. (11.& 12.)See CHAPTER TWENTY #11. (13.) Authorities: "History of Isma'il," by E.Renan; "Literature of the Old Testament" and Bibliography therein, by G.F.Moore; also see CHAPTER EIGHT #4. & 5. (14.) A.C.n.2176, 2178, 2179. (15.) A.B.V.Surah 39:72.   (16.) A.B.V.Surah 55:41. (17.) A.B.V.Surah 25:13. (18.) A.B.V.Surah 25:14. (19.) A.B.V.Surah 36:63-64. (20.) A.B.V.Surah 22:22.
(21.) A.B.V.Surah 32:20. (22.) A.B.V.Surah 78:30. (23.) Daniel 8:16-17.   (24.) A.B.V.Surah 17:71-77. (25.) "Musnad," by Ahmad ibn Hambal; Suyuti; Tabarani; ibn Asakir; "Hilyat al-Awlia," by Abu Nu'aym'; "Tafsir Kabir," by Fakhrud-Din Muhammad al-Razi; ibn Hatim. (26.) A.B.V.Surah 10:35.   (27.) "Tafsir," by Manhajus Sadiqeen.

CHAPTER TWENTY-FIVE
(1.) "Seerah," by ibn Hisham, Vol.1, pp.438-444; "Tabaqat," by ibn Sa'd, Vol.1, pp.221-223. (2.)A.B.V.Surah 9:40. (3.) "Tarikh," by al-Tabari, Vol.3, p.1234.

CHAPTER TWENTY-SIX

(1.) A.B.V.Surah 28:85. (2.) "Bihar ul-Anwar," by al-Majlisi,Vol.19, p.116. (3.) "Al-Bidayah wa'n-Nihayah," by ibn Kathir, Vol.3, p.213.

CHAPTER TWENTY-SEVEN
(1.) John 16:12-13. (2.) Matthew 5:17. (3.) Matthew 15:24. (4.) "Yanabi ul-Mawaddah," by al-Qunduzi, Vol.1 p.55. (5.) A.B.V.Surah 23:1-11, 57-92.　　　(6.) A.B.V.Surah 47:1-3, 7-11, 14. (7.) See CHAPTER EIGHT #4.& 5.

CHAPTER TWENTY-EIGHT
(1.) A.B.V.Surah 25:54. (2.) A.B.V.n.1635, p.1114. (3.) "Musnad," by Ahmad ibn Hambal, Vol.2, p.259. (4.) "Al-Maghazi," by Muhammad al-Waqidi, Vol.1, p.48. (5.) "Tarikh," by al-Tabari, Vol.2, p.140; "Seerah," by Halabi, Vol.2, p.160; "Bihar ul-Anwar," by al-Majlisi, Vol.19, p.217. (6. & 7.) "Tarikh," by al-Tabari, Vol.2, p.140; "Seerah," by ibn Hisham, Vol.1, p.615. (8.) "Seerah," by ibn Hisham, Vol.2, p.621. (9.) A.C.n.353.

CHAPTER TWENTY-NINE
(1.) "Kitab al-Irshad," by Shaykh al-Mufid, p.394. (2.) "Al-Maghazi," by Muhammad al-Waqidi, Vol.1, p.176. (3.) A.C.Com.no.89, p.413. (4.) A.C.Com.no. 92, p.430. (5.) "Al-Mustadrak," by al-Hakim, Vol.3, p.111. (6.) "Tarikh," by al-Tabari, Vol.1, pp.1395-1396; "Tarikh," by ibn Athir, Vol.2, p.107. (7.) "Seerah," by Hisham, Vol.2, p.83. (8.) A.B.V.Surah 4:1-5, 36-42, 44-50, 59-61, 77-78, 82, 87, 163-171. (9.)See CHAPTER EIGHT #4. & 5.

CHAPTER THIRTY
(1.)　A.C.Com.no.243,　p.1475.　(2.)　A.C.Com.no.249,　p.1515. (3.) A.C.Com.no.283, p.1692. (4) A.C.Com.no.287, p.1703
 (5.)　A.C.Com.no.289,　p.1707.　(6.)　A.C.Com.no.238,　p.1441.　(7.) A.B.V.Surah 83:7-23. (8.) A.B.V.Surah 52:7-14. (9.) A.B.V.Surah 61:1-9. (10.) See CHAPTER EIGHT #4. & 5.

CHAPTER THIRTY-ONE
(A) God is the Greatest x4, I bear witness that there is no god but THE GOD x2, I bear witness that Muhammad is the Prophet of God x2, Hasten to prayer x2, Hasen to success x2, Hasten to the best deeds x2 *, God is the Greatest x2, There is no got but The God x2. *This phrase was part of the original call to Prayer, during the Phrophet's lifetime.
(1.)　A.C.Com.no.242,　p.1470.　(2.)　A.C.Com.no.186,　p.1054. (3.)　A.C.Com.no.208,　p.1219.　(4.)　A.C.Com.no.185,　p.1044.　(5.) A.B.V.Surah 59:1-4,18. (6.) A.C.n.3680. (7.) Ibid. (8.) A.C.n.3693. (9.)

A.B.V.n.1835, pp.1247-1250. (10.)A.C.n.3701. (11.) Deteronomy 20:13-14. (12.) A.C.n.3704. (13.) A.C.n.3706.

CHAPTER THIRTY-TWO
(1.) A.B.V.Surah 22:26-38, 73-78. (2.) Maulvi Syed Ali's commentary in, "Umdatul Byan"; "Holy Qur'an," translation/commentary by Badsha Hussain, Vol.2, pp.134-135. The Eleven sons are the eleven other Holy Imams descended through Ali and Fa'timah. Also see, "Yanabi al-Mawaddah," by al-Qunduzi, Vol.3, p.99; "Tarikh ul-Khulafa," by Suyuti; "Fath-ul-Bari," by ibn Hajar al-Asqalani; "Shifa," by Qazi Ayaz; "Musnad," by Ahmad ibn Hanbal; "Early History of Islam," by S.S.Husayn, 1933 edition. The number is also reported by al-Bukhari, Vol.4, p.164; and, by Muslim, p.119, in their sahihs. (3.) "Sawa'iq ul-Muhriqah," by ibn Hajar, p.148; "Majma al-Zawa'id," by al-Haythami, Vol.9, p.163; "Yanabi al-Mawaddah," by al-Qunduzi, p.41; "al-Durr al-Manthur," by Suyuti, Vol.2, p.60; "Kanz ul-Ummal," by al-Muttaqi al-Hindi, Vol.1, p.168; "Usd al-Ghabah," by ibn Athir, Vol.3, p.37; "Abaqat al-Anwar," Vol.1, p.184. (4.) "Tafsir," by al-Tabari, Vol.13, p.108; "Mustadrak," by al-Hakim, Vol.3, p.129; "al-Durr al-Manthur," by Suyuti, Vol.4, p.45; "Tafsir," by ibn Kathir, Vol.2, p.502, and others. (5.) "al-Jami al-Kabir," by al-Tabarani; "Tarikh," by ibn Asakir, Vol.2, p.99; "al-Isabah," by ibn Hajar al-Asqalani; "Kanz ul-Ummal," by al-Muttaqi al-Hindi, Vol.6, p.155; "Majma al-Zawa'id," by al-Haythami, Vol.9,p.108; "Mustadrak," by al-Hakim, Vol.3,p.128; "Hilyat al-Awliya," by Hafiz Abu Nu'aym, Vol.4, p.349; "Ihqaq al-Haqq,"by al-Tustari,Vol.5, p.108. (6.) A.C.n.690. (7.) A.C.n. 4878. (8.) A.C.n.4881. (9.) A.C.n.4886. (10.) A.C.n.217. (11.) "Tarikh," by al-Tabari, Vol.2, pp.274-275; "Seerah," by ibn Hisham,Vol.2, p.314. (12.) "Seerah," by Halabi,Vol.3, p.24. (13.) "Bihar ul-Anwar," by al-Majlisi, Vol.20,p.353. (14.) "Majma ul-Byan," Vol.9,p.117. 15.) "Seerah," by Halabi, Vol.3, pp. 25-26. (16.) "al-Shurut," by al-Bukhari, Vol.2, p.122: fully describes Umar ibn Khattab's doubts about the legitimacy of Muhammad's Prophethood; also see "Tafsir," by Abul Futh. (17.) A.B.V.Surah 48:1-3, 23-25. (18.) See CHAPTER EIGHT #4. & 5.

CHAPTER THIRTY-THREE
(1.) "Kitab al-Irshad," by Shaykh al-Mufid, p.84. (2.) Ibid. (3.) "Sahih," by al-Bukhari, Vol.4, pp.5,12, and Vol.5, pp.76-77; "Sahih," by Muslim, Vol.7, p.121. (4.) A.C.n.1816. (5.) A.C.n.1817. (6.) A.B.V.Surah 33:9-11, 22-24. (7.) "Sahih," by al-Bukhari, Vol.5, pp.22-23; "Sahih," by Muslim, Vol.5, p.195. (8.) "Tafsir al-Kabir," by al-Thalabi. (9.) Khaybar's Battle is paraphrased from "Kitab al-Irshad," by Shaykh al-Mufid, pp.84-86. (10.) "Tarikh al-Kabir," by al-Bukhari, Vol.2, p.281; "Tarikh al-Khulafa," by Suyuti, p.173;

"Mustadrak," by al-Hakim, Vol.3, p.123; "al-Khasa'is," by an-Nisa'i, p.27; "Sawa'iq al-Muhriqah," by ibn Hajar, p.74; "Tarikh Dimashq," by ibn Asakir, Vol.2, p.234. (11.) "Yanabi al-Mawaddah," by al-Qunduzi, Bombay edition, p.107. (12.) A.C.n.3476. (13.) A.B.V.Surah 33:33. (14.) "Mustadrak," by al-Hakim, Vol.3, p.127; "Tarikh," by ibn Kathir, Vol.7, p.358. (15.) "Mustadrak," by al-Hakim, Vol.3, p.151; "al-Jami al-Saghir," by Suyuti, Vol.2, p.132; "Musnad," by Ahmad ibn Hanbal, Vol.3, p.17 and Vol.4, p.366; "Hilyat al-Awliya," by Hafiz Abu Nu'aym, Vol.4, p.306; "Mu'jam al-Saghir," by al-Tabarani, Vol.2, p.22; "al-Sawa'iq al-Muhriqah," by ibn Hajar, pp.136, 227; "Yanabi al-Mawaddah," by al-Qunduzi, pp.30, 370. (16.) "Sahih," by Muslim, Vol.2, p.362; "Sahih," by al-Tirmidhi, Vol.5, p.328; "al-Khasa'is," by an-Nisa'i, Vol.1, p.44; "Musnad," by Ahmad ibn Hanbal, Vol.5, p.189; "Mustadrak," by al-Hakim, Vol.3, p.148; "Sawa'iq al-Muhriqah," by ibn Hajar, p.148; " al-Tabaqat al-Kubra," by ibn Sa'd, Vol.2, p.194. (17.) A.C.Com. no.297, p.1719. (18.) A.C.Com.no.278, p.1677. (19.) A.C.Com.no.295, p.1719. (20.) See CHAPTER EIGHT #4. & 5. (21.) A.C.Com.no.14, p.4. (22.) C.Kingley's words in "Hypatia". (23.) See CHAPTER EIGHT #4. & 5.

CHAPTER THIRTY-FOUR
(1.) Paracletos is contended by Scholars as a corrupted reading for the Greek word PERICLYTOS, which closely translates "Ahmad" or "Muhammad". In John 14:16, 15:26, 16:7, the word "Comforter" in the English version is for the Greek word Paracletos, which means Advocate rather than Comforter. Prophet Muhammad, who Advocated Truth and God's Oneness can easily be reconciled as PERICLYTOS. See A.C.n.5438. (2.) Kedar, the second son of Isma'il, (Genesis 25:13), firstborn of Abraham: God promised Abraham to make his progeny a great nation, (Genesis 17:20), of whom Muhammad is a direct descendant. (3.) See CHAPTER EIGHT #4. & 5. (4.) A.C.Com.no.72, p.255. (5.) A.C.Com.no.80, p.327. (6.) A.C.Com.no.147, p.794. (7.) A.C.Com.no.94, p.446. (8.) A.C.Com.no.102, p.498. (9.) A.C.Com.no.51, p.99. (10.) A.C.Com.no.57, p.143. (11.) A.C.Com.no.78, p.309. (12.) A.C.Com.no. 89, p.413. (13.) A.C.Com.no.58, p.158. (14.) A.C.Com.no.59, p.165. (15.)A.C. Com.no.64, p.206. (16.) A.C.Com.no.60, p.175. (17.) A.B.V.Surah 3:2-6, 102-103, 149-150, 26-27. (18.) A.C.Com.no.156, p.859. (19.) A.C.Com.no.239, p.1451. (20.) Luke 9:20-21, 4:41. (21.) "Seerah," by ibn Hisham, Vol.2, p.409. (22.) Ibn Asakir reports Jabir ibn Abdullah Ansari reported the Holy Prophet Muhammad's actions and words upon the First Holy Imam, Ali ibn Abi Talib's arrival. (23.) Introduction to "Sharh an-Nahj," by Abu Hadid. (24.) "Bihar ul-Anwar," by

al-Majlisi, Vol.1, p.111. (25.) "The Message," by Ayatullah Jafar Subhani, pp.652-653.

CHAPTER THIRTY-FIVE
(1.) A.C.n.1275. (2.) "Kitab al-Irshad," by Shaykh al-Mufid, p.96. (3.) Reported by Jabir ibn Abdullah Ansari. Also, see "Kanz ul-Ummal," by al-Muttaqi   al-Hindi. (4.) Mark 7:6-7. (5.) John 14:28. (6.) Romans 8:14. (7.) Ezekiel 37:1-9. (8.) A.B.V.Surah 23:23-30, 51-56, 93-109, 115. (9.) See #2, pp.113-114; "Tafsir," by Ali ibn Ibrahim. (10.) "Sahih," by Muslim, Vol.2, p.360 and Vol.15, p.175; "Sahih," by al-Bukhari, Vol.2, p.305 and Vol.6, p.3; "Sunan," by ibn Majeh, Vol.1, p.44. (11.) "Seerah," by ibn Hisham, vol.1, p.39.   (12.) "Mustadrak," by al-Hakim, Vol.3, p.139; "al-Isabah," by ibn Hajar   al-Asqalani,Vol.1, p.25; "Yanabi al-Mawaddah," by al-Qunduzi, p.233; "Kifayat al-Talib," by al-Kanji,p.334; "Ihqaq al-Haqq," by al-Tustari,Vol.6, p.37.   (13.) "Tarikh," by Suyuti, p.78; "Musnad," by Ahmad ibn Hanbal,Vol.6, p.33; "Mustadrak," by al-Hakim,Vol.3, p.121. (14.) "Sahih," by Muslim,Vol.1, p.61; "Sunan," by an-Nisa'i,Vol.6, p.177. (15.) "Sawa'iq ul-Muhriqah," by ibn Hajar. (16.) "Zad al-Ma'ad," by Hafiz ibn Qayyim,Vol.3, pp.13-14.   (17 .) A.C.Com.no.95,   p.451.   (18.)   A.C.Com.no.96,   p.459.   (19.) A.C.Com.no.98, p.473. (20.) A.B.V.Surah 9:60-63, 70-72, 100, 115-116. (21.) "ad-Durr   al-Manthur," by Suyuti; "Musnad," by Ahmad ibn Hanbal; "Kanz ul-Ummal,"   al-Tirmidhi; an-Nisa'i, and others. (22.) A.B.V.Surah 9:1-13.   (23.) Deuteronomy 18:15. (24.) Matthew 5:17. (25.) Deuteronomy 18:19.
(26.) Matthew 17:12. (27.) John 1:21. (28.) Gospel of Saint Barnabas, section 17. (29.) Deuteronomy 27:15. (30.) Ezekiel 37:1-10. (31.) Matthew 12:18. (32.) Matthew 15:24. (33.) A.B.V.Surah 3:59-60. (34.) A.B.V.Surah 3:61. (35.) A.B.V.Surah 3:64-71. (36.) The Authorities used for the Sacred event of the Historic Mubahala: The Holy Ahlul Bayt Version of Holy Qur'an, notes 376-378, pp.300-308; "Iqbal," by ibn Tawus, pp.496-513; "Tafsir al-Kashshaf," by az-Zamakhsari,Vol.1, pp.282-283; "Tafsir Mafatihul Ghayb," by ar-Razi,Vol.2, pp.481-482; "Tarikh al-Kamil," by ibn Athir,Vol.2, p.112; "Seerah,' by Halabi,vol.3, p.239; "Sahih," by Muslim,Vol.15, p.176.

CHAPTER THIRTY-SIX
(1.) A.B.V.Surah 5:55. (2.) "Ali the Magnificent," by Yousef N.Lalljee, pp.21-22. (3.) al-Tabari,Vol.1, pp.1395-1396; "Tarikh al-Kamil," by ibn Athir,Vol.2, p.305; "Bihar ul-Anwar," by al-Majlisi,Vol.21, pp.360-363. (4.) "Sahih," by   al-Tirmidhi,Vol.5, p.201; "Mustadrak," by al-Hakim, Vol.3, p.126; "Tarikh," by ibn Kathir,Vol.7,p.353; "Kanz ul-Ummal," Vol.15, p.3. (5.) "Sahih," by   al-Tirmidhi,Vol.5, p.300;

"Sunan," by ibn Majeh,Vol.1, p.44; "Jami al-Usul," by ibn Kathir,Vol.9, p.47. (6.) "Sawa'iq ul-Muhriqah," by ibn Hajar, p.234; "Uyun ul-Akhbar," Vol.1, p.211; "Mustadrak," by al-Hakim,Vol.3, p.151; "Mishkat ul-Masabih," by al-Tabrizi, p.523; "Fara'idu's-Simtayn," by al-Hammuyi. (7.) "Mustadrak," by al-Hakim,Vol.3, p.128; "Tarikh," by ibn Asakir,Vol.2, p.95. (8.) See #3. (9.) "al-Maghazi," by al-Waqidi; "Fath ul-Bari ," by ibn Hajar,Vol.6, pp.170-172; "al-Bidayah wa'n-Nihayah," by ibn Kathir; "Izalat al-Khifa," by Shah Waliullah. (10.) A.B.V.Surah 5:67. (11.) A.C.Com.no.1, p.1. (12.) "Sahih," by al-Tirmidhi,Vol.5, p.328: "Sahih," by Muslim,Vol.15, p.176; "Musnad," by Ahmad ibn Hanbal,Vol.5, pp.181-182; "Mustadrak," by al-Hakim,Vol.3, p.148. (13.) "Sahih," by al-Tirmidhi,Vol.2, pp.296, 329. (14.) "Sahih," by al-Tirmidhi,Vol.5, p.296; "Musnad," by Ahmad ibn Hanbal,Vol.1, p.119 and Vol.4, p.281; "Mustadrak," by al-Hakim,Vol.3, p.109. (15.) "Sahih," by Muslim,Vol.2,p.362; "Musnad," by Ahmad ibn Hanbal,Vol.3, p.116 and Vol.5, p.25; "Mustadrak," by al-Hakim,Vol.3, p.109. (16.) A.B.V.Surah 5:3. (17.) A.B.V.n.703, p.499. (18.) "Musnad," by Ahmad ibn Hanbal,Vol.4, p.281; "Tafsir al-Kabir," by ar-Razi,Vol.3, p.636; "Sawa'iq ul-Muhriqah," by ibn Hajar. (19.) A.B.V.n. 703, p.493. (20.) "Muntakhab Kanz ul-Ummal," by al-Muttaqi al-Hindi,Vol. 5, p.34. (21.) A.B.V.n.1879, pp.1276-1277. (22.) "Mustadrak," by al-Hakim, Vol.3, p.149. (23.) "Sahih," by al-Bukhari,Vol.7, p.29. (24.) "Sahih," by al-Bukhari,Vol.1, pp.37, 44, 171. (25.) "Sahih," by Muslim,Vol.7, p.117. (26.) "al-Bidayah wa'n-Nihayah," by ibn Kathir. (27.) A.B.V.Surah 17:55, 2:253. (28.) A.B.V.Surah 81:19. (29.) A.B.V.Surah 53:2. (30.) A.B.V.Surah 68:4. (31.) A.B.V.Surah 33:21. (32.) A.B.V.Surah 16:83. (33.) Paraphrased from "To be with the Truthful," by Muhammad al-Tijani al-Samawi, p.125. (34.) al-Tabari. (35.) "Seerah," by ibn Hisham,Vol.1, p.39. (36.) "Mustadrak," by al-Hakim,Vol.3, p.122; "Tarikh Dimashq," by ibn Asakir, Vol.2, p.488. (37.) "Mustadrak," by al-Hakim, Vol3, p.139. (38.) "Sahih," by Muslim, Vol.6, p.24. (39.) "Sunan," by ibn Majeh,Vol.2, no. 3993; "Musnad," by Ahmad ibn Hanbal,Vol.3, p.120. (40.) "Sahih, by al-Bukhari,Vol.7, p.209. (41.) "Sahih," by Muslim,Vol.6, p.4. (42.) "Seerah," by ibn Hisham, Vol. 2, pp.600-601. (43.) Ibn Sa'd, series 2, Vol.2, p.41; "Seerah," by Halabi,Vol.3, p.207; "Tarikh," by al-Tabari,Vol.3, p.226; "Tarikh," by ibn Athir,Vol.2,p.137. (44.) "Sahih," by Muslim,vol.5,p.75; "Tarikh," by al-Tabari,Vol.3, p.193. (45.) "Seerah," by ibn Hisham, Vol.1, p.39; "Tarikh," by al-Tabari,Vol.3, p.193; "Sahih," by Muslim,Vol. 5, p.75. (46.) A.B.V.Surah 53:3-4. (47.) A.B.V.n.2335, p.1533. (48.) "Sunan,"by ibn Majeh, no.143. (49.) "Tarikh al-Kamil," by ibn Athir,Vol.3, p.120. (50.) "Kitab al-Irshad," by Shaykh al-Mufid, p.21. (51.) "Sahih," by al-Bukhari,Vol.3, p.92. (52.) The Holy Prophet Muhammad's last days were paraphrased from "Kitab al-Irshad," by Shaykh al-Mufid, pp.127-133.

CPSIA information can be obtained
at www.ICGtesting.com
Printed in the USA
BVHW041246120719
553289BV00017B/789/P